TRACES OF TEXAS HISTORY

Traces of Texas History

Archeological Evidence of the Past 450 Years

Daniel E. Fox

Corona Publishing Company, San Antonio

Copyright © 1983
by DANIEL E. FOX

Library of Congress Cataloging in Publication Data

Fox, Daniel E.
  Traces of Texas history.

  Bibliography: p.
  Includes index.
  1. Texas--Antiquities. I. Title.
F388.F68 1983   976.4'01   83-70811
ISBN 0-931722-24-1
ISBN 0-931722-23-3 (pbk.)

Printed and bound in the United States of America

Table of Contents

List of Figures

Acknowledgements

I began the task of writing *Traces of Texas History* at the invitation of Corona Publishing Company in March, 1982. The final draft was completed in January, 1983. Several of my colleagues in anthropological archeology and various personal friends and associates who are familiar with the science and business of doing archeology and history provided advice, constructive criticism, and encouragement. Most supportive were my mother, Anne A. Fox, Archeologist, Center for Archaeological Research, The University of Texas at San Antonio; John W. Clark, Jr., Archeologist, Texas Department of Highways and Public Transportation, Austin, Helen Simons, Editor, Texas Historical Commission, Austin; and my business associates, Bill Hood, Wildlife Biologist, Chris Jurgens, Archeologist, and Hayden Whitsett, Archeologist, Texas Department of Water Resources, Austin.

I am indebted to Susan Tyree and her family in San Antonio, who provided support and encouragement without which I might not have been able to complete the book within the necessary time limits. Susan typed most of the final drafts of the manuscript. My children, James C. and Karen E. Fox, were incredibly understanding of my moodiness during the limited time I had to spend with them. I also am grateful to the civil engineers and others on the staff of the Construction Grants and Water Quality Management Division of the Texas Department of Water Resources, who understood the time I was spending on the book at home on week nights, weekends, and holidays, and were patient while I struggled to live up to their expectations in the performance of my duties at work.

Much needed information, encouragement, and advice was given to me by the following friends and colleagues: Texas Anderson, Rice University, Houston; Art Black, Texas Parks and Wildlife Department, Austin; Shawn and David Carlson, Texas A&M University, College Station; Eddie Guffee, Museum of the Llano Estacado, Plainview; Billy Harrison, Panhandle-Plains Historical

Museum, Canyon; Elton Prewitt, Prewitt and Associates, Inc., Austin; Carolyn Spock, Texas Archeological Research Laboratory, The University of Texas at Austin; Al Wesolowsky, The University of Texas at San Antonio; and Jim Word, Floydada.

I appreciate comments on the manuscript offered by Bob Mallouf, State Archeologist and editor of the *Bulletin of the Texas Archeological Society*; T. R. Fehrenbach, historian; Jim Mitchell, editor of *La Tierra*; George Miller of the Council on America's Military Past; and Al Wesolowsky, Archeologist, The University of Texas at San Antonio.

I am grateful for the permission granted by the following organizations for the use of excerpts from their published works: Knights of Columbus, Austin; Macmillan Company, New York; Texas Historical Foundation, Austin; University of Texas Press, Austin. The following individuals, institutions, and organizations helped me find illustrations for the book and granted permission for their use: Catholic Archives of San Antonio; Center for Archaeological Research, The University of Texas at San Antonio; Mr. Thom Evans, Photographer, San Antonio; Houston Archeological Society; Library of the Daughters of the Republic of Texas at the Alamo; San Antonio; Lone Star Archeological Services, Georgetown; Museum of the Llano Estacado, Plainview; Mr. George Nelson, Uvalde; Panhandle-Plains Historical Museum, Canyon; Mr. John Poindexter, The University of Texas at San Antonio; Prewitt and Associates, Inc., Austin; Mr. Larry Sheerin, San Antonio; Southern Texas Archaeological Association; Stephen F. Austin State University, Nacogdoches; Texas Antiquities Committee, Austin; Texas A&M University, College Station; Texas Archeological Research Laboratory, The University of Texas at Austin; Texas Archeological Society; Texas Archeological Survey, The University of Texas at Austin; Texas Department of Highways and Public Transportation, Austin; Texas Historical Commission, Austin; Texas Parks and Wildlife Department, Austin; Trammell Crow Company, Austin; Uvalde County Historical Commission.

Finally, David Bowen, Publisher, and Alice Evett, Editor, of San Antonio, and Fred and Barbara Whitehead, Graphic Designers, of Austin, are to be thanked for their personal encouragement and for getting *Traces of Texas History* into print.

Introduction

SINCE I BEGAN TO WRITE this book in the spring of
1982, I have conceived of it as a study that would present Texas
history from an archeological point of view to a large and varied
audience. I hope that the final product of my work is interesting to
people who are not familiar with the scientific discipline of archeology, enlightening to students of Texas history and cultural geography, and satisfactory to my colleagues in anthropology.

For those who have had little experience with the study of
past peoples through the careful, scientific recovery and examination of the traces of their activities, I have tried to show what the
evidence of the past four and a half centuries of human life in Texas
looks like with the dirt still on it, how the material evidence of
history is collected archeologically, and how—unfortunately—
much of it is being destroyed by the activities of modern Texans
who either are not concerned or are unaware that they are eliminating forever the only real, tangible remains of their heritage.

For Texas historians, I have attempted to show how archeology can be used to expand the meaning of written history and test
the accuracy of historical accounts.

For Texas archeologists—ranging from scholarly university
anthropologists and professionally-employed archeologists to avocational archeologists interested in preserving the traces of Texas
history—I have tried to review what has been accomplished by the
archeological investigation of historic places in such a way as to
avoid the usual academic arguments about method and theory,
about whether historical archeologists are anthropologists with
history books or historians with shovels.

For everyone who reads this book, I have tried to demonstrate the value of the archeological evidence of Texas history and
the need to preserve it as an irreplaceable part of our heritage.

Archeologists are detectives trained to uncover the finger-
prints of the remote and recent past. Because human beings live in
environments by means of adaptive systems of learned behavior

known as cultures, archeologists, as anthropologists, see artifacts and the other physical evidence of human activity as material culture. Archeological sites are the places where people lived in the past, leaving artifacts and other traces of their cultural behavior. For the study of the Prehistoric Period in Texas, before history was written down and before European technology appeared, the history of the original human inhabitants of Texas and the processes by which their cultures changed can only be reconstructed from the material culture contained in archeological sites. For the Historic Period, archeological evidence can provide cultural information not contained in written histories, which have been subject to their writers' interpretations.

But digging into the historical accounts is just as much a part of the archeological investigation of the Historic Period as digging into the archeological sites. Placed within the context of documented history and folklore, the archeological sites and material culture of the Historic Period can be used to enrich our knowledge of the unknown, as well as the famous, people in history and the ways they left their imprints on our present world. Historical archeologists in America study the spread of Europeans and their culture to the New World, the impacts they had on the indigenous peoples of North America, and the ways in which Anglo-American culture developed from the sixteenth and seventeenth centuries into the modern American culture of today. Historical archeologists in Texas study the movement of European and Anglo-American peoples into Texas, how they replaced the original inhabitants and how the culture we think of as Texan came to be.

I have tried to organize *Traces of Texas History* in such a way that the results of the various historical archeological investigations that have been done in Texas can be seen as a series of historical perspectives. In some cases, I found it necessary to elaborate on the historical background of the archeological evidence somewhat, and in others I had to elaborate on the results of the archeological investigations. So in places my treatment of the history might appear superficial to historians and in others my explanation of the archeology may seem somewhat naive to archeologists, particularly specialists in certain periods of Texas history in certain parts of Texas in which I have had little personal experience doing historical archeology.

As general historical references, I have relied on two of what I consider to be the most appropriate published perspectives on Texas history—T. R. Fehrenbach's *Lone Star* (1968), a culture history, and D. W. Meinig's *Imperial Texas: An Interpretive Essay in Cultural Geography* (1969). I have used more specific sources for the development of the historical backgrounds focusing on archeological investigations into specific areas and time periods.

I have been as exhaustive as possible in my review of historical archeology in Texas, within reasonable limits of time and resources. Any biases that may be noticeable in my treatment of the historical archeology of the state stem as much from the difficulties I met in obtaining the most recent published and unpublished reports on investigations as they do from my lack of association with the archeologists and archeological practice in certain areas of the state. What may seem like glaring historical omissions simply result from the absence of archeological work in particular areas.

Instead of footnotes, I have set off by parentheses within the text references to authors and dates of the published and unpublished materials I have used, for each of which full bibliographic information is provided in References Cited at the end of the book. The references acknowledge the authors of works dealing with archeological sites and historical topics discussed and refer the reader to sources of additional background information.

There are two topics of interest to historical archeology that I found impossible to develop in full detail—archeological field methods and the wide variety of historic artifacts and other kinds of archeological evidence used in historical archeology. A formal explanation of archeological field methods and techniques would require a considerable amount of space and could distract attention from the discussion of the results of historical archeology and its manifestation of Texas history. However, I have tried to show the variety of methods and techniques that are involved in doing historical archeology in Texas as my discussion of the archeological evidence proceeds from one investigation, in one place and time, to another. Unfortunately, no "how-to" books on historical archeology in Texas have been written yet, and the only really comprehensive one for historical archeology in America is Ivor Noel Hume's *Historical Archaeology* (1969, also in a 1975 edition). One study of methods and techniques of prehistoric archeology in Texas has been published, T. R. Hester's *Digging Into South Texas*

Prehistory (1980), and there are the old standbys for prehistoric archeology in North America, like *An Introduction to Prehistoric Archaeology*, by Hole and Heizer (several editions), *Invitation to Archaeology*, by J. Deetz (1967), and *Field Methods in Archaeology*, by Hester, Heizer, and Graham (6th edition, 1975).

A thorough description and classification of the great variety of kinds of material culture and other cultural resources (archeological and historical) used by the historical archeologist would be unmanageably long and probably would be done much better as a separate study, as Hume did in his book, *A Guide to Artifacts of Colonial America* (1970). However, I have tried to give an impression of the basic types of cultural resources used in the many different archeological investigations I discuss and, in passing, I have referred the reader to some basic sources on artifacts, architecture, and the other physical remains of history. I also have provided an appendix at the end of the book with suggested readings pertaining to various topics related to historical archeology in Texas.

To my mother,
Anne Fox,
Archeologist

FIG. 1.1 *Works Progress Administration works at San José Mission, San Antonio.* (From *The San Antonio Light* Collection, University of Texas Institute of Texan Cultures at San Antonio. Courtesy Center for Archaeological Research, The University of Texas at San Antonio.)

Prehistoric and Historical Archeology in Texas

THE HISTORY OF HUMAN LIFE in Texas dates back some 12,000 years. Of this span, only the last 450 years or so have been documented by written records, beginning with the accounts of the first European explorers in the sixteenth century. This is known as the Historic Period.

For the Prehistoric Period, there are, of course, no written records of the diversity of human societies that inhabited the wide range of environmental areas that came to be called Texas. Their early lifeways and their cultural adaptations to changing environmental conditions can only be reconstructed through the careful scientific examination of the physical archeological evidence of their activities and the environments they lived in. There are a variety of historical ethnographic descriptions of the various aborigines that survived the first part of the Historic Period. But only a few Historic Indian sites have been found. Combined with the ethnographic accounts, the archeological evidence that has been recovered from Historic Indian sites presents a picture of rapid cultural change responding to environmental disruption, beginning with the intrusion of Europeans, continuing with the arrival of Anglo-Americans, and ending ultimately with the extinction of all of the original human cultures of Texas.

Besides the sites and artifacts that were left by the Texas Indians, there are archeological sites of the Historic Period that contain evidence of our own cultural heritage as Texans. There are Spanish shipwrecks, missions and presidios, French settlements and trading posts, Mexican and Anglo-American settlements and communities, slave quarters and Afro-American settlements, battlegrounds, frontier forts, towns, European immigrant farmsteads, early urban neighborhoods, early industries, dumps, and other historic sites of the settlement and development of our state. Texas history has been written and rewritten since the first European intruders began to record it in the sixteenth century. And many take it for granted that our written history is complete and accurate enough. In recent years, scientists have begun to realize that historic sites are resources of archeological evidence that can be used to verify, refine, and expand the written record of how different ethnic and cultural elements came to be Texans as family members in a sovereign republic, then as citizens of an American state, and more recently as human resources in the modern world community.

The History of Texas Archeology

Certainly in prehistoric and early historic times people have happened upon ancient artifacts and wondered who the people were who made them. Prehistoric peoples may have collected relics from the past, like modern people today collect arrowheads, bottles, barbed wire, and other antiquities and mementos of bygone days. But it was not until the nineteenth century that scholars began the scientific investigation of the human past in North America as it can be reconstructed from archeological evidence. They focused their attention first upon the more impressive monumental archeological sites left by the more complexly organized, technologically advanced Indian societies. The earliest published scientific studies of this sort that touched on Texas archeology began to appear in the late nineteenth century and the early twentieth century (Mallery 1886; Bandelier 1892; Fewkes 1902; Moore 1912; Pearce 1919).

In the 1920's, public interest in Texas archeology was stimulated by the news of man-made chipped stone implements found in unquestionable association with the fossil bones of animals known to have been extinct since the end of the last ice age in the Pleistocene geologic epoch (Cook 1927). Suddenly, there was real, hard evidence that mankind has existed in the New World much longer than had been believed. Besides the few university professors and students who studied natural history and the evolution of human society, more and more private citizens from different walks of life began to search for the archeological remains of Texas' earliest human inhabitants. Many of the first amateur archeologists were interested primarily in collecting ancient relics. But some were more curious, more conscientious. They wanted to know the history of the peopling of America as it might be documented archeologically.

In 1928, the Texas Archeological and Paleontological Society was founded by a group of amateur enthusiasts led by a chiropractor and naturalist named Cyrus N. Ray of Abilene, Texas (Wendorf 1978; Davis 1979). In 1929, the Society began the publication of an annual journal, or *Bulletin*, which became the means of reporting archeological discoveries made by university scientists and by amateur archeologists interested in the scientific investigation of human prehistory. Gradually, the Texas Archeological and Paleontological Society grew to include members from across the state and the *Bulletin* began to receive national recognition. Regional archeological societies were founded in the 1930's, such as the Dallas Archaeological Society with its journal, *The Record*, and the Central Texas Archaeological Society with its publication, the *Central Texas Archaeologist.*

As the number of citizens interested in Texas archeology grew, schools for the study of man were established within the state's universities. During the Great Depression, the federally-funded archeological recovery programs of the Works Progress

FIG. 1.2 *Excavations in front of the Alamo Shrine, San Antonio, viewed from the roof.* (Courtesy Center for Archaeological Research, The University of Texas at San Antonio.)

Administration employed several professionally-trained archeologists to direct large-scale excavations at selected archeological sites in Texas. There was growing concern for the professional quality of archeological investigations. Amateur and professional archeologists tended to divide into separate groups, as specially-trained archeologists who made their living and their reputations doing archeology began to claim archeological sites as their territory, suggesting that they were the only scientists who knew the proper methods of investigation.

As an organization dedicated to maintaining scientific standards and to the preservation of the state's archeological resources, the Texas Archeological and Paleontological Society became the meeting ground where the professionally-employed archeologist could gain public support for his work and the interested amateur could learn professional methods and techniques of archeological investigation. The important distinction was not between amateurs and professionals but between archeologists and relic collectors. Archeologists are concerned with the careful recovery and examination of the material evidence of human behavior and meticulous documentation of the situations, or contexts, in which the evidence is found. Relic collectors, or "pot-hunters," are content to simply dig up rare or collectible objects without concern for the irreplaceable information they destroy by removing artifacts from their archeological contexts.

Following World War II, the membership of the Texas Archeological and Paleontological Society increased rapidly. In 1952, the term "Paleontological" was dropped from the Society's name. Paleontology never had been an important part of the work of the Society, except in cases where archeological investigations of the sites of early man involved the study of fossil remains of extinct animals. By the 1950's, Texas archeology involved the study of the entire range of sites that had been inhabited by human societies in different regions at different times during the more than 10,000 years since the end of the Pleistocene, including some of the places lived in by Indian groups who survived the arrival of the Europeans in the early Historic Period.

In the postwar years, regional archeological societies became active in Houston, central Texas, Dallas, and El Paso. Amateur and professional archeologists across the state became more and more concerned about the need to preserve archeological sites and

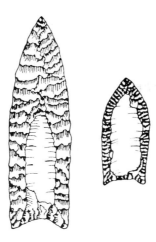

FIG. 1.3 *The traditional shapes and flaking patterns of two of the oldest known projectile point types (Clovis and Folsom) found in Texas.* (Courtesy Texas Historical Commission.)

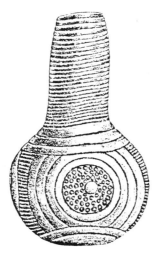

FIG. 1.4 *A decorated earthenware pottery bottle from a late prehistoric archeological site in the Red River Valley of northeastern Texas.* (Courtesy Texas Historical Commission.)

salvage information from the rapidly increasing number of sites being destroyed by postwar urban development, relic collecting, and the construction of highways, reservoirs, and other large-scale earthmoving projects. The state's universities were encouraged to employ and train professional archeologists in the 1950's to support federally-funded programs for the salvage of archeological resources doomed to be destroyed by government financed projects.

But the destruction of archeological sites continued to increase at an alarming rate. The Texas Archeological Society began to recruit new members. In 1962, it sponsored its first annual field school, where interested people could learn scientific methods of archeological recovery, analysis, and preservation. The activities of amateur and professional archeologists increased the public's awareness of the scientific and historic values of archeological resources, as American society became caught up in the processes of rapid social, economic, and environmental change, and more and more Americans began to cherish their cultural roots. The increase in the public's concern for preserving prehistoric and historic sites as unique and non-renewable resources of America's cultural heritage became a part of our society's attempts to preserve and protect our total human environment.

The federal government became actively involved in the protection of America's historic sites as early as the late nineteenth century, particularly in efforts to preserve well-known historic buildings and neighborhoods. In 1906, the National Antiquities Act was passed to regulate the unauthorized looting or other disturbance of historic and prehistoric ruins, monuments, and objects of antiquity located on federal lands. The Historic Sites Act of 1935 expanded the policies of the 1906 Act.

The National Historic Preservation Act of 1966, Executive Order 11593 (1971), and the Archeological and Historic Conservation Act (Moss-Bennett Bill) of 1974 clarified the federal government's responsibilities regarding management of historical and archeological resources on federal lands and in other areas that would be affected by projects involving federal funding or licensing. The National Historic Preservation Act of 1966 authorized the establishment of the National Register of Historic Places—an official list of cultural resources determined to be worthy of preservation because of their significance to local, state, and national history. The owner of a property listed in the National Register is eligible for federal grants-in-aid administered through state programs for preservation-related undertakings. The Tax Reform Act of 1976 provides certain tax incentives for the preservation of properties listed in the National Register of Historic Places.

Realizing the need for leadership in state government for the preservation of archeological sites, the Texas Archeological Society began as early as 1956 to promote the establishment of a state archeologist position and a state archeological salvage program (Word 1979). The Texas Historical Survey Committee had been created in 1953, but its primary concern was the public recognition of historic places, focusing upon old historic structures instead of archeological sites. Finally, in 1965, Governor John Connally recommended to the Texas Legislature that an Office of the State Archeologist be established and a bill passed creating the Office as part of the State Building Commission. In 1967, the Texas Legislature passed the Historic Sites and Structures Act and in accordance with it the Texas Parks and Wildlife Commission adopted a program for the acquisition, development, interpretation, and preservation of historic sites and structures.

In 1969, the Office of the State Archeologist was transferred from the Building Commission to the Texas Historical Survey Committee, which continued to designate historic landmarks and administer the state's part of the federal National Register program. In 1969, the Texas Antiquities Code was enacted as a result of widespread public anger over the looting and destruction of a treasure-laden Spanish shipwreck in Texas coastal waters by a treasure-hunting corporation from outside Texas. The Antiquities Code created the Texas Antiquities Committee with the authority to protect historic and archeological sites by designating them as Texas Archeological Landmarks. According to the Antiquities Code, sites ". . . located in, on or under the surface of any land belonging to the State of Texas or to any county, city, or political subdivision of the state are state archeological landmarks and are the sole property of the State of Texas." In 1972, the Texas Historical Survey became the Texas Historical Commission, which continues to serve as the headquarters for the state historical landmark program, the Office of the State Archeologist, the federal National Register program, and the operations of the Texas Antiquities Committee.

In the 1970's, there was an increase in the number and size of publicly-funded programs for locating, investigating, reporting, and protecting archeological resources, and an increase in the number of academically- and professionally-trained archeologists employed in the business of doing what has become known as "cultural resource management." This encouraged the growth of research programs in academic institutions and, in some cases, became the basis for the creation of large divisions of archeology within university anthropology departments. The requirements of the antiquities legislation of the 1960's and the early 1970's were responsible for this trend and also have encouraged the staffing of cultural resource management positions within state government agencies obliged to comply with federal and state antiquities laws.

The public funding made available for compliance with antiquities laws has been limited in comparison with the amounts appropriated for civil engineering and the administration of various development-oriented government programs. But when combined with the funding available for the various scientific studies required by the National Environmental Policy Act of 1969 and other environmental programs, public funding for cultural resource management has created business opportunities for private consulting firms. These organizations often can respond more quickly than academic institutions to emergency situations requiring archeological work and can lighten the work loads on government agencies that always have been hesitant to support their own cultural resource management programs beyond the minimum required for compliance with laws and regulations.

One of the more recent developments in the history of Texas archeology has been the establishment of the Council of Texas Archeologists as an organization to foster communication between archeologists employed by government agencies, universities, and private consulting firms. The members of this professional organization argue amongst themselves about whether the name of their profession should be spelled "archaeology" or "archeology" and struggle to come up with means of improving the effectiveness of managing the state's cultural resources within their complex systems of business and bureaucracy; meanwhile, the Texas Archeological Society and regional and local archeological organizations continue to be the meeting grounds for interaction between professionally-employed archeologists and the hundreds of private citizens interested in Texas archeology. These amateur/professional organizations continue to be the most effective vehicles for demonstrating the societal values of the state's archeological resources and for encouraging greater public involvement in the preservation of the archeological evidence of Texas history.

Texas Prehistory

Given the physiographic diversity of the vast area that has come to be called Texas in historic times, and considering the environmental changes that occurred throughout the more than 11,000 years of prehistory during which the area was the habitat of untold generations of stoneage human populations, it should not be surprising that a wide variety of prehistoric archeological evidence has been found in Texas. What is difficult to comprehend is the ever-increasing rate in which the archeological remains of prehistoric societies are being damaged and destroyed. Despite the efforts of hundreds of avocational and vocational archeologists who have worked diligently during the past 60 years to salvage, preserve, and interpret the evidence of Texas prehistory, the non-renewable resources of the prehistoric cultural heritage of Texas are disappearing much faster than Texas prehistory can be reconstructed. Archeologists have been forced to spend more of their energies identifying and protecting archeological sites and less time studying the cultural remains that they contain.

Prehistoric Indian sites include camps, villages, ceremonial centers, localities where game animals were killed and butchered, and other activity areas where prehistoric peoples quarried flint and extracted other naturally-occurring materials. The most common physical traces of prehistoric cultural behavior usually are the most durable artifacts, like simple tools, weapons and ornaments of stone, bone, and shell, and the debris that was produced by the manufacture and reconditioning of these artifacts. Snail shells, clam shells, and the bones of different animals are the evidence of some of the foods that were processed and consumed by prehistoric peoples. Other archeological evidence includes hearth areas of burned rock and charcoal, storage pits, midden concentrations of discarded debris, and other occupational features, such as stains in the soil that were left by posts, trenches, and other architectural elements of simple prehistoric structures. The bones of prehistoric peoples themselves also occur in single, isolated graves and in special cemetery areas. Evidence of prehistoric environments includes pollen grains and other lasting remains of different species of plants, bones of vertebrate animals, and shells of invertebrate animals, all of which were sensitive to certain environmental conditions.

For artifacts and other archeological evidence to be useful for reconstructing human prehistory, their positions in space and time must be recovered. The stratigraphy of soil layers and prehistoric cultural remains within an archeological site contains the history of environmental and cultural factors that contributed to the accumulation of the soils and the archeological deposits that comprise the site. The ways in which prehistoric human societies lived at different times and in different environments are observable in the horizontal and vertical distribution of archeological and paleoenvironmental evidence, in the spacial relationships between certain kinds of artifacts and occupational features within archeological sites, and in the location of archeological sites with respect to water sources, gravel outcrops, uplands, lowlands, and other natural resource areas.

Scientific investigation of prehistoric archeological sites in Texas and the material evidence of human cultural behavior recovered from them has revealed bits and pieces of a long, complicated history of human adaptation to changing environmental conditions (Suhm, Krieger, and Jelks 1954; Jelks, Davis, and Sturgis 1960; Hester 1980; Prewitt 1981). From a widespread Paleo-Indian tradition in which bands of people lived a nomadic hunting and gathering existence by following herds of big game during the end of the Pleistocene geologic epoch, prehistoric human societies adapted in separate ways as they settled into different physiographic regions. These Archaic peoples developed different systems of social organization, settlement pattern, religion, language, and other cultural elements. But in general, they all continued to live as groups of hunters and gatherers who moved about seasonally within territorial ranges. Their technology remained rather primitive. The principal weapon and hunting device was the *atlatl*, or spear-thrower, a short wooden implement used to hurl short spears or darts.

It was not until the Christian era, in the Neo-American Period, that prehistoric Texans began to use the bow and arrow and pottery containers. In eastern Texas, in parts of northern Texas, and in certain areas along the Rio Grande, societies had begun to live by gardening as well as by hunting and gathering. They lived in permanent and semi-permanent hamlets and villages and were integrated into systems of social, economic, and political organization that were much more complex than those of their nomadic neighbors. The most advanced of the early agriculturally-based

FIG. 1.5 *Skeletal remains of an adult female member of one of the earliest human societies to inhabit central Texas.* This archeological feature, found recently at the Wilson–Leonard Site, Wilson County, has been dated to about 8,000 B.C. (Courtesy Texas Department of Highways and Public Transportation D-8A.)

societies inhabited northeastern Texas, where relatively large populations lived in stratified societies, with upper and lower classes, and were governed by religious and secular officials. They built large houses, ceremonial centers, and burial mounds, and they participated in trade networks that linked them with different societies hundreds of miles away. In most regions of Texas, however, the Late Prehistoric peoples continued to live as stoneage hunters and gatherers, even after the arrival of European technology in the beginning of the Historic Period, and never completely adopted the Formative lifeway of the more advanced aboriginal cultures.

Historical Archeology

In 1620, an exploratory party of Pilgrims dug into some Indian mounds on Cape Cod and found aboriginal items mixed with European objects (Young 1841:109–110), and other archeological sites of the Historic Period in America were excavated by curious historians and relic collectors in the eighteenth and nineteenth centuries. But it was not until the mid-twentieth century that historic sites were excavated systematically, or scientifically, and only within the past 20 years or so has historical archeology become an accepted scholarly discipline in America (Schuyler 1978:1). The Society for Historical Archaeology was founded only 15 years ago.

In the mid-nineteenth century, Americans began to protect historic sites, particularly places of patriotic significance, and the historic-preservation movement continued to grow out of a popular enthusiasm for the memory of the American past. In the early twentieth century, American archeologists were interested primarily in the study of the cultural remains of American aborigines. Some were drawn into historical archeology when they investigated Indians sites of the Historic Period, and the European trade goods that they found became a part of the archeological evidence to be examined. Some archeologists were employed by the National Park Service in the 1930's to manage historic monuments (Hosmer 1978), but prior to World War II, archeological investigations at historic sites were undertaken as a prelude to the restoration or reconstruction of historic shrines and tourist attractions, rather than for the purposes of studying history as it is reflected in historic sites and artifacts (Woodward 1937; Hume 1969:10–11).

Even after the war, when more historic sites were investigated archeologically and there was more support for archeologists to pursue the scholarly goals of anthropology, some still viewed historical archeology as a handmaiden to history (Harrington 1955; Russell 1967). But other archeologists recognized the possibilities for creating broader, more meaningful images of the historic past through archeological investigation than can be generated from the study of documentary history alone (Cotter 1958; Griffin 1958; Fontana 1965).

The growing ecological awareness of Americans in the 1960's brought archeology, as a branch of anthropology, into a broadly-based movement for the protection of the total natural and cultural environment. Historians and anthropologists began to argue about who should do historical archeology. Historians claimed that anthropologically-trained archeologists are not proficient enough at historiography and either ignore history or have not mastered the historical record before doing historical archeology (Hume, 1968; Dollar 1968; Walker 1974). On the other hand, historians have been accused of not understanding anthropological objectives (Hume 1978:32), of being indifferent and openly hostile toward archeology and ignoring the findings that have been produced by hundreds of archeological investigations at historic sites (Schuyler 1978:2). In recent years, some outspoken American archeologists have begun to promote their beliefs that historical archeology should be done as a branch of anthropology, and not as a branch of history, by pursuing anthropological methods for abstracting answers to relevant questions about cultural evolution and the processes that govern human behavior (e.g., South 1977a, 1977b). But these relatively narrow viewpoints have not been accepted by all historical archeologists (e.g., Schuyler 1980) and cannot be applied to many archeologists whose work is restricted, for practical reasons of one sort or another, to cultural resource management and historic preservation.

The development of historical archeology in Texas has progressed in much the same way as it has on the national scene, but it began much later. Texas archeologists, both amateur and professional, always have been more interested in the archeological evidence of Texas Indians than in the archeological remains of the cultural heritage of modern Texans. Of the various articles published in the first 50 volumes of the *Bulletin of the Texas Archeological Society* prior to 1980 (Simons 1981), only 20 or so dealt with archeo-

FIG. 1.6 *Archeological investigations at Mission Concepción, San Antonio, in 1972.* (Courtesy Texas Historical Commission.)

logical sites of the Historic Period. Most of these were concerned with isolated Indian burials, caches, and house sites (Humphreys and Singleton 1978:76–77). Only three or four had to do with archeological investigations at non-Indian sites, and these were done in the 1970's.

Actually, several historic sites investigations have been done in Texas since about 1950. But most have been done since the enactment of the National Historic Preservation Act of 1966 and the Texas Antiquities Code of 1969, and were fostered by the establishment of the Office of the State Archeologist and cooperation between the Texas Historical Commission and other agencies and public groups interested in preserving the archeological resources of history. The archeological recovery and cultural resource management programs of the Texas Parks and Wildlife Department and the Texas Highway Department became actively involved in investigating historic sites in the 1970's, as did regional archeological societies and the research and cultural resource management programs of various academic institutions.

But historical archeology in Texas has been restricted as much as it has been encouraged by legal, financial, and political factors (Bond 1978:17). As yet, historical archeology in Texas does not have an organized system of method and theory, although some historic site investigations have applied some of the more current scientific concepts and methods of American anthropological archeology (e.g., Gilmore 1969, 1973; Fox and Livingston 1979; Freeman and Fawcett 1980; Moir 1982). Even while historic preservation, cultural resource management, historical and archeological research face cutbacks in public and private funding, more and more people are becoming aware of the contributions historical archeology can make by preserving our cultural heritage and expanding the meaning of Texas history.

FIG. 2.1 *Physiographic map of Texas.*

II

Texas at the Beginning of Written History

THE HISTORY OF TEXAS began with the first written accounts of travels through a new environment. From the time of Piñeda's exploration of the Gulf coastline and Cabeza de Vaca's fortuitous journey, more than two centuries passed before the first truly permanent settlements of the Spanish Colonial Empire were established in the Province of Texas. During this period from 1519 to the early eighteenth century, travellers and explorers recorded their impressions of the countryside. They described the landscape, the rivers and creeks they crossed, the menacing insects and inclement weather they endured, the plant and animal life they saw and learned to use as dietary supplements, and the different human societies they encountered. The travellers' written observations, though often sketchy and usually biased, offer interesting pictures of the constantly changing environments that had supported native peoples for more than 10,000 years and became the setting for the development of Texas that we read about in our history books.

Of course there were many people who travelled Texas long after it was first mapped and settled and recorded their experiences. Traders, speculators, refugees, military agents, and others with different motives saw Texas from different perspectives. Some still explore it. Historians and anthropologists have been studying the travellers' writings, interpreting and re-interpreting the locations of the places the first historical observers described, the routes they took, and what they really must have seen (e.g., Bolton 1959; Hodge and Lewis 1953; Krieger 1961; Donoghue 1936; Skeels 1972). Various researchers have been trying to reconstruct what the early Texas environments were like, who the inhabitants were, and how Texas' environmental and cultural setting has changed (e.g., Inglis 1964; Sibley 1967; Newcomb 1961; Berlandier 1969; Campbell 1975, 1977; Fehrenbach 1968; John 1975; Weniger n.d.).

The Environmental Setting

Texas is made up of an enormous diversity of environments and physiographic regions. The pine forests of eastern Texas, the prairies and marshlands along the coast, and the brush country of southern Texas are a continuation of the Gulf Coastal Plain—a physiographic region that includes the rolling downstream country, the coastal estuaries and bays from Cape Cod to the Yucatán Peninsula. Lush pine forests extend into eastern Texas from the southeastern United States. Further west, open grassy prairies and belts of hardwood thickets run southward across east-central Texas. Desert environments extend into Texas from the south and west. The rolling woodlands and prairies of north-central Texas are the southern part of the interior lowlands of the Midwest. The mountains of western Texas are the southern extension of the Rocky Mountains. The vast tableland of the Panhandle Plains, or Llano Estacado, rises out of the Great Plains. Bounded by the Cap Rock escarpments on the east and the mountains on the west, these high plains merge imperceptibly into the Edwards Plateau, which sweeps southward and eastward to the Hill Country and the Balcones Escarpment.

Since the earliest part of the historic period, travellers have crossed southern Texas, which some scientists now think did not become the "brush country" with its charcteristically dense cover of chaparral until the nineteenth century (Inglis 1964; Hester 1980: 31–37). In the spring of 1716, on his expedition to establish missions in the Spanish Province of Tejas, Captain Don Domingo Ramón noted a well-pastured country containing mesquite and lots of cactus south of the Nueces River in southern Texas (Foik 1933:9–10). Further north he found beautiful canyons with oak trees and fragrant wild flowers, land with much vegetation, and stream banks with large pecan trees and a variety of other timber.

On another Spanish *entrada* known as the Aguayo Expedition, Padre Bachiller Juan de la Peña, who kept a diary of the journey, described southern Texas as it looked in the spring of 1722 (Forrestal 1935:11–14). He found the land north of the Rio Grande and south of the Nueces River to be densely covered with mesquite brush, rough and hilly in some areas, flat and open in others, with large numbers of wild turkeys, quail, rabbits, and hares. North of the Nueces the expedition travelled through country carpeted with a variety of wild flowers. Dense woods, brush, and briars grew along the Frio River. Further north the country became open and was covered with flowers again. The travellers saw large numbers of deer, antelope, turkeys, rabbits, and quail.

The numerous springs, clear water, and lush vegetation along the Balcones Escarpment have always impressed newcomers. Captain Ramón's caravan, after having some trouble crossing the Medina River, travelled over prairies covered with mesquite and reached San Pedro Springs at the base of the Escarpment in May, 1716, north of what was to become San Antonio.

There was sufficient water here for a city of one-quarter league, and the scenery along the San Antonio River is very beautiful, for there are pecan trees, grape vines, willows, elms and other timbers. We crossed said stream; the water, which was not very deep, reached to our stirrups. We went up the river looking for a camping place and we found a very fine location. There were beautiful shade trees and good pasturage, as we explored the head of the river. Here we found, in the estimate of twelve ultra-marines, hemp nine feet high and flax two feet high. Fish were caught in abundance for everyone, and nets were used in the river with facility (Foik 1933:12).

And later, after crossing rolling prairies below the Escarpment, the Ramón expedition came upon the Guadalupe River.

It is the most beautiful stream that can be imagined, because from the passage to its source it is not greater than a shot with bow and arrow. It has such an abundance of water that it can hardly be crossed without swimming, being very broad. It would seem very strange without water, because on its banks and at its head were found maiden hair ferns, mulberries with leaves like the fig tree, and grapes in quantity. The rocks in the bottom of the river were transparent without any bitumen, which indicates that the water is healthful; and also it is very cold (Foik 1933:12–13).

Many travellers have commented on the eastern Cross Timbers, a dense woodland ranging from 30 to 50 miles in width and stretching for hundreds of miles from north to south across east-central Texas. Advancing northeastward in June, 1716, over rough and broken land and then open and level country, the Ramón expedition entered the Cross Timbers, or Monte Grande.

This day I travelled through a dense wooded region of oaks. The forest was so impenetrable that we could not pass through on horseback without cutting down some trees with axes and knives. We lost two knives. We advanced seven leagues with great difficulty, arriving in the afternoon in an open spot, that God had placed there for us to rest after such a painful journey (Foik 1933:15).

In eastern Texas, the Spanish travellers found lush forests and woodlands of pines, oaks, pecans, walnuts, and other trees. They described numerous streams, lakes, meadows, hills, and rich bottomlands. They mentioned deer, bear, fish, and other wildlife and reported the difficulties of travel in this country, particularly during wet weather when the rivers and creeks were on the rise. They assessed the potential uses of timber for construction materials, springs and streams for water supplies and irrigation, land for pasturage and farming, and mineral resources such as *salinas* for mining salt (Foik 1933:19–23; Forrestal 1935:39–59).

Few early travellers commented in detail about the mountains that were a geographic obstacle to travel in western Texas, but many described the high plains of the Panhandle. In search of Quivira, Coronado crossed the Llano Estacado in 1541 and Oñate crossed it in 1601 (Donoghue 1936). Both commented on its featureless, level plains with innumerable buffalo. Few early travellers could foresee how its sea of grasses would eventually support large ranches and later how its rich soils and high groundwater table would encourage extensive agricultural enterprises. In the mid-nineteenth century, Randolph Barnes Marcy described the Llano Estacado as

one vast, dreary, and monotonous waste of barren solitude. It is an ocean of desert prairie, where the voice of man is seldom heard, and where no living being permanently resides. The almost total absence of water causes all animals to shun it; even the Indians do not venture to cross it except at two or three points, where they find a few small ponds of water (Marcy 1874:169).

Besides the diversity of natural resources that the early travellers and explorers found, they also met many different human societies that inhabited the countryside at the beginning of Texas history. The early travellers' accounts describe Indians that ranged from primitive "savages" with simple technologies, to sophisticated, more complexly organized, sedentary agriculturalists (Hodge 1907; Newcomb 1961; Winfrey, *et al.* 1971; Skeels 1972). Just as Texas was a meeting place of environmental regions, so it was an area of transition between very different human cultures. Hunters and gatherers in southern Texas had cultural ties with peoples beyond the Rio Grande. In western, or Trans-Pecos, Texas, there were peoples related to the Pueblo cultures of the Southwest. Peoples affiliated with the agricultural societies of the Mississippi Valley inhabited eastern and southeastern Texas. The indigenous peoples of the Edwards Plateau and later immigrants to northern and central Texas were a part of the Plains culture area.

Hunters and Gatherers

In the semi-arid environments of southern Texas and northern Mexico, small groups of foragers wandered from place to place gathering wild plant foods, hunting small game, fishing, and collecting almost anything they could find to subsist on (Newcomb 1961:29–81; Hester 1980:39–51; Gatschet 1891). Cabeza de Vaca was probably the first European to describe some of these peoples in their native state before their lifeways were upset by pressures from other Indian groups moving down from the north and by Europeans, their diseases and technology. "Coahuiltecan" became the term used to refer to the language they spoke, although recent studies have found that several different languages probably were spoken by a variety of distinctively different aboriginal groups in southern Texas and northeastern Mexico (Campbell 1977:2; Hester 1980:39–40, Table 3.1).

In general, the original South Texans can be divided into two groups. The Coahuilteco inhabited the inland areas while the Karankawa livelihood was focused on the coastal lowlands and littoral. The basic social and economic unit of both the Coahuilteco and Karankawa populations was the small family group. During the various seasons for harvesting native plant foods, they assembled into bands of as many as 100 or more, each moving within its own territory and sometimes overlapping the territories of neighboring bands. Feuding and small-scale warfare often occurred.

Carried out within well-understood customary practices, territorial conflict among the hunters and gatherers of southern

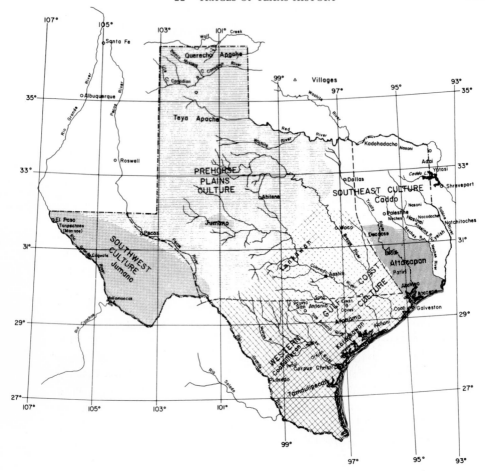

FIG. 2.2   *Location of Texas Indians in the sixteenth and seventeenth centuries.*
(From Skeels 1972: Fig. 3. Courtesy Texas Historical Commission.)

Texas, sometimes involving ritual cannibalism, was a natural part
of their environmental adaptation. Far more devastating were the
Apache raids that began in the late 1600's. The need to move about
in search of food prohibited the Coahuilteco from establishing
strongholds. If they congregated for protection too long in a particular place they would starve; if they dispersed and foraged
for food in their usual subsistence rounds they risked being
slaughtered.

   To make matters worse, the Coahuilteco were troubled by activities to the south. Spanish slavers preyed upon them before In-

dian slavery became illegal in New Spain. Coahuilteco visitors to Spanish frontier settlements south of the Rio Grande brought back smallpox, measles, and other diseases. It is no wonder that by the late 1600's, the Coahuilteco began pleading for missions to be established in their homelands. The Karankawa peoples managed to hold out for a while in their refuges along the coast.

When the Spanish were exploring Texas during the sixteenth and seventeenth centuries, a number of independent groups of hunters and gatherers occupied much of central Texas, including the Edwards Plateau, parts of the coastal plain to the south, and parts of the Brazos River drainage to the east. Unfortunately, the most detailed accounts of these people were not recorded until after they organized into a tribe known as the Tonkawa in order to confront the environmental and cultural changes of the Historic Period (Hoijer 1946; Sjoberg 1953a; Jones 1969). The origins and lifeways of their ancestral groups are obscure, but it is possible that a complex of archeological materials identified in central Texas might be the late prehistoric remains of the Tonkawa (Newcomb 1961:134–135).

Although they are considered to have been a plains culture with a technology based on buffalo hunting, the Tonkawa were dependent upon many of the same plant and animal resources as their Coahuilteco neighbors to the south. Some groups may have spoken Coahuiltecan dialects. The basic cooperative unit of Tonkawa tribal society was the clan, composed of groups of kin who traced their descent back to a mythical ancestor. Tonkawa groups may have practiced agriculture, at least after European colonial settlement began, but agriculture was never an important part of their lifeway.

Like the hunters and gatherers of southern Texas, the Tonkawa were caught from the beginning of the historic period between overpowering outside forces. They suffered from European-introduced diseases, struggled against the onslaught of Indians from the north, and asked for Spanish missions during the eighteenth century. Some Tonkawa bands joined other Indian peoples such as the Karankawa on the coast. Other Tonkawa were gathered along with Indians from different cultures into missions that operated for a while in east-central Texas. In 1859, a few of those who were left were moved to the Oklahoma Indian Territory (Hester 1980:51–52; Kelley 1971:164). Others were employed as scouts for the U.S. Cavalry during the 1870's (Neighbors 1973).

At the time of Coronado and Oñate, nomadic Apache bands inhabited the Llano Estacado and adjoining areas. Regarded as the original Plains Indians of Texas (Newcomb 1961:103–131; Sjoberg 1953b), the Eastern Apache were bison hunters, although many groups practiced farming from spring until harvest time in small, scattered communities and other groups carried on extensive trading and raiding. After they acquired horses and intensified their raiding of settlements in New Mexico, the Spanish mounted numerous retaliatory campaigns against them. Also with horses and with guns supplied by the French, the Comanche and the Wichita began attacking the Apache. Pressured by bitter enemies on all sides, they were driven into Mexico, Trans-Pecos Texas, and central Texas, where they intruded upon the already troubled native hunters and gatherers and raided the Spanish Colonial settlements of the area. Known as the Lipan Apache, the groups that survived into the nineteenth century became enemies of Mexicans and Americans on the frontier and raided them as the opportunity arose.

Although they were among the last Indians to be "pacified" in Texas, the Apache lifeway of the eighteenth and nineteenth centuries was not what it was before the advent of Europeans. In Newcomb's terms,

> An aura of the romantic and tragic clings to the Lipans, as it does to all Apaches. But apart from the intangibles of such a characterization, the dominant, recurring theme of later Lipan culture is its descent from something better. From their high estate as recent conquerors of the southern plains, they became dispossessed and harried remnants. Once a gardening and hunting people, they next became hunters, and finally poverty-stricken hunters and gleaners. From the proud and independent warriors Coronado met in the sixteenth century they became the skulking, beggarly riffraff of the Texas frontier (1961: 130–131).

Hunters and Gardeners

At the beginning of historic times, more than two dozen tribes of agricultural peoples who spoke a language known as "Caddo" lived in eastern and northeastern Texas and adjoining

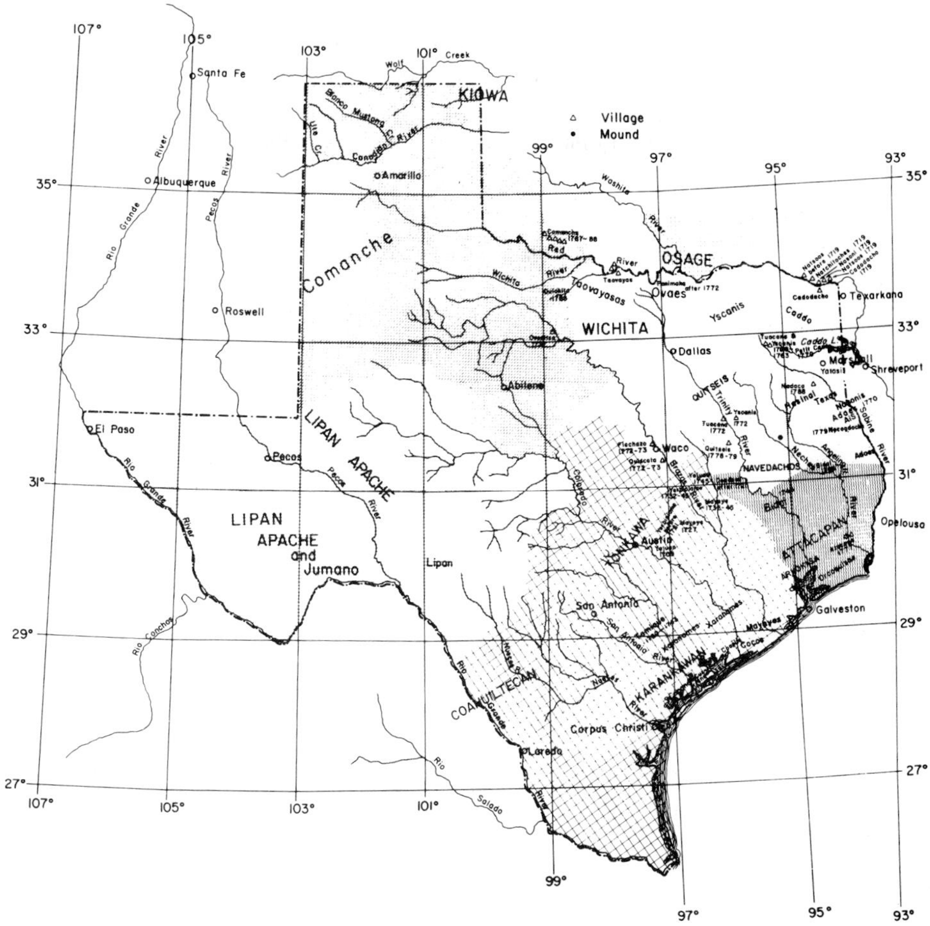

FIG. 2.3   *Location of Texas Indians in the eighteenth century.* (From Skeels 1972:Fig. 7. Courtesy Texas Historical Commission.)

areas of Louisiana, Arkansas, and Oklahoma. Their tribes were joined into three principal Caddoan confederacies, the largest of which was the Hasinai. They referred to each other as *Tayshas*, meaning "friends" or "allies." The Spanish recorded it as "Tejas" which since has been transformed into the name Texas.

Caddo culture apparently had a long heritage in the piney wood of Texas. Archeological evidence suggests that the impressive Caddo society of the historic period descended from a more spectacular prehistoric civilization that thrived long before De

Soto entered Caddo country in 1541. The historic and prehistoric Caddo probably achieved the highest level of social and economic development of the Texas aborigines. The forests of eastern Texas provided a relatively stable, rich environment to support a well ordered and productive society (Newcomb 1961:279–313; Swanton 1942).

Encouraged by the attractiveness of the Kingdom of Tejas and by concern about French intrusion into their territory, the Spanish established missions for the Caddo in the last part of the seventeenth century. Problems developed and the Province of Texas was ordered abandoned in 1694, but increasing French activity among the Caddo provided cause for the Spanish to reestablish settlements in eastern Texas in the early eighteenth century. Caddo populations continued to decline due to epidemics and their great confederacies rapidly collapsed.

South of the Caddo lived tribal groups of people who were gardeners but made considerable use of marine resources, freshwater fish, and other animals and plants they found in the marshes, thickets, and woodlands of southeastern Texas. During the 1700's, the Atakapa proper lived in southwestern Louisiana and across the Sabine River in southeasternmost Texas. The Orcoquisa (or Akokisa) occupied villages in the lower Trinity and San Jacinto river valleys and on the eastern shores of Galveston Bay. Upstream, to the north, were the Patiri and the Bidai, and further north were the Deadose (Newcomb 1961:315–329). Very little is known about these people who apparently numbered less than 3,500 in the early historic period. The Choctaw name "Atakapa" means "man-eaters," and the use of it to refer to the historic aborigines of southeastern Texas echoes the misunderstanding that many outsiders had about the ritual cannibalism practiced by various Texas Indians during the territorial struggles that took place in historic times.

A complex of archeological materials, left by prehistoric hunters, gatherers, and fishermen, known as the Galveston Bay Focus may be the evidence of the ancestors of historic Atakapa groups. Cabeza de Vaca may have lived with the Orcoquisa in 1528. A French trading post operated in their territory until the Spanish put an end to this illegal activity and established a military post and a mission there in the mid-eighteenth century.

A hunting and gardening people who were immigrants to Texas were the Wichita, ancestors of the people Coronado found at Quivira in central Kansas in 1541 (Newcomb 1961:247–277; Newcomb and Field 1967). Oñate visited Quivira in 1601 but there are few accounts of the Wichita between then and the early eighteenth century, when they already were drifting southward into north-central Texas under pressure from their Osage and Comanche enemies. Various Wichita subgroups were forced to form politically cohesive tribes by the second half of the eighteenth century. The Waco and Tawakoni were the southernmost Wichita tribal groups.

In early times the Wichita had close ties with the Caddo agriculturalists of eastern Texas. Their Wichita language was a member of the Caddoan linguistic family. As they acquired horses and began to move, they became more like Plains peoples, although gardening remained the basis of their lifeway. Farming villages were inhabited from spring until fall and were abandoned during the winter buffalo-hunting season.

The Wichita were preoccupied with raids and wars with Indians and Europeans throughout the historic period. They kept records of their scalping, horse-stealing, and other feats of war. They took captives to be used as slaves and concubines, and like other Indians the Wichita tortured and ritually ate their enemies. They fought their traditional enemies, the Osages and the Plains Apache, and warred with the Comanche until the French negotiated a treaty between them. As they entered Texas the Wichita intruded upon the Lipan Apache and the Tonkawa. Known as the Norteños, they participated with other Indian groups in an attack on the Spanish on the San Saba River in 1758. Brought on by constant warfare, the disintegration of the Wichita lifeway was hastened by epidemics of European diseases.

The Spanish probably heard their first embellished stories of the Kingdom of Tejas from the Jumano in the early seventeenth century (Newcomb 1961:225–245). They were a friendly people who ranged from western to eastern Texas, trading with the pueblos of New Mexico, participating in the trade fairs of the Caddo, and hunting buffalo on the southern plains. Cabeza de Vaca probably visited the Jumano, or Cow Nation as he called them, at La Junta at the confluence of the Rio Conchos and the Rio Grande. In the late seventeenth century the Jumano began asking for protection against the marauding Apache, and the Spanish established missions for these peoples who desired conversion, had contacts with the Tejas, and knew of freshwater pearls in the western headwater tributaries of the Colorado River.

Despite the early and long-standing acquaintance the Spanish had with them, very few details are known about the Jumano lifeway. To make matters worse, *jumano* and variations of the word were used in Spanish accounts to refer to other Indians besides these peoples contacted by Cabeza de Vaca in the Rio Grande Valley downstream from El Paso as far as the Big Bend country and up the Rio Conchos in Mexico. Prehistorically they probably were related to the Jornada Branch of the Mogollon pueblo culture of the Southwest. Historically the mysterious Jumano appear to have been an indigenous mixture of western Texas hunter, gatherer, trader, and gardener.

Plains Nomads and Warriors

Originally hunters and gatherers of a land far from Texas, north of the headwaters of the Arkansas River, the Comanche spoke the Shoshonean branch of the Uto-Aztekan linguistic family. They did not call themselves "Comanche," which comes from a Ute word meaning "enemy," a name applied to them by the Spanish and later by Americans. The Comanche acquired horses at some time during the seventeenth century and moved out onto the plains as nomadic bands of buffalo hunters. By 1705 they reached New Mexico and by the mid-eighteenth century they had taken control of the southern plains. There, they conquered the Eastern Apache, the Tonkawa, and other original Indian inhabitants of the Llano Estacado and central Texas and went on to fight Spaniards, Mexicans, Texans, and Americans until the late nineteenth century (Wallace and Hoebell 1952; Newcomb 1961:155–191; John 1975: 306–312).

The flexible organizational structure of the Comanche was well suited for their nomadic warring and hunting existence. The size and leadership of Comanche bands changed as situations changed. They never were a unified tribe. Each family group had its own headman or peace chief who emerged as a leader gradually as he demonstrated his ability. A council of peace chiefs dealt with the affairs of the band of family groups.

Like the Comanche, the Kiowa and the Kiowa Apache were late invaders of Texas, and even after they began to range into the Panhandle-Plains in the nineteenth century, most of their territory was to the north and east (Newcomb 1961:193–221; Mooney 1898; Marriott 1945; Richardson 1940). Like the Lipan, the Kiowa Apache may have been descendants of the Eastern Apache. By the nineteenth century most of them had been driven from the southern plains and no longer were typical Plains Indians in the ways they lived. Only the Kiowa Apache survived as Plains nomads, probably because they became so closely associated with the Kiowa.

The Kiowa apparently inhabited the headwaters of the Yellowstone and Missouri rivers in western Montana in early historic times and may have had their prehistoric roots there. They were driven out of the Black Hills of South Dakota during the late eighteenth century by the Sioux and the Cheyenne. During the early nineteenth century, the Kiowa and the Kiowa Apache moved southward into eastern Colorado and areas along the Arkansas River and began raiding into the Texas Panhandle-Plains.

Unlike the Comanche, the Kiowa and the Kiowa Apache formed into tribal groups, but their populations were too few in number for their more organized social structure to help them fight off the armies that pursued them on the frontier and finally placed them on reservations in the 1870's, ending their proud history as nomads of the Plains.

Traces of the Original Texans

As significant a part of the environment as they were and despite their long heritage as the native human inhabitants, most Texas Indians were well on the way to extinction by the beginning of the nineteenth century. Today not one of the original Indian cultures survives within the borders of the state (Newcomb 1961:25). The search for material evidence of historic Indians has long been of interest to Texas archeologists. Linking the early travellers' descriptions with the actual physical traces of the peoples they saw can help us locate where various Indian groups were at different times and uncover details about their lifeways that were misinterpreted or overlooked by the historical observers. Because people's traditional cultural behavior is reflected by the things they leave behind, we can compare the archeological evidence of historic Indian occupations with prehistoric cultural remains and we should be able to identify the living areas and artifacts of the ancestors of historic Indian groups and study the cultural changes the original Texans went through in their adaptation to the forces of history.

Unfortunately few archeological sites have been found which can be associated reliably with specific historic Indian groups in Texas (Skeels 1972; Humphreys and Singleton 1978:75–77; Fox 1980). Some historic Indians, like the Wichita and the Comanche, had homelands outside Texas, making it difficult to study their heritage archeologically. And because the cultures of the native Texas Indians changed so drastically in early historic times, it is difficult to see any transition between the archeological evidence of the late prehistoric cultures and the archeological evidence of their overwhelmed and acculturated descendants.

Distinctive triangular flint arrow points known as Garza points, and other stone tools and black pottery sherds found with them, are thought to be the archeological evidence of Apache occupations on the Llano Estacado in Texas and northeastern New Mexico. Several archeological sites containing Garza materials have been dated to the late prehistoric period because no European trade goods were found in them. At a site on the outskirts of the city of Lubbock, investigations found Garza materials and the bones of buffalo, antelope, rabbits, and other small game at a food processing area in a shallow drainage basin and at upland campsites surrounding the draw. Radiocarbon dates obtained from charcoal samples indicate that these Garza living areas at the Lubbock Lake Site were occupied repeatedly during the "protohistoric" period, when the first Europeans visited the Llano Estacado but before the Apache acquired European trade goods and were forced off of the southern plains by the Spanish, the Comanche, and the Wichita (Johnson, Holliday, Kaczor, and Stuckenrath 1977).

Although some archeological sites in central and southern Texas have been found that contain metal arrow points and glass trade beads (Hester 1980:161; McReynolds 1982), few sites have been recognized specifically as historic Coahuilteco, Karankawa, Tonkawa, or Lipan Apache occupations. Recent excavations by the Texas Archeological Society have found some evidence of the protohistoric Indian occupation of a campsite on the San Gabriel River in central Texas (Prewitt 1982). The flint tools and other artifacts, fire hearths, food processing areas, and other features uncovered in the upper soil layers of this buried river terrace, known as the Rowe Valley Site, are similar in many ways to archeological materials found in late prehistoric sites in the central Texas area. But the occurrence of fragments of historic period Caddoan trade pottery and other differences in the evidence recovered by the Society's first phase investigations indicate that the occupation occurred sometime between 1650 and 1750. Rowe Valley is located only a few miles from the sites of the San Xavier Missions, established by the Spanish in 1748 and 1749 for the Tonkawa and other Texas Indians who inhabited the San Gabriel River Valley and surrounding areas.

Most of the archeological sites that have been investigated intensively so far which are known to have been occupied by the different hunters and gatherers of central, southern, and coastal Texas are the Spanish Colonial missions located in those aboriginal homelands. In many cases the Spanish accounts document which Indians lived in each Texas mission. But because Indians from various cultural groups were gathered together and quickly integrated into mission societies, it is extremely difficult to identify mission artifacts that are representative of specific Coahuilteco, Karankawa, Tonkawa, or Lipan Apache peoples. By the time the missions were established, the Texas aborigines had been forced to adapt to population decline, territorial displacement, and separation from their relatives. They were confronted with new ideas, languages, and technologies, and many were forced to join invading populations (Campbell 1973:2). Mission technology and European tools quickly replaced the hunting and gathering technology of native Indians groups. The mission converts used tools, weapons, ornaments, and clothing imported from supply centers in Europe and New Spain. Under the missionaries' super-

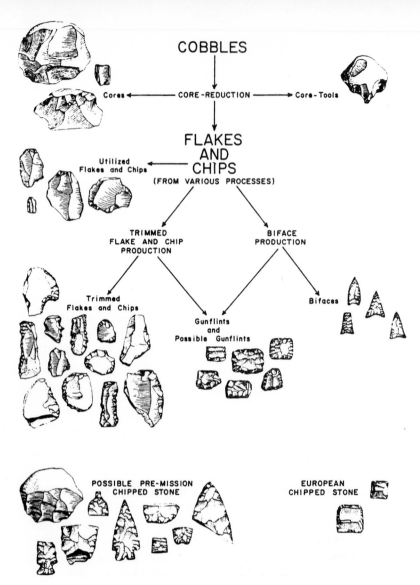

FIG. 2.4 *The products and by-products of lithic tool production at the Spanish Colonial missions of San Antonio.* (From Fox 1979: Fig. 12. Courtesy Center for Archaeological Research, The University of Texas at San Antonio. Drawing by D. E. Fox.)

vision, they fashioned imported and native materials into implements and structures that conformed to European technological specifications.

Certain artifact forms do occur at mission sites that we usually think of as "Indian," such as chipped flint tools and the chip-

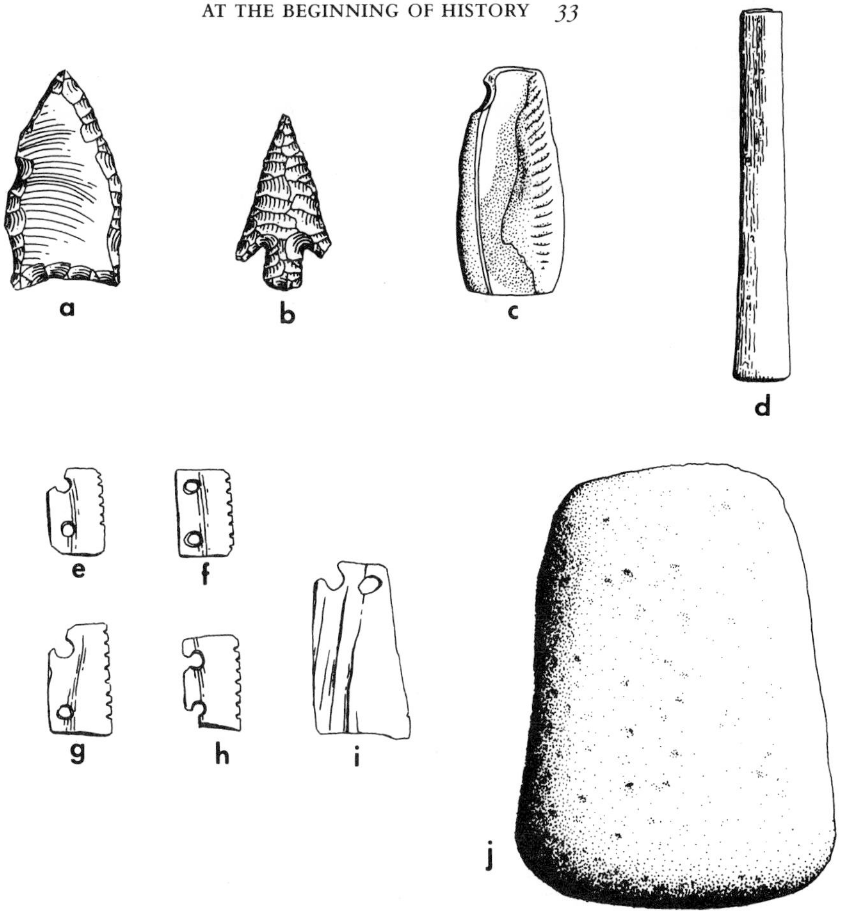

FIG. 2.5   *Mission Indian artifacts from Alamo Plaza, San Antonio (site of Mission San Antonio de Valero).* a, typical "mission" type projectile point; b, stemmed projectile point typical of the Late Prehistoric Period in central Texas; c, Olivella shell bead; d, bird bone bead; e–h, mussel shell beads; i, mussel shell bead from a Late Prehistoric burial site in San Antonio; j, basalt pestle, probably imported from Mexico for use by Texas mission Indians. (From Fox, Bass, and Hester 1976:Fig. 24. Courtesy Center for Archaeological Research, The University of Texas at San Antonio. Drawing by D. E. Fox.)

ping debris from their manufacture. We can try to identify assemblages of chipped flint, or lithic, artifacts that are typical of the mission Indians as a group and then we can compare this evidence with collections from late prehistoric archeological sites and hope to find out how Indian lithic technology changed from the prehistoric period into the historic period. But there are problems in-volved in identifying artifacts that are typical of mission Indian lithic technology. Many of the missions were built on sites that had been occupied by prehistoric peoples—for thousands of years in some cases—and implements made by the mission Indians sometimes are mixed with the flint artifacts of earlier occupants. The possibility that Spaniards as well as Indian mission inhabitants collected and reused prehistoric Indian artifacts makes it even more difficult to identify the chipped flint and the lithic technol-ogy that are truly mission Indian.

Based on a small sample of artifacts from four San Antonio missions, one study has managed to isolate a series of chipped flint artifacts which probably are the evidence of historic mission In-dians (D. Fox 1979). The remnants of the flint cobble stones from which flakes were struck to make tools, the flint flakes that were used as cutting and scraping tools, and the trimmed and shaped flint implements that were used as arrow points and for cutting, scraping, boring, and engraving—all seem to have been produced in much the same way as the chipped stone implements of pre-historic peoples. But the assemblage also includes gunflints made for European flintlock rifles and other tool forms that are different from the artifacts found in prehistoric sites. The standardized, mass-produced appearance of the mission assemblage suggests that the lithic technology of the mission Indians probably was sup-plementary to the European technology of metal, stone, and glass, more than it was a carry-over from traditional Indian technology.

There are, of course, other mission artifacts which would seem to be of traditional Indian manufacture. Shell and bone orna-ments and tools were produced and used by Indians at the mis-sions (Schuetz 1969:75–77, Plates 32 and 33), although some may have been carried in by Indian converts or obtained through con-tacts with Indian groups not living at the missions (Fox, Bass, and Hester 1976:70–71, Figure 24). Similar shell and bone artifacts have been found in late prehistoric archeological sites, but no thor-ough studies have been done comparing prehistoric and historic shell and bone artifacts.

Pottery sherds and other ceramic objects found at mission sites are another sort of artifact that can be thought of as "Indian." In fact, Goliad Ware, a smooth-surfaced, orange-colored earthen-ware pottery with white specks of crushed bone temper in it, com-

FIG. 2.6   *A historic Indian pictograph (rock painting) on the wall of a cave in Val Verde County, southwestern Texas.* Note the artist's conceptualization of foreign religion, technology, animals, and dress. (See also Kirkland and Newcomb 1967:Plate 64. Photo courtesy Texas Archeological Research Laboratory, The University of Texas at Austin.)

monly is found at the missions in central, southern, and coastal Texas and is quite similar to pottery found at late prehistoric archeological sites in the same physiographic regions (Schuetz 1969: 62–67). But detailed comparisons of the mission wares and the prehistoric pottery have not been done and there are pottery forms at the missions that do not have counterparts in prehistoric sites, such as the clay "furniture" used in firing pottery, miniature pots, pottery whistles, candle sticks, and pottery vessels shaped like European-made containers (Schuetz 1969:66–67, Figures 34 and 36, Plate 28). This may indicate that mission Indian ceramics were more a part of European mission technology than a carry-over of traditional Indian pottery-making.

During archeological investigations at mission San Juan Capistrano in San Antonio in 1967, several mission Indian burials were excavated (Schuetz 1969:116–124). The skeletal remains were determined to be from at least 63 individuals, including the bones of approximately 10 infants. Most of the burials were young adults

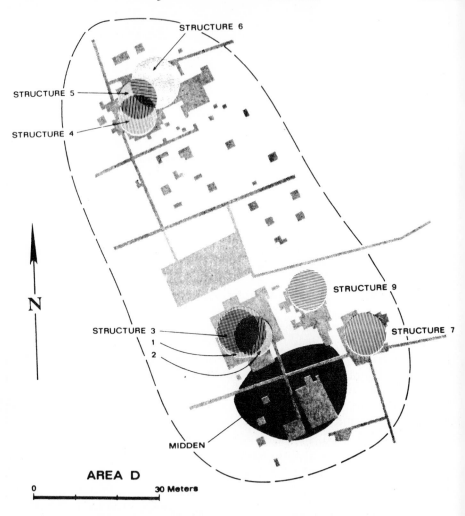

FIG. 2.7 *A historic Caddoan Indian residential occupation area at the De-shazo Site, Nacogdoches County.* (From Story 1982: Cover. Courtesy Texas Antiquities Committee.)

and middle-aged people; very few were elderly. The analyses of the bones found that the population varied in physical characteristics, particularly in head shape and size. Some individuals were broad-headed and others were long-headed, reflecting the variability in the ethnic population of the mission. At least one skull had been deformed during infancy by pressure against a cradle-board for an extended length of time. The average adult male rep-

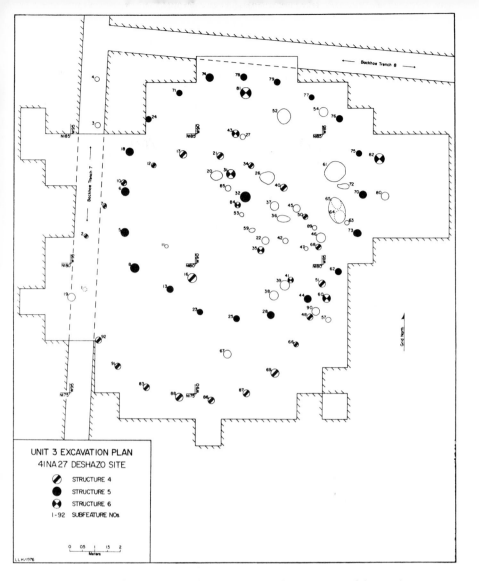

FIG. 2.8 *Plan of archeological features uncovered in one part of the Deshazo Site, Nacogdoches County.* Note rings of post molds marking the locations of historic Caddoan Indian houses built at different times on the same spot. (From Story 1982:Fig. 18. Courtesy Texas Antiquities Committee.)

resented by the skeletal remains was 5 feet 7 inches tall. The adult female was 5 feet 4 inches tall.

The bones commonly showed evidence of fractures, arthritis, and other diseases. The bones of one individual showed symptoms of syphilis. The skeletal remains also showed signs of tooth decay,

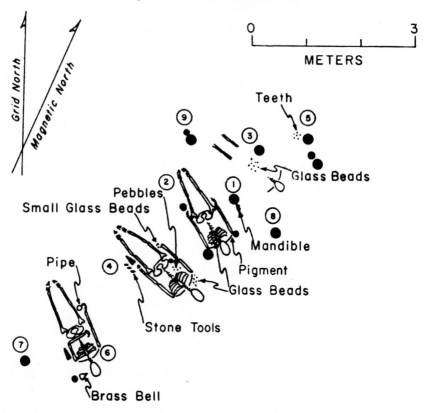

FIG. 2.9   *Plan showing historic Caddoan Indian cemetery details at the De-shazo Site, Nacogdoches County.* The circled numbers mark each of the nine burials found in this location. The black dots mark the locations of pottery vessels. The black triangles mark the locations of iron knives. Other burial offerings are labelled. (From Story 1982:Fig. 28. Courtesy Texas Antiquities Committee.)

gum disease, and abscesses. An unusually high incidence of diseases was noted in the skeletal materials, although it seems likely that there were many mission Indians who went on to become members of the Spanish Colonial community and did not die in the mission hacienda.

The archeological investigation of the original inhabitants of central, southern, and coastal Texas is still in the beginning stages. Most mission investigations have concentrated on the analysis of European-introduced materials because they can be associated more easily and reliably with particular uses and time spans. The mission-Indian evidence we have found and studied so far seems only vaguely similar to prehistoric archeological materials; its limited, standardized appearance reflects a dependence upon European technology and an adaptation to the settled, hierarchically-organized life of the mission, more than a continuation of Indian cultural traditions. It is quite possible that mission artifacts are evidence of a mixture of peoples who were no longer Texas Indians, but were instead a part of the newly acculturated laboring class needed to support the hacienda system of the Spanish Colonial Empire during the eighteenth century (Chevalier 1966; Fehrenbach 1968:65).

Archeological investigations of the agriculturalists of eastern Texas have focused primarily on prehistoric sites and only recently have Texas archeologists begun to study the archeological evidence of historic Caddo occupations (Webb 1960:53; Williams 1961). At the site of the mission Dolores de los Ais, near San Augustine, Texas, archeological investigations have found that sherds of Indian-made pottery outnumber sherds of European ceramic vessels by about nine to one (Corbin, Kalina, and Alex 1980:209–216). The principal historic Caddo Indian ceramic types found at Mission Dolores include Natchitoches Engraved, Emory Punctate-Incised, Ebarb Incised, and Patton Engraved. These are handmade earthenwares that have been categorized into types based on technique and pattern of decoration, on paste (the texture, tempering agent, color, hardness, and surface finish of the wall of the pottery vessel), and on vessel form (including the thickness of the wall, the shape of the base, the shape of the rim, vessel size and overall shape, and the kinds of handles, nodes, and other appendages added to the exterior of the vessel).

The engraved, incised, and punctated Indian-made pottery sherds found at Mission Dolores are of the same decorative types and vessel forms as pottery found at the site of Presidio de los Adaes on the Red River in Louisiana (Gregory 1980) and at a couple of Caddo occupation sites in eastern Texas (Jones 1968). Some of this pottery also occurs at Wichita village sites in northeastern Texas (Bell, Jelks, and Newcomb 1967:226–227; Duffield and Jelks 1961:138–139). But the tempering agents recognizable in the potsherds from Mission Dolores are different from the temper added to the pottery found at sites in different areas and it seems that certain ceramic traditions and trade relationships occurred within river drainages in eastern Texas (Corbin, Kalina, and Alex 1980:210–214).

Although paste, form, and decorative technique of pottery found at the Spanish Colonial sites appears generally to reflect a continuation of prehistoric traditions, it also shows signs of European influence. Some rim sherds and basal sherds of historic Caddo pottery found at Mission Dolores and Presidio de los Adaes are fragments of flatware, like plates and saucers, which are more typical of European vessel forms than the bowl, pot, and bottle shapes typical of prehistoric Caddo pottery vessels (Corbin, Kalina, and Alex 1980:214).

A series of archeological surveys and test excavation projects carried out in the 1970's where a lake was proposed to be constructed found several archeological sites that contained evidence of historic Indian occupation near Nacogdoches in eastern Texas (Prewitt, Clark, and Dibble 1972; Elton Prewitt, personal communication, September, 1982). The sites were marked by pottery sherds and other Indian-made artifacts and European trade goods on elevated areas scattered up and down the bottomland of Bayou Loco, a tributary to the Angelina River. Excavations in the 1930's and the 1940's at one of the larger archeological sites, called Deshazo, found Indian burials with grave goods that included glass trade beads, metal knives, Caddoan pottery, and other historic period artifacts. Various kinds of French trade goods were found at Deshazo and other sites in the Bayou Loco Valley. Recent studies at Deshazo have uncovered the stains of postholes and other archeological evidence of the beehive-shaped dwellings of poles and thatch that were built by one of the historic Indian family groups of the Bayou Loco settlement area. The possible site of a French trader's habitation area also was found.

Comparison of the archeological evidence recovered from the Bayou Loco area and the historical accounts of Spanish and French travellers through the Angelina River Basin in the late 1600's and the 1700's indicates that the historic Indian inhabitants probably were a part of the well-established village of the Hasinai Confederacy of the Caddo. Rather than living in concentrated villages, the Hasinai had adapted a settlement pattern of interrelated but independently situated family hamlets that shared common cemeteries, ceremonial centers, and public meeting houses (Prewitt

FIG. 2.10   *Some historic artifacts from the area of Spanish Fort on the Red River in Montague County.* Chipped flint projectile points, cutting and scraping tools, Indian pottery sherd, rolled metal "tinklers," a gunflint, a gun part, and a cannon ball. (Courtesy Texas Archeological Research Laboratory, The University of Texas at Austin. Photo by R. King Harris.)

1975). Much of the material recovered during the archeological investigations still is being analyzed and interpreted and will provide an interesting new look at the village of El Loco which existed when the French and Spanish arrived in the Angelina Valley in the late seventeenth century and continued to be a stronghold in the early nineteenth century for what was left of the Caddo peoples of that part of eastern Texas and for others who inhabited the Nacogdoches area.

The southern Wichita tribes that inhabited Texas during the eighteenth and early nineteenth centuries were probably not Texas Indians originally. But they did leave a number of recognizable archeological sites, some of which are documented in the historical accounts. The Spanish Fort Site, on the south bank of the Red River in Montague County, Texas, probably was a large eighteenth-century Taovayas tribal Wichita village which was referred to in several historical accounts and was a prominent place in the struggle between the Spanish and French over the control of Texas (Witte 1938; Harris and Harris 1961; Duffield and Jelks 1961: 69–75). The Stansbury Site, now beneath Lake Whitney on the Brazos River, was a Tawakoni Wichita village referred to as Flechado by the Spanish in the late 1700's (Stephenson 1947, 1970; Jelks 1970). Other southern Wichita sites include the Pearson Site, now under Lake Tawakoni on the Sabine River (Duffield and Jelks 1961), the Gilbert Site on the upper Sabine River in Rains County (Jelks 1967), the Womack and Sanders sites on the south bank of the Red River in Lamar County (Harris, Harris, Blaine, and Blaine 1965), the Vincent Site in Limestone County, and the Stone Site near Waco on the Brazos River.

From the archeological investigations of these village sites, a series of artifacts of native manufacture found in association with European trade goods has been designated as the Norteño Focus— the archeological evidence thought to be characteristic of historic Wichita Indians in Texas (Duffield and Jelks 1961). The Norteño materials include triangular, chipped-flint arrow points, a type of snub-nosed flint scraping tool, Womack Engraved pottery (a ware that follows the Caddoan pottery-making tradition), undecorated Goliad Ware (like the mission pottery), and tobacco pipes made from fired clay and from ground stone. The Norteños apparently also made other varieties of pottery besides Womack and Goliad wares and they used pottery vessels they obtained through trade with the historic Caddo.

Other artifact forms of native manufacture found at Norteño Focus sites include an assortment of chipped and polished stone implements and various bone and shell tools and ornaments (Jelks 1967:112–219). Some artifacts similar to Norteño materials have been found at Henrietta Focus sites of the late prehistoric period in north-central Texas, leading some to think that the Wichita may have had at least some roots in Texas (Duffield and Jelks 1961:74–75).

The Spanish began settling northeastern Texas by 1690, and by 1700 the French were becoming well established in settlements further to the east. The Norteño Focus dates to the period of economic influence when European trade goods were available in quantity to the Wichita and other Indians in north-central and northeastern Texas. An impressive array of European trade goods has been recovered during archeological investigations of Norteño

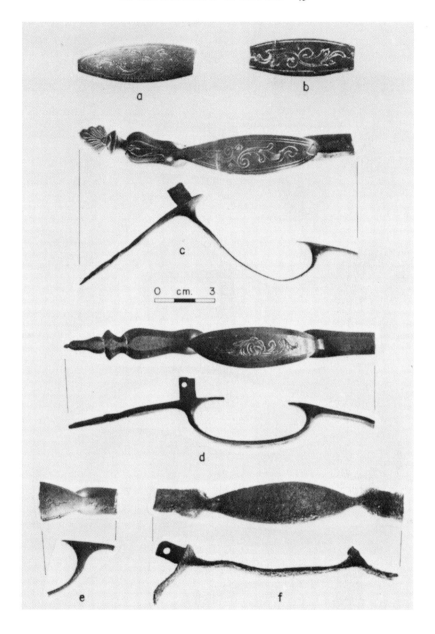

FIG. 2.11 *Trigger guards from flintlock muskets, from the Gilbert Site, Rains County.* (From Jelks 1967: Fig. 40. Courtesy Texas Archeological Society.)

FIG. 2.12 *Assorted European trade beads from the Gilbert Site, Rains County.* (From Jelks 1967: Fig. 45. Courtesy Texas Archeological Society.)

Focus village sites. For example, the metal artifacts collected from the Gilbert Site (Jelks 1967) include metal knives and knife handles, axes, splitting wedges, kettle fragments, awls, chisels, scissors, buttons, flintlock gun parts, bullets and shot, bridle parts, and metal ornaments such as bells, finger rings, and bracelets.

Some metal artifacts were fashioned by the Wichita from European materials or adapted to uses other than those for which they were originally designed. Examples include sheets of brass rolled up into cone-shaped ornaments known as tinklers, pendants made from sheet metal and from French coins, and metal arrow points made from odd pieces of brass and iron. European gunflints of honey-colored French flint and Indian-made gunflints of local stone were found at the Gilbert Site. Also common were hundreds of glass trade beads of different colors and types which stylistically place the occupation of the Gilbert Site in the mid-1700's (Jelks 1967:97–104).

The semi-permanent nature of historic Wichita villages is attested to by the relatively large size of Norteño archeological sites and by the kinds of occupational features found in them. Several trash accumulations, or middens, were found at the Gilbert Site (Jelks 1967:11–15), each of which contained considerable numbers of artifacts, fragments of food bones, charcoal, ash, and other discarded occupational debris. Oval to roughly circular in outline, as much as 35 feet in diameter, and up to a foot thick, these features are evidence of intensive, concentrated village habitations and may actually have been the floors of Wichita lodges. Some of the Gilbert Site middens and similar middens at the Vincent Site had been capped with layers of clay. Storage pits have been found, as have large pit-house depressions which are the remains of fairly substantial dwellings at the Vincent and Spanish Fort sites. Lumps of fire-hardened clay impressed with the molded outlines of thatching found at Norteño Focus sites probably are the remains of the clay plaster that coated Wichita houses.

Studies of animal bones found at the Gilbert Site indicate that white-tailed deer was the major source of animal protein for the Wichita village inhabitants, although the sample also contains bones of buffalo, black bear, puma, bobcat, raccoon, skunk, jackrabbit, cottontail rabbit, and opossum. Horse and dog bones also were found. The patterns in which the villagers butchered the deer they harvested can be recognized in the bone sample. Judging from the ages the animals were when they were killed and brought home, the Gilbert Site probably was occupied during the spring, summer, and fall.

The aboriginal nomads of central, southern, and coastal Texas were the first to disappear during the historic period. The more organized, semi-sedentary Wichita immigrants endured a while longer. The Comanche were the last to surrender to domination. But because their history on the plains of Texas began late and was of short duration, and because they did not settle anywhere for very long, archeological evidence of the Comanche is scattered and limited primarily to a few isolated burials in northwestern Texas, most of which were disturbed before they were reported to properly trained archeologists (Newcomb 1955; Word and Fox 1975; Willey, Harrison, and Hughes 1978).

An example of a Comanche burial site is the Cogdell Burial, found in a small niche or cave in the Cap Rock Escarpment on the eastern edge of the Llano Estacado (Word and Fox 1975). Although the burial had been dug up before it could be properly investigated, parts of it could be reconstructed and an interesting assortment of burial goods was collected.

The body had been placed on its side in a depression or pit about two feet wide and six feet long and oriented so that the head was on the south end. Grave goods were arranged in the pit. Then rocks were placed over the body to form a cairn and a small fire was built on top of it. An analysis of the skeletal material found that the bones were those of a male between 35 and 45 years of age and about 5 feet 7 inches tall (Doran and Malina 1975).

Artifacts in the burial included clothing such as a cotton shirt, beaded leggings and other beaded garments, a pair of moccasins with the imprints of the feet of their owner, and fragments of wool blankets and a buffalo robe (Word and Fox 1975). Other personal items included brass bracelets, hair ornaments, a gold-plated finger ring, silver *conchas*, the remains of a weasel pelt, a small rectangular hand mirror, trade beads of various colors, a part of a silver buckle, pendants made from elk teeth and Pacific coast abalone shell, and an iron hoe. Saddle parts of wood and leather and iron saddle hardware were found in the burial, along with fiber cordage, parts of what possibly was a Spanish bridle, and the wooden poles and fastener of a *travois*—the horse-drawn carrier used to

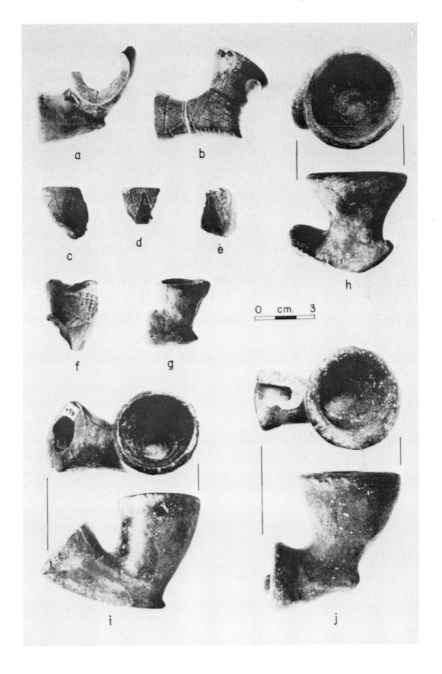

FIG. 2.13 *Native-made tobacco pipes from the Gilbert Site, Rains County.*
(From Jelks 1967: Fig. 66. Courtesy Texas Archeological Society.)

transport belongings from camp to camp. Food offerings were represented by buffalo (or possibly cow) bones, some of which showed signs that the offering had been cooked. The analysis of the artifact collection indicated that the deceased was a Comanche who apparently was buried some time between 1850 and 1860.

Several Comanche burial customs reported in the historical accounts were verified by archeological evidence from the Cogdell Burial and its comparison with other historic burial sites (Word and Fox 1975:48, Table 5). Among these customs, the body was flexed (its knees bent and brought up toward the chest) and bound in position, painted with vermillion, dressed in the finest clothes, and wrapped in a robe or blanket. The corpse was buried in a crevice, or some other secluded lonely place, along with the deceased's possessions, including his saddle, bridle, and favorite horse. The grave was covered with rocks and a ceremonial fire was built over it. In this way the Comanche was laid to rest so that his spirit would live on in the perfect afterworld where there was no sorrow or suffering (Newcomb 1961:189).

After the Louisiana Purchase in 1803, Spain gave land in eastern Texas to some of the Indian groups who were migrating westward under pressure of Anglo-American frontier settlement, such as the Choctaw, Cherokee, Alabama, and Coushatta. The Mexican government granted land to Shawnee in the 1820's, and remnants of other Indian peoples of the eastern United States lived for a while in Texas. But by the time Texas became a state, most of these peoples and many native Texas Indians had been removed to Arkansas and Oklahoma. Fragments of the Puebloan societies of the Southwest who were brought into the Spanish missions of the El Paso area had been acculturated by the beginning of the twentieth century, and even though some of their descendants survive today, most of their culture is extinct (Newcomb 1961:24). Some Kickapoo Indians live today near the International Bridge in Eagle Pass after migrating through various parts of Texas and Mexico during the nineteenth and twentieth centuries. The Alabama and Coushatta remained in Texas and managed to maintain their ethnic identity during the early nineteenth century, but became acculturated with Anglo-American values by 1854 when a reservation was established for them in southeastern Texas and the two Indian groups merged (Peebles 1968; Marsh, Martin, and Jacobson

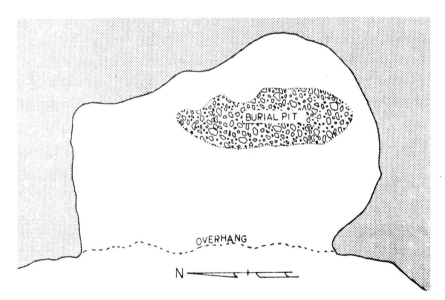

FIG. 2.14   *The Cogdell Burial Site.* Cross-section and plan of burial niche. (From Word and Fox 1975:Fig. 3. Courtesy Texas Archeological Society.)

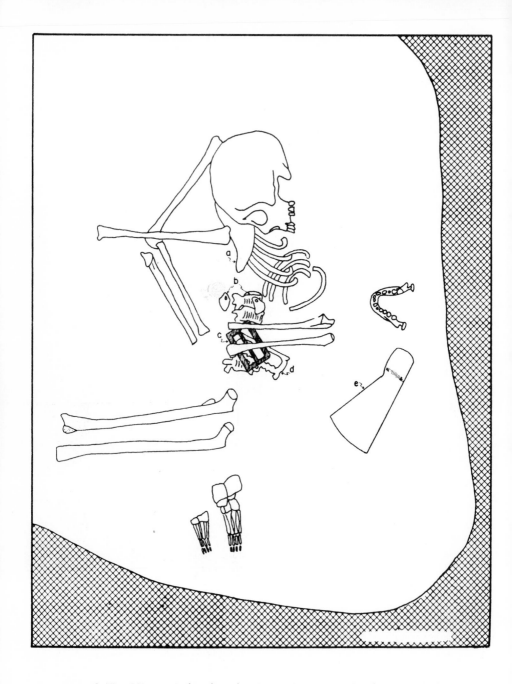

FIG. 2.15 *Historic Indian burial, Morgan Jones Site, Crosby County, Texas.* a, whelk shell artifact; b, elk tooth pendants; c, brass buckle; d, brass cinch buckle; e, axe. (From Parsons 1967: Fig. 22. Courtesy Texas Historical Commission.)

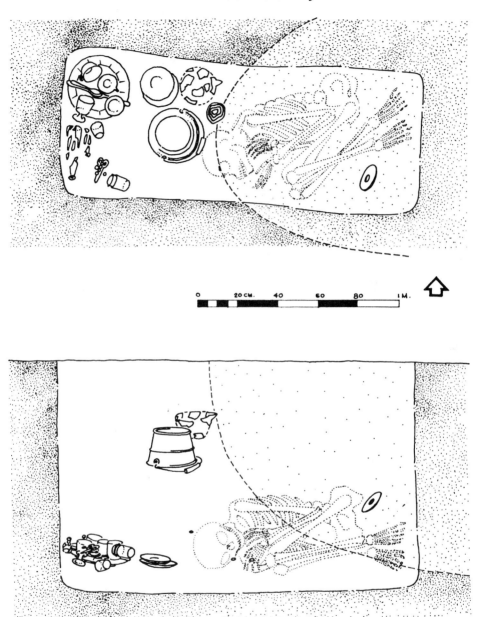

FIG. 2.16 *Nineteenth-century Indian burial, possibly Alabama-Coushatta.* Plan and section showing position of grave offerings. (From Hsu 1969:Fig. 4 and 4A. Courtesy Texas Historical Commission.)

1974). Eventually their reservation was reduced in size, restricted primarily to a secluded part of the Big Thicket region of southeastern Texas.

At least 14 Alabama-Coushatta village sites in Texas are mentioned in the historical accounts. Five of these were located on the Trinity River, but others scattered across southeastern Texas included agricultural settlements, hunting camps, and a fishing village on the coast. In the late 1960's interested members of the Houston Archaeological Society and an archeologist from the Archeological Program of the State Building Commission conducted careful excavations of an Indian cemetery site that had been disturbed by relic collectors (Hsu 1969). The cemetery was located on a prominent point overlooking the bottomland of the Trinity River in San Jacinto County about 50 miles from the present-day Alabama-Coushatta Reservation in Polk County. Six burials were studied, only three of which remained intact after the disturbance of the cemetery by artifact hunters. The cemetery's location with respect to Indian lands referred to in property records and the kinds of grave goods indicated that the burial ground and a possible village site nearby probably were used by the Alabama-Coushatta between 1842 and 1877.

The burial pits were oriented east-west with the heads to the west. As probably was traditional for the Alabama and the Coushatta, grave offerings of tools, clothing, weapons, food containers, and other possessions needed in the afterlife were placed in special positions in the graves. But instead of traditional Indian-made goods, the graves contained mid-nineteenth-century British-made dishes, glass tableware, clothing buttons, finger rings, *conchas* made from Mexican and American silver coins, a bone-handled knife, glass medicine bottles, a metal bucket, a tin can, a coffeepot, a sewing kit with buttons and scissors, coins dated 1792, 1842, and 1852, and other non-Indian artifacts. Obviously the Alabama-Coushatta had adopted Anglo-American technology by the mid-nineteenth century, but the ways these goods were placed in the burials suggest that several traditional beliefs and lifeways were retained by these native American peoples through generations of pressures for cultural change.

III

The First Europeans

SPANISH EXPLORERS made more than 40 expeditions into Texas and to its coast during the sixteenth and seventeenth centuries. It was not until the 1680's that the first actual Spanish settlements were founded at El Paso and near Presidio—which at that time were a part of the Colonial Province of New Mexico. Historians and archeologists have argued about the routes of the first European explorers and have searched for evidence of their visits. Some treasure ships were lost off the Texas coast along their homebound route to Spain, and treasure hunters and archeologists have found some of their remains. But the first Europeans left very few traces of their two centuries of exploration in Texas.

The French influence in Texas history has been important to historians and archeologists. The Spanish Colonial occupation of eastern Texas began in 1690 with the establishment of two missions for the Christianization of the Hasinai Caddo Indians and, more importantly, to control French intrusion into the borderlands of New Spain. These first missions quickly failed and the Province of Texas was abandoned until the resurgence of French activity in the early eighteenth century encouraged the Spanish to establish six missions and a military garrison, or presidio, in eastern Texas. In 1719 the French invaded eastern Texas and drove the Spanish out. The response was an imposing expedition in 1720 led by Marqués de San Miguel de Aguayo, who reestablished the missions of eastern Texas, founded a new presidio which became the first capital of the Province of Texas, and went on to establish another presidio and mission settlement on the Texas coast in 1722.

The Routes of the Earliest Intruders

Cabeza de Vaca, Coronado, and Moscoso entered Texas before 1550 and were the first Europeans known to have recorded what they saw there (Hodge and Lewis 1953). Alvar Núñez Cabeza de Vaca, two fellow Spaniards, and a Moorish black companion were the only survivors of a shipwreck on the Texas coast in

1528. After being held captive by Indians near the coast for almost six years, they made their way across southern Texas and northern Mexico before finally reaching European civilization and Mexico City in 1536. In 1541, Captain General Francisco Vásquez de Coronado led an expedition northeastward out of New Mexico across the Texas Panhandle-Plains in search of Quivira, an Indian province which was said to have a large population and a large amount of gold, but turned out to be a village of gardeners and buffalo hunters who lived in grass huts. In the same year, Luis de Moscoso de Alvarado led De Soto's men through northeastern Texas, across the Trinity River, and down the Brazos River as far as present-day Waco. During the next 150 years, several other Spanish explorers, traders, and slavers ventured into Texas from the south and west. And by the end of the seventeenth century, French traders began moving in from the east.

Many of these *entradas* were relatively short trips. Others covered more of Texas and encountered more of its native peoples. Taken together, the various European visits during the sixteenth and seventeenth centuries probably had little direct impact on the Texas environment and its native human inhabitants at the beginning of written history. But the indirect effects of the introduction of Spanish horses and French guns upon the lifeways of the Texas Indians is well-known history. The disruption of their lifeways by technological changes and the devastation of their populations by European diseases and invasions by outside peoples are impossible for most modern Americans to comprehend.

For the last hundred years, historians have been challenged to retrace the routes of the earliest explorers in Texas, especially the first and most famous ones like Cabeza de Vaca and Coronado. Based on translations and interpretations of the travellers' descriptions of the countryside they crossed and the landmarks they observed, so many different routes have been postulated for Coronado's trip to and from Quivira that when superimposed on a modern map of the Texas Panhandle, Coronado's possible lines of travel crisscross just about every part of the Plains north of Amarillo (Skeels 1972:7–8, Figure 4). The Quivira that Coronado finally found in 1542 and Oñate visited in 1601 has been placed everywhere from the Canadian River Valley in Texas to areas in Oklahoma and north of the Arkansas River in Kansas, Nebraska,

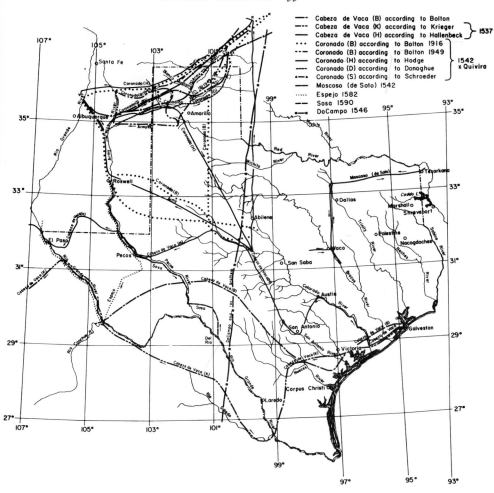

FIG. 3.1 *Routes of Non-Indians in sixteenth-century Texas.* (From Skeels 1972: Fig. 4. Courtesy Texas Historical Commission.)

and Missouri (Donoghue 1936). Historians' attempts to retrace Cabeza de Vaca's route also have been numerous and no two are in complete agreement. One route runs as far north as present-day San Angelo (Hallenbeck 1940). Most of the others run farther south (Bolton 1959).

Of course, because the first European travellers in Texas were on the move most of the time and carried only the minimum provisions with them, they probably left little actual archeological evidence of their visits. But some historians and archeologists have been able to use the ethnographic information recorded by Cabeza de Vaca and Coronado and by later explorers who travelled through the same areas to supplement the topographic descriptions in the narratives used in reconstructing the travellers' routes. To an anthropologist studying the native peoples of Texas at the beginning of written history and the changes their later generations went through, the descriptions of the Indians recorded by the European explorers in the sixteenth and seventeenth centuries are of considerable interest. But first the routes of the travellers must be reconstructed so that the ethnographic information can be placed appropriately in space and time.

In the 1950's, Alex D. Krieger, an American anthropologist who studied for his doctoral degree in Mexico, set out to accomplish this for the route of Cabeza de Vaca. Krieger's (1961) reconstruction is probably the most reputable because he approached the problem with a better understanding of the geography of northern Mexico and southern Texas. He had more of an awareness of the geographical knowledge that probably was available in 1527 and 1528 to the Narváez expedition of which Cabeza de Vaca was a member, and his study did not suffer from the subjectivity and possessiveness exhibited by so many American and Texas historians who could not allow Cabeza de Vaca's route to cross the Rio Grande until it reached El Paso. Also, Krieger was one of the only scholars to reconstruct Cabeza de Vaca's route using both of the original narratives—Cabeza de Vaca's own story, entitled *Los Naufragios* (The Castaways), written some time after he returned to Spain in 1537 and before he left to become governor of Paraguay in 1541, and the other account by the sixteenth-century historian Fernando Oviedo y Valdez, whose work was written in 1543 or 1544 and was published in the 1850's (Krieger 1961).

Except for the first two or three hundred miles in southern Texas, the route that Krieger postulates was entirely within Mexico. The trek began in November, 1528, when about 250 men of the Narváez expedition, attempting to sail five barges along the Gulf Coast from Florida to the Pánuco River settlements on the Mexican coast, became shipwrecked on Mal-Hado, or Galveston Island. Except for Cabeza de Vaca, who was left behind, the survivors of the wrecks set out along the coast for Pánuco, but only three survived and were captured by coastal Indians known as the Mariame. Cabeza de Vaca lived for four years as a trader among the Indians of Mal-Hado. When he finally set out along the coast, he also was captured by the Mariame but was reunited with the three other European castaways. Krieger places the homeland of the Mariame east of the Guadalupe River around Lavaca Bay.

As prisoners, the four Europeans moved inland every summer with the Mariame and neighboring hunting and gathering Indian bands on their seasonal migrations to the prickly pear cactus fields, and there they met several other Indian groups who came to harvest the cactus *tunas*. At the end of the *tuna* harvest in late September or early October, 1534, the four castaways managed to escape and were taken in by a friendly Indian group in an area Krieger places south of the Atascosa River about 30 or 40 miles south of present-day San Antonio. They moved south with the Avavares, crossing the Nueces River, and after spending about eight months in their homeland, Cabeza de Vaca and his companions resumed their attempt to reach the Pánuco. It was in this area of southern Texas that the Spaniards began curing sick and wounded Indians and were sought after as gods by hundreds and sometimes thousands of the people of the region.

Next, the four foreigners crossed a river so large that Cabeza de Vaca compared it to the Guadalquivir in Spain. This must have been the Rio Grande. Krieger places the crossing in the area of present-day Roma in Starr County. The next day they saw their first mountains in the New World. Krieger identifies these as the Sierra de Cerralvo which are visible today from either side of the Rio Grande between Laredo and Rio Grande City. Then the travellers turned inland, possibly for fear that they would meet fierce coastal Indians again if they ventured to go southeastward directly toward the Pánuco. They actually turned northwestward, probably because of the barrier formed by the Sierra Madre Oriental, near present Monterrey.

Eventually they may have reached Texas again where they met the "People of the Cows," who were bison hunters and gardeners living in permanent villages. Several historians agree that this was at La Junta de los Rios, where the Rio Conchos meets the Rio Grande in eastern Chihuahua, and where the Spanish continued to meet the Jumano more than a century later. After Cabeza de Vaca and his companions made their way up the Rio Grande for some distance, they turned westward and crossed the continent to the Gulf of Baja, and then they travelled southeastward all the way to Mexico City. So favorable was Cabeza de Vaca's report of the journey that less than four years later Coronado set out to explore the southwestern and central plains areas of what later became the United States.

One archeologist has attempted to assess the archeological evidence for the route of Cabeza de Vaca (Taylor 1960). While not actually proving the locations of any of the various routes proposed by the historians, he did provide an interesting evaluation of the proposed routes in the light of the archeological evidence found up until the 1950's, and he presented some archeological problems that he thought could be investigated in attempts to reconstruct Cabeza de Vaca's journey. He found three descriptions in *Los Naufragios* that can be studied archeologically. For one part of the journey, Cabeza de Vaca described Indians who organized into a line to drive rabbits out in the open so that they could be knocked down with short clubs "three palms in length." Rabbit sticks, as archeologists call them—short, flat, slightly-curved wooden implements rather like the Australian boomerang—have been recovered from several prehistoric archeological sites, particularly around the mouth of the Pecos River, in the Big Bend area, and in northern Coahuila and Nuevo León, Mexico. Although this distribution seems to support the more southern routes proposed, like Krieger's, the actual distribution of rabbit sticks may have been wider. The geographic region which has environmental conditions favorable for the preservation of wooden artifacts is rather restricted in area. Most of the archeological specimens have been found in dry caves in southwestern Texas. It is possible that Indians in other areas used rabbit sticks that did not survive to be found by archeologists hundreds and thousands of years later (Chelf 1946).

Cabeza de Vaca described the disciplining of a child by Indians living in the same area where he referred to the use of rabbit clubs. A child who had begun crying was carried off some distance away from the band, where the Indians scratched his body with mice teeth. In 1936, a "medicine bundle" containing several rodent jaws was found near the mouth of the Pecos River (Butler 1948:18; Taylor 1949:111–112). Of course, this by no means is proof that Cabeza de Vaca was in this area. There is historical and archeological evidence that rats and mice were a part of the diets of many of the prehistoric and historic Indians of Texas and northern Mexico.

But Cabeza de Vaca's reference to the Indians' use of mice teeth does provide an interesting bit of support for the more southern routes postulated.

The third location of a part of Cabeza de Vaca's route is the area of La Junta de los Rios, where the travellers found their first agricultural communities. Not only was this probably the only area in western Texas and adjacent northern Mexico that had the soils, water, and other conditions to support simple agricultural communities, but some archeological evidence recovered in the La Junta area indicates that villages of agriculturalists did exist there in late prehistoric times (Kelley 1952:382–383). The Presidio area became the site of Spanish Colonial settlements for the Jumano more than 150 years after Cabeza de Vaca and his companions visited the area.

Taylor (1960:282–287) also pointed out references in Cabeza de Vaca's Los Naufragios that could be investigated archeologically. Perhaps the most interesting is the location of the island called Mal-Hado where Cabeza de Vaca and his companions were first shipwrecked. Relocating this place has been the subject of considerable debate, and Mal-Hado has been located by different scholars in places scattered all the way from the mouth of the Mississippi River to Padre Island. However, Cabeza de Vaca specifically mentions oyster shell mounds with huts built on them, located on the mainland opposite Mal-Hado. Shell mounds, or middens, are a distinctive type of archeological site on the upper Texas coast, although few remain that have not been disturbed. Most have been destroyed by modern development of the coastline.

According to Cabeza de Vaca's account, the Indians from Mal-Hado lived on the mounds, probably from February to April of each year, and a number of the shipwrecked Spaniards were employed collecting oysters during the season in 1529. Considering the accounts that of the 80 to 95 shipwrecked Spaniards, the 15 or 16 who survived the winter were in the possession of a considerable amount of European goods and equipment, Taylor suggests that the remains of some of these materials may be buried in shell middens along the coast and their archeological recovery could help to pinpoint the location of Mal-Hado and the places the Spaniards occupied in 1528 and 1529. Taylor acknowledges that this would be like searching for a needle in a haystack, however. Not only would many of the Europeans' goods, such as those made of leather and wood, have perished due to climatic conditions, but many of their supplies could have been picked up and used by the Indians at occupation sites scattered along the Gulf coast. And even if artifacts dating to the early sixteenth century could be found it might be difficult to determine whether they were evidence of occupation by the castaways or by the Indians.

Treasures of the Gulf

In April 1554, a small group of Spanish ships laden with treasure to be delivered to Spain set sail for Havana after becoming separated from a larger homebound fleet. Under the command of Antonio Corzo, the flotilla included his ship, the *San Andrés*, and three other vessels—the *Santa María*, the *San Esteban*, and the *Espíritu Santo*. Twenty days after leaving Vera Cruz, the ships were lost in a storm off Padre Island. More than half of the estimated 300 passengers and crew drowned. Those who made it ashore set out in small boats and on foot to return to Mexico. The *San Andrés* managed to escape the storm and limped into Havana where she was scrapped and her cargo transferred to other vessels.

The people who attempted to follow the coast to the Pánuco River and Spanish settlements there included five Dominican friars, several women and children, and others who had been passengers and crew, servants, and slaves on the wrecked ships (McDonald and Arnold 1979:218–219). Only two made it to safety. One was a Spaniard who had left the main group and returned to the shipwreck site to be found later by the salvage expedition sent to retrieve the valuable cargos from the wrecked ships. Most of the others died from the wounds of Indian arrows.

The castaways suffered from hunger, thirst, and exposure to the harsh environment of the barren coastline (Dávila Padilla 1596). The Indians attacked them all along their trip south. The Spaniards had only two crossbows with which to defend themselves and these were lost when the group was crossing one of the rivers that were major obstacles to their travel. At one point the unfortunates stripped themselves of all their clothing, thinking that clothing was all the Indians wanted. But this mistake resulted only in more exposure to the elements and in embarrassment. All the women and children had been killed by the time the helpless travellers reached the first river south of the Rio Grande. The rest

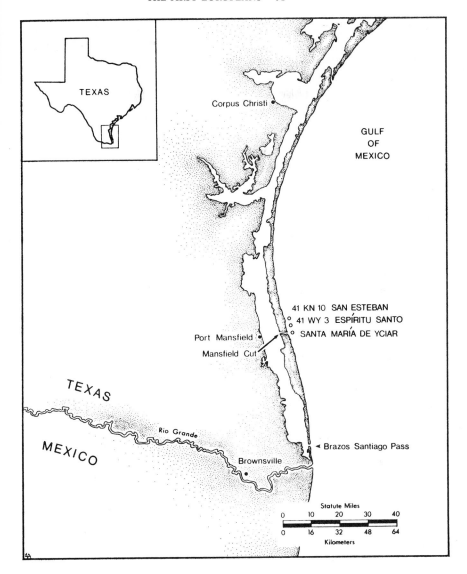

FIG. 3.2 *The sites of the Spanish shipwrecks of 1554, off South Padre Island, Texas.* (From McDonald and Arnold 1979: Map 3. Courtesy Texas Antiquities Committee.)

of the Spaniards were killed at the next river crossing before reaching the Pánuco, except for Friar Marcos de Mena. He had been buried alive in the sand by his companions so that he would not be found by the Indians and could die peacefully from the several arrow wounds he had received, one in the tear duct of his right eye. Eventually Friar Marcos managed to revive himself and struggle southward until he was found by friendly Indians who took him to Tampico. Learning of the disaster, Spanish officials immediately organized a salvage expedition which found the wrecks within two months and recovered a large portion of the valuable cargo. But the rest had to be left on the bottom of the Gulf (Arnold 1978a:25).

More than three and a half centuries later, beach-combing and treasure-hunting became a favorite pastime of vacationers along the Texas coastline. The search for old Spanish coins and other relics was rewarded because a number of shipwrecks occurred during and after the Spanish Colonial Period and bits of wreckage are continuously washed ashore. The largest and most destructive treasure hunt was made in 1967 by an incorporated group of divers who looted the wreckage of the 1554 flotilla from the tidelands that belong to the people of Texas. Legal arguments ensued over ownership of the materials taken from these earliest shipwrecks that have been found in this hemisphere. Nonprofit organizations searched for more evidence of the wrecks in the early 1970's (Hays and Herrin 1970; Scurlock 1974). Eventually, the loot from the 1554 flotilla was given proper cleaning and analysis (Olds 1976).

Much of the Platoro collection apparently was taken from the wreck of the *Espíritu Santo*. The artifacts included an assortment of wrought iron artillery and shot, a crossbow with its wooden stock still intact, parts of hammers and other tools, ceramic olive jars, a gold crucifix, gold and silver coins and bullion, and ship's hardware such as a block-and-tackle, chains, nails, and ballast stones. Also in the collection were navigational instruments such as cast brass astrolabes (which were the forerunners of the modern sextant), and lead sounding weights, which were used to judge the water's depth.

The Texas Antiquities Committee's investigations began in 1972 at the site tentatively identified as the wreck of the *San Esteban*. A detailed survey was conducted using a proton magnetometer—an instrument sensitive to distinctive, localized variations, or anomalies, in the earth's magnetic field. The magnetometer, a computer system, and other sophisticated electronic gear were mounted aboard a survey boat which made passes over specific

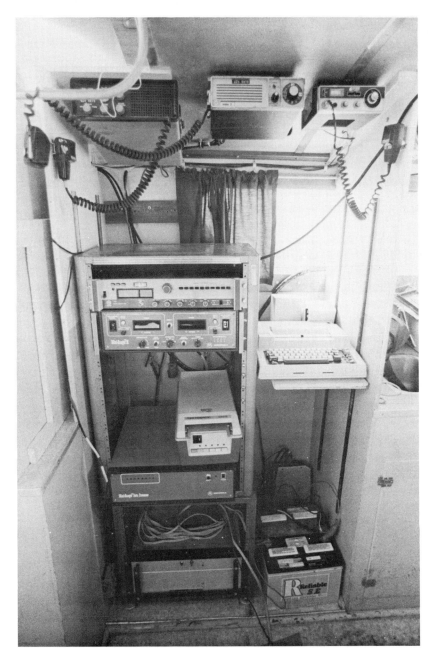

FIG. 3.3 *Proton magnetometer and other electronic equipment used in the search for shipwrecks off the Texas Gulf Coast.* Courtesy Texas Antiquities Committee.)

areas systematically so that a map could be made of anomalies on the Gulf's floor (Clausen and Arnold 1976). Three months of controlled underwater archeological excavations followed, which involved the use of a blower device that diverted the prop wash from the divers' boat to the bottom where it could be directed to erode away the overburden of sand and shell covering the artifacts resting on the clay floor of the Gulf. Careful records were kept of the horizontal position of each archeological specimen by means of a grid system keyed to known points on the coastline so that the wreck could be reconstructed from its archeological remains and its location could be plotted accurately.

A larger team returned to the site in 1973, organized as a training expedition, or field school, in underwater archeology. Further excavations were carried out and a search was made of Padre Island near the wreck in the hope of locating the camps of the survivors of the wrecks or possibly those of the salvage expedition. But definite evidence of these temporary occupations could not be found.

More than 13 tons of encrusted artifacts were recovered during the two archeological field seasons (Arnold 1978a: 27; Arnold and Weddle 1979). This collection included wrought iron anchors, cannon, tools, ship's hardware and fittings, silver bullion and coins, and artifacts of aboriginal manufacture such as blades of obsidian, or volcanic glass, and a mirror made from a polished nodule of iron pyrite. Also found during the investigations were the aft section of the ship's keel and part of the sternpost. From this evidence experts have estimated that the *San Esteban* was at least 66 feet and perhaps 97 feet long and had a capacity of from 164 to 286 tons.

Meticulous study of the artifacts recovered from the Texas tidelands has resulted in the detailed description of a sample of sixteenth-century Spanish cargo from the New World. Many of the artifacts were found as conglomerates, or clusters of objects that had become attached to each other along with sand and shells in the saltwater environment. Techniques had to be developed to carefully analyze the conglomerates, such as by x-raying them, and to separate and preserve the metal artifacts they contained (Olds 1976; Hamilton 1976).

The location, identification, and underwater excavation of the 1554 wrecks of the Spanish flotilla resulted in further development

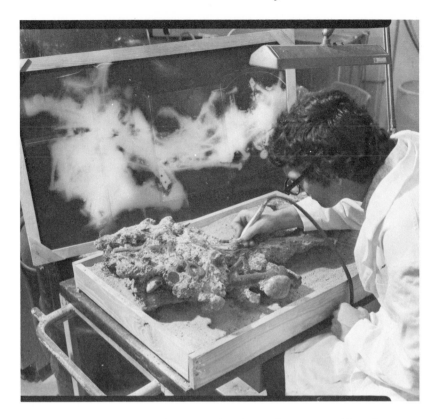

FIG. 3.4   *Dr. Donny Hamilton removing sixteenth-century artifacts from a conglomerate recovered from one of the three Spanish shipwrecks found off Padre Island, Texas.* Note the x-ray of the conglomerate in the background. (Courtesy Texas Antiquities Committee.)

of technological innovations, such as the proton magnetometer, for use in later archeological investigations (Arnold 1976, 1978b). A considerable amount of historical documentary research was done at archives in the United States, Mexico, England, France, and Spain as part of the studies of the shipwrecks (McDonald and Arnold 1979). Public interest in the finds and in the underwater excavations encouraged several academic publications, public exhibitions, a motion picture, and a popular book (Arnold and Weddle 1979). The archeological techniques and technology developed have great potential for the investigation of shipwrecks and other underwater sites, and also for the archeological investigation of sites on dry land.

FIG. 3.5   *Nails, spikes, coins, and other artifacts arranged as they occurred in a conglomerate recovered from one of the Spanish shipwrecks of 1554 off Padre Island, Texas.* (Courtesy Texas Antiquities Committee.)

The Search for the French

In July 1684, René Robert Cavelier, Sieur de La Salle, departed France with four vessels loaded with colonists and supplies and bound for the mouth of the Mississippi River. He intended to establish a port there to secure French control of the area and expand the French trade empire.

The expedition had trouble from the beginning. There was dissension among the leaders. One of the ships was captured by the Spanish, exposing La Salle's plans. To make matters worse, the party sailed past the Mississippi and arrived instead on the Texas coast at Matagorda Island. La Salle explored the area and located a suitable settlement site on the bank of a creek entering the bay. But the colonists became stranded when one of their ships sailed for France and the remaining two ran aground. With the materials they salvaged from the wrecked vessels and from what little timber they could haul in from the countryside, they erected a pal-

FIG. 3.6   *Coins from one of the Spanish shipwrecks of 1554 found off Padre Island, Texas.* (Courtesy Texas Antiquities Committee.)

isaded settlement and named it Saint Louis. The colony suffered hunger, sickness, and Indian attacks. Eventually, while La Salle was gone in search of the Mississippi and help from the French settlements in the Illinois River Valley, the stockade was overrun by the Indians and most of its remaining inhabitants were massacred (Joutel 1962).

Aware of French plans to colonize the Gulf coast, 11 Spanish expeditions were sent by sea and by land to find La Salle's colony (Weddle 1973). The Alonso de León expedition finally found it in April 1689. The houses had been sacked. Chests and furniture had been broken apart. The pages of books, other articles, and decomposed bodies were found scattered across the settlement area (Bolton 1959:398–399).

Still suspicious of French activity in Spanish territory, De

León was ordered to return and establish missions in eastern Texas, destroy La Salle's fort, and search for evidence of other French intruders. After burning the fort in April 1690, De León's party noticed objects offshore that looked like buoys—possible evidence that the French were still coming into the bay. In 1691, a sea expedition was sent to find the buoys, map the bay, and search for the French. But no evidence was found, except for some of the remains of La Salle's colony, and the expedition returned to Vera Cruz (Gilmore 1973:15–17).

After the La Salle fiasco, the French ignored the lower Mississippi Valley until competition with the British encouraged the French settlement of Louisiana in the early eighteenth century. Responding to the resurgence of French activity, expeditions were sent to reestablish the Spanish presence in eastern Texas and to strengthen defenses there. After this was accomplished, the Aguayo expedition built a presidio on the site of La Salle's fort (Forrestal 1935). The presidio Nuestra Señora de Loreto, and the mission Nuestra Señora del Espíritu established nearby, operated until 1716 when they were moved inland.

The site of La Salle's Fort Saint Louis was forgotten, for the most part, until twentieth-century historians became interested in the search for the French in Texas. Using the Spanish map from the 1691 search, Bolton (1924) found a possible location of La Salle's settlement on Garcitas Creek near Lavaca Bay in Victoria County. Other historians contested his claims (e.g. Cole 1946).

In 1950, the Texas Memorial Museum conducted archeological excavations that recovered early European artifacts at Bolton's site, now known as the Keeran Site. But they did not demonstrate that this was the location of La Salle's fort. None of the artifacts recovered were identified as being positive evidence of late seventeenth-century French occupation and until recently there was doubt as to the location of Fort Saint Louis. In 1970, a magnetometer survey plotted 16 anomalies, two of which might possibly mark the wrecks of La Salle's ships (Briggs 1971).

Using a combined historical and archeological approach, Kathleen Gilmore (1973) worked out a concept of what the remains of La Salle's fort should look like. She researched the historical accounts to reconstruct the geography, physiography, and topography of the site's location. She studied archeological materials

FIG. 3.7 *The Cardenas map of 1691 showing the Matagorda Bay area.* Note the reference to the location of "Pueblo de los Franceses"—La Salle's Fort. (From Gilmore 1973: Fig. 4. Courtesy Texas Historical Commission; from J. P. Bryan Collection, The University of Texas at Austin.)

from sites of the appropriate time periods to get an idea about what the occupational debris of the French colony and the later Spanish presidio should be.

The site of Fort Saint Louis was described in the accounts as situated on a small hillock two leagues, or about five miles, up the smallest stream that enters the bay. Gilmore found that Garcitas Creek fits the description. The Keeran Site is located about five miles above its mouth and on the highest land form in the area. Even the plant and animal life in the vicinity today are similar to those mentioned in the historical accounts. The shorelines drawn on maps by the Spanish while searching for the French in 1691 compare rather closely to the configuration of islands, estuaries, streams, and bays depicted on modern maps of the Matagorda Bay area.

Gilmore had little trouble finding collections of Spanish artifacts from colonial sites occupied concurrently with the Spanish presidio built on the site of La Salle's fort. And the eighteenth-century artifacts in the Texas Memorial Museum collection from the Keeran Site compared well with those from other Spanish Colonial sites. But it was not easy to find a comparative collection of French artifacts of the same time period as La Salle's colony that could be considered truly reliable evidence of French occupation. So many French-made trade goods had been in circulation by that time that different peoples could be represented by various kinds of French artifacts. Even more of a problem, the main French settlement area of the Keeran Site may not have been excavated during the 1950 investigations, and positive evidence of French occupation might not be included in the Museum collection.

Funding was not available for a full-scale archeological investigation of the Keeran Site. So Gilmore concentrated on the study of sherds of French pottery types as a more sensitive indicator of actual French habitation than gun parts, tools, and other French-made artifacts. In the collection from the 1950 excavations of the Keeran Site she found one type of French pottery that is very similar to pottery found at the French sites of Fort Michilimachinac in Michigan and Louisbourg in Nova Scotia. This green-glazed earthenware pottery is the best material evidence we have so far that the Keeran Site is most probably the location of La Salle's Fort Saint Louis.

As important as they were in the Spanish Colonial Period in eastern Texas, few of the places the French actually occupied have been found. French trade goods are common at archeological sites of Indian occupation and Spanish Colonial settlements. Archeological investigations have found that the further east and closer to French Louisiana the sites are located, the greater are the proportions of French-made artifacts that occur (Tunnell and Ambler

1967:26–27; Corbin, Kalina, and Alex 1980:215). But these materials are evidence of trade and of Spanish and Indian habitation rather than French habitation. Even though it was against the law of New Spain, the Spanish settlers in Texas traded often with the French during the eighteenth century.

By 1731, the Spanish Colonial Empire had strategically placed several military posts and missions in the Province of Texas in response to continued threats of French intrusion. The capital of Texas became the Presidio de los Adaes across the Red River from French Nachitoches in Louisiana, and there were other Spanish settlements at Nacogdoches, San Antonio, and La Bahía (present-day Goliad). Southeastern Texas was not secure, however, and rumors of French infestation of that area led to searches for French traders and the establishment of the presidio San Agustín de Ahumada and the mission Nuestra Señora de la Luz nearby in 1756 on the lower Trinity River in the homeland of the Atakapa-speaking Orcoquisac Indians. The presidio was built on the site of the trading post of Joseph Blancpain, a Frenchman who was arrested by the Spanish in 1754 for practicing illegal trade.

The site of Blancpain's trading post, along with the sites of the Spanish presidio and mission, and some Indian campsites, have been found on the edge of Lake Miller on the lower Trinity River and have been designated officially as a Historic District. In the late 1960's, the Houston Archaeological Society made collections from the surface of the sites and conducted some limited test excavations. They found French-made pottery sherds on an elevated area near the lake shore that probably are evidence of Spanish and French occupations.

In 1979 the Center for Archaeological Research of The University of Texas at San Antonio, with the help of members of the Houston Archaeological Society, conducted archeological investigations in search of a wharf and the wreck of Blancpain's boat, which according to the historical accounts were located near the French trading post and the Spanish settlement that succeeded it (Fox, Day, and Highley 1980:85–93). Soil cores were taken systematically from the low-lying areas along the shore of Lake Miller to determine the nature of the lake deposits and the depth of the silt covering the original sandy lake bottom of the eighteenth century. A test was made to determine the feasibility of undertaking an intensive survey using a magnetometer to find buried magnetic

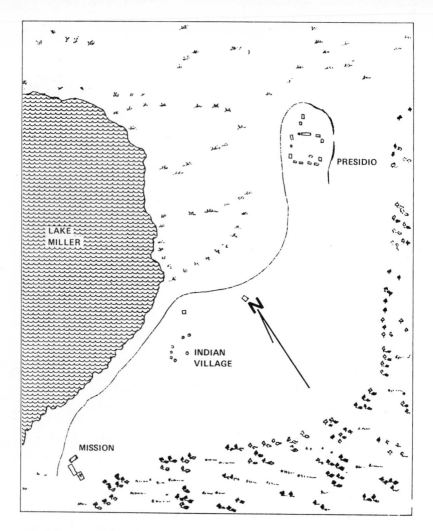

FIG. 3.8 *Spanish settlement areas on Lake Miller in 1776.* Redrawn from original Spanish document. (From Fox, Day, and Highley 1980:Fig. 25. Courtesy Center for Archaeological Research, The University of Texas at San Antonio.)

signs of Blancpain's boat and other possible features near the site of the trading post and the presidio. Although no trace of the wharf or the boat could be found, the investigation concluded that the remains of both probably are present somewhere in the area and can be found by future, more intensive archeological investigation.

Late in the year 1718, a French trader arrived in Texas to establish a trading post among the Caddo Indians in northeastern Texas

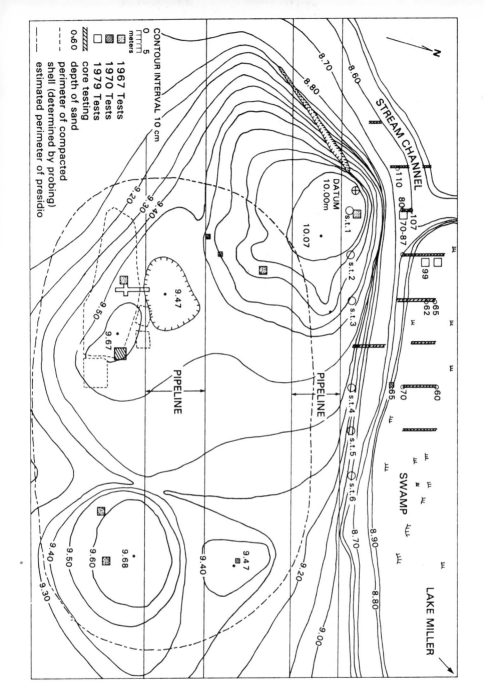

FIG. 3.9 *Map of the first site of Mission La Luz and Presidio Ahumada (41CH57), showing disturbances and archeological excavations.* (From Fox, Day, and Highley 1980:Fig. 24. Courtesy Center for Archaeological Research, The University of Texas at San Antonio.)

FIG. 3.10 *Map of La Harpe's route up the Sulphur River and overland to the location of his Nassonite Post (41BW5). From Miroir et al.* 1973:Fig. 1. Courtesy Texas Archeological Society.)

(Smith 1958). From New Orleans, Benard de La Harpe canoed up the Mississippi to the mouth of the Red River and then on to the French outpost of Natchitoches in Louisiana. In March 1719, he and six companions left the outpost to explore the frontier. In April, La Harpe's expedition beached their pirogues on the banks of the Sulphur River and began an overland journey northeastward to the village of the Nassonites, members of the Kadohadocho Confederacy of the Caddo. After he arrived and was well received by the war chief and other officers of the Nassonites, La Harpe spent several days looking for a good location for his trading post. He selected the spot for it on the south bank of the Red River, about a musket shot from the river channel. In July 1719,

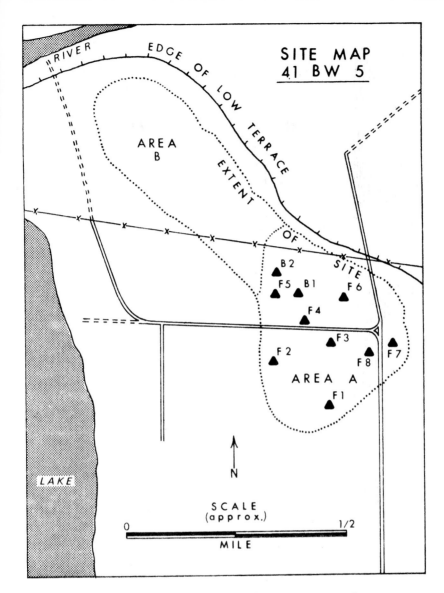

FIG. 3.11 *Map of Site 41BW5, the probable site of La Harpe's Nassonite Post.* "B" indicates burial location; "F" indicates location of occupational feature. (From Miroir *et al.* 1973: Fig. 2. Courtesy Texas Archeological Society.)

the Indians helped him build a structure that measured about 110 feet long and 20 feet wide.

La Harpe left later in 1719 and little is known about what happened at the Nassonite Post after that. Most of the eighteenth-century history of the post is based primarily on depositions made in 1805 before Dr. John Sibley, Indian agent for the Orleans Territory, by former residents of the trading post (American State Papers 1832). Alex Grappe settled at the post in 1737 and built a small fortified settlement and trading house there. The post remained in operation until 1765, when Grappe and his family moved away, two years after Louisiana had been ceded to Spain. A small French and Indian population occupied the site in 1770 when Athanase de Mézières passed through the area (Bolton 1914:71–74). But by 1778 the French settlement had been abandoned.

During the 1960's and the 1970's, a group of amateur archeologists conducted investigations at a site on the south bank of the Red River in Bowie County which they have determined to be the remains of La Harpe's Nassonite Post (Miroir, Harris, Blaine, and McVay 1973). Located on a slightly elevated rise in the floodplain of the river, the Rosebrough Lake Site was found as two primary areas—one in which both Indian and European artifacts were found as well as artifact concentrations and human burials, and the other in which only artifacts of Indian manufacture were found.

The investigators were careful to preserve the integrity of the historic site, carefully recording what they took from its cultivated and eroded surface, and digging only in limited areas in order to study the stratigraphy of the site and to recover the contents of a couple of burial pits that had become exposed. The graves contained the remains of Indians who had been buried fully extended on their backs with offerings including native-made pottery of several varieties and jewelry native-made from glass trade beads and polished pieces of conch shells, probably obtained through trade from the Gulf coast. Several "spoons" fashioned from freshwater clam shells were found with one of the burials.

The artifacts collected from the surface that were made from native materials included historic period aboriginal pottery of various Caddoan types, clay figurines (one of a horse), clay tobacco pipes, chipped flint arrow points and other tools, polished stone pendants and a celt, or axe-like tool, and five ornaments of olivella marine shell imported through trade networks all the way from the Pacific coast. European trade goods and artifacts made from European-produced materials included iron axes, or tomahawks, metal arrow points, glass bottle fragments, glass mirror fragments, sherds of French, Spanish, and British pottery, fragments

FIG. 3.12   *European trade axes from archeological site 41BW5, probable site of La Harpe's Nassonite Post, on the Red River, Bowie County.* (From Miroir *et al.* 1973: Fig. 7. Courtesy Texas Archeological Society.)

of Spanish bridle bits, metal knife blades (some stamped with their makers' names), scissors, metal ornaments and tools, iron kettle fragments, the latch from an eighteenth-century French briefcase, "strike-a-lights" used to spark fires, a large number of glass and shell trade beads, and a variety of flintlock gun parts and gunflints possibly of European origin and also of aboriginal manufacture.

One comparatively large assortment of glass trade beads was found in one of the artifact concentrations and the estimated dates of their manufacture have led the investigators to suggest that the concentration marks the site of Alex Grappe's trading house built in 1737. The metal gun parts included the whole range of gun cocks, frizzens, springs, barrel parts, breech sections, side plates, butt plates, and trigger guards. A large sample of lead shot also was recovered which appeared to have been fired and had been produced for use in fowling pieces and for other hunting purposes. Several lead musket balls also were found. All of the European materials appeared to date to the period of occupation of the Nassonite Post, between 1719 and 1778. Further, more problem-oriented investigation of the Rosebrough Lake Site and the material from it should provide additional information about the history of the occupation of the Nassonite Post and its place in eighteenth-century French trade networks in Spanish Texas.

IV

Remains of the Spanish Colonial Empire

THE HAPPENINGS during the initial period of Spanish colonization were the first in a series of adaptations that the Colonial system underwent in its attempt to secure the Texas frontier, removed and isolated as it was from the core cities of New Spain (Casteñeda 1936). The mission system evolved originally as an agent of the government to occupy Spanish borderlands and to "pacify" the native inhabitants of an area into a work force that could be managed by the civil authorities as part of the Empire (Bolton 1960:47).

During the Spanish Colonial Period in Texas, the Empire's attempts to control French encroachments had to be adapted from the initial system of establishing missions by themselves, to a later arrangement of missions accompanied by presidios, and finally to the establishment of actual civil colonies of Spanish settlers (Hatcher 1905). After the failure of the first missions in eastern Texas in the late seventeenth century, mission settlements were reinforced with presidios. The mission-presidio combination became the most common and widespread form of Spanish Colonial settlement in Texas (Moorhead 1975), but in many ways the only successful approach was the creation of civil communities such as San Antonio de Bexar, which eventually replaced the Presidio de los Adaes on the Red River as the official center of governmental affairs in Texas in 1773.

Nineteenth-century travellers in Texas were impressed by the permanence and mystery of the ruins of the Spanish Colonial Empire. Public interest during the early twentieth century encouraged restorations, historical research, and—unfortunately—a lot of destruction of the archeological deposits at the early historic sites. Only within the last two decades have systematic, properly controlled archeological investigations been conducted at Spanish Colonial sites in Texas. Archeologists have undertaken a variety of short-term and some intensive excavations at the more spectacu-

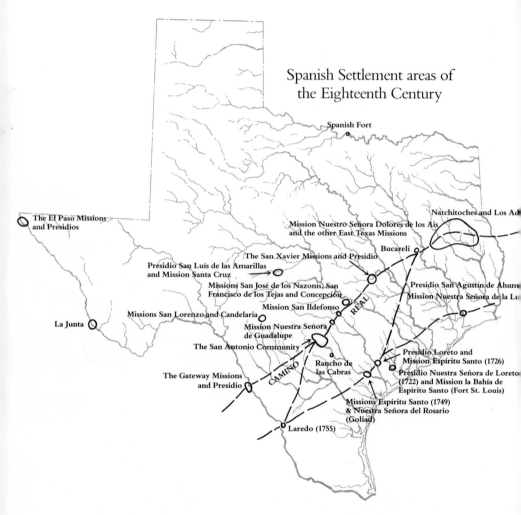

Spanish Settlement areas of
the Eighteenth Century

Spanish Fort

The El Paso Missions
and Presidios

Natchitoches and Los Ad

Mission Nuestro Señora Dolores de los Ais
and the other East Texas Missions

Bucareli

Presidio San Luís de las Amarillas
and Mission Santa Cruz

The San Xavier Missions and Presidio

Missions San José de los Nazonis, San
Francisco de los Tejas and Concepción

Presidio San Agustín de Ahum
Mission Nuestra Señora de la Lu

Mission San Ildefonso

Missions San Lorenzo and Candelaria

La Junta

Mission Nuestra Señora
de Guadalupe

REAL

The San Antonio Community

Rancho de
las Cabras

Presidio Loreto and
Mission Espíritu Santo (1726)

The Gateway Missions
and Presidio

CAMINO

Presidio Nuestra Señora de Loreto
(1722) and Mission la Bahía de
Espíritu Santo (Fort St. Louis)

Missions Espíritu Santo (1749)
& Nuestra Señora del Rosario
(Goliad)

Laredo (1755)

FIG. 4.1   *Spanish settlement areas in eighteenth-century Texas.*

lar, best preserved, and better known missions and presidios, particularly those in San Antonio. More recently, archeological research has been extended to include the location and evaluation of the more obscure, almost forgotten sites of the Spanish Colonial Period.

Mission and Presidio Sites in Eastern Texas

A couple of the Spanish Colonial settlements of eastern Texas have received preliminary archeological study. In 1979, at the request of the Louisiana Division of Culture, Recreation, and Tourism, exploratory excavations were conducted by Northwestern State University at the site of the Presidio de los Adaes on the Red River near Robeline, Louisiana (Gregory 1980). The purpose of this project was to obtain information about the areal extent of the site and collect a sample of its contents for use in interpretive exhibits and in park planning and development.

Founded by the Aguayo Expedition in 1721, Los Adaes was

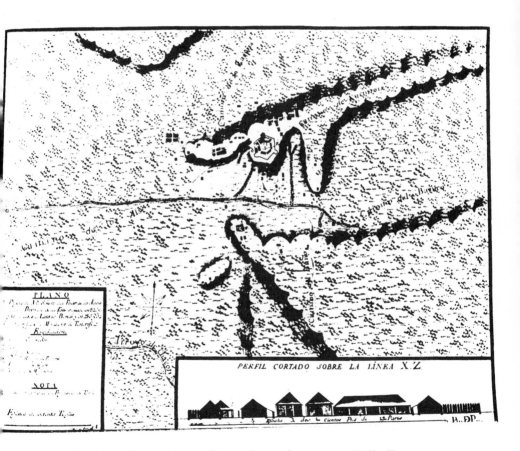

FIG. 4.2 *Joseph Urrutia's map of Los Adaes settlement area, 1768.* (From Gregory 1980: Fig. 2.)

the capital of the Province of Texas from 1731 until 1773. The presidio was a wooden stockade, hexagonal in shape and surrounded by a moat. It was constructed to control French activity in Texas, but it became a major center for social and economic interaction between French, Spanish, and various Indian peoples.

The most numerous artifacts recovered during the excavations at Adaes were wrought iron nails, which reflect the primarily wooden construction of the various structures of the presidio community. Evidence of the structural makeup of the Spanish Governor's house was found, including the large sandstone slabs of its central hearth. The possible locations of a powder house, a cooking and food preparation area, a stable, a shot tower (from which molten lead was dropped to form spherical ammunition), and the lines of the moat, palisade, and bulwark fortifications of the presidio were located.

A large number of Indian-made pottery sherds, the most common of which were historic Caddo ceramic types, were found, along with a variety of sherds from imported ceramic vessels of French, Spanish, Mexican, German, Chinese, and English origin. Studies of these ceramics and the stratigraphic and spacial relationships in which they were found indicated that the French trade influence increased toward the end of the Spanish occupation of the Presidio de los Adaes. Some pottery sherds and other artifacts were found that were representative of reoccupation of the site after the presidio was abandoned. This later occupation apparently lasted well into the nineteenth century.

Another Spanish Colonial site in eastern Texas that has been archeologically investigated is the site of Mission Nuestra Señora de los Ais, which was established in 1717 by members of the Ramón expedition for the conversion of the Ais Caddo Indians. The settlement was occupied for only a couple of years before it was abandoned under the threat of French invasion of eastern Texas, and then it was reestablished at a new location by the Aguayo Expedition in 1722.

In contrast to the busy capital at Presidio de los Adaes, Mission Dolores was a small, struggling settlement that apparently barely managed to survive until 1773. The Indians would not live at the mission but instead occupied scattered villages, or *rancherias*, in the surrounding forests. The missionaries were hesitant to bap-

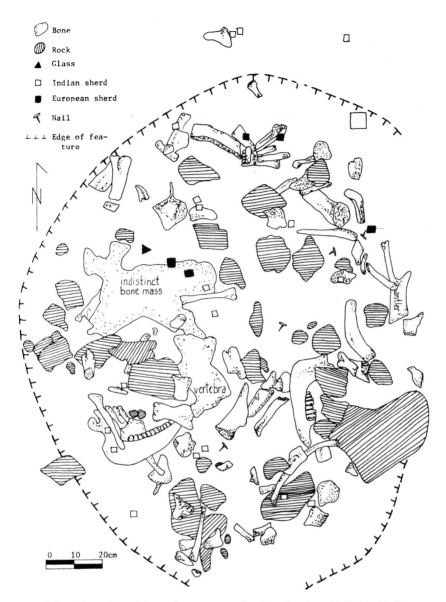

Bone
Rock
Glass
Indian sherd
European sherd
Nail
Edge of feature

N

indistinct
bone mass

vertebra

antler

0 10 20cm

FIG. 4.3   *Plan of an eighteenth-century trash pit at the site of Mission Dolores de los Ais; San Augustine County.* (From Corbin, Kalina, and Alex 1980: Fig. 35. Courtesy Stephen F. Austin State University.)

tize the Ais because they were not serious enough about becoming Christians. Spanish travellers and inspectors passing by noted the poor conditions at Mission Dolores and questioned the need for the settlement, particularly after the Treaty of Paris of 1763, when

Spain's eastern border became the Mississippi River and the presidios and missions of eastern Texas were no longer essential for protection against French intrusion. In 1767, Gaspar José de Solís commented that there was no hope for the "reduction" of the Ais (Kress 1932:67).

Since 1972, several short-term archeological investigations have been focused on Mission Hill near San Augustine, Texas, where Mission Dolores was thought to have been located. In 1976, 1977, and 1978, the Stephen F. Austin State University Archaeological Field School conducted excavations which demonstrated that this is in fact the mission site. They also recovered some archeological data about historic Caddo mission Indians and some physical remains of the 50 years of Spanish Colonial occupation of the piney woods of eastern Texas (Corbin, Kalina, and Alex 1980). The investigations were able to recover preliminary information about the southern perimeter wall of the mission compound, three mission dwellings, four trash pits, and possibly a section of the Camino Real—the main route linking the settlements of the Province of Texas with San Antonio de Bexar and Mexico in the eighteenth century.

The collection of European artifacts recovered from Mission Dolores offered few real surprises. The sherds of Spanish and Mexican tin-enameled earthenware pottery, or majolica, that were found are of the types to be expected for the period, like the ceramics from Spanish Colonial sites located elsewhere in Texas. The French-made tin-enameled earthenware pottery, or faience, of the eighteenth century occurred in the proper proportions to Spanish wares as archeologists predicted they would at sites in close proximity to the French settlements of Louisiana. Chinese and English ceramics were found at Mission Dolores as they have been at other Spanish Colonial sites, but in greater proportions than at sites further west, suggesting a greater influence of English trade than might be expected, long before the movement of Anglo-Americans and their supply systems into the area in the early nineteenth century.

Mission-Presidio Settlements on the Coastal Plain

Spanish Colonial occupation of the Gulf coastal plain began with the establishment of Presidio Loreto on the site of La Salle's

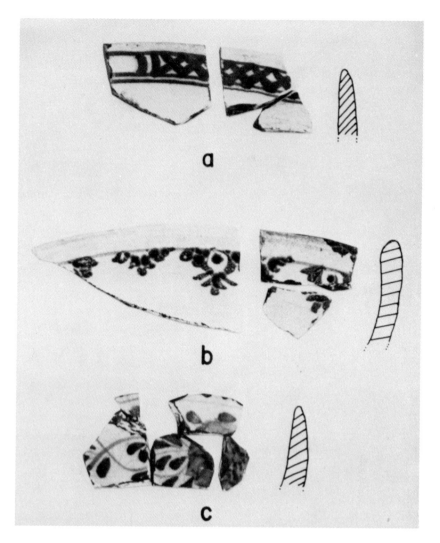

FIG. 4.4 *Sherds from three different vessels of eighteenth-century French tin-enameled earthenware, or faience, pottery from the site of Mission Dolores de los Ais, San Augustine County.* (From Corbin, Kalina, and Alex 1980: Fig. 56. Courtesy Stephen F. Austin State University.)

Fort Saint Louis and the founding of Mission Espíritu Santo de Zuñiga nearby in 1722 for the Karankawa and other coastal Indians. Commonly referred to as the La Bahía mission and presidio, they were moved inland in 1726 among the Aranama and other Coahuilteco groups on the Guadalupe River in the area of present-day Victoria. Then they were relocated again in the mid-

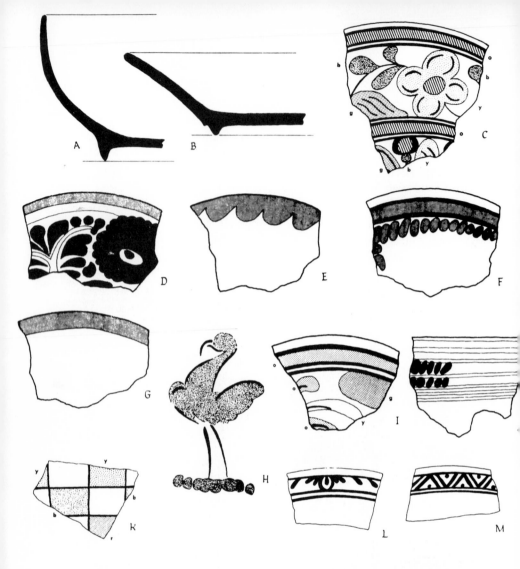

FIG. 4.5 *Various sherds of eighteenth-century Spanish Colonial tin-enameled earthenware, or majolica, pottery from Mission San Antonio de Valero (the Alamo), and sherds of eighteenth-century French tin-enameled earthenware, or faience, pottery from the site of Presidio San Agustín de Ahumada, Chambers County.* A–B, typical cross-sections of majolica bowls and plates; C–G, I–J, various majolica decorative patterns, most commonly painted in shades of blue on white (E, G, J), but also in polychrome designs of orange, yellow, green, and brown on white; H, bird motif (blue and brown on white) found on the bottom of some majolica plates; K–M, decorated sherds of French faience (K, yellow, brown, and red on white; L and M, blue on white). (From Tunnell 1966: Figs. 1, 2, & 3; Tunnell and Ambler 1967: Fig. 7. Courtesy Texas Historical Commission.)

eighteenth century to the San Antonio River where a community grew up that became known as Goliad. In 1754 the Mission Nuestra Señora del Rosario was established near the La Bahía community.

Excavations at the Keeran Site in 1950 recovered a general sample of evidence of the Spanish Colonial occupations of the Presidio Loreto and Mission de Zuñiga on the coast (Gilmore 1973). Their second sites near Victoria have been found but have only received preliminary archeological investigation. Excavations at the presidio site by members of the Texas Archeological Society found some structural remains, a sample of Spanish Colonial artifacts, and skeletal remains of people buried in the consecrated ground of the presidio. Some of the burials are the remains of Texans who were laid to rest there in the nineteenth century, long after the presidio was abandoned (Anne A. Fox, personal communication).

FIG. 4.6 *Mission Nuestra Señora del Espíritu Santo de Zuñiga, Goliad State Historic Park, Goliad.* (Courtesy Texas Parks and Wildlife Department.)

The second site of the La Bahía mission also has been located but as yet it has not been archeologically investigated. At their final locations in Goliad, the La Bahía mission and presidio have been reconstructed and are maintained as historic parks with public and private funding. Archeological investigations at Presidio La Bahía at Goliad recovered a large collection of artifacts, including evidence of the nineteenth-century use of the Spanish Colonial fortification, but a report on these investigations has not yet been published.

Excavations were conducted at Mission Rosario near Goliad in 1973 and 1974 by archeologists from North Texas State University under contract with the Texas Parks and Wildlife Department (Gilmore 1974). The first objective of these investigations was to determine the nature and extent of disturbance to the mission site and its stone ruins by relic collectors, stone robbers, and poorly controlled and poorly recorded excavations done in 1940 and 1941. The various phases of construction of the mission could be figured out by using a combination of excavated materials, stratigraphy, and historical descriptions. Only a comparatively small number of artifacts could be found, and most of those were not in their proper stratigraphic positions because of the degree to which the site had been disturbed. Evidence of an original wooden wall and later stone walls of the mission compound were found. The foundation outlines of the original and later mission churches were identified and found to contain several burial pits, caliche-plaster floors, and segments of fallen stone walls with remnants of painted murals on them. The *campo santo*, or mission cemetery, also was found. Activity areas were identified within the mission compound where the eighteenth-century inhabitants prepared food, made tools, and carried on other daily activities of mission life.

Like the La Bahía mission and presidio, the Presidio San Agustín de Ahumada and the Mission Nuestra Señora de la Luz were established on the site of a previous French occupation. Their initial locations on the lower Trinity River were to be temporary. Plans were made to find a suitable site for a civil settlement in the area and, once it was functioning, to relocate the mission and presidio to the new community. But the civil settlement never took place, primarily because not enough families in New Spain could be found who were willing to commit themselves to life in such a

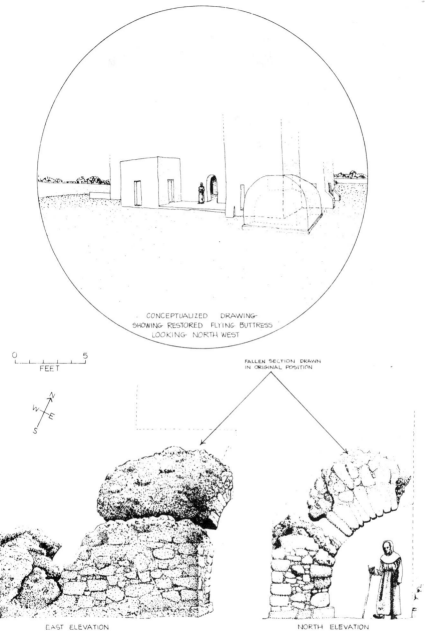

FIG. 4.7 *Artist's reconstruction of the church of Mission Rosario, Goliad County.* (From Gilmore 1974: Fig. 20. Courtesy Texas Parks and Wildlife Department. Drawings by George Nelson.)

remote frontier location. The mission was moved to a more favorable site a short distance from its original location in 1759, and after a destructive hurricane in 1766 the presidio was moved to higher ground near its original location.

The first sites of Mission de la Luz and Presidio de Ahumada on the lower Trinity River were surface-collected and tested by members of the Houston Archaeological Society in 1966, 1967, and 1970, and during studies by the Center for Archaeological Research of The University of Texas at San Antonio in 1979 to determine the possible effects of the proposed construction of a lake. Much of the historic occupation area was found to have been disturbed by pipeline construction and other earthmoving activities. However, there were indications that parts of the original mission and presidio sites may still be preserved and recommendations were made to protect them from relic hunters and from the wave action of the lake (Fox, Day, and Highley 1980:83–93, 98–100).

Archeological testing was carried out at the second site of Presidio de Ahumada in 1966 (Tunnell and Ambler 1967), which found little left of the Spanish Colonial occupation but demonstrated that it was the presidio site. The hill on which it once was located was almost completely removed in the 1950's for use as fill in the construction of Interstate Highway 10.

Scattered Spanish Colonial Settlements in Central Texas

The first Spanish Colonial settlements in the central Texas area were Mission San Antonio de Valero and the Presidio San Antonio de Bexar in 1718 near the headwaters of the San Antonio River. The Mission San José y San Miguel de Aguayo was established there in 1720. Three missions originally established in eastern Texas were removed to the Colorado River in 1730, probably somewhere in the vicinity of Barton Springs in present-day Austin. But in 1731 these missions—San Francisco de los Neches, Nuestra Señora de la Purísima Concepción de los Hainai, and San José de los Nazonis—were moved permanently to the San Antonio River downstream from the Bexar settlement. The locations of their temporary sites on the Colorado River have not been found, and they probably have been obliterated by urbanization and other land uses.

After the first missions and presidios had been firmly established in eastern Texas, on the coastal plain, and in the San Antonio area, there was a lull in new colonial activity. But around 1745, renewed interest in colonization was caused by the need for the missionaries to find new Indians to convert, by the real or imagined fear of French intrusion, and by the government's standard plan to develop new outposts (Bolton 1915:42).

One attractive area for new Spanish Colonial mission settlements was the Ranchería Grande. This was the campground of a conglomeration of Tonkawa and various other Indian groups who, in order to escape the pressures of the Apache and the Spanish, had moved into an area between the Colorado and Brazos rivers. For the Indians of the Ranchería Grande, which may have numbered 2,000 persons, the missions San Francisco Xavier de Horcasitas, San Ildefonso, and Candelaria were established in 1748 and 1749 near the confluence of the San Gabriel River (then the San Xavier) and Brushy Creek (Bolton 1915:227–230). The Presidio San Francisco de Gigedo was supposed to be established as part of the colonial community, but the historical accounts suggest that, although soldiers were garrisoned among the missions, a formal fortified presidio may not actually have been built. A civil settlement was planned but was never established (Gilmore 1982:6).

The San Xavier community was plagued with disputes between soldiers, missionaries, and Indians and with epidemics and droughts. In 1755 the entire mission complex was moved to the San Marcos River, where Mission San Ildefonso was established and operated, until the property of the San Xavier missions was transferred in 1757 for use in the establishment of a mission on the San Saba River. In 1756 the Mission Nuestra Señora de Guadalupe was established on the Guadalupe River in the area of present-day New Braunfels as a place for Indians from Mission San Xavier de Horcasitas who refused to join Mission San Antonio de Valero. However, the Guadalupe River mission was withdrawn in 1758 in order to prevent its possible destruction by the Comanche and other Indians who inhabited the hills to the north.

Minimal archeological investigation has been done at the San Xavier mission sites. Their temporary locations on the San Marcos and Guadalupe rivers are thought to be known but probably have been obliterated by urbanization. A study that combined research into the historical accounts of the topography, geography, and physiography of the original locations of the San Xavier missions with archeological test excavations has located one of the original sites in Milam County (Gilmore 1969). The excavations found remnants of *jacal* walls constructed of poles and brush plastered with clay, or adobe. Also found were sherds of Mexican-made pottery, beads, triangular flint arrow points, French gun parts, and Christian burials, all of which probably are evidence of the Spanish Colonial occupation of Mission San Francisco Xavier de Horcasitas. Archeological testing in the area also found limited evidence of the possible sites of the other two missions and the garrison area, but further investigations will be necessary to verify these locations.

Because of Indian attacks on Spanish Colonial settlements in central Texas, the government in New Spain was asked to establish a presidio in Apache territory and to attempt to make peace with the Lipan. In 1749, 167 Apache were taken captive and held hostage in San Antonio until a peace agreement was reached between the Indians and the presidio garrison. Events finally led to the founding of the Presidio de San Luís de las Amarillas and the Mission Santa Cruz on the San Saba River in 1757. But at first no prospective Apache converts came into the mission and some that eventually did come only stayed temporarily. In March, 1758, the mission was overrun and destroyed by an alliance of Tonkawa, Wichita, and Caddo Indian groups (Weddle 1964). Spanish military campaigns against the Indians followed, including an unsuccessful assault on Spanish Fort which was a major Indian *ranchería* and trading center on the Red River.

Some Lipan groups in central Texas were still interested in missionization but not at the ill-fated Mission Santa Cruz, and in 1762 the missionary and military leaders of the San Saba community set out to find a suitable location for a new mission, which they established as San Lorenzo de la Santa Cruz on the upper Nueces River in present Real County. A few months later a sister mission, Nuestra Señora de la Candelaria del Cañon, was dedicated downstream on the Nueces in present Edwards County and soldiers were stationed there for defense. But Indian raids, desertion, epidemics, and unproductive gardens soon spelled failure for the Nueces River settlements, and they were abandoned by 1771 (Cook 1981).

By the time archeologists found the Spanish Colonial presidios and missions on the San Saba and Nueces rivers, their sites had been badly disturbed by relic collectors, uncontrolled excavations, various twentieth-century land uses, and natural processes (Gilmore 1967). The Presidio San Saba is now a crumbling ruin near Menard, Texas. Walls reconstructed in the 1930's are again collapsing into the surrounding rubble (Ivey 1981).

The site of Mission San Lorenzo, now a roadside park at Camp Wood, Texas, has received the most intensive archeological investigations, although only about 30 percent of the site was found to be undisturbed (Tunnell and Newcomb 1969). Archeological excavations were able to locate the walls of the mission compound, which measured roughly 175 feet east to west and 165 feet north to south. Adobe floors of various mission structures were found. Some architectural information concerning the construction of the mission church and sacristy was recovered, even though their ruins had been bulldozed. Artifacts sampled included pottery sherds, glass bottle fragments, metal artifacts (including religious medals found with burials beneath the adobe floors of the

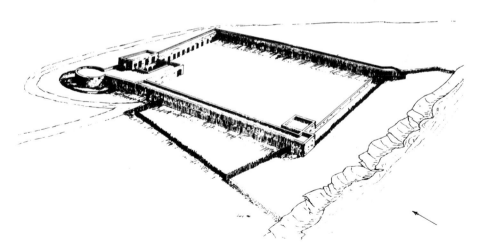

FIG. 4.8 *Artist's reconstruction of Presidio San Saba.* (From Ivey 1981: Fig. 3. Courtesy Southern Texas Archaeological Association. Drawing by Jake Ivey.)

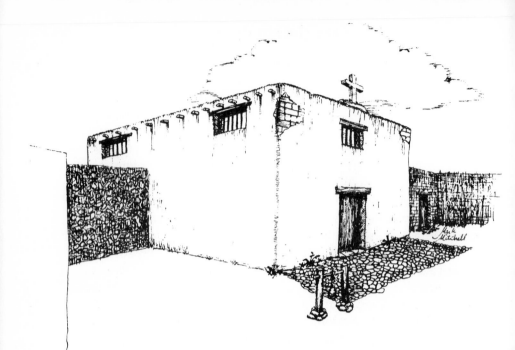

FIG. 4.9 *Idealized view of Mission San Lorenzo de la Santa Cruz.* From Cook 1981: Frontispiece. Courtesy Southern Texas Archaeological Association. Drawing by Mark A. Mitchell.)

mission church), glass beads, bone and shell tools and ornaments, and chipped flint tools and tool-making debris. These Spanish Colonial archeological materials are similar to occupational evidence from other Spanish Colonial sites of the same time range. But the collection is an important one because it is almost the only sample of physical evidence that has been properly recovered that can be identified reliably with the Lipan Apache mission Indians of the eighteenth century.

One other Spanish Colonial settlement in central Texas is worthy of mention. Some colonists were dissatisfied with the orders given them in 1773 to close their settlements in eastern Texas and move to San Antonio. They obtained permission to establish a community on the Trinity River at the crossing of the Camino Real. Founded in 1774, Nuestra Señora del Pilar de Bucareli prospered for a while, possibly because of illegal trade with the French. An epidemic in 1777 and Comanche raids in 1778 caused the settlers to move back to the old mission site near the old Hasinai

Caddo village of El Loco in eastern Texas where they, without official permission, established the community that became present Nacogdoches. Although possible archeological sites of Bucareli have been found in Madison County, none have been verified archeologically.

The Gateway Missions and Presidio

At the turn of the eighteenth century, a few years after the failure and abandonment of the first Spanish Colonial missions in eastern Texas, a few dedicated Franciscans moved, unauthorized, to the Rio Grande on the hostile northern frontier of New Spain. The missionaries soon realized that they needed military protection, and in 1703 the Presidio San Juan Bautista was established for missions San Juan Bautista, San Francisco Solano, and San Bernardo. This "gateway to Texas" (Weddle 1968) was the most easily travelled and best known route across the Rio Grande into the *monte* of southern Texas. Downstream from present-day Piedras Negras, Coahuila, and Eagle Pass, Texas, the mission-presidio complex and the settlement that grew up around it became a listening point for French activities and a staging point for supply trains, inspection trips, and other expeditions along the Camino Real. San Francisco Solano ceased effectively to be a mission in 1717, but San Juan Bautista and San Bernardo continued to operate throughout the Spanish Colonial Period.

In 1975 and 1976, under a permit issued by the Mexican government and with funds provided by private foundations and the National Endowment for the Humanities, archeological and ethno-historical investigations were undertaken at the gateway missions by the Center for Archaeological Research of The University of Texas at San Antonio (Adams 1975, 1976; Almaraz 1979; Campbell 1979). This project was preceded by an architectural survey of the eighteenth-century mission sites and the stone buildings of the presidio which now are a part of the town of Guerrero, Mexico. Of the three missions, only San Bernardo still has standing structural remains, the most notable of which are the massive stone walls of the mission's second church, which was begun in the 1760's but was never completed. The remains of the other mission structures at San Bernardo and San Juan Bautista were found as rows and mounds of stone rubble and soil.

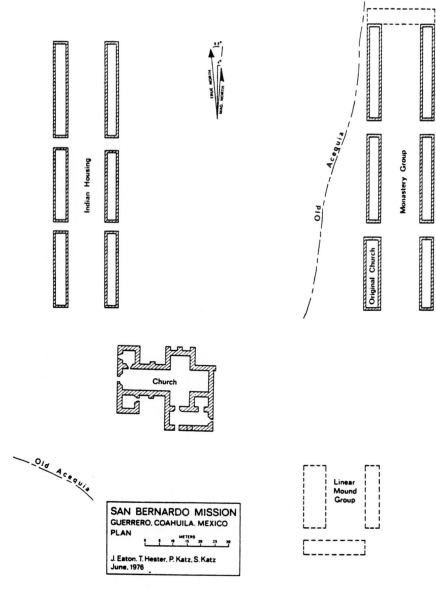

FIG. 4.10 *Plan of San Bernardo Mission, Guerrero, Coahuila, Mexico.*
(From Adams *et al.* 1976: Fig. 7. Courtesy Center for Archaeological
Research, The University of Texas at San Antonio.)

The archeological investigations found the structural remains
of the original church of San Bernardo, which probably was used
until the secularization of the mission in the late 1770's. Some of

the footings of the walls of the monastery also were uncovered. Archeological evidence indicates that the church was constructed of cut travertine limestone blocks quarried nearby and with large slabs set in place with a lot of rubble masonry. The church probably was plastered and whitewashed. Various architectural details found archeologically compare very well with historical accounts of the mission structures. Evidence of two parallel rows of mission Indian houses also was found. A large mound of rubble which may be the remains of the mission granary has yet to be investigated.

Mission San Juan Bautista, probably originally established where the town of Guerrero now stands, was moved in the early 1740's and now all that remains of it are slight elevations in the ground surface. The highest mound was tested and found to be the remains of the mission church. Like the San Bernardo church, it was constructed of cut travertine blocks and its walls were plastered, whitewashed, and probably decorated with painted designs. The floor of most of the church was laid with locally-made red ceramic tiles, except in the transept where evidence of wood planking was found. Human burials were found beneath the floor of the nave of the church. The skeleton of a young person, possibly a woman, was found under a thick deposit of rubble on the tile floor in front of the altar. Apparently, the deceased was buried there after the abandonment of the church but before its final collapse.

The archeological investigation also found the probable structural remains of the mission's monastery, along with its well or water storage cistern, the mission granary, and the locations of the textile mills, a blacksmith shop, a carpenter shop, and possibly other workshops mentioned in the historical accounts. The remains of a long narrow building with many apartments was found which probably was the mission Indian housing. A circular bastion probably stood as a fortification at the end of this linear structure.

A large sample of artifacts was recovered during the investigations at missions San Bernardo and San Juan Bautista. Similar to the cultural materials found at Spanish Colonial sites in Texas, the sample included chipped 'flint tools, ground and polished stone implements, and artifacts of shell, bone, iron, brass, copper, and glass. Potsherds from unglazed utility wares, polished and decorated earthenwares, lead glazed pottery, and tin-enameled majolica styles were found which are similar to the ceramics that occur at

Texas Spanish Colonial mission sites. Porcelain from China and a few sherds of British pottery were also found, but the simple bone-tempered earthenware mission Indian pottery so common at mission sites in central and coastal Texas was not found by the gateway mission investigations.

The food bones sampled included the remains of a variety of domesticated and wild animals, such as cattle, goats, pigs, sheep, rabbit, deer, buffalo, rodents, and snakes. Snails and freshwater clams apparently also were collected and eaten by the mission inhabitants. The bones of draft animals such as horses and burros also were found.

The Alamo Chain of Missions

The Spanish Colonial settlement of the San Antonio area may have begun as early as 1715 when a small group of families from northern Mexico reportedly settled on the banks of the San Antonio River (Hatcher 1905:191–192). But as yet this occupation has not been verified. The official beginnings of the San Antonio community occurred in 1718 with the establishment of Mission San Antonio de Valero (known today as the Alamo), the Presidio of San Antonio de Bexar and a *villa*, or civil settlement (Habig 1968: 29). In 1720 the Mission San José y San Miguel de Aguayo was founded downstream on the San Antonio River. In 1731 the three missions that were removed from eastern Texas were placed permanently in the San Antonio area where they became known as Missions Concepción, Espada, and San Juan Capistrano. Also in 1731, families of colonists from the Canary Islands in the Atlantic Ocean moved into the San Antonio community.

Learning from their experiences in eastern Texas, the missionaries at the San Antonio missions began to congregate Indians into pueblos, or villages, within walled mission compounds, rather than leaving prospective converts to live in their own *rancherías* in the countryside. The construction of dams and irrigation ditches was begun early to supply water for well-planned fields. Ranches were established on the rolling prairies of southern Texas to support each mission.

Although some Indians ran back to the *monte*, most of the Coahuilteco and other hunting and gathering peoples brought into the San Antonio missions did not resist conversion as much as the

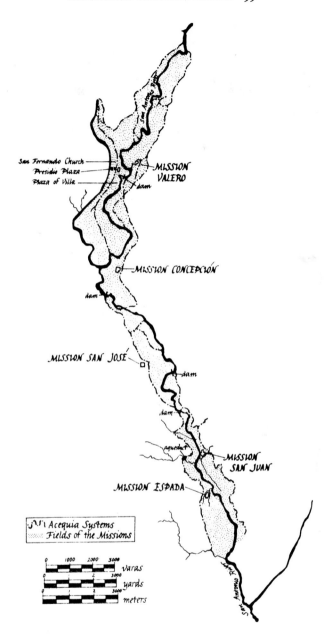

FIG. 4.11 *Map of the San Antonio missions, farmlands, and acequias.* (From Scurlock, Benavides, Isham, and Clark 1976: Map 1. Courtesy Texas Historical Commission.)

native peoples of eastern and southeastern Texas. Several epidemics took their toll on the mission Indian populations and there were bad and good years for the missions' farming and ranching enterprises. The San Antonio community was constantly harassed by the raids of the Lipan Apache and later the Comanche. Relations between the missions and the military and civil community were strained when the missionaries refused to allow their Indians to be used as laborers and servants for the soldiers and Canary Islanders, who considered themselves to be of more privileged status. But the missions managed to operate until the end of the eighteenth century and in some years fared better than the civil community.

The San Antonio missions were finally removed from the authority of the missionary colleges of evangelization of New Spain in 1793 and 1794. Many mission Indians claimed to be of Spanish descent in order to climb the social ladder of New Spain with its hierarchy of classes, and there was intermarriage of missionized Indian, or *Ladinos*, and the Spanish military and settlers in the San Antonio community. There were changes in ownership and use of the mission lands. The care of the mission churches became the responsibility of the church authorities of the civil community of San Antonio.

In the late 1800's, Father Francis Bouchou became interested in the ruins of Mission Espada and reconstructed the chapel and portions of the *convento* there (Habig 1968:225–226). In 1917, Bishop John W. Shaw cleared rubble from the church at Mission San José (Clark 1980:6). In the 1930's, funds provided by the Works Progress Administration supported excavations and reconstructions at Missions Concepción, San José, San Juan, and Espada, but these investigations were architecturally rather than archeologically oriented. Detailed records of archeological features were not kept and artifacts were not collected systematically so that they could be used in a meaningful reconstruction of the histories of the missions.

Properly controlled archeological investigations of the sites of the Spanish Colonial community of San Antonio began in 1966 with excavations designed to salvage archeological remains that would be affected by trenching for the installation of electrical lines in the courtyard of Mission San Antonio de Valero (the Alamo). Reports on historical research (Schuetz 1966), the archeological field techniques employed and features encountered during

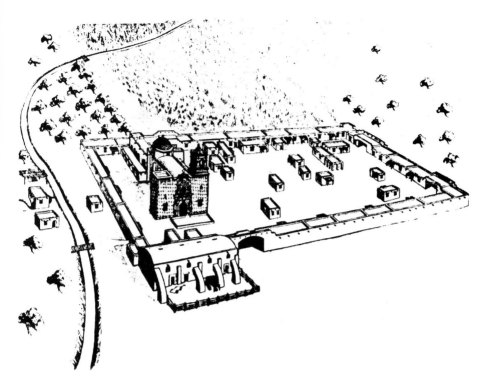

FIG. 4.12   *Artist's reconstruction of Mission San José in the late eighteenth century.* (From Clark 1978: Cover illustration. Courtesy Texas Historical Commission. Drawing by Sharon Roos.)

the excavations (Greer 1967), and study of Mexican-made tin-enameled earthenware pottery, or majolica, (Tunnell 1966) resulted from this project.

Other short-term archeological investigations were done at Mission Valero in the late 1960's and the early 1970's in areas where various sorts of construction projects would disturb archeological deposits. These excavations uncovered remains of parts of the mission water supply ditch, or *acequia*, and foundations of nineteenth-century structures that once stood on the eighteenth-century mission site (Sorrow 1972; Adams and Hester 1973), as well as bits of information about mission Indian workshops within the mission compound (Schuetz 1973).

Short-term investigations at San Antonio de Valero in 1975, 1977, 1979, and 1980 found remnants of the footings of the southern compound wall of the mission (Fox, Bass, and Hester 1976), architectural information about the foundations of the west wall of the mission *convento* (Fox 1977a), and evidence of the north patio wall of the mission (Fox and Ivey n.d.).

In 1980 intensive excavations were conducted by the Center for Archaeological Research on the west side of Alamo Plaza, where a major construction project had been proposed (A. Fox, personal communication, July, 1982). These investigations found the adobe foundations of the west compound walls of the mission beneath the floors and foundations of the modern buildings on the west side of the plaza. The outer wall of the mission was more than three feet (a Spanish vara) thick. Built along the interior of the wall was a row of Indian apartments and an arcade that shaded the front of this structure which faced the mission courtyard. A large archeological deposit was found which contained thousands of bones from cows, goats, and various other domesticated and wild animals that were butchered for food by the mission inhabitants. Within the Indian quarters, small fire hearths and pits containing charred corn cobs were uncovered.

Short-term excavations were conducted at Mission San José in 1968, 1969, and 1970 to salvage archeological information from areas where a sprinkler system was to be installed (Schuetz 1970) and where other, more limited earthmoving activities were planned (D. Fox 1970). A relatively large number of artifacts were found which dated from the early mission occupation to the present. Also found were portions of the mission Indian quarters, which once stood near the *convento*. Filled postholes, trenches, rubble, and other evidence of the 1930's restoration of the mission church were found.

Additional short-term investigations were conducted at Mission San José in 1974 by the Texas Parks and Wildlife Department and the Texas Historical Commission (Clark 1976, 1978, 1980). Test pits were excavated adjacent to standing mission structures, such as the church, the granary, and the mission water supply ditch, to determine soil moisture conditions that could affect the foundations and the preservation of the structures. Information concerning the methods of construction of the church, the sacristy, and other structures was obtained and remains of the mission's gristmill, sugar mill, and a possible lime-slaking vat were given preliminary study.

Artifacts from these and earlier test excavations at Mission

FIG. 4.13   *Theodore Gentilz's "La Purísima Concepción de Acuña."* Gentilz was an Alsatian immigrant, an artist and surveyor who lived in Henri Castro's colony on the Medina River and in San Antonio and travelled about southern Texas and northern Mexico in the nineteenth century. This is Gentilz's image of the ruins of San Antonio's Mission Concepción in the mid-nineteenth century. (Courtesy Library of the Daughters of the Republic of Texas at the Alamo, San Antonio.)

San José indicated that the mission site was occupied for some time after it ceased to be a mission and began to fall into ruins in the nineteenth century. Animal bones recovered during the 1974 excavations were studied and at least 27 different species of animals were identified, including cow, goat, and deer, which probably were the main sources of meat, and turtles, fish, chicken, and pig, which probably supplemented the diet of the mission populations. The bones of other animals also were found, such as snakes, fox, mockingbird, rats, burro, and horse, which may or may not have been used for food. Interestingly enough, the butchering marks found on the cow bones indicated that the butchering techniques of the mission inhabitants were similar to those of prehistoric peoples in Texas, but different in the amount of bone left on the cuts of meat. These supplies were evidently brought in from butchering areas located outside the mission.

The most recent archeological investigations at Mission San José also were short-term in scope. Historical accounts, notes on restoration drawings from the 1930's, and evidence recovered during the 1974 excavations indicated that a blacksmith shop may have been located on the western side of the mission granary. In 1979 the Texas Parks and Wildlife Department contracted with Prewitt and Associates, Inc., Consulting Archeologists, to evaluate the archeological sensitivity of that area because drainage improvements were proposed to be constructed there. Stratified archeological deposits from the mission and later occupations were encountered during the archeological testing, as were middens containing artifacts and large amounts of butchered animal bones. Portions of a flagstone floor and the remains of a stone and lime mortar wall also were found. Because of the archeological potential of the area, the plans for the French drain were abandoned, but unfortunately no detailed studies have been done on the archeological features (Clark and Prewitt 1979; Clark 1980).

The first archeological investigations at Mission Concepción were done in 1971 and 1972 by archeologists from the Texas Historical Commission in order to obtain information about soil moisture conditions that might cause deterioration of the walls of the mission church and other structural remains. Test pits placed along the church walls found that the foundations were dry and the source of the deterioration of the wall above them was determined to be from the watering of plants on the mission grounds (Scurlock and Powers 1975; Olsen and Tunnell 1975).

The other purposes of the 1971 and 1972 investigations were to locate the west wall of the Concepción mission compound and to collect a controlled sample of artifacts that could be compared with artifacts from the other San Antonio missions (Scurlock and Fox 1977; Cook 1980). The entire mission site was mapped, and detailed architectural drawings were made of the various standing mission structures. The archeological testing along the walls of the church found a nineteenth-century burial, trash accumulations, and construction debris from various periods, and other archeological features. Test excavations on the western edge of the mission grounds found the limestone quarry which was the source of building stone for the major mission structures. Seventeen archeological features were recorded, including midden heaps, adobe brick foundations and clay and plaster floors of possible Indian dwellings within the mission compound, and two parallel lines of irregularly-shaped limestone rocks which were believed to be the

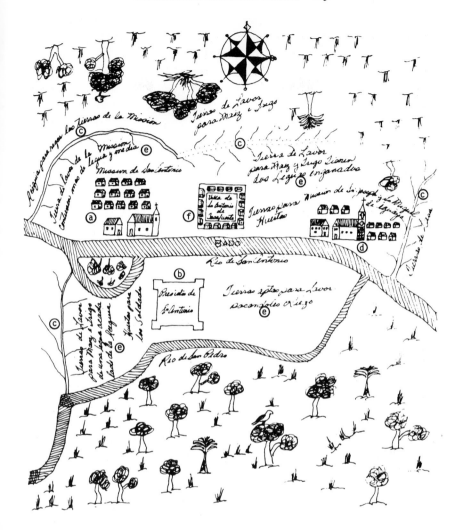

FIG. 4.14 *Hand-drawn copy of the Marquis de Aguayo's map of San Antonio in the late 1720's, before missions Concepción, San Juan Capistrano, and Espada were relocated from eastern Texas to the Upper San Antonio River.* Spanish Colonial features depicted include: a, Mission San Antonio de Valero (later to become known as the Alamo); b, the Presidio San Antonio de Bexar; c, acequia systems leading from the San Antonio River and from San Pedro Springs; d, Mission San José y San Miguel de Aguayo; e, farmlands for various crops; f, the proposed site for the civil settlement of Canary Islanders who arrived in San Antonio in the early 1730's. (From Schuetz 1970: Fig. 1. Courtesy Texas Historical Commission.)

FIG. 4.15 *Theodore Gentilz's picture of people washing along an acequia in San Antonio in the nineteenth century, possibly in the area of San Pedro Springs.* (Courtesy Larry Sheerin, San Antonio.)

remains of the foundations of the western wall of the mission compound.

A considerable number and variety of artifacts dating from the Spanish Colonial Period to the present were recovered during the excavations. The sample included earthenware, stoneware, and porcelain ceramic sherds, fragments of bottles and other glass containers, firearm-related artifacts, household items, tools, harness trappings, building hardware, and other metal objects, and bone and shell ornaments and buttons. Freshwater clam, or mussel, shell fragments and the bones of fish, deer, cow, turkey, turtle, birds, rodents, reptiles, and other wild and domesticated animals were found.

More recent investigations have been conducted at Mission Concepción by the Center for Archaeological Research of The University of Texas at San Antonio (A. Fox, personal communication, July, 1982; Ivey n.d.). The location of the compound west wall was verified and the north and east walls were located. Evidence of the mission granary was found, as were some interesting artifacts and structural features that could be the remains of Mission San Francisco de Najera which was founded by the Aguayo Expedition in 1722 and was abandoned in 1726, five years before Mission Concepción was established there (Habig 1968:78–81).

Intensive archeological investigations were undertaken in 1967 at Mission San Juan Capistrano by Mardith Schuetz of the Witte Memorial Museum in San Antonio and by members of the Texas Archeological Society (Schuetz 1968, 1969). Supported in part by the Texas Historical Commission, the excavations were prompted by plans for restorations of parts of the mission by the Archdiocese of San Antonio. The goals of the investigation were to recover a sample of artifacts that could be considered the occupational evidence of Coahuilteco Indians, to recover actual skeletal remains of the Coahuilteco who lived in the mission, and to obtain information about building techniques and the building sequence of the mission complex.

The older mission church, several rooms in the mission compound walls, and portions of the mission plaza were excavated. Further excavations were done in 1969 to recover evidence with which to date the present-day chapel at the mission site (Schuetz 1974). Almost all of the standing structures were found to have been disturbed to varying degrees by relic hunters and burrowing animals, but other parts of the mission site were found to be relatively well preserved. A large midden deposit about 50 feet long and 4 feet thick was found and excavated outside the south wall of the mission compound, but it turned out to be the pile of fill removed from a room in the compound wall which was used in the 1930's and the 1940's as a parish hall. Several burials were recovered from the old mission church. Possible evidence of rows of *jacales*, which were the quarters of some of the mission Indians, was found in the open plaza area.

A considerable quantity of historic artifacts was collected during the investigations at Mission San Juan, which represented different occupations and visits to the site from the 1730's to the 1960's. Similar to the sample of artifacts from the more recent excavations at Mission Concepción, the collection from San Juan included ornaments, coins, copper, brass and iron artifacts, European, Mexican, and American pottery sherds, and glass beads (all of which are commonly found at Spanish Colonial mission sites), as well as sherds of pottery, flint tools, shell and bone ornaments, and tools produced by the mission Indians.

Downstream on the San Antonio River, the last in the Alamo chain of missions was Mission San Francisco de la Espada. Until the recent urban expansion of the San Antonio metropolitan area, Espada was one of the more remote mission ruins, situated in a rural community of Bexar County residents, many of whom an anthropologist would swear must be of mission Indian descent. During the first half of the twentieth century, the plan of the mission could still be seen (Smith 1931) and those who restored it recognized its scheme as a place for worship, for conversion, and for refuge in a vast, unfriendly land (Smith 1980).

Only a couple of short-term archeological investigations have been done at Espada. Limekilns, or furnaces used to make lime mortar, and a corner bastion of the mission compound have been investigated (Fox and Hester 1976). Like San Juan, Mission Espada has been disturbed in various places by the activities of relic collectors, restoration workers, and others. But because of its remoteness, it appears to be better preserved than many of the other sites of the Spanish Colonial community of San Antonio and probably has much to offer to the understanding of the mission period in Texas. It is to be hoped that it will be preserved and investigated carefully following a well-developed research design, rather than having to be salvaged like the other San Antonio missions in the wake of urbanization.

The San Antonio Community

Besides the numerous missions and presidios, there are other sorts of archeological sites of Spanish Colonial occupations in Texas. Some of the first organized activities that took place during the establishment of the San Antonio community involved the engineering and construction of systems of ditches, or *acequias*, designed to transport water from dams on the San Antonio River and from San Pedro Springs to supply the domestic needs of the missions and the civil settlements as well as for irrigation of the mission fields and the farmlands of the civil settlements. By

FIG. 4.16 *Artist's reconstruction of the Spanish Governor's Palace, San Antonio.* (From Smith 1981: Frontispiece. Courtesy Southern Texas Archaeological Association. Drawing by Harvey P. Smith, Sr.)

the mid-eighteenth century, several dams, *acequias*, and aqueducts were in use and rights to the water they supplied had been established for the farmland along the San Antonio River from its headwaters to the fields downstream from missions San Juan and Espada (Scurlock, Benavides, Isham, and Clark 1976:27–32; Minor and Steinberg 1968; Holmes 1962). The *acequia* systems fell into disrepair during the revolutionary period of the early nineteenth century but were cleaned out, stone-lined, and reopened for use by the San Antonio community of the mid-nineteenth century (Corner 1890:50; Chabot 1937:406). Large sections of the different *acequias* of San Antonio, ruins of some of the mission dams, and the Espada aqueduct are still in existence (Scurlock, Benavides, Isham, and Clark 1976:145–155; Fox n.d.). The Espada *acequia* system is still in use. Portions of the San Juan *acequia* are being restored to use by the National Park Service in an attempt to recreate the atmosphere of the mission period.

Short-term archeological investigations have been done at different *acequias* of Spanish Colonial San Antonio. Two sections of the Valero, or Alamo, ditch in downtown San Antonio were studied in 1966 (Schuetz 1970). Sections of *acequias* have been found during archeological excavations at the different mission sites. Sections of the Alazán and San Pedro *acequias*, which ran through the civil settlement of San Antonio, have been studied (Fox 1978; Valdez and Eaton 1979; Frkuska 1981). These brief archeological investigations have recovered details about the construction of the different *acequias*, with their masonry of quarried limestone blocks, many of which have been removed, or "borrowed," since the mid-nineteenth century for use in the construction of houses and other structures. The histories of use of sections of the different *acequias* were found to be reflected by the artifacts and stratigraphy of the deposits within them. However, because it was common practice for San Antonio residents to clean their sections of the *acequia* system periodically, some sections that have been investigated archeologically were found not to contain artifacts from the periods during which they were in use.

Another important element of the Spanish Colonial Period of Texas history was the mission "rancho" where cattle, sheep, goats, horses, and other livestock were raised to support the mission haciendas. Several mission ranchos controlled rangelands of rolling prairies and river valleys south of San Antonio. The possible sites of some of the ranch headquarters have been located but few have been archeologically investigated. Recently, under an agreement with the Texas Parks and Wildlife Department, archeologists from the Center for Archaeological Research of The University of Texas at San Antonio have begun to investigate the probable headquarters site of the Rancho de las Cabras—the ranch that belonged to Mission Espada and, according to historic records, probably operated from about 1740 until the official closing of the mission in 1797 (Ivey and Fox 1981).

The Rancho de las Cabras site is situated on a prominent point of land overlooking the bottomlands of the San Antonio River Valley near Floresville. Ruins of sandstone rock walls and piles of stone rubble form an irregularly-shaped, four-sided compound with stone ruins of buildings inside it. During the first season of archeological investigations, the site was mapped and 14 small test excavations were placed so as to expose the remains of different structural features and the architectural and stratigraphic record of their histories. Samples of artifacts were collected systematically as the material evidence of life at Las Cabras.

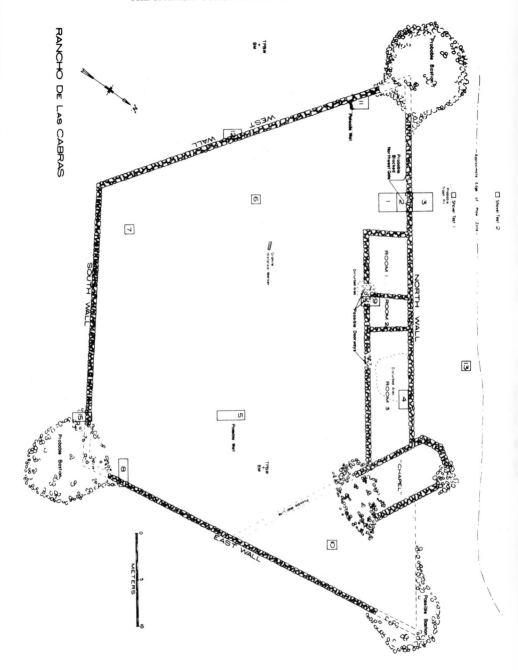

FIG. 4.17   *Plan map of the ruins of Rancho de las Cabras, Wilson County.*
(From Ivey and Fox 1981: Fig. 2. Courtesy Center for Archaeological
Research, The University of Texas at San Antonio.)

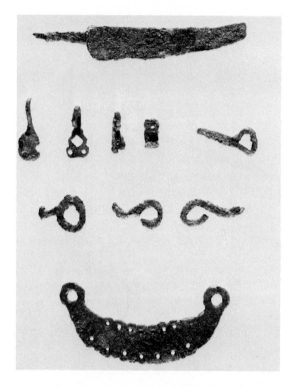

FIG. 4.18 *Metal artifacts from Rancho de las Cabras on the San Antonio River in Wilson County—the ranch of San Antonio's Mission Espada.* From left, top to bottom, iron knife blade; "jinglers" from Spanish bridle bits; spur attachment; rusted furniture or cabinet hinge; chain links from Spanish bridles; chin piece from Spanish bridle. (Courtesy Center for Archaeological Research, The University of Texas at San Antonio.)

The archeological investigations found indications that the Spanish Colonial occupation of the ranch headquarters began at least as early as 1760 with the construction of the sandstone compound walls and three or four rooms and possibly a chapel along the north wall. The compound had a hard-packed clay surface and one main entrance, or gateway, in the north wall. A plaster floor and other archeological evidence indicates that adobe or *jacal* structures were built within the compound, possibly to accommodate an increase in the number of people who lived there. Bastions probably stood as fortifications on three corners of the compound. The need for increased protection against Indian attacks may be indicated by some rough masonry construction that was added to

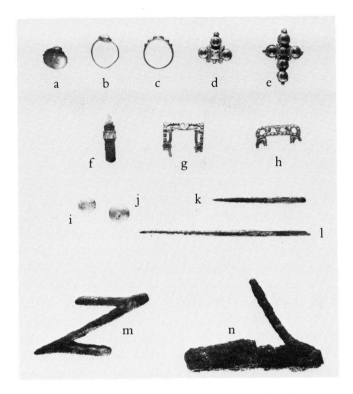

FIG. 4.19   *An assortment of Spanish Colonial Period artifacts from Rancho de las Cabras on the San Antonio River in Wilson County—the ranch for San Antonio's Mission Espada.* a, metal button; b, c, rings with glass insets; d, e, crucifixes; f, part of possible writing implement; g, h, brass shoe—or clothing—buckle fragments; i, j, musket balls; k, l, metal awls (punch); m, n, fragments of iron livestock brands. (Courtesy Center for Archaeological Research, The University of Texas at San Antonio.)

reduce the opening of the gateway to the size of a doorway in the north compound wall.

The archeological evidence found so far at Las Cabras conforms to a brief historical account (Saenz de Gumiel 1772:1371–1373) which indicates that the rancho was supplied with the minimum frontier necessities. The sample of animal bones recovered shows that, in addition to cattle and sheep, a variety of wild game was eaten by the inhabitants, such as fish, turtles, squirrels, rabbits, and several kinds of birds. The artifacts suggest that the occupants of Las Cabras were of relatively low economic status. The historical accounts indicate that Rancho de las Cabras served as a *visita*, or sub-mission, where the Indians of the surrounding area were taught Christianity and the Spanish way of life (Scurlock, Benavides, Isham, and Clark 1976:32–33). Perhaps the material remains found at the Las Cabras site are the archeological evidence of Coahuilteco Indians as well as *Ladinos* who had been Hispanicized at Mission Espada and its ranch.

There are undoubtedly many archeological sites of the civil settlements of Spanish Colonial Texas that have been covered up, surrounded, and "contaminated," in the archeological sense of the word, by urban development during the nineteenth and twentieth centuries. Like the sections of the Spanish Colonial *acequias* that keep turning up here and there in the older San Antonio neighborhoods, a few other early traces of the original settlement of Bexar have been investigated archeologically.

Limited test excavations were carried out in 1976 by the Center for Archaeological Research of The University of Texas at San Antonio next to the Spanish Governor's Palace, where the City of San Antonio proposed to build a small park (A. Fox 1977b). Although the Governor's Palace was reconstructed and has been well maintained by the citizens of San Antonio as a monument to their heritage, the 1976 archeological investigations found that in most places the archeological deposits of the Spanish Colonial occupation of this part of the Presidio of San Antonio de Bexar had been thoroughly disturbed by construction activities during the nineteenth and twentieth centuries.

One of the more interesting sites of the civil settlement of Spanish Colonial San Antonio is the church, Nuestra Señora de la Concepción y Guadalupe, which was constructed between 1738 and 1749 (Habig 1968:260). The church served the people of the presidio and the villa of San Antonio de Bexar, which by then was called San Fernando de Bexar. At the end of the eighteenth century this church of San Fernando became a warehouse for equipment removed from the secularized mission churches. It was neglected during the revolutionary period and was almost in ruins in 1841, when it was restored. San Antonio's population grew from about 1,650 in 1839 to about 8,235 in 1860, and in 1868 the decision was made to enlarge the old San Fernando church. Construction soon began and in 1873 the church was reopened as the San Fernando Cathedral.

Archeological investigations were conducted at the San Fer-

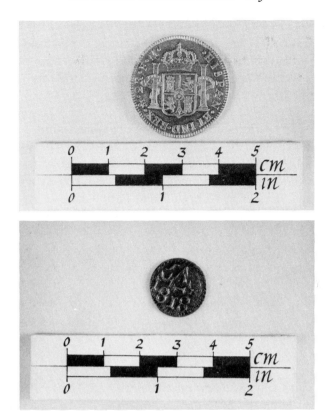

FIG. 4.20   *Two coins found during archeological excavations at the San Fernando Cathedral, San Antonio. A Spanish two real piece, dated 1777, and a de la Garza coin, minted in San Antonio in 1818. (Courtesy Texas Historical Commission.)*

nando Cathedral by archeologists from the Texas Historical Commission in 1975 (Fox, Scurlock, and Clark 1977). Several test pits were excavated in areas where air-conditioning ducts were to be installed beneath the floor of the cathedral nave. Another test excavation was placed in the apse, or altar area, of the church to investigate the nature of deposits there.

Archeological and architectural features encountered by the excavations included pits, burials, postholes, foundations, and floors dating from the Spanish Colonial Period to the present. Spanish Colonial features included plaster and dirt floors associated with the eighteenth-century church, the limestone and masonry foundations of the nave and bell tower of the Colonial church which were torn down during the construction of the Gothic revival nave in the nineteenth century, postholes that apparently were dug for scaffolding used during construction of the Colonial church, and two burials located near the foundation remains of the original church.

More than 1,600 artifacts of pottery, glass, metal, shell, bone, stone, wood, fabric, and other materials were found during the controlled excavations. Dating from the early 1700's to the present, this sample of artifacts contains evidence of activities associated with the construction, maintenance, and use of the church. The artifacts of the Spanish Colonial Period are similar to those found at other eighteenth-century sites in the San Antonio area. One interesting kind of artifact, however, is the sample of chipped flint that was found. Chipped stone tools are not the type of artifacts one would expect to be left by Spanish soldiers, settlers, or even Hispanicized mission Indians. Although it is possible that the chipped flint actually is evidence of occupation of the area by Indians prior to the construction of the San Fernando church, chipped stone artifacts also have been found at archeological investigations at Alamo Plaza and at the Governor's Palace. The historic accounts indicate that supplies of metal for the manufacture of tools was limited on the Spanish Colonial frontier in Texas. Perhaps the Spanish settlers of San Fernando de Bexar resorted to the use of stone when metal was not available (A. Fox 1977b:16).

In addition to the artifacts recovered from the San Fernando church, more than 3,700 bones and bone fragments were collected during the 1975 investigations. Most of the sample was made up of human bones from graves that had been disturbed and scattered during the various construction activities in and around the church. Some bones were from bats and rats that inhabited the church. And food remains were represented by the bones of animals such as fish, chicken, turkey, cow, pig, and goat.

V

Sites of Mexican Texas, the Revolution, and the Republic

As THE EIGHTEENTH-CENTURY colonization of Texas struggled to develop and then declined, a sparse framework of frontier Spanish Colonial settlements became anchored upon the more firmly established communities of San Antonio (de Bexar), Goliad (La Bahía), and Nacogdoches. In the early nineteenth century, confusion, greed, and bloodshed had disastrous effects on Texas. Aggravated by foreign political interference and mercenary activities, the conflicts between traditional Spanish and revolutionary Mexican elements resulted in the reduction of the Spanish population of Texas and the destruction, neglect, and deterioration of farms and communities (Fehrenbach 1968:114–131). San Antonio was almost deserted in 1816 (Yoakum 1856:183). Spanish occupation between San Antonio and eastern Texas was almost non-existent.

Finally, in 1820, the royal government decided that careful recruitment of foreign colonists was the only means of occupying the Spanish province and maintaining the Empire's control of its borderlands (Barker 1969:34). But by then it was too late, and the new independent Mexican regime set out to establish its control by encouraging the settlement of the unoccupied void between San Antonio and Nacogdoches (Meinig 1969:24–28).

Although land grants were to be given to foreigners, it was thought that the conditions, the regulations, and the required civil and religious commitments imposed on the colonists by the empresario system would guarantee foreign settlers' allegiance to Mexico. Austin's colony was the first to be authorized, and his Anglo-American settlers took over the lower Brazos and Colorado river drainages from the Camino Real, then called the San Antonio-Nacogdoches Road, southeastward across the coastal plain to the Gulf. Before long, Austin's colony was joined by other empresario endeavors. DeWitt's colony of Anglo-Americans set-

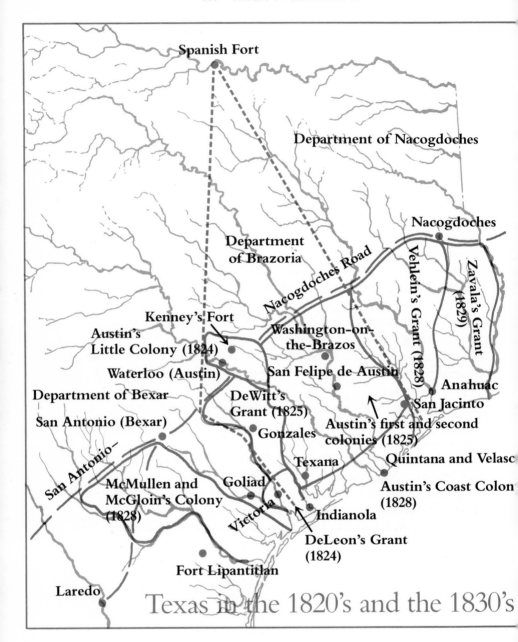

FIG. 5.1 *Texas in the 1820's and 1830's.*

tled the rich Guadalupe River Valley south and west of Austin's grant and became centered around Gonzales. DeLeon's colony, the principal grant for Mexican settlement, established itself south of Austin's colony and became centered around Victoria and Goliad. Further south and west, a broad area of southern Texas and the coastal plain was granted for a colony of Irish Catholics, but many of them died of cholera before reaching their new lands and the remaining ones were satisfied to settle in communities near the coast, such as San Patricio and Refugio.

Several grants were loosely settled above the San Antonio-Nacogdoches Road, but they barely survived the distance from supply depots and the exposure to the Comanche. Three empresarios received grants for colonies to be settled in the area between the lower San Jacinto and Sabine rivers in southeastern Texas. Known as the Atascosito district, these settlements asked to be incorporated into Austin's colony and, although this was never authorized officially by the Mexican government, Austin's civil, judicial, and military jurisdiction was extended to include the Atascosito area (Fox, Day, and Highley 1980:51).

After less than a decade of foreign colonization, the non-Indian population of Mexican Texas grew to more than 25,000, including mostly Anglo-Americans and their slaves (Meinig 1969: 31–32; Fehrenbach 1968:151). The risk of losing control became apparent. Mexico suspended colonization between 1830 and 1834 and divided Texas into three departments, each with one military garrison on the San Antonio-Nacogdoches Road and another fort near the Gulf coast to enforce the order to stop immigration. But there were not enough soldiers, not enough loyal settlers, and with the reopening of Texas to foreign colonization it was not long before the Mexican outposts found themselves surrounded to the point of being absorbed by the Anglo-American frontier.

At the time of the Texas Revolution, there were only about 4,000 people concentrated in the settlements of the Department of Bexar, mostly at San Antonio and Goliad, while more than 20,000 settlers were scattered across the departments of Brazoria and Nacogdoches. The disasters the Anglo-Americans suffered at the Alamo and at Goliad took place in what was still Mexican Texas, ethnically and politically. The ultimate victory at San Jacinto was won well within Anglo-American territory (Meinig 1969:36–37).

Much of written Texas history has been devoted to the folklore about the Revolution and the Republic of Texas. Texans' pride in the sovereignty of their State finds historic basis in the drama of their "Texican" forefathers' clashes with Mexican armies and their struggle to carve a new republic out of a vast, hostile frontier environment. Little has been done with the history of the first years of the nineteenth century, before Mexico achieved her independence, when the Province of Texas was a buffer area that the Spanish government could not adequately protect from the westward expansion of the development of the Mississippi Valley or from the movements toward insurrection centered in the Lower Rio Grande Valley (Almaraz 1971:ix).

As monuments to the Revolution and the Republic, which so many Texans consider to be the real beginning of their heritage, many of the best-known historic sites of battles, birthplaces, frontier towns, and capitals have been maintained as historic parks and shrines. Unfortunately, this patriotic interest in the preservation and development of historic sites of the first half of the nineteenth century has neglected and inadvertently disturbed the archeological deposits which often contain the only material evidence of the historical events that Texas preservationists commemorate, as well as the evidence of earlier history. And although most of the well-known sites of Mexican Texas, the revolutionary period, and the Anglo-American frontier have been afforded preliminary research and evaluation, few have been carefully and thoroughly investigated archeologically.

Early Nineteenth-Century San Antonio

There has been archeological investigation of many of the Spanish Colonial sites in the San Antonio area that were occupied before, during, and after the Texas Revolution, such as the Spanish missions, the Governor's Palace, and the San Fernando church. But archeological evidence of early nineteenth-century occupations at these sites is difficult to identify amidst the complexity of remains of earlier and later occupations, and in many cases archeological deposits of the early nineteenth century have been disturbed by later activities. Few archeological sites have been found that were occupied exclusively during the time of the Revolution and the Republic.

Several short-term archeological investigations at the Alamo

FIG. 5.2   *Theodore Gentilz's "El Alamo," showing how the unfinished church of Mission San Antonio de Valero looked in the 1840's, after it had been used as part of the defensive fortifications during the siege of the Alamo in 1836.* (Courtesy Library of the Daughters of the Republic of Texas at the Alamo.)

have recovered bits and pieces of evidence of the 1836 battle, such as a fortification ditch outside a gate in the old mission wall (Fox, Bass, and Hester 1976), a palisade trench (Eaton 1980), and even a human skull (Fox and Ivey n.d.). Lead musket balls have been found by several different archeological salvage projects at the Alamo shrine. Excavations in the summer of 1979 by the Center for Archaeological Research of The University of Texas at San Antonio recovered a large number of musket balls and some cannonballs along the foundations of what must have been a main defensive position on the west wall during the revolutionary battle (A. Fox, personal communication, July 10, 1982).

Some archeological investigations and related historical research have been done in the area of La Villita—the little village of settlers and military families in Spanish Colonial and Mexican San Antonio that continued to develop as an urban neighborhood throughout the nineteenth century. Most of the investigations have been conducted in the area immediately south of the surviv-

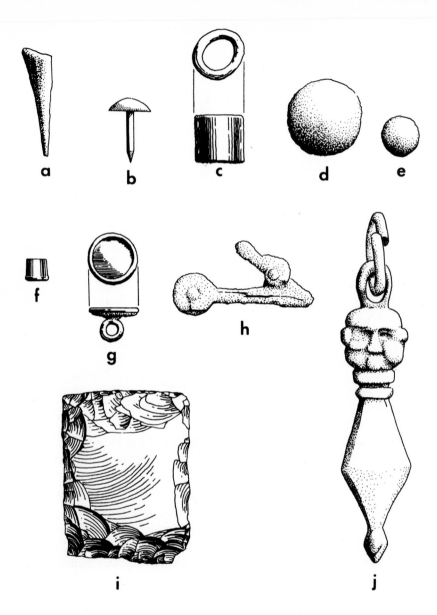

FIG. 5.3 *Artifacts from Alamo Plaza, San Antonio.* a, pointed fragment of brass; b, copper tack; c, brass ferrule or bead; d, lead musket ball, .68 inch diameter; e, lead pistol or rifle ball, .35 inch diameter; f, percussion cap, brass; g, brass sleeve button; h, sear spring from flintlock rifle; i, musket flint made of local stone; j, brass drawer of cupboard pull. (From Fox, Bass, and Hester 1976: Fig. 26. Courtesy Center for Archaeological Research, The University of Texas at San Antonio. Drawings by D. E. Fox.)

ing part of La Villita that has been preserved by the people of San Antonio as a historic neighborhood near Hemisfair Plaza. Historical research (Santos 1967) and short-term archeological investigations (Schuetz n.d.) led some to suggest that the ruins of an old stone stable building may have been a part of a military barracks, or *cuartel*, possibly constructed in the La Villita area in 1809 and destroyed prior to the siege of the Alamo in 1836. But the artifacts sampled during the archeological excavations dated from the late nineteenth century instead of the early 1800's, and additional historical research led another investigator to question the claims that the *cuartel* existed in the stable ruins area (Luckett n.d.).

Archeological and historical investigations were conducted in 1976 by the Center for Archaeological Research of The University of Texas at San Antonio in the same general area within the southern part of the officially designated and legally protected La Villita Historic District. The purpose of these investigations was to assess the nature and significance of archeological resources that would be disturbed by the construction of a luxury hotel (Katz 1978). Some of the test excavations were placed in the vicinity of the stable ruin in an attempt to resolve the question as to whether the *cuartel* was ever constructed, and if so, where it was located. The earliest archeological evidence found was from occupations during the late nineteenth century and not from the period during which the *cuartel* would have been occupied. Eliminating the stable ruin area archeologically as a possible site of the Spanish and Mexican barracks, archival research indicated that if the *cuartel* existed it would have been located where a later nineteenth-century structure, known as the German-English School, now stands.

Several late nineteenth-century and early twentieth-century residential and commercial structures once stood on the city lots comprising the hotel project area, most of which was cleared and paved in recent years for urban renewal and for parking lots. Archival research found that the hotel project area probably was not occupied until after Mission San Antonio de Valero was secularized in 1793 and its lands were partitioned to the mission Indians, to refugees from Los Adaes, and to the residents of the civil settlement of San Antonio. Apparently a part of the area had belonged to Cayetano Dominguez, a revolutionary in the short-lived Casas Rebellion which occurred in San Antonio de Bexar in 1811. And there are also records which show that next to Dominguez's parcel

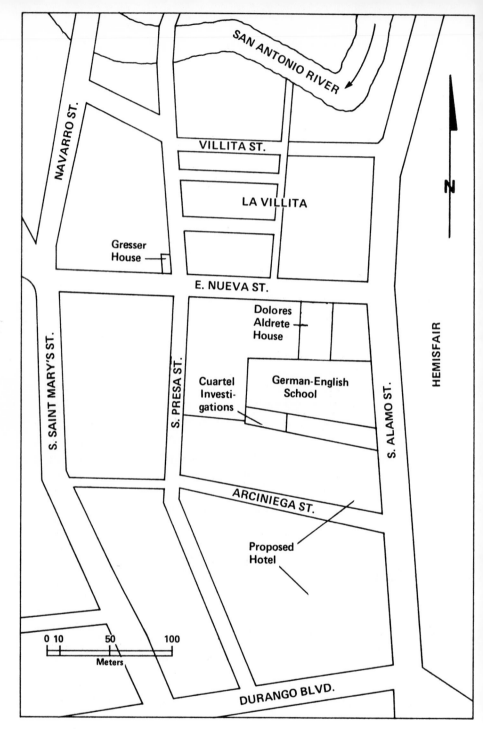

FIG. 5.4 *Map of the La Villita neighborhood, downtown San Antonio.*
(From Fox, Valdez, and Bobbitt 1978: Fig. 1. Courtesy Center for Archaeological Research, The University of Texas at San Antonio.)

of land was a lot owned from 1811 until 1841 by Gregorio Arciniega, a retired Spanish soldier. His son, Miguel Arciniega, became *alcalde* of Bexar in 1830, founded the town of Bastrop in 1832, acted as interpreter when General Cos surrendered to the Texans under Edward Burleson at Bexar in 1835, and was appointed Judge of the Municipality of San Antonio in 1836.

It was hoped that evidence of early nineteenth-century occupations by these historic figures could be found. But the results of the archeological test excavations indicated that the Dominguez and Arciniega properties probably were not occupied until the late nineteenth century. Nowhere in the entire hotel project area could buried architectural remains or artifacts be found that pre-date 1840. Apparently the area, which was served by the Spanish Colonial *acequia* system, continued to be used for agricultural purposes at least until the time of the Revolution, and Dominguez and Arciniega must have lived somewhere else.

In 1978, on Nueva Street on the southern edge of La Villita, a preliminary archeological and historical investigation was conducted at the Dolores Aldrete House (Fox, Valdez, and Bobbitt 1978). Two historic buildings stand on the property which consists of three small lots on a city block in this old neighborhood of downtown San Antonio. The Caile House, a mid-nineteenth-century two-room stone structure with later additions, is situated on the front of the property near the street. The early nineteenth-century post and mud, or *palisado*, Dolores Aldrete House is located on the back of one of the lots. A prominent San Antonio family purchased the property and planned to restore it as a historic site. The objectives of the archeological investigation were designed to find buried structural details, assess the archeological potential of the property, and recover samples of artifacts and information about architectural and archeological features that might be buried there.

The test excavations yielded information that substantiates and supplements the historical records indicating that the property has been occupied more or less continuously since before Dolores Aldrete received formal title to it as a Spanish land grant in 1818. Construction materials found consisted of the debris produced by nineteenth- and twentieth-century carpentry, masonry, electrical, and plumbing work which was done during several periods of construction, maintenance, and renovation of the early and mid-nineteenth-century structures. The household garbage found re-flects the residential nature of the site up until the time it became a commercial property in the twentieth century. The bones of a pet dog and pet cats were found. Clothing fasteners, beads, comb frag-ments, pencils, fish hooks, and other items recovered probably were lost or discarded by the site's many occupants and visitors throughout the nineteenth and twentieth centuries. A relatively small proportion of firearm-related materials, parts of machinery, and artifacts related to agriculture and transportation were recov-ered, probably because of the urban residential nature of the site's various occupations since the early nineteenth century. Chipped flint artifacts and some pottery sherds from mission Indian Goliad Ware and Mexican-made tin-enameled majolica and lead-glazed wares were found in the deposits pre-dating the construction of the Dolores Aldrete House and may be evidence of eighteenth-century occupation of the La Villita area.

One little-known site offers an astonishing example of how an archeological find can confirm written records. In 1968 a hu-man skeleton was found eroding out of a ditch along an unpaved road in a rural area of southern Bexar County. The discovery of the skeleton on Blue Wing Road was reported to the Witte Memo-rial Museum of San Antonio (A. Fox n.d.). The bones were rest-ing in a dense clay subsoil only a few inches below the natural ground surface of the area, indicating that the body had been placed in a shallow grave. The bones of the lower legs and the top of the skull had been scraped away by road machinery. A thor-ough search found no other bones or other archeological evidence along the road or in the farmland surrounding the grave site, in-dicating that it probably was a single, isolated burial.

Careful excavation of the loose soil and hard clay covering the undisturbed parts of the skeleton revealed seven brass buttons near the waist, on the pelvis, and at the knees. No other artifacts could be found. When it became impossible to remove the hard clay from the fragile bones without damaging them, the investigators removed the burial as large chunks still encased in clay and took them to the laboratory where the soil could be more easily and efficiently removed with water. When the mud was washed from the skull area, a lead ball was found under the chin. It measured

FIG. 5.5   *The remains of an adult male as they were exposed archeologically in Blue Wing Road, southern Bexar County.* Note shallowness of the grave pit. (Photo by A. A. Fox.)

more than an inch in diameter, weighed more than four ounces, and must have been fired from something larger than a musket. Although the bones of the skeleton were not fractured in the area where the ball was lodged, the impact of such a projectile must have been a cause of death.

Scientific analysis determined that the skeleton from Blue Wing Road probably was that of an adult male, possibly in his mid-20's and about 5 feet 7 inches tall (Butler 1974). He apparently had good teeth with no cavities or other dental problems. His right forearm had been broken and then healed at some time during his lifetime. The arrangement of the buttons found with his skeleton indicated that the man was wearing breeches, perhaps as part of a uniform, that were buttoned at the waist, at a flap in front and at the knees. Although the undecorated brass buttons and the lead ball could not be dated precisely, they are of the types found in other archeological deposits dating to the late eighteenth century and early nineteenth century. This evidence suggests that the skeleton is that of a soldier who died in one of the Mexican revolutionary battles that occurred in the San Antonio area around 1812 or 1813.

Considering the large number of men who died in those clashes, historical research (A. Fox n.d.) has turned up information about the possible identity of the "Blue Wing Road Burial." The Battle of Medina occurred not far from this burial site on August 18, 1813, between a force of loyalist Spanish soldiers under the command of Arredondo and a force of Mexican revolutionaries and Americans who sought to take over Texas. One of the revolutionary leaders of this insurgent force was Colonel Miguel Menchaca, who may have been a member of a prominent family of Spanish Colonial San Antonio and may have been involved in previous revolutionary activities in San Antonio and at Goliad (Gulick and Allen 1924:71–72). According to the accounts of the battle, Menchaca acted against the advice of his commander, General Toledo, and led his soldiers into an attack against a detachment of loyalist troops sent up to lure the insurgents into a trap. Menchaca reportedly was struck in the neck by a ball. He was carried off by his fleeing comrades, but he died on the way and was buried on the "Seguin Road" (Menchaca 1937). Could the skeleton found beneath Blue Wing Road in southern Bexar County be the remains of Miguel Menchaca himself?

The Departments of Brazoria and Nacogdoches

Archeological surveys of river valleys where lakes have been proposed and similar searches for historical sites in other project areas have located and identified a variety of early nineteenth-century homesteads, plantations, communities, and cemeteries. Many sites of Austin's and DeWitt's colonists have been found during reservoir surveys in Jackson, DeWitt, and Gonzales counties on the coastal plain (Mallouf, Fox, and Briggs 1973: Fox, Mallouf, O'Malley, and Sorrow 1974). An archeological survey of the Wallisville Lake area of Chambers and Liberty counties located the site of some of the first family homesteads of the Atascosito area between the lower Sabine and San Jacinto rivers (Fox, Day, and

FIG. 5.6 *Brass trouser buttons found near the lower parts, and the large lead ball found in the neck area of the Blue Wing Road burial, southern Bexar County.* (Photo by A. A. Fox.)

Highley 1980). Although several of these historic sites may be relatively well preserved and might contain enlightening evidence of the Anglo-American colonization of Mexican Texas and the early years of the Texas Republic, few of them as yet have been archeologically investigated, and most of the archeological evidence that has been recovered pertains to developments that took place years after the Revolution (e.g., Freeman and Fawcett 1980).

The historic cemeteries and the sites of the early nineteenth-century coastal towns of Quintana and Velasco have been found at the mouth of the Brazos River near present-day Freeport where the U.S. Army Corps of Engineers has proposed the construction of a series of maritime navigational improvements (Baxter and Ippolito 1976; Lynn n.d.). But despite initial impressions and hopes that substantial parts of these early seaports and coastal resorts still remained intact, more intensive archeological investigations have found that the town sites have been badly disturbed by tropical storms and modern development of the area, and not much can be recovered archeologically (Hole 1980; Fox, Ivey, and Markey 1982).

Another early-nineteenth-century town site that has been investigated is that of Texana, located near the confluence of the Lavaca and Navidad rivers in what is now Palmetto Bend Reservoir. First settled in 1832 as the tiny village of Santa Anna by families of Austin's "Old Three Hundred," the community began to grow and the townspeople changed its name in 1835 when Santa Anna's name was no longer appreciated (Webb 1952:730). Two speculators from the United States offered to purchase Texana and the surrounding area so they could develop it into an inland deepwater port. But when the townspeople wanted too much for the land, the Allen brothers predicted that Texana would never amount to anything and went on to develop a much less expensive piece of Mexican real estate that eventually came to be the Houston metropolitan area. Texana grew after the Revolution and by 1882 became an important inland port with a prosperous business district. But in 1883, a railroad line was constructed that bypassed the town and most of its residents moved away, leaving Texana a deserted ghost town.

In the early 1970's, when archeologists found the town site, the tops of the underground stone cisterns once used to collect rainwater to supply Texana's households were found protruding above the farmland and pastures of the area. It was hoped that more evidence of Texana's streets, buildings, and perhaps even the town's wharf area might still be preserved (Mallouf, Fox, and Briggs 1973). In 1974 archeological test excavations were conducted at the town site by the Texas Archeological Survey of The University of Texas at Austin (Jackson 1977) and a thorough study of the architecture of Texana was done based on some of the town's surviving buildings, which were moved to other locations when Texana was abandoned (Crosby 1977). But the archeological investigations were relatively unproductive. Apparently most of the town's building foundations, streets, and the other archeological features had been disturbed by bulldozing, erosion, and plowing.

Another historic town, Washington-on-the-Brazos, was laid out in 1835 on a land grant held by one of Austin's colonists. On March 1, 1836, delegates from each municipality in Texas met there in an unfinished frame building to determine Texas' political future. This convention declared Texas' independence from Mex-

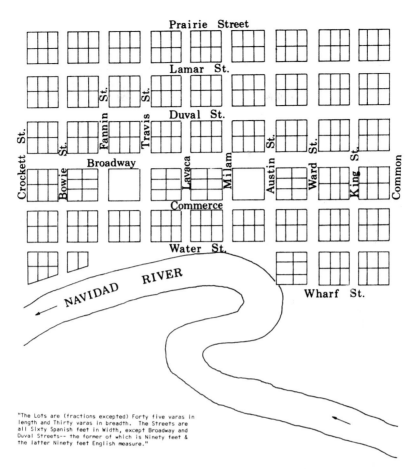

FIG. 5.7 *Township plan of Texana, Jackson County, filed on record on April 25, 1837.* (From Mallouf, Fox, and Briggs 1973: Fig. 15. Courtesy Texas Historical Commission. Adapted from transcribed Deed Record, Jackson County.)

ico, established the Republic with a new constitution, and organized an interim government before the delegates and the residents of the town fled to avoid Santa Anna's advancing troops. After the Republic's capital was established there in 1842, Washington began to grow. But, like Texana, the railroad bypassed the town in the mid-1850's. Washington's importance as a commercial center dwindled and by the end of the nineteenth century little visible evidence of the town remained (Texas Parks and Wildlife Department 1977).

Archeological investigations were first done at Washington-on-the-Brazos State Historical Park in 1964 in search of the precise location and structural details of Independence Hall (Parsons, Corbin, and Tunnell n.d.). This short-term project found only a couple of postholes, trash pits, and other features that provided minimal information about the structure's possible location. In 1966 several trenches were excavated in search of the town's major streets (Davis and Corbin 1967). Once streets were located it would be easier to find the sites of buildings that stood along them. But the results of this short-term investigation were negative and the researchers recommended that large-scale excavations, instead of small trenches and limited test pits, would be necessary to find the appropriate archeological and architectural remains.

In 1968 more extensive excavations were opened in which a section of a brick walkway or sidewalk was found along what probably was Ferry Street, and artifacts were recovered that probably were evidence of the location of Independence Hall (Texas Parks and Wildlife Department 1977). Finally, in 1969, another more intensive investigation was conducted, excavating a series of large, open trenches that ran back from Ferry Street (Lorrain and Jackson n.d.). The archeological remains of at least five buildings, a hand-dug well, brick sidewalks, and an alleyway were found, as well as a large trash pit containing thousands of artifacts from the early nineteenth century. Once these features were located and identified, it was obvious that other valuable archeological and architectural features are preserved, and disturbance of them by the park's development and public use can be avoided. The Texas Parks and Wildlife Department found that the acreage along Ferry Street in Washington-on-the-Brazos provides a significant resource of information about life in one of the most important historic sites of the Revolution and the Texas Republic. A research and management plan has been developed for the preservation and careful recovery of the historical and archeological information that the site contains.

The site of Kenney's Fort is an example of the few early fortified settlements dating from the time of the Republic which somehow have been spared from the complete destruction by relic hunters, urbanization, and alteration of the rural landscape. Kenney's Fort was built in 1839 by Dr. Thomas Kenney and other settlers of Austin's Colony as a small complex of two or three log houses surrounded by a stockade on the bank of Brushy Creek

FIG. 5.8 *Washington-on-the-Brazos in 1865.* (From Texas Parks and Wildlife Department 1977: Fig. 7. Courtesy Texas Parks and Wildlife Department.)

FIG. 5.9 *Aerial view of Washington-on-the-Brazos State Historic Park, 1965.* (From Texas Parks and Wildlife Department 1977: A-90. Courtesy Texas Parks and Wildlife Department.)

near present-day Round Rock (Webb 1952:949, 729; Pierce 1969: 81–83; Scarbrough 1976:83–85). Settlers of the area successfully defended the stronghold against an Indian attack in 1840.

In July of 1841, the ill-fated Texan Santa Fé Expedition began its march toward New Mexico from Camp Cazneau at Kenney's Fort. The expedition, which included a military force, merchants, teamsters, and others totalling 321 people, intended to establish trade and political relations between Texas and New Mexico. But the travellers got lost and suffered from limited provisions and harassment by Indians on their journey across north-central Texas and the Llano Estacado. The expedition became a total failure when it finally reached Santa Fé. The Texans were taken prisoner and were marched to Mexico, finally to be released in April, 1842.

After Adrian Woll's Mexican army captured San Antonio in 1842, President Sam Houston ordered a company of Texas Rangers to remove some of the Republic's archives from Austin to Washington-on-the-Brazos. A vigilance committee from Austin overtook the Rangers at Kenney's Fort (also called Fort Dunnington by this time) and, after only a few shots were fired, recovered the documents and returned them to Austin.

Some of the original buildings at Kenney's Fort were reported to be in fairly good condition in the 1860's. Foundations of the fort's cabins, some cedar posts, and a portion of the flagpole reportedly could be seen in the early twentieth century. When the site was found by archeologists in 1981, no structural remains could be seen, but iron building hardware and household evidence dating from the first half of the nineteenth century were found. Although the historic site has been altered by clearing and cultivation, foundation remains and other archeological evidence of the 1840's occupation of the site may still be buried there (Fox, Whitsett, and Jurgens 1981), and one hopes that the Kenney's Fort site will be protected from vandalism, relic hunters, urbanization, and other effects of the development of the area around it.

The French Legation in Austin was the site of one of the first scientifically conducted historical archeological investigations in Texas (Olds 1967). The historic property was sold by Anson Jones to Alphonse de Saligny, chargé d'affaires of the King of France, in 1840. The embassy and residence was built of pine lumber and had foundations and chimneys of local limestone. Its doors, windows, and hardware were imported from France. Saligny sold the property to Bishop John Marri Odin of San Antonio with the agreement that Saligny would occupy the place until April, 1842, and that he would complete the construction of the house and build a kitchen and a stable on the grounds nearby. The short-term archeological investigations, carried out by the Texas Archeological Research Laboratory of The University of Texas at Austin, were designed to find physical evidence of the location of the kitchen building, which had been erected as a separate structure behind the embassy residence. The Daughters of the Republic of Texas, who manage the historic landmark today, planned to reconstruct the kitchen and wanted it to be located on its original site. Carefully controlled hand-excavated trenches uncovered the remains of the kitchen's floor, its fireplace hearth area, and a lime-filled pit, as well as an assortment of ceramic, glass, and metal artifacts and food bone refuse associated with the embassy's kitchen operations and later occupation of the French Legation property.

Mexican Texas

Besides the historic sites of San Antonio, only some of the more historically well-known Mexican sites of the early nineteenth century have been studied archeologically. Most of the Mexican forts have been located, such as the site of the fort and customs-house of Anahuac on Galveston Bay, where William B. Travis was imprisoned in 1832, and the site of Fort Velasco at the mouth of the Brazos River, where the first real battle between Mexicans and Texans was fought in 1832 and where Santa Anna signed the treaty that ended the war. The site of Fort Lipantitlan also has been found on the lower Nueces River near San Patricio. Lipantitlan was captured by the Texans in 1835, was ordered destroyed by the Mexican army in 1836, and later was defended by the army of the Texas Republic against a Mexican attack in 1842 (Pierce 1969:93).

The brick ruins of Fort Anahuac have been afforded preliminary study but have not been archeologically investigated (Fox, Day, and Highley 1980). Archival research and test excavations have found that little remains of the structure of driftwood posts set in rows with sand filled in between them that once was Fort Velasco (Fox, Ivey, and Markey 1982). The site of Fort Lipantitlan is now a State Historic Site and preliminary archeological inves-

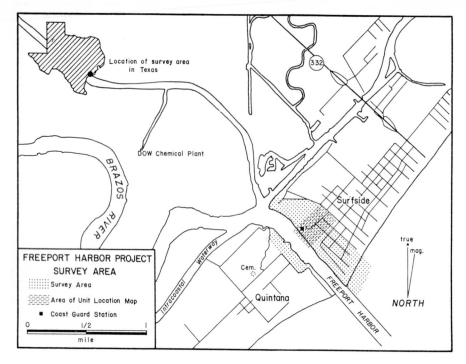

FIG. 5.10 *Map of the historic sites of Quintana and Velasco (now Surfside) on the Texas coast.* See also map of archeological test units, Fig. 5.11. (From Fox, Ivey, and Markey 1982:Fig. 1. Courtesy Center for Archaeological Research, The University of Texas at San Antonio.)

tigations have concluded that most of the fort site area has been disturbed by mechanical clearing, although European and Mexican pottery sherds, bottle glass, and a possible gunflint were found that date to the appropriate periods during which the fort was occupied (Ing 1976).

Most Texans are familiar with the Mexican holiday, Cinco de Mayo, which commemorates the day in 1862 when Mexican forces defeated the French in Puebla, Mexico. But not so many know that Ignacio Zaragosa, the military hero who led the Mexican forces in that decisive battle, was born in Mexican Texas. The stone building near Presidio La Bahía in Goliad where Zaragosa was born in 1829 has been designated as a State Historic Site. Archeological excavations were conducted there in the 1970's, but unfortunately the field notes and other important records and collections from the investigation were destroyed in a fire shortly after the archeological fieldwork was completed.

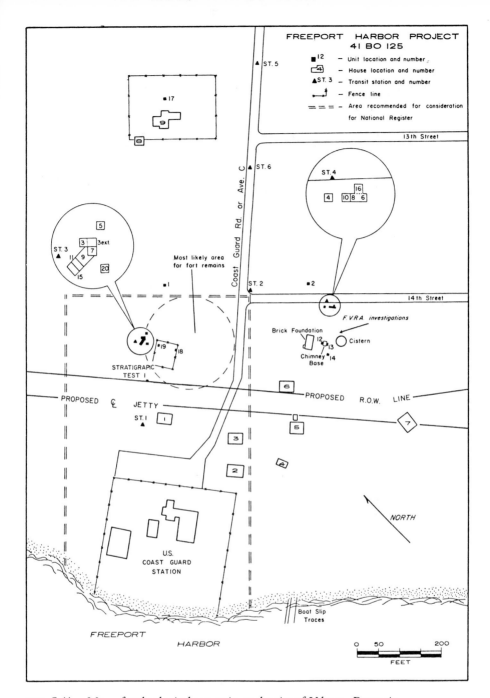

FIG. 5.11 *Map of archeological test units at the site of Velasco, Brazoria County, showing most likely location of Fort Velasco and other features.* (From Fox, Ivey, and Markey 1982: Fig. 8. Courtesy Center for Archaeological Research, The University of Texas at San Antonio.)

There still is a considerable amount of archeological investigation to be done in the study of the history of Mexican Texas. Of course most of the historical research into the happenings in early nineteenth-century Texas has focused on the lives of Anglo-American and Texan colonists, military heroes, and political leaders of the period. And it follows that most archeological investigations of the early nineteenth century have concentrated on the places that these people occupied. Little is known historically and archeologically about the mixture of Spanish Colonial military, settler, and acculturated Indian peoples that evolved into Mexican society in early nineteenth-century Texas. And even though one of the first Europeans to see Texas was a black man who accompanied Cabeza de Vaca on his journey in the early sixteenth century, and black people played a role in the history of Spanish Colonial Texas and were a major part of the population of Anglo-American Texas in the first half of the nineteenth century, only a

FIG. 5.12 *Ignacio Zaragoza's birthplace (1829) at Presidio La Bahía, Goliad, restored by the Texas Parks and Wildlife Department as a State Historic Site.* (Courtesy Texas Parks and Wildlife Department.)

few slave quarters sites have been identified and the archeology of Afro-American Texans is virtually unknown.

Artifacts of Early Nineteenth-Century Texas

The archeology of Mexican Texas, the Revolution, and the Republic is in the early stages of development. Its primary objectives have been the identification, preliminary investigation, and preservation of the best-known archeological sites and structures of the first half of the nineteenth century, and the study of the various kinds of material evidence of that period of Texas history. The dates of manufacture and the functions of many of the types of artifacts have been determined, particularly for the period after 1820 when most of the settlements of Texas were supplied from sources in Europe and the United States.

Certain types of pottery were used most commonly in pre-Civil War Texas and generally are accepted as evidence of occupations that took place during that period. The soft-paste, tin-enameled majolica styles, the tan, brown, and greenish lead-glazed earthenwares, and the mission Indian Goliad Ware pottery of the Spanish Colonial period were quickly replaced by the harder, more consistently shaped, clear-glazed white paste earthenwares, or pearlwares, imported from England in large quantities and brought into Texas with the Anglo-American colonists after 1820. The English ceramic wares have been described in detail in several published studies (e.g., Godden 1964, 1967; Hume 1970:128–133; Davis and Corbin 1967:15–27; Greaser and Greaser 1967; Mankowitz and Haggar 1975), and sherds from the decorated portions of these wares have been used effectively to help identify archeological sites and specific features and soil deposits within sites dating to the pre-Civil War period in Texas (Mallouf, Fox, and Briggs 1973; Fox, Mallouf, O'Malley, and Sorrow 1974; Fox, Bass, and Hester 1976; Scurlock and Fox 1977).

Edged, or shell edged, wares were plates and other flat vessels with molded feathered or scalloped rims sometimes unpainted, but usually painted in blue and less commonly in green or yellow along the molded edge. Another common decorated ware of the period has simple, bold, hand-painted floral designs in a mixture of green, blue, rose, yellow, and brown, often accented with black dots and lines and with bands near the rim. Banded slip, or mocha, wares also were popular and are easily recognizable as sherds from cups and bowls with painted bands of blue and brown that rise noticeably above the flat white surface of the vessel and by swirling, or wormed, designs in shades of brown, tan, and blue. Sponged, or spatter, ware, has simple spattered or randomly dotted areas of red, blue, purple, or green in much the same hues as the decorations on hand-painted ware. Transfer ware is another common decorative type. On these white paste earthenware vessels, landscapes and other scenes were transferred onto the vessel surfaces and appear as patterns of dots, like the halftone pictures in newspapers. Blue transfer patterns apparently were the most common in the early nineteenth century, but patterns printed in a variety of colors such as red, brown, black, purple, and green were popular in the 1840's and the 1850's. "Flown blue" is similar to blue transfer printed ware, but it usually is darker in color and was produced intentionally to have a smeared, blurred, or "flown" appearance.

The most common forms of glass artifacts of the first half of the nineteenth century are fragments of alcoholic beverage bottles and medicine bottles, although glass drinking vessels and other containers and serving wares also occur occasionally. Because the technology of bottle-making advanced through time, the dating of bottles and bottle fragments is based mostly on mold marks, or the lack of them, and on the shape of the base of the vessel and details about the way that the neck and rim were formed (Lorrain 1968; Newman 1970; Kendrick 1970; Mallouf, Fox, and Briggs 1973; Deiss 1981).

Most bottles manufactured before the Civil War were made entirely by hand. A glob, or parison, of glass was taken from the furnace with a blowpipe, then inflated into a slowly cooling globe. Another metal pole or rod, called a pontil, was pressed into the bottom of the parison to form an indented base, or kick-up, so that the bottle would stand upright. Adhering to the bottom, the pontil was used to hold the beginning form of the bottle so that the neck of the vessel could be drawn out, the blowpipe could be removed, and then the lip and rim could be finished to the appropriate size and shape. Rings of glass were often added to the rim to reinforce it for the later insertion of a cork closure. Then the pontil was broken off, usually leaving a jagged scar in the center of the kick-up. The attributes of these free-blown bottles, then, are the lack of mold seams, a pontil scar, rather uneven wall thicknesses,

FIG. 5.13 *British-made white paste earthenware, typical evidence of household occupations in the first half of the nineteenth century in Texas.* a, edgeware; b, e, transfer printed ware; c, h, k, mocha ware; d, sponged ware; g, l, sponged and hand-painted ware; f, i, j, hand-painted ware. (Courtesy Center for Archaeological Research, The University of Texas at San Antonio.)

somewhat asymmetrical vessel shapes, stretch marks on the neck portions, and an entirely hand-finished rim and lip.

During the mid-1800's, methods were invented so that pontil scars could be avoided or improved, such as the use of the snap case which held the body of the bottle while the lip was finished. Reheating, or annealing, of the newly shaped bottle sometimes was done to improve the pontil base. And also during the mid-nineteenth century, molds came into use for glass bottle production which left mold seams on the body of the vessel. But the neck was still drawn from the body by hand and had no mold marks, and the rim and lip were hand finished. Most alcoholic beverage bottles from the first half of the nineteenth century were green, ranging from olive green to almost black. Medicine bottles and vials were almost clear or aquamarine in color. Fancier free-blown, partially molded, and pressed glass objects usually were of clear glass.

Metal artifacts as a general category are not as easy to date to specific time periods. One reason is that molded, or cast, metal forms lasted longer than ceramic dishes and glass bottles and sometimes were more difficult or more expensive to obtain and to replace. The functional shapes developed for metal items that could be produced in large quantities and served their purpose well enough had no reason to be changed, unless technological development was more or less revolutionary.

Nails are an example. Although various methods of mass producing nails were developed at different times during the nineteenth century, there are three basic types of nails (Nelson 1968; Fontana and Greenleaf 1962). During the early nineteenth century, wrought iron nails were used. Handmade on an anvil, they had a sharp point and an asymmetrical, battered head. Wrought nails preceded standardized, mass-produced, machine-cut square nails with their chisel-shaped points and rectangular heads. Wire nails, like those used today, apparently were not used commonly in Texas until around the beginning of the twentieth century, even though they were first produced in the nineteenth century.

There are other sorts of ceramic, glass, and metal artifacts that can be dated to specific time periods, such as clay tobacco pipes, glass beads, metal coins, and gun parts. But it would take many pages to describe all of them. The use of various artifacts and classes of archeological materials for assigning dates to archeological deposits and for identifying the activities carried on can vary from site to site. In many cases the dates and functions of various artifact types have been identified by previous archeological research. In other cases the time in which an object was produced and the nature of its use is unknown and can only be determined from new research and through the study of the archeological context within which the artifact is found.

VI

The Settlement of American Texas

DURING THE YEARS between the Revolution and the Civil War, Texas received thousands of immigrants, mostly from the Old South, but also from other parts of the United States and from Europe (Fehrenbach 1968:270–324). The success of the economy of early Texas depended upon population growth. The Republican and state governments did whatever they could to encourage immigration, including providing for squatters' rights and homesteading, and reopening the old empresario system of colonial settlement in untamed areas not naturally rich or secure enough to attract scattered settlement by individual frontier families. The well-watered pine and hardwood forests of eastern Texas and the rich prairie lands of the coastal plain were the first areas to be settled and became an extension of the Cotton Kingdom with its working class of thousands of Afro-American slaves. Traders and merchants took advantage of the new demands for supplies in the new state. Some hauled goods. Others established businesses in the growing coastal ports and inland towns.

East Texas Farms and Plantations

By the time the Republic became a state, eastern Texas was no longer the frontier sanctuary for fugitives and refugees from the United States that it had been in the early nineteenth century (Meinig 1969:47–51). The native Indian inhabitants and transplanted Indian groups had been eradicated or removed, and the pine and hardwood forest region became more stable in settlement pattern. Its landscape, although thinly settled, became an established patchwork of poor and prosperous farmers and scattered plantation owners (Collier 1982). By the time of statehood, the pioneer families of the original empresario colonies on the coastal plain had developed their large tracts of wilderness into productive estates and plantations. Joining them were new immigrants, in-

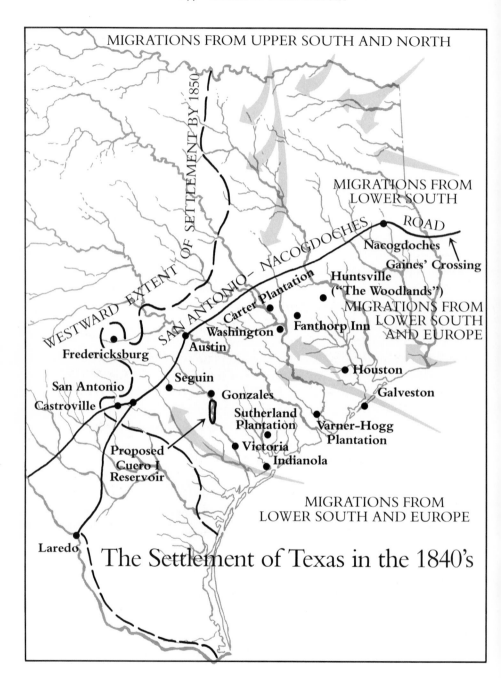

FIG. 6.1 *The settlement of Texas in the 1840's.*

cluding influential planters whose economic success and social prestige were based on huge landholdings and hundreds of slaves. By 1860, slaves accounted for almost a third of the more than 600,000 people in what was called Texas (Fehrenbach 1968:287). In the broad, rich valleys and in the upland areas where the soils and climate were right for corn and cotton, more than half of the population was Afro-American.

There were many slaves and there were many large plantations in Texas between the 1830's and the 1860's, but the old romantic assumptions about the antebellum South should not be applied to pre-Civil War Texas. An interesting study has been put together by an archeologist based on historical research into Texas plantations and on information gathered during archeological surveys conducted in areas where a lake and large strip mines have been proposed in Hill, Freestone, and Rusk counties (Jackson 1982). The study concluded that, except for those plantations that had early beginnings during the 1820's in the heart of Austin's Colony (Curlee 1932; Bornhorst 1971), the plantation era included less than 30 years in deep eastern Texas and less than 10 years in areas behind the frontier further west. Large slave-run farming operations in Rusk County were located in areas that were similar environmentally to the Old South. They were more numerous and had more time to mature before the Civil War than plantations located in counties further west.

The study found that the large plantation operations in Texas were much more diversified than the typical Southern plantations of the Cotton Kingdom, which were based primarily in the production of one or two cash crops. More important, the typical Texas slave-owner was the small farmer with three slaves or less, a modest family dwelling, and very little capital. These settlers filled the broad gap between the rich planter class, usually thought of as plantation owners, and the forgotten poor farmers, or "white trash," who owned no slaves (Fehrenbach 1968:309–310).

The study also concluded that the classic image of blacks in the antebellum South as field hands and house servants is unfair and inaccurate. On an 1850's plantation in Hill County, for example, a wealthy cattleman and industrialist named James J. Gathings had slaves who were accomplished millwrights, tanners, bootmakers, brickmakers, masons, and furniture makers. Together

Gathings and his slaves established the town of Covington which became one of the most prosperous towns on the western frontier.

Several historic buildings and building complexes in varying degrees of preservation and deterioration have been marked as historic plantation sites in various old Texas counties. Among these are the Stratton Place in Brazoria County, the Braches Home in Gonzales County, the A. W. Hill House in Bastrop County, the William Garrett House Plantation in San Augustine County, the Hatfield Plantation, and the Asa-Hoxay Home in Washington County, the Polley Mansion in Wilson County, and the Edgemont Plantation, Locust Grove, Mimosa Hall and the Dial-Williamson House in Harrison County.

Most of these historic places have been recognized because of their distinctive homes, ranging from impressive Greek Revival mansions to simpler double log cabins, or dog-runs, with two log rooms separated by a breezeway and covered by a common roof. Most were built and occupied as the residences and headquarters for farming operations and other activities during the period from the early 1820's until the 1860's. Unfortunately, few of them have been thoroughly investigated archeologically, even though such investigations might discover the real diversity that existed in the early rural agrarian settlement of American Texas.

Archeological surveys of areas proposed to be overtaken by the construction of reservoirs, strip mines, and other projects have located a variety of sites of pre-Civil War farmsteads which ranged from true large Southern plantations with impressive mansions and hundreds of slaves to the more common "plantations" with fewer acres, simpler family residences, and only a few slaves. In areas south of Gonzales where a large water supply reservoir was proposed to be constructed, an archeological and historical survey found the foundations of a large house and some associated outbuildings, and an old family cemetery on an upland slope overlooking the broad, rich bottomlands of the Lower Guadalupe River Valley (Fox, Mallouf, O'Malley, and Sorrow 1974:254).

These architectural features turned out to be the remains of a plantation that belonged to a family named Carroll who controlled hundreds of acres in the area before the Civil War. Some descendants of the plantation owners showed the investigators an old painting of what the place was like when it was in operation. The painting shows a large two-story mansion with white columns, a landscaped front garden and walkways, a carriage house, and other nearby buildings. When the site was found in 1973, an abandoned late nineteenth-century Victorian-style house and its associated farm and ranch buildings stood where the Greek Revival plantation house and its front garden had been located decades before. There was no apparent relationship between the plantation's foundations and the later building complex, reflecting the changes in land tenure and land use practices that occurred following the Civil War.

Several other nineteenth-century historic sites with the remains of simple log and frame buildings and others with substantial brick and stone foundations, cisterns, and other structural features were found in the proposed reservoir area that may well have been slave-run farms and plantations. Unfortunately, the objectives of the reservoir survey were limited to locating, identifying,

FIG. 6.2   *Theodore Gentilz's "Stick Stock," showing surveyors at work in nineteenth-century Texas.* (Courtesy Larry Sheerin, San Antonio.)

and evaluating archeological and historical sites, and time was not available for more intensive study of the Carroll place and other pre-Civil War sites in the proposed reservoir area. Fortunately, the Cuero I Lake has not been constructed and perhaps the plantation site along that stretch of the Guadalupe will be preserved.

Other Texas plantation sites have been located archeologically and historically identified, particularly in the old, rich farming areas around Brazoria County. The Ellerslie Plantation is an example. Found during a survey of the general area where oil pipelines and storage facilities were to be constructed, the Ellerslie site consists of a large complex of structural features of handmade brick, including the remains of a sugar refinery, an intact house, large subterranean cisterns, and several unidentifiable foundations (Texas Archeological Survey 1974). Originally established in the 1820's, the Ellerslie Plantation reportedly had one of the earliest steam-driven sugar mills in Texas and produced high quality sugar throughout the 1850's and the early 1860's. Like other plantation sites, Ellerslie has not been thoroughly investigated, but its significance has been recognized and it is listed in the National Register of Historic Places.

Marked only by a scatter of pre-Civil War artifacts, the site of another plantation has been found near the mouth of the Trinity River in southeastern Texas (Fox, Day, and Highley 1980:64–82). The plantation was owned by Nicolas Labadie, a doctor who served as surgeon of the Mexican garrison at Anahuac and opened a mercantile store there. He acquired the plantation in the early 1830's and served as surgeon for the First Regiment of Texas Regulars at the Battle of San Jacinto. The Labadie plantation was used as a stop-over point during the Runaway Scrape of 1836, when most Anglo-American colonists fled toward the Sabine River in fear of the advancing army of Santa Anna. Although there are no standing remains of the plantation, the preliminary archeological investigation found that important evidence is buried there. The U.S. Army Corps of Engineers has been made aware of the site's location and significance so that it may be protected from the activity associated with Wallisville Lake.

In part of the Navidad River Valley to be inundated by the waters of Palmetto Bend Reservoir in Jackson County, archeological excavations were conducted in 1977 at the site of the Sutherland

FIG. 6.3 *Artist's reconstruction of the Jim Hogg birthplace, Cherokee County, in the mid-nineteenth century.* Note that the kitchen is separated from the living quarters. (From Jensen 1968: Frontispiece. Drawing by Gene Mobley.)

Plantation. This was the homestead of one of the prominent members of a group of families who migrated to Texas from Alabama and Tennessee and became neighbors again in the early 1830's as Austin's Third or Coast Colony (Freeman and Fawcett 1980).

Born in Virginia in 1787, George Sutherland moved his family to Texas from Alabama in 1830. He soon resumed his career as a merchant while developing his land grant on the Navidad. He entered into a partnership with an early firm of Texas merchants and financiers who helped him gain access to the import network that supplied the people of the Alabama Settlement with the sorts of clothing, household goods, and other materials that fit their Southern lifestyle. Like other pioneers, the Sutherlands' first home probably was a dog-run log cabin. But within the first couple of years, trade connections were established along new overland routes leading to neighboring inland communities and along the navigable Navidad and Lavaca river channels leading to the coast.

Then the materials could be imported with which to improve their original house or build a new one.

Sutherland was a leader in the establishment of the agrarian economy of his community and became influential in the politics of Anglo-American Texas during the years before and after the Revolution. By the 1840's, Sutherland's slave plantation, known as Spring Hill, and other large farmsteads and plantations in the Alabama Settlement were well established and the new Texans developed a lifestyle that combined elements from two Southern cultural traditions. Their earliest roots were in the Upper South, where yeoman farmers owned few, if any, slaves and raised corn and tobacco, swine, cattle, and horses, and where the typical family dwellings were dog-run cabins (Newton 1974). With their migration to Alabama in the late 1800's, they were introduced to the agrarian tradition of the Lower South and Tideland plantations, typified by slave labor, the cultivation of cotton, and the manufac-

FIG. 6.4   *Theodore Gentilz's "Colored Home," typical slave quarters in American Texas.* Note the method of construction of the chimney and the limited number of windows in this small household structure. (Courtesy Larry Sheerin, San Antonio.)

ture of brick for the construction of large masonry homes (Jordan 1964; Kniffen 1965:574).

Reflecting a mixture of these cultural traditions, the farms and plantations of the Alabama Settlement in Texas produced corn and cotton as major crops and also grew tobacco, potatoes, millet, oats, and other crops. By the early 1840's, Sutherland and other members of the colony were experimenting with sugar-refining, and sugarcane became another important crop of the farms and plantations on the coastal plain in Texas. With the benefit of slave labor, Sutherland also became a successful cattle rancher in the 1840's, reflecting an adaptation from the emphasis on raising hogs, sheep, cattle, and other livestock back in Alabama and representing a part of the Anglo-American tradition that contributed to the development of the Texas cattle industry (Jordan 1969).

The days of the Spring Hill plantation ended with Sutherland's death in 1855. The place remained a community center and the estate was controlled by the Sutherland family until around the end of the nineteenth century. By the 1960's, few traces remained of the Sutherland house, outbuildings, sugar refinery, and other features that once were a part of one of the most productive plantations in the Jackson County area. Land use practices since 1900 thoroughly altered the bluff overlooking the Navidad where Spring Hill stood. The Sutherland family cemetery and an early twentieth-century house were the prominent standing structures on the plantation site when the archeologists arrived. But excavations uncovered a fireplace foundation of handmade bricks and some postholes and remnants of brick piers that probably had supported the original Sutherland house. The brick remains of Sutherland's early sugar refinery also were found.

Despite the disturbed condition of the surface of the area and the limited amount of structural remains, a large collection of artifacts was recovered from the plantation site. Analysis of the different kinds of artifacts and their distribution enabled the archeologists investigating the Sutherland site to date the different structural features, to determine the nature of construction of the house, and to estimate the area enclosed within the building and its orientation with respect to prevailing wind patterns and other environmental conditions.

Several archeological dating techniques were experimented with, including two that have been developed to study historic sites in other parts of the United States (South 1964, 1977). In one of these analyses, sherds of various kinds of porcelain, stoneware, and earthenware pottery from the Sutherland site were assigned ranges of dates based on the known dates of archeological deposits in which the same kinds of ceramics have been found at other nineteenth-century sites. The other borrowed dating technique involved the statistical comparison of the dimensions of bricks from sites of known time periods with the dimensions of the bricks found at the Sutherland site.

Another archeological technique was attempted which involved comparison of the ratios between the numbers of bottle glass fragments and the number of pottery fragments found at the plantation site with the ratios of the same sorts of artifacts found at other historic sites. Based on the assumption that the household use of glass containers increased during the late eighteenth and nineteenth centuries while the use of ceramic tablewares remained relatively constant, the higher the ratio of bottle glass to ceramics found in a collection of household artifacts, the later the occupation that the artifacts represent.

Taken together, the results of the different artifact analyses and other information recovered by the archeological investigation indicated that the Sutherland house site was occupied from the 1830's to the 1870's, and that sometime early in that period a large frame house stood there which either replaced the original log cabin or grew out of its renovation and expansion. The collection of artifacts recovered from the Sutherland Plantation Site will provide a resource of comparative information to be used in continuing investigations of the sites of other early Texas farms and plantations which will help to explain the history of antebellum life on the coastal plain.

Recently, concerned residents of College Station have supported preliminary historical and archeological investigations by students from Texas A&M University at an early Anglo-American homesite in their community where land development has been planned (Carlson 1982). The homesite was occupied by Richard Carter after he received a Mexican land grant in 1831 as one of the last group of colonists settled by Stephen F. Austin. Carter did not acquire the fame that so many other Anglo-American Texans did who settled in Mexican Texas, but intensive historical research provided an outline of his life in Texas.

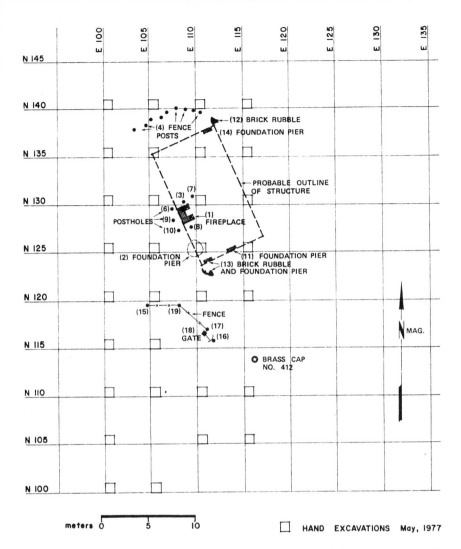

FIG. 6.5 *Plan of excavation units, structural features, and the grid system used to maintain horizontal control of the archeological investigations at the site of the Sutherland Plantation, Jackson County.* (From Freeman and Fawcett 1980: Fig. 9. Courtesy Texas Archeological Survey, The University of Texas at Austin.)

Apparently, Carter moved with his family from Alabama to his land grant in the Brazos River Valley in 1831. After occupying their frontier home and being isolated from almost everyone except friendly Indians and a couple of distant pioneer neighbors, they moved in 1835 to a small settlement at the Navasota River Crossing on the old San Antonio Road. But by the end of 1841, the Carters were back on their land grant in Brazos County, living in a one-room log cabin. Throughout the years of the Republic and early statehood, Carter succeeded in developing his frontier homestead into a prosperous rural estate. Judging from old county tax rolls, he was able to increase the value of his real and personal property from $1,300 in 1842 to $30,000 in 1860, primarily through the accumulation of cattle, horses, and slaves. By the time of the Civil War, he was among the top producers of cotton and corn and was one of the wealthiest owners of slaves, cattle, and land in the county. From the time Carter died in 1863 until his wife died in 1877, the estate dwindled in value. The Carter family continued to control parts of it, but by about 1920 the old homesite was abandoned.

Although the only visible remains of the Carter homesite was a stone-lined well on a prominent point overlooking Carter Creek, the investigating archeologists hoped to recover evidence of Carter's actual occupation of the site and artifacts illustrating his socioeconomic status and his early agricultural and ranching activities. Surveys using a proton magnetometer found only a few metal artifacts and the footings of the fence that once enclosed the family cemetery. Long, narrow trenches and series of small shovel probes were placed strategically in the area near the well where buried remains of the Carter house should be and in a different part of the old estate where the outbuildings and slave quarters were likely to have been located.

The most significant feature that was found was a large "sheet midden," or broad, thin scatter of occupational debris, that was most concentrated in the area nearest the well. No structural features were found, but fragments of limestone, probably from masonry structural elements, and an assortment of square nails and other building hardware found in the sheet midden suggest that it marked the location of a household structure. The ceramic and glass artifacts from the midden date generally from the period between 1830 and 1920, corresponding to the period of occupation of the homesite by the Carters and then by others after 1877.

Because his historical records indicated that Carter was in the highest economic bracket in Brazos County, the investigators assumed that this affluence would be indicated archeologically by the presence of a relatively high percentage of sherds of expensive ceramic tablewares. Archeological investigations have found this to be true at a plantation in Georgia (Otto 1977:98–99), where inexpensive pottery wares occurred at the habitation sites of the plantation's slaves and overseer, while the more expensive ceramic wares were found at the planter's homesite. But apparently this sort of evidence of social and economic stratification does not occur in Texas, or at least not at the Carter homesite. The kinds of nineteenth-century ceramics found there are of the same general types that are found at other sites of about the same time periods in Texas. Perhaps wealth was exhibited differently in a frontier community of scattered family homesteads, where household articles, no matter how expensive, were not as noticeable to one's neighbors and to travellers as impressive amounts of land, cattle, and slaves.

One large Texas plantation that has been preserved and is being maintained and interpreted is the Varner-Hogg Plantation State Historic Park in Brazoria County. Martin Varner joined Austin's Colony in 1822 and established a farm on his land grant in the Brazos River bottom in 1824. By 1829 he was distilling rum from sugarcane grown on his farm.

In 1834 Varner sold his headright strip of land to Columbus Patton, whose family established a plantation there. Santa Anna reportedly was held prisoner at the Patton Plantation for a short time in 1836. The sugar and cotton enterprise prospered during the 1840's and the early 1850's, but after 1854, when Columbus Patton was declared insane, the plantation's productivity declined because of bad weather, poor economic conditions and, of course, the Civil War. In the 1870's the land was still used to produce sugarcane and cotton, but by then it was owned and operated by a land corporation instead of a Southern aristocratic family. The operation was not productive enough and in 1901 former Texas Governor James S. Hogg purchased the place and used it as a second home. The Hogg family maintained ownership of the property and visited it as a weekend retreat until 1958, when Miss Ima Hogg gave the estate to the people of Texas to commemorate Governor Hogg and other historically prominent Texans and Americans.

Historical research, architectural studies, and some preliminary archeological investigations have produced information about the architectural and occupational history of the Varner-Hogg building complex (Texas Parks and Wildlife Department n.d.). Although no historic records have been found that describe how

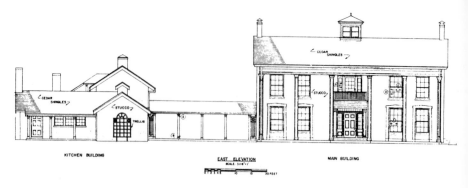

KITCHEN BUILDING   EAST ELEVATION   MAIN BUILDING

FIG. 6.6 *Elevation of the Varner-Hogg Mansion, Brazoria County.* (From Texas Parks and Wildlife Department n.d. Courtesy Texas Parks and Wildlife Department.)

Varner developed his land in the 1820's, archeological evidence indicates that his residence probably was located in the vicinity of the present plantation house which was built by the Pattons after they acquired the property in the 1830's. The Patton house and other plantation buildings were constructed of hand-formed brick made by slaves from local clay. A creek flows through the plantation site, separating the main residential area from the industrial area which included a sugar mill, farm storage and work areas, and the slave quarters. A wooden bridge probably linked the residential and working areas of the plantation. Brick walls enclosed a small family cemetery which was shaded by some of the large pecan trees on the plantation grounds.

The Patton's house was built of slave-made brick in the Greek Revival style. It is rectangular in shape and two stories high, with a tall attic space and galleries of columns along front and back. Even though it is a large brick building, its plan of rooms separated by a central hallway resembles the dog-run log structures of the early eastern Texas frontier. Fireplaces were used to warm the house during the winter months. The kitchen was built of a combination of wood and brick and stood separate from the house, as was typical of frontier farmsteads and established mansions of the day. This was intended not so much to separate the servants from the living quarters of the family, but as a means of isolating the heat of the stoves and the risk of fire from the main household.

Archeological test excavations at the ruins of the sugar mill found that two or three construction episodes took place there,

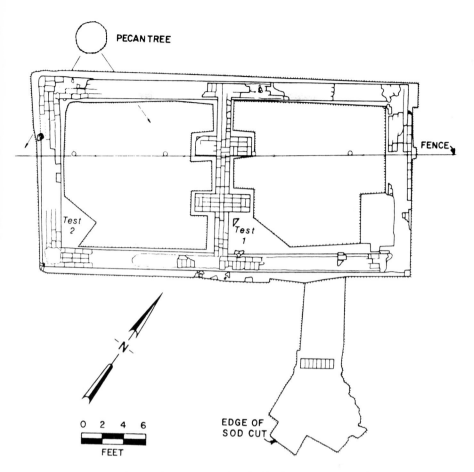

FIG. 6.7 *Plan of brick foundations of probable slave quarters at the Varner-Hogg Plantation State Historical Park, as exposed by archeological test excavations. Note small living area and central double fireplace hearth foundation.* (From Crouch 1982: Fig. 24. Courtesy Texas Parks and Wildlife Department.)

and that the sugarcane was crushed at one end of the mill, while the molasses was separated from the raw sugar in the "purgery" at the other end. The foundation remains and other evidence of a row of slave quarters buildings were found on the same side of the creek as the mill, but even further away from the plantation house. Each of the slave quarters buildings apparently had two small rooms and a central double fireplace.

The archeology of the Varner-Hogg Plantation is only partially understood. The abundant remains uncovered so far indicate that valuable archeological information is preserved at the park that can contribute to our understanding of what life was like for the people who owned a true Texas plantation and for those who actually made it work. The information obtained can be compared to the historical and archeological evidence recovered from other pre-Civil War slave-run farms and plantations to help explain the social and ethnic distinctions that existed and clarify the history of how the Southern agrarian economic system developed and then declined in early American Texas.

A different sort of pre-Civil War plantation has been archeologically and historically investigated in the core settlement area of Anglo-American Texas. Now owned by Sam Houston State University, an estate known as The Woodlands was constructed around 1847 by Sam Houston and his slaves on the outskirts of Huntsville (Clark 1980). Houston maintained the residence until 1853, when he went off politicking. Various people owned the estate, with its main two-story, dog-run log house and associated log kitchen, law office, and slave quarters, throughout the rest of the nineteenth century. Houston tried to buy it back once, but he was unsuccessful. In 1876, The Woodlands was converted into a girls' boarding school and several structural additions were erected. In 1901 the original house was moved away from the estate; in 1911 it was moved back.

The primary purpose of the archeological investigation was to find physical evidence that demonstrated whether or not the house is now located on its original 1840's site. The excavations were placed near the foundations of the house and in other nearby areas, and evidence of the original wooden posts and sandstone rock piers was found that indicated the house had been put back, more or less, in its original place. The artifacts recovered were representative primarily of the period following Houston's sale of the property in the 1850's, including doll parts, a gold-plated pendant inscribed "Momma," and other jewelry, which probably were lost by the occupants of the boarding school. But some sherds of British-made pottery dishes of transfer printed ware, sponged ware, and mocha ware and other artifacts found during the investigation probably are the material evidence of the period of Houston's ownership and occupation of The Woodlands estate.

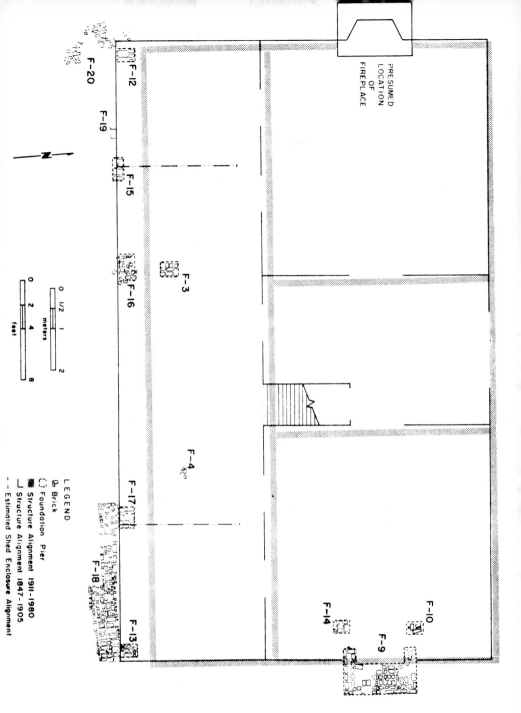

FIG. 6.8 *Plan of Sam Houston's home at "The Woodlands" in Huntsville, showing the location of the structure in relation to archeological features.* (From Pevey 1981: Fig. 6. Courtesy Prewitt and Associates, Inc., Austin.)

Boat Landings, River Crossings, and Inns

Transportation systems, and the lack of them, were crucial to the patterning of settlement in American Texas, particularly to the location of cash crop enterprises, like plantations, that were dependent upon reliable systems for the exportation as well as for the importation of goods (Fehrenbach 1968:285–286, 318–319). For the rate of growth early American Texas was experiencing, roadways, seaports, and railroads were inadequate, to say the least. Steamboats, barges, and other water craft reached into northeastern and southeastern Texas. River traffic moved for some distance up the Trinity River and even up the Rio Grande, although the naturally sluggish waterways of Texas were not always a reliable means of transport due to variable water levels and obstacles to navigation that often occurred (Puryear and Winfield 1976; Collier 1982).

The Gulf coast, with its shallow bays and sand bars, had no natural deep harbors. The hazardous nature of the Texas coast had been known since the early Spanish and French seamen's first encounters with it. The largest ports in pre-Civil War Texas were in Galveston and Matagorda Bays and served southeastern Texas settlements, primarily. Indianola, which became the main port for the western frontier in central and southern Texas, later was destroyed by a hurricane.

An archeological and historical survey of the Trinity River Basin has found several abandoned towns and boat landings, and numerous ferry crossings documented in the historic literature (Richner and Bagot 1978:184–200, 247–248). The sites of 13 towns, with names like Alabama, Buffalo, and Cincinnati, were found during the survey. Many were established by the mid-nineteenth century and became important population centers and shipping points. They all were located on elevated areas near the river and all had associated boat landings. Some prospered for several decades, while others were deserted before the Civil War. Many declined in the 1870's and the 1880's after the railroads came to replace river navigation as the most efficient means of transporting freight.

Other factors influenced the development of river towns. For example, the development of Cincinnati, in Walker County, declined after a yellow fever epidemic killed many of its residents in 1853 and most of its survivors moved to another nearby Trinity

River town called Tuscaloosa. In its early years, Cincinnati was a small community (Hollen and Butler 1956:292), but in its heyday the town had ferries, schools, saloons, churches, a post office, a bowling alley, warehouses, and other establishments (Bowman 1966). Cincinnati's population dropped after the railroads took over, and by 1884 the town had only about 35 residents (Webb 1952:347). The archeological survey of the Cincinnati town site found concentrations of nineteenth- and early twentieth-century artifacts, an old wagon road, and two graveyards in a pastureland which are all that is left of a once thriving river town (Richner and Bagot 1978: 189–191).

The probable site of a boat landing has been located near the mouth of the Trinity River (Fox, Day, and Highley 1980:53–55). Robert McManus came to Texas in 1832 and worked as a surveyor for several early empresarios. He was awarded 320 acres of land on the Trinity River after the Battle of San Jacinto and settled there in 1838. Sometime around 1850, McManus acquired a fleet of boats which he used to transport people and goods up the Trinity. An old map dated 1873 shows the location of plantations and steamboat landings, including McManus' landing on the lower Trinity. Archeological investigation found that the area where the landing was located had been flooded frequently, eliminating all traces of structures, including McManus' dock and related buildings, and probably also obliterating the evidence of the residential occupation that took place there.

The sunken wreck of one of the steamboats that navigated the Trinity River has been located and archeologically evaluated (Arnold 1974). The wreck was that of the *Black Cloud*, which steamed up and down the Trinity in the 1850's and the 1860's. The boat was about 150 feet long and 45 feet wide. In the spring of 1869, on one of its month-long round-trip journeys up the Trinity, the *Black Cloud* hit a snag and sank near the Atascosita Road Crossing in Liberty County. The ship's bell was recovered by the owner, who donated it to the First Methodist Church in Liberty where it still is in use. The wreck was hit during the laying of a pipeline in 1965 and many objects were looted from it.

When another pipeline was proposed in 1974 which would cross the same area, the precise location of the wreck had to be determined so that further damage could be avoided. A proton magnetometer survey was conducted which found the location of the *Black Cloud*. The magnetic data, combined with what could be observed from artifacts known to have been plundered from the wreck in 1965, indicated that although it was damaged to an undetermined degree by the pipeline construction, much of the ship's fittings and other structural remains of both wood and metal may be well preserved. The boat apparently was headed downriver when it sank and so its cargo probably consisted primarily of agricultural products, instead of the more impressive manufactured goods and luxury items it would have carried upstream which would offer much more significant archeological information about the nature of trade on the Trinity. For this reason and because of the estimated high cost of conducting an intensive underwater excavation, the recommendation of the preliminary archeological survey was to protect the wreck of the *Black Cloud* from further damage so that it can be thoroughly and properly investigated in years to come, when conditions and scientific interest warrant.

Overland routes for travel and for transportation of goods were important to the location of settlement in early Texas. Roads varied in direction and width on the open countryside but converged at stream crossings. Suitable crossings were few and far between, particularly on large rivers. Well-known and heavily travelled ferry crossings provided opportunities for other business enterprises such as inns and stores.

The Anglo-American immigrants crossed into Texas along two major overland routes. One crossed the Red River in the northeastern corner of the state. The other crossed the Sabine River in the same general area that the old Spanish Colonial Camino Real, and the early nineteenth-century San Antonio-Nacogdoches Road, once did (Collier 1982). Frederick Olmsted crossed there in cold winter weather in 1854 on a ferry operated by an old Negro man. The slave reported that "he had taken many a man to the other side, before annexation, who had ridden his horse hard to get beyond the jurisdiction of the states" (Olmsted 1978:64).

After crossing the Sabine, Olmsted and his party saw their first Texas house, which once was the homestead of a man named Gaines, the ferry's original operator, but had become the property of a neighboring planter by the name of Strather. "His log house had two stories, and being the first we had met having glass windows, and the second, I think, with any windows at all, takes high rank for comfort on the road" (Ibid 1978:65).

Mr. Strather boasted of his two upland plantations, located some miles back from the river, which were run by an overseer and produced abundant crops of corn and cotton. He complained about his poor white neighbors who tended small patches of land and subsisted much of the time by stealing hogs from the wealthier folks. Olmsted went on to note (1978:66), "The Negro quarters here, scattered irregularly about the house, were of the worst description, though as good as local custom requires. They are but a rough inclosure of logs, ten feet square, without windows, covered by slabs of hewn wood four feet long. The great chinks are stopped with whatever has come to hand—a wad of cotton here, and a corn-shuck there."

Archeological investigations were conducted in 1968 at the well-known crossing on the Sabine that Olmsted visited in the 1850's. The project attempted to salvage what little remained there after bulldozers cleared the area and before the rising waters of Toledo Bend Reservoir inundated it (Simons n.d.). Related research found that the site originally was the home of James Gaines, a signer of the Texas Declaration of Independence. Gaines constructed the log house in 1819. Walter Strather owned it later and others occupied it after the Civil War. Known as the Gaines-McGown House, the original log structure, with its later additions and alterations, stood until 1965.

The bulldozers destroyed all but a few faint traces of the structures of the early homestead and ferry crossing. But an interesting sample of ceramic artifacts was recovered which reflects the general trend of trade throughout the nineteenth and twentieth centuries in Texas. The industrialization of British pottery-making by the beginning of the nineteenth century is reflected by the early mass-produced transfer-printed, hand-painted, banded, and molded-edge wares commonly found at archeological sites of pre-Civil War Texas, when Gaines' Ferry and the roads that focused on it linked the Anglo-American frontier in Texas with Louisiana and the European markets. After 1870, railroads changed the trade patterns, opening the Texas market to the growing American ceramic industry. At Gaines-McGown, more American than British makers' marks were found on the bottoms of dishes from the last decade of the nineteenth century. Sherds of ceramic wares of the twentieth century were predominantly from the American Midwest and also from increasingly worldwide markets, particularly Japan.

There were not many true hotels in pre-Civil War Texas. Those few stately hotels that were in operation, like the famous Menger Hotel in San Antonio, were far too expensive and extravagant for the average traveller on the road, who often spent the night in wagon yards (Fehrenbach 1968:321). Overnight accommodations along the primitive roads of that day usually were stopovers at family homes along the way. Some farmsteads developed into popular hostels, or lodging houses, and inns. A fine example, known as Fanthorp Inn, is now a State Historic Site near Anderson in Grimes County.

Henry Fanthorp was an Englishman who arrived in Texas in 1832 and acquired a quarter league of land at the intersection of the old roads between Houston and Springfield and between Nacogdoches and San Felipe. Fanthorp became involved in the mercantile business and was the first postmaster of the settlement of Alta Mira that grew up around his home. The family house originally was a double log cabin and later was enlarged with additions of frame construction, including a second story which was added around 1850.

Merchants, carpenters, stone masons, stage drivers, and several prominent travellers stayed at Fanthorp's Inn, including Texas Presidents Sam Houston and Anson Jones, U.S. Presidents Zachary Taylor and Ulysses S. Grant, Generals Robert E. Lee and Stonewall Jackson, Jefferson Davis before he became President of the Confederacy, and even a lady-in-waiting for Queen Victoria. In 1860, Fanthorp owned 30 slaves and large areas of improved and unimproved farmland that produced livestock and crops of corn and cotton. He donated a townsite for the Grimes County seat in 1846 and suggested it be named "Anderson" for the last vice-president of the Republic, who died at the inn in 1845. Fanthorp and his wife died of yellow fever in 1867, possibly contracted from a stagecoach driver. The inn was operated by their descendants for several years and then occupied as a family residence until 1977, when it was purchased by the Texas Parks and Wildlife Department.

FIG. 6.9   *The Fanthorp Inn, Grimes County, as it looked in 1982.* (Courtesy Texas Parks and Wildlife Department.)

Archeological investigations were conducted at the historic property in 1978 to determine if any important features would be disturbed by the construction of a parking lot for the park, to search for the remains of a structure reported to have been an attachment on one side of the inn, and to evaluate the archeological deposits in other parts of the State-owned property (Burnett 1981). Because the parking lot area is located away from the inn and the activity areas concentrated around it, machine and hand-dug excavations found no occupational features and only scattered bits and pieces of glass bottles, windowpane glass, and some other trash. The investigation concluded that the construction of the parking lot would not disturb significant archeological deposits.

Horizontally and vertically controlled hand-dug test excavations placed near the inn found large quantities of artifacts east of the building and evidence of an early wing that once was attached to the north side of the structure. Only a few artifacts were found in test pits on the west side, but they included such things as a military button dating to the period from 1829 to 1834 and indicated that early deposits could be preserved in that area. In the yard south of the inn, test excavations placed on the edge of a circular depression found twentieth-century artifacts such as an icebox hinge and children's toys near the ground surface but then encountered a pattern of old wooden beams which sloped toward the center of the depression, indicating that it had originally been a cistern that was later used as a trash dump.

This was enough evidence to recommend that disturbance to this area by park development activities should be preceded by archeological investigation. The cistern apparently had been abandoned and used as a trash disposal area for many years. It could contain considerable quantities of artifacts representative of the people who lived at Fanthorp Inn and the activities that took place there.

Test excavations placed in an old cellar ruin found a mixture of twentieth-century and nineteenth-century artifacts and evidence that most of the soil deposits within the structure had been disturbed. However, the structural remains of the cellar and some of the fill deposits within it appeared to be preserved, and the investigators concluded that earthmoving activities associated with park development in the cellar area should be preceded by archeological investigation.

More recent investigations at Fanthorp Inn have found evidence of two more structures that once were a part of the inn complex (Smith-Savage and Ing 1982). Both were wooden structures that were used during the mid-nineteenth century when the inn played an important role in the transportation–communication network in developing American Texas. The function of one of the buildings has yet to be determined. The other probably was a kitchen that was detached from the main living quarters. Within its stone wall foundations was the original dirt floor, covered with a thick layer of soil and kitchen debris that accumulated on it, such as food bones, fragments of glass containers, and pieces of pottery dishes, which can be used to study the cooking and eating habits of the mid-nineteenth-century occupants at Fanthorp Inn.

Some other early Texas hotels have received preliminary archeological investigation. The large two-story stone barn behind the old Nimitz Steamboat Hotel in Fredericksburg has been studied (Brooks and Baskin 1976). The hotel operated from 1858 until 1926 and was well known for its hospitality and for its exterior design, incongruously appearing as a steamboat on a main street in a German frontier town. The sturdy stone barn was the most prominent of a series of stables and outbuildings that were part of a walled wagon yard behind the hotel. Historical research and the archeological evidence found during the test excavations indicated that, besides being used as a storage building, the barn may have been used as a brewery and as a hostelry, or living quarters, for the men who cared for the livestock, carriages, and wagons belonging to the hotel patrons—and probably also for travellers who could not afford the comforts of the hotel. Now known as the Admiral Nimitz Center, the hotel and its associated grounds are a State Historic Landmark and a museum operated by the State under the

FIG. 6.10   *The barn and enclosure behind the Admiral Nimitz Steamboat Hotel, Fredericksburg.* (From Brooks and Baskin 1976: Fig. 2. Courtesy Texas Historical Commission.)

Northwest Elevation

Vance Hotel

SCALE IN FEET

Southeast Elevation

FIG. 6.11 *The Vance Hotel on the Medina River, Landmark Inn State Historic Site, Castroville.* (Courtesy Historic Sites and Restoration Branch, Texas Parks and Wildlife Department.)

auspices of the Fleet Admiral Chester W. Nimitz Memorial Naval Museum Commission.

Another early Texas inn that has been afforded preliminary archeological investigation is the Vance Hotel, now known as the

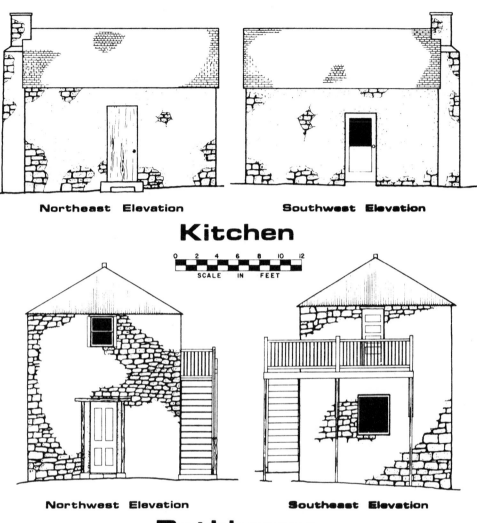

Northeast Elevation   Southwest Elevation

Kitchen

Northwest Elevation   Southeast Elevation

Bathhouse

FIG. 6.12   *The kitchen and bathhouse at Vance Hotel on the Medina River, Landmark Inn State Historic Site, Castroville.* (Courtesy Historic Sites and Restoration Branch, Texas Parks and Wildlife Department.)

Landmark Inn State Historic Site on the Medina River in Castroville, one of the Alsatian immigrant towns established in the 1840's by Henry Castro on the frontier west of San Antonio (Texas Parks and Wildlife Department 1976). Like other frontier boarding-houses, the Landmark Inn originally was a household on a major roadway.

A settler named Cesar Monod acquired two of the original lots in Castroville. In 1853 an Irish immigrant named John Vance purchased Monod's homestead with its European-looking building complex that included a one-story stone house with an attached store structure and a detached kitchen. Because of the location of the house and store on the road from San Antonio to Laredo, Vance began renting overnight accommodations to travellers as well as outfitting them with supplies. Vance added a second story to the main structure and later constructed other buildings on the property, including a new one and one-half story stone house for his family and a bathhouse in the courtyard of the inn. One room of the hotel building served as the local post office for a while when Vance was postmaster of Castroville.

During the development of the property in the 1850's, Vance and neighbors named George Haass and Laurent Quintle built a stone and wood dam across the Medina River and diverted water into a millrace leading to the two-story gristmill that they constructed. They also built a cotton gin and other industrial facilities that served the growing agrarian economy of the community. Later, other families purchased Vance's hotel and associated buildings. The inn remained in operation until after World War II. The property was donated to the Texas Parks and Wildlife Department in 1974. So far, preliminary archeological investigations have been focused primarily on the mill complex. The deposits in and around the inn are being preserved for future archeological and historical interpretation.

VII

The Movement West

THE WESTWARD EXPANSION of Texas settlement was slowed by hostile Indians and by the distance from supply centers. During the mid-nineteenth century, the U.S. Army pushed the Indians further west and northwest up the river valleys and by 1860 the Texas frontier had advanced to a line running roughly through the center of the State (Meinig 1969:38–62).

Frontier people moved into the wilderness areas wherever there were adequate water resources and lands suitable for farming, where there was protection from hostile Indians, and where there were transportation routes that linked the frontier with the core areas of settlement back east. Families of subsistence, or yeoman, farmers from the South and native Texans from established settlements on the coastal plain spread westward to the edge of the Edwards Plateau and southwestward as far as the Nueces River. Anglo-American immigrants from Missouri and other states of the Border South settled the Upper Trinity River area of north-central Texas. Germans, Alsatians, and other immigrants of a variety of European nationalities began to establish family farmsteads and communities on the coastal plain and along the frontier in central Texas.

By the time of the Civil War, the old Spanish and Mexican community of San Antonio had become a cosmopolitan town where only a few Anglo-Americans controlled the political power and where European immigrants outnumbered even the native Hispanic population (Fehrenbach 1968:285, 320). Victoria's population became similarly mixed, greatly influenced by a large population of German immigrants, but also with a miscellany of Afro-Americans, French, Alsatians, Hispanic Texans, Poles, Irish, English, Swiss, Danish, Canadians, and other immigrants (Victoria Sesquicentennial 1974:43).

Some towns and ranches grew up along the northern bank of the Rio Grande near military posts established as a result of the Mexican War, and a dominant American class developed to manage

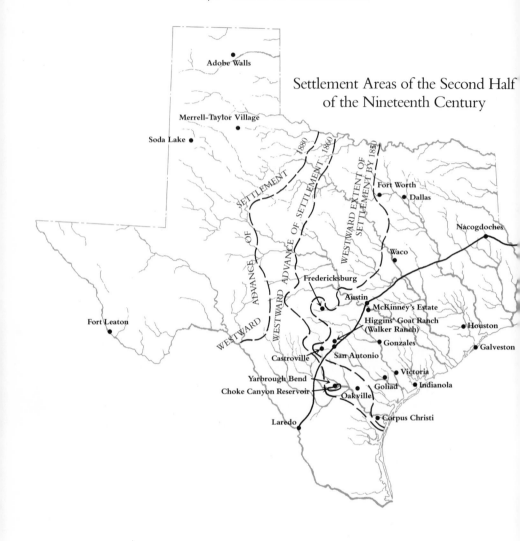

FIG. 7.1 *Settlement areas of the second half of nineteenth century*

the predominantly Hispanic population. In north-central Texas, a large group of French immigrants, who attempted unsuccessfully to establish a Fourier socialist colony on the Upper Trinity River in 1855, moved to the young town of Dallas, and contributed to the cultural variety of the developing community (Meinig 1969:48).

Central Texas Settlements and Rural Estates

Anglo-American farmers, planters, and businessmen were quick to follow the westward advance of Texas frontier settlement during the 1840's and the 1850's. The plantation economy and its Negro slavery tended to fall behind in the movement west as the climate became more arid, the soils too rocky for cash crops, and the rivers too shallow for navigation (Fehrenbach 1968:285–286, 297). Where archeological surveys have covered large areas of the countryside in central, north-central, and southern Texas, evidence of this pattern of westward-moving settlement has been found. Generally, the further west one looks, the later the archeological evidence of frontier settlement, followed within a few years by the evidence of the first permanent farmers and ranchers, and later by towns and large-scale agricultural enterprises.

Anglo-American frontier settlement in north-central Texas began after the establishment of the Peters Colony authorized by the Republic in 1841. By 1848 the Texas Emigration and Land Company brought more than 2,000 families into the colony's lands, which included parts of present-day Tarrant and Johnson counties.

But the real settlement of north-central Texas took place between 1855 and 1875, during what archeologists who have studied the area call the Initial Cash Crop Period (Richner and Lee 1976, 1977), when cotton was the principal crop and a principal economic source of encouragement for the use of the Trinity River as a major transportation route. Named after a military outpost established in 1849, the frontier community of Fort Worth developed as a distribution center on the upper Trinity. Other communities were settled in the mid-nineteenth century along military roads and other communication routes. Some archeological sites of farmsteads and communities of the Initial Cash Crop Period have been identified in north-central Texas and future archeological and historical investigations will help to explain the settlement of that part of the mid-nineteenth century Texas frontier.

Several investigations already have been done in the Anglo-American frontier areas of central Texas, where the movement westward began earlier than it did in north-central and southern Texas. Austin's colony was firmly established and frontier settlement already had spread westward to the edge of the Hill Country by the time of the Revolution. Archeological surveys along Onion Creek, which enters the Colorado River below the present-day city of Austin, found scattered traces of frontier settlement that occurred during the 1830's and the 1840's (Whitsett and Fox n.d.).

Because the first frontiersmen lived by a farming and hunting subsistence, they were attracted first to the extensive, rich bottomlands along the major streams. These settlement areas provided an abundance of wild plant and animal life that the earliest pioneers depended upon to supplement their farming and livestock raising. But the pattern of settlement was restricted by other environmental forces. No matter how resourceful and self-sufficient they were, even the most daring frontier families of the 1830's and the 1840's in central Texas were dependent upon their pioneer neighbors, as well as on the established communities back east, for subsistence needs and for support against the hostile Indians that inhabited the Edwards Plateau. The first wave of Anglo-American settlement was restricted primarily to the major river valleys at the foot of the Balcones Escarpment.

As pioneer settlement secured the countryside in central Texas, farmers and large-scale planters moved in behind them, bringing slaves, livestock, and other forms of Anglo-American "civilization." Slave-run farms were established on the fertile blackland prairie soils along the Colorado River below Austin in areas still within reach of markets back east. Where transportation routes converged at reliable stream crossings, small communities developed, and if conditions warranted, stores and other enterprises were established.

In 1839, the shallow hard-rock crossing on Onion Creek, which Spanish caravans used as a ford more than a century before, became the property of Thomas F. McKinney, a prominent figure in Texas history (McEachern and Ralph 1980:17–19). McKinney was one of the original settlers in Austin's Colony, a political leader and a "hero" of the Texas Revolution. He was a businessman, rather than a planter, and had cross-country dealings at trade centers in Chihuahua and San Antonio during the 1820's (Ralph and McEachern 1974:1–2).

At Galveston in 1834, McKinney and Samuel M. Williams entered into a partnership and obtained a charter for the first legally-incorporated private bank in Texas (Franz 1952). Their firm financed more than ten percent of the cost of the Revolution and their merchant ships became a part of the Texas Navy. After the Revolution, McKinney, Williams, and some other associates were involved in various business interests, including banking, land speculation, and railroad development ventures. Although McKinney was elected to three different legislatures by those who could vote in Texas, he apparently was not well liked by Texans in general. The cotton business was ruinous for him after the Civil War and McKinney was hopelessly in debt when he died in 1872.

McKinney moved to Travis County by 1849. In the early 1850's he established horse-training and horse-racing facilities and a flour mill on his Onion Creek property and then began the construction of a large stone house. His mill was destroyed by a flood in 1869. His horse trainer moved away a year before McKinney's death. The McKinney house was occupied by his relatives until the 1880's and after that by other families, black and white. In the 1940's the house was abandoned and later was burned by vandals.

During the 1970's, the Texas Parks and Wildlife Department and the Texas Archeological Society conducted archeological investigations at McKinney Falls, which now is a State Park as well as the grounds for the Parks and Wildlife Department's central headquarters (McEachern and Ralph 1980, 1981). First McKinney's house and mill complex were surveyed intensively. The entire estate was mapped accurately to show all structures and other archeological features and their relationships to each other, the terrain, vegetation patterns, soil types, and other visible environmental characteristics of the property. Archeological prospecting was done to identify hidden features of the complex, without unnecessarily disturbing the soil deposits at the historic site. A proton magnetometer and metal detectors were used as a means of remote sensing to search for signs of buried features. Small samples of soil were taken systematically from different parts of the residential area and tests were run on the samples to look for variations in the ground's chemical characteristics that might help to locate specific activity areas, such as the site of McKinney's kitchen building where food preparation and garbage disposal would be expected to leave a distinctive pattern of residues.

Interviews were arranged with some of the surviving black residents of the lower Onion Creek community who recalled their family histories in the area—as well as those of their white neighbors—and related their folklore about the places and events of the McKinney Falls area. The archeological mapping and prospecting, combined with the historical accounts, provided a detailed layout of McKinney's estate that can be superimposed over an aerial photograph or a map of the present-day park area.

The central feature, of course, was McKinney's two-story house, located on the edge of a broad, flat plain, or stream terrace, elevated just above the suspected flood level on the north side of Onion Creek, south of Austin. Two large stone-lined cisterns which stored water supplies for the household were constructed on the edge of the terrace near the house. Several outbuildings, including slave quarters, a barn, corncribs, stock pens, and outhouses, were arranged in their appropriate positions around the house. McKinney's flour mill and its millrace were built into the base of the stream terrace a short distance down the creek bank. A dam was constructed that retained the stream flow of the creek at a certain elevation and diverted portions of the flow into the millrace leading into the mill. A stone quarry was located on the south bank of the creek, downstream from the estate. The house of McKinney's horse trainer was across the creek from the residential area. The horse racetrack was upstream in an area that is now a golf course. And, of course, the hard-rock crossing at McKinney Falls is still there today, near the ruins of McKinney's house and mill.

The second stage of the archeological investigation involved the actual excavation of the McKinney house ruin area, its two nearby cisterns, and the mill ruins, using conventional horizontally- and vertically-controlled soil removal, screening, and artifact sampling techniques. Extensive historical research was conducted as well as an archeological survey of the land surrounding the McKinney Falls building complex. The ruin of McKinney's horse trainer's cabin also was studied archeologically and historically. Another study attempted to relate various fence lines on the property to different structures and activity areas.

A large collection of artifacts was recovered from carefully-recorded locations during the archeological investigations. Fragments of porcelain tableware, which would have been rather expensive in nineteenth-century Texas, were found in high proportions to other, more common ceramic wares, reflecting the aristocratic image of Thomas McKinney suggested in the historical accounts

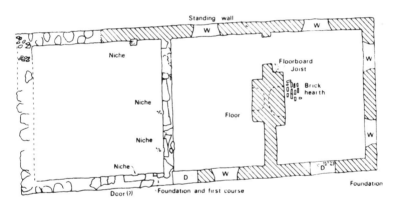

FIG. 7.2   *Drawing and plan of the McKinney House ruins on Onion Creek,*
McKinney Falls State Park, Travis County. (From McEachern and Ralph
1980:Fig. 14 and Fig. 15. Courtesy Texas Archeological Society.)

(McEachern and Ralph 1980:52). The functions of the different
structures at McKinney's estate were verified by the kinds of artifacts, and other archeological and architectural information was
recovered during the investigations that can be used, along with
the information derived from historical research, in the ongoing
development of the State Park.

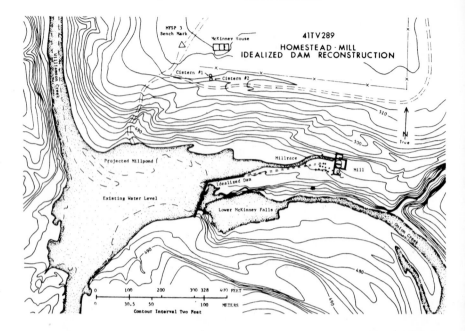

FIG. 7.3 *Map of the McKinney Estate on Onion Creek, McKinney Falls State Park, Travis County, showing the locations of the house, the cisterns, the mill and its millpond.* (From McEachern and Ralph 1980:Fig. 2. Courtesy Texas Archeological Society.)

Another mid-nineteenth-century frontier homestead and ranch complex has been studied on the Balcones Escarpment, more than 60 miles southwest of McKinney Falls, in the hills north of San Antonio. This site was known for its stone building ruins, but more interest was attracted to it when two massive carved stone pillars were found there which were inscribed with what appeared to be Spanish brands and the numbers "1786," which indicated that the site may have been occupied in the Spanish Colonial Period. The pillars reportedly were found about 100 yards from the ruins by the twentieth-century owners of the ranch property.

The monoliths were four-sided with pyramidal tops, or obelisk in shape, and stood about six feet tall. Two other carved limestone objects reportedly were found in the area. They were much smaller than the pillars and looked like grave markers, but could have been used as boundary markers or road markers during the Spanish Colonial Period or in the nineteenth century. The ruins had been protected from encroaching subdivision development until the early 1970's when the Walker Ranch on which the ruins were located was purchased by developers and became accessible to vandals.

A group from Trinity University was allowed to dig test excavations at the ruins in 1971, but apparently no records were kept of the excavations. Additional preliminary investigations carried out in 1973 at Walker Ranch by the Texas Historical Commission could not find any evidence of eighteenth-century Spanish Colonial occupation that would correspond to the stone pillars, but did recover enough information with which to nominate the ruins and several prehistoric Indian campsites on the Walker Ranch property to the National Register of Historic Places (Scurlock and Hudson 1973; Hudson, Lynn, and Scurlock 1974).

Subdivision development on the ranch property began in earnest in 1977, and in 1979 the Center for Archaeological Research of The University of Texas at San Antonio conducted the first phase of an intensive archeological and historical investigation of the Walker Ranch ruins (A. Fox 1979). The second phase of the investigation was carried out in 1981 (Fox and Cox n.d.).

When the historic building complex was first investigated in the early 1970's, it appeared as a group of stone building ruins and possible cisterns surrounded by a stone wall on a low hill overlooking a deep, permanent waterhole on Panther Springs Creek, above where it joins Salado Creek in northern Bexar County. The walls of two of the building ruins apparently had been constructed entirely of quarried limestone blocks, many of which had been robbed for use by later occupants of the area. An old limestone quarry known to have been used in the mid-nineteenth century is located within a mile of the historic building complex. Further study found that the stones used in the Walker Ranch ruins probably came from the quarry. The stone-cutting techniques and the style of construction of the ruins were typical of the mid-nineteenth century. No artifacts dating earlier than the 1840's were found. This was to be expected, though, since the foothills of the Lomeria Grande, as the Spanish called the Hill Country, were the home of hostile Indians and were not at all safe for settlement during the Spanish Colonial Period, or for that matter, during the first half of the nineteenth century.

Historical research conducted as part of the archeological in-

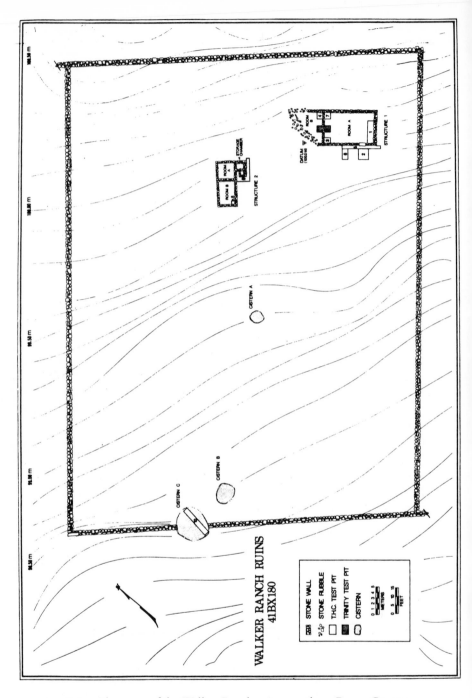

FIG. 7.4 *Plan map of the Walker Ranch ruins, northern Bexar County.* (From Hudson, Lynn, and Scurlock 1974: Fig. 4. Courtesy Texas Historical Commission.)

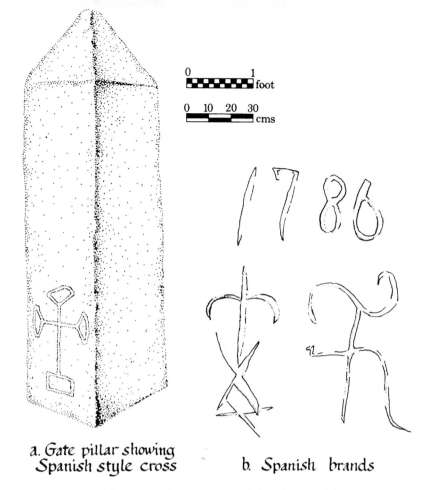

a. Gate pillar showing
   Spanish style cross

b. Spanish brands

FIG. 7.5 *Measured drawings of a limestone obelisk and some of the rock carvings from obelisks found at the Walker Ranch ruins, northern Bexar County.* (From Hudson, Lynn, and Scurlock 1974:Fig. 7. Courtesy Texas Historical Commission.)

vestigations of the Walker Ranch ruins (Fox and Cox n.d.) found that the site was granted in 1838 to Sterling N. Dobie, an ancestor of the renowned Texas folklorist and historian J. Frank Dobie. But it is doubtful that Dobie ever lived on the north Bexar County property. He sold it to a merchant named Joseph Crews, who evidently bought it for land speculation, which dominated the economy of the San Antonio area between 1837 and 1842. Crews probably did not live on the property either. He was captured along with several San Antonio court officials by General Adrian Woll's Mexican forces when they took over San Antonio in 1842, and he later died in a Mexican prison.

FIG. 7.6 *Walker Ranch ruins in 1974, northeast corner of Structure 1.* Note small window in right wall. Hole in north wall may not be an original opening. (Courtesy Texas Historical Commission.)

A Frenchman named Peter Odet purchased the Crews place in 1846. Although he also was a merchant and a speculator and owned property in downtown San Antonio, Odet apparently did provide the financial support for improvements to the Crews property and he may have lived there.

In 1858, Odet sold the place to Edward Higgins, who had been a U.S. Navy midshipman, led attacks on cities along the California coast during the Mexican War, and later worked with a steamship line before he moved to San Antonio. Higgins regis-

FIG. 7.7   *One of the stone-lined, subterranean storage chambers at the Walker Ranch ruins, northern Bexar County.* (From Hudson, Lynn, and Scurlock 1974:Fig. 5b. Courtesy Texas Historical Commission.)

tered his livestock brand with the county and by 1859 he had purchased additional land which doubled the size of his goat ranch. He also owned a lot in downtown San Antonio, not far from the headquarters of Major General David E. Twiggs, also a veteran of the Mexican War and commander of the U.S. Army's Department of Texas.

In December, 1859, General Twiggs left for New Orleans on leave of absence; soon after that, Higgins sold his downtown lot and promptly mortgaged his ranch to Eliza H. Thompson, mother-in-law of Dr. Charles Ganahl, a signer of the articles of

Texas Secession and later a surgeon in the Confederate Army. This transaction is the last known formal record of Higgins' presence in Texas.

Twiggs returned the day after Lincoln was elected in November, 1860, to relieve Colonel Robert E. Lee and resume command of the Department of Texas. In February 1861, before he could be relieved of his command under orders given by suspicious military superiors in Washington, Twiggs surrendered the Department of Texas to a loosely-organized army of secessionists in what turned out to be the first Confederate victory of the Civil War. He was dismissed from the U.S. Army for his treachery and departed for New Orleans, where he was appointed a Brigadier General in the Confederate Army and selected Captain Higgins to be his aide. After the war, the Ganahl family gained legal title to Higgins' ranch. The Ganahls apparently did not live in the stone structures, but instead built a home on the opposite side of Panther Springs Creek at the turn of the century, using stone borrowed from the ruins of Higgins' place.

The first phase of the intensive archeological investigations by the Center for Archaeological Research found that the principal structures of the Walker Ranch ruins included the stone wall, which probably was originally four to five feet high and enclosed an area of more than an acre near the creek, and the stone ruins of three structures clustered within the enclosure. The nature and function of the possible cisterns identified during previous investigations have not been determined, although they may actually have been shallow hand-dug wells or, more likely, natural depressions, or sinkholes, in the limestone slope (Anne Fox, personal communication, October, 1982). Although most of the soil deposits within the ruins had been disturbed by vandals searching for rumored Spanish gold and by previous archeological investigations, enough evidence was found by the Center for Archaeological Research archeologists to suggest that the larger of the two standing stone ruins probably was a barn with an attached room that may have been used as the kitchen for the complex. The other walled ruin, located about 45 feet away, evidently was a residence with two main rooms. Layers of ash and other debris covering the original nineteenth-century ground surface and other evidence indicated that the structure burned during or shortly after its occupancy in the mid-nineteenth century.

Attached to the corners on one side of the house ruin were small stone-lined chambers. Both had been built into holes in the ground and apparently were intentionally constructed as part of the original structure. The nature of the fill deposits archeologically excavated from within them and the mixture of artifacts found throughout the deposits indicated that the chambers had been filled with soil and debris which apparently had been scraped up from the surrounding area. A porch probably spanned the area between the two mysterious corner structures.

The third structural feature at the Walker Ranch site was located about 30 feet from the stone house ruin. It was found to be the remains of a chimney and fireplace that apparently were part of a simple log cabin or frame house with a dirt floor. The artifacts found in the settlement area indicated that all three structures were occupied at about the same time during the mid-nineteenth century. But later disturbance to the area by stone-robbing, vandalism, and heavy machinery made it difficult to interpret the archeological features or to reconstruct the history of the site's occupation in detail.

Many intriguing questions are still unanswered. What was the origin of the odd, carved, stone pillars with the Spanish-looking inscriptions and what was the function of the "storage chambers" built into the walls of the house ruin? The historical accounts indicate that Higgins and Twiggs were associates when they were in San Antonio and probably were strongly sympathetic with, if not active supporters of, the slave-holding interests at work in Texas before the Civil War. What was a naval officer and sea captain like Higgins doing goat-ranching on the central Texas frontier? Could Captain Higgins and Major General Twiggs have been involved with the Knights of the Golden Circle (Webb 1952:970–971), a secret organization that included several prominent Texans and schemed to strengthen the slave-holding sugar and cotton kingdoms of the South by forcibly including Mexico, Central America, and the West Indies? Who was the Frenchman, Peter Odet, who apparently began the development of the ranch complex and sold it to Higgins in 1858? Could Higgins' ranch complex have been a staging area for the organization of the force that Twiggs surrendered to, which included several members of the Knights of the Golden Circle?

Perhaps the mysterious Spanish-looking stone pillars and the possible road markers were produced during the mid-nineteenth-century development of the ranch complex from the stone quarry about a mile away. But the obelisks apparently were not of the same stone and were not shaped by the same methods as all of the blocks from the quarry, and the carvings on the monoliths do look very "Spanish" (Hudson, Lynn, and Scurlock 1974:19). Could the pillars have been taken from an old Spanish rancho in the San Antonio area or could it even be possible that they were hauled back from the Rio Grande Valley after one of the two aborted attempts by the Knights of the Golden Circle to mount an invasion of Mexico in 1860? Between 1767 and 1810, several large tracts of land were granted to colonists for ranching and one of the acts of possession officially recognized by the Spanish Crown was the arrangement of cornerstones demarcating property boundaries (Scott 1966:66–69).

In the spring of 1860, after a tour of the Lower Rio Grande Valley, Robert E. Lee reported that most of the ranchos along the river had been abandoned or destroyed by the famous Mexican bandit Juan Cortina, and by the Texas Rangers and U.S. Army regulars who pursued him. John Salmon (Rip) Ford, who led the Texas Rangers against Cortina in 1859, was a Knight of the Golden Circle (Fehrenbach 1968:374, 520–521). If Higgins was a member of one of the groups that reached the Rio Grande Valley with the intent of invading Mexico in 1860, he probably would have met little resistance if he decided to take boundary markers back with him for use at his Bexar County "goat ranch."

The Walker Ranch ruins may once have contained archeological evidence that could help to solve some of these mysteries. But as so often happens to historic sites that are subject to legends and are in the path of urbanization, vandalism and careless construction activities have left very little for the archeological investigators of history to go by.

Cattlemen's Settlements on the Southwestern Frontier

In 1828 the Mexican government authorized Irish empresarios McMullen and McGloin to colonize a large area of southern Texas between the San Antonio and Nueces rivers and west of the DeWitt and DeLeon colonies on the coastal plain. Many Irish immigrants came to Texas and selected large headrights extending back from the Nueces, Frio, and Atascosa rivers. But they never occupied their grants. Instead they settled in communities near the coast where they could be within reach of supply centers and protected from the Indians and other forbidding elements of the interior frontier. Although the Laredo-San Antonio Road was well established through the middle of southern Texas, travellers and explorers who recorded their journeys across southern Texas in the 1840's found it to be a vast, unoccupied region of prairies and brush (Hendricks 1919:121, 139; Hollon and Butler 1956:351–370; Bender 1933:130–131).

Throughout the first half of the nineteenth century, large herds of feral cattle and mustangs thrived in the brush country and became an attractive resource to enterprising Anglo-American

FIG. 7.8   *A "Texan Cattle-Drover" in the 1870's.* (From King 1974.)

frontiersmen from the older Texas communities and from the southeastern United States. The town of Oakville was founded in 1856 as the first true town in the region. Located on the north side of the Nueces River about 75 miles inland from the coast, Oakville became the principal base out of which to settle the Nueces, Frio, and Atascosa river valleys further west.

Archeological surveys and later more intensive investigations have recovered a good sample of information about the frontier settlement of a large area where a dam recently has been constructed to retain water as a lake on the Lower Frio River just above its confluence with the Atascosa and the Nueces (Lynn, Fox, and O'Malley 1977; Everett 1981; Bandy 1981; D. Fox 1982). The archeological studies found evidence of the first settlers who took up residence in 1857 and 1858 along the Frio downstream from the Laredo-San Antonio Road. Where the Frio Valley makes a large bend through resistant outcrops of Lipan sandstone, John Swanson Yarbrough, N. H. Walker, Dr. George Dilworth, John Moore, and Joe Walker, and possibly other "squatters" with their families, built a series of homesteads along the river bank in places that were elevated above the suspected flood level. They were located far enough apart to preserve the independence of the frontier family enterprise but close enough together to maintain the security and interdependence of the community. Most of the earliest Yarbrough Bend homes apparently were of a temporary sort, constructed of *jacal*, or picket, walls, like a picket fence chinked with mud, and they probably had either stone or stick and mud chimneys and shingle roofs. Scattered sandstone rocks, stone fireplace foundations, burned lumps of clay containing impressions of twigs, and scattered pre-Civil War ceramic, glass, and metal artifacts are just about all that remains of the first frontier settlements.

Besides the usual British-made pottery sherds and fragments of mid-nineteenth-century bottles, sherds of nineteenth-century Mexican majolica were found which are similar to the type of pottery made during the Spanish Colonial Period and probably are evidence that the frontier cattlemen traded with the people of northern Mexico for some of the supplies they needed to sustain their settlements so far removed from the supply centers in San Antonio and toward the coast. Sherds of Mexican-made, tin-enameled pottery also were found at the archeological sites of post-Civil War cattle and goat ranches along the Frio River, reflect-

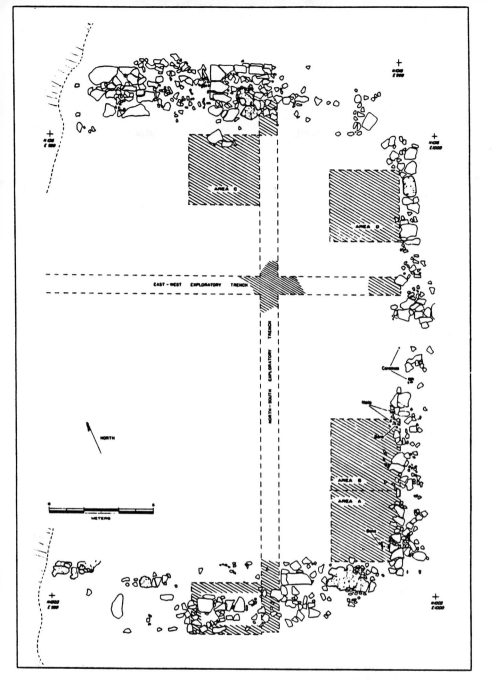

FIG. 7.9 *Plan of the foundation remains and archeological excavation units at the King Place, 41LK202, a frontier homestead occupied circa 1857–1882, on the Lower Frio River, Live Oak County.* (From Fox 1982:Fig. 19. Courtesy Center for Archaeological Research, The University of Texas at San Antonio.)

ing continuous interaction with Mexico and in some cases probably representing the family habitations of Mexican ranch hands in
the area.

But at one site on the north side of Yarbrough Bend the occurrence of majolica sherds has raised some intriguing questions
about the history of the area. The only Mexican-made pottery
found at this house site consisted of sherds from at least three kinds
of majolica that previous research in other parts of Texas indicated
were not in use after the Spanish Colonial Period, and yet virtually
all of the other datable ceramic, glass, and metal artifacts found are
representative of an 1870's and 1880's occupation of the place. It
seems highly unlikely that an eighteenth-century occupation of the
site would be represented by only a few sherds of pottery. There
are no springs, rock formations, or other notable natural features
in the area which might have attracted settlements more than 75
years apart to be focused on the same precise spot, and yet the majolica sherds were found within the same restricted area in which
the post-Civil War occupational evidence was found. The principal structural remains found were the disturbed sandstone foundations and rubble from a fireplace and chimney not unlike the remains of other post-Civil War houses in the Yarbrough Bend
settlement area, and it does not seem probable that a Spanish Colonial structure stood abandoned throughout the nineteenth century to become the focal point of a much later occupation. Could
the post-Civil War occupants of the site have been a Mexican family who still used majolica pottery that had been in their family for
generations? Or is it possible that the majolica types that were no
longer popular or accessible to the Spanish Colonial people of
Texas by the end of the eighteenth century were, in fact, still being
produced or still were available somehow to Anglo-American settlers of the Lower Frio River Valley in the 1870's?

Most of the original settlers of the Frio Valley were squatters
in the sense that they did not own the land where they pursued
their livelihoods. By the time of the Civil War, however, the community of Rio Frio, later known as Dog Town and then Tilden,
was established by some of the Yarbrough Bend people and by
other settlers, and became the basis for the organization of Mc-
Mullen County, the population of which was about 100 persons in
1860.

The isolation of Yarbrough Bend and Dog Town from the people, goods, and services of American civilization served to strengthen relationships between families as they worked together to defend their territories on the open range. Once or twice a year they drove herds north, south, or east to trade for subsistence needs such as salt, flour, sugar, and coffee. In Laredo they traded for various supplies, including Mexican jackets and hats, which were considered real finery. European and American goods were obtained during excursions to San Antonio, Goliad, Indianola, Rockport, and Corpus Christi. Archeological evidence indicates that they obtained foodstuffs, household necessities, medicines, alcoholic beverages, and other things from these American market centers. But the evidence also indicates that most essentials were produced on the family farm and gathered from the surrounding countryside.

A few miles back to the east and downstream on the Frio from Yarbrough Bend was the homestead of John G. King, who apparently was the son of a farmer in DeWitt's Colony in the Guadalupe River Valley. King and his family settled on the Frio in 1858 with their five slaves. They established a farm and ranch complex there and leased their cattle that grazed on the open range.

The archeological investigation found the remains of at least two habitations in this area (D. Fox 1982). One was marked by sandstone foundation walls which were the remains of a rather large wooden house. A stone-lined well was found in the river bank nearby. The other structural feature, located about 150 yards down the river, appeared to be the site of a smaller, less substantial household marked only by the foundation remains of two fireplaces which probably were located on each end of a dog-run structure.

Although the artifacts found at the homestead site are typical of the period from the 1850's to the 1880's, they definitely reflect the frontier nature of the King's settlement. The archeological evidence represents a subsistence based on open-range ranching and probably some farming, supplemented by hunting. The Kings ate foods and used other materials and equipment produced on the farmstead, extracted from the countryside, and imported from trade centers on the Texas coastal plain, in south-central Texas, and possibly on the Rio Grande. Characteristic of this subsistence were large quantities of domesticated and wild animal foods, a

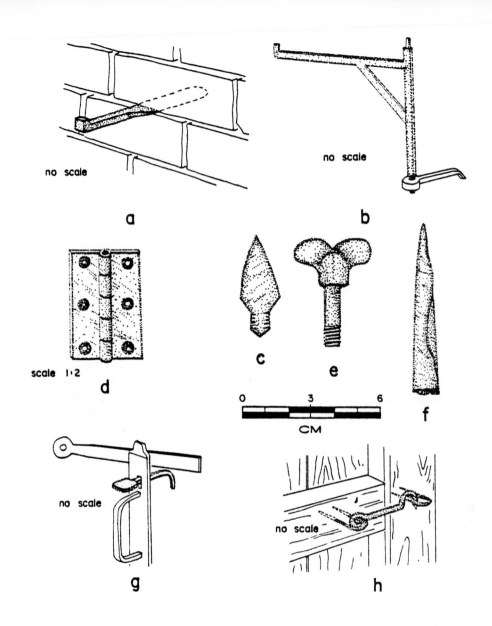

FIG. 7.10 *Metal building hardware and other objects from the King Place, 41LK202 and 41LK31/32, on the Lower Frio River, Live Oak County.* a, wrought iron tool or fireplace hardware; b, heavy wrought iron door or fireplace crane pintle; c, metal arrow point; d, butt hinge; e, iron adjustment wing bolt; f, rolled, pointed tin cone; g, door latch fragment; h, wrought iron staples. (From Fox 1982:Fig. 20. Courtesy Center for Archaeological Research, The University of Texas at San Antonio. Drawings by D. E. Fox.)

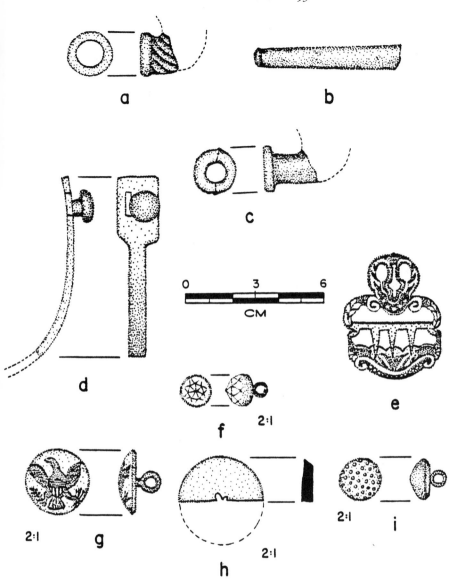

FIG. 7.11   *Personal items from the King Place, 41LK202 and 41LK31/32, on the Lower Frio River, Live Oak County.* a, c, clay pipe fragments; b, clay pipe stem fragment; d, spur fragment; e, suspender buckle; f, red multi-faceted glass button (or bead); g, Scovill & Co. U.S. Army button; h, black glass button fragment; i, brass shoe button. (From Fox 1982: Fig. 25. Courtesy Center for Archaeological Research, The University of Texas at San Antonio. Drawings by D. E. Fox.)

sufficient supply of bitters, schnapps, and other spirits, a variety of medicines, and an extensive arsenal of firearms ranging from flint-lock rifles to more technologically advanced rifles and pistols. A rusty iron arrow point found near the house site could pre-date the Kings' occupation but might represent an encounter with Indians while the Kings were living there. Food bones found were identi-fied as the remains of domesticated livestock, including cow, sheep or goat, and pig, and game animals, such as deer, antelope, wild turkey, rabbit, aquatic turtle, and possibly wild cow or buffalo. Not only special cuts of meat but also various body portions were represented by cut and unaltered food bones.

An interesting aspect of the archeological remains of the King place was the evidence distinguishing the Kings' house from the habitation site located down the river bank. As mentioned earlier, the King house evidently was much more substantially con-structed and larger than the one downstream, judging from the amounts of sandstone structural debris and iron building hard-ware. The possible dog-run structure apparently did not have glass windows like the King house did, and the evidence suggests that the structure may have been the dwelling for the Kings' slaves. The dates of the artifacts found there were restricted pri-marily to the 1850's and the 1860's, which would correspond to the period between the Kings' arrival on the property and the abolish-ment of slavery during the Civil War. Various agriculturally re-lated implements and harness trappings were found at the King house site, while none of these kinds of evidence were found at the other house site.

If the less substantial structure was indeed the quarters for the Kings' slaves, some of the occupational evidence found there sug-gests that the relationships between slaves and their owners were much closer than those between slaves and their masters on plan-tations back east. It seems logical that the frontier existence would encourage closer ties and perhaps slaves were given more freedom and responsibilities. The household artifacts found there, although more limited in quantity and variety than the occupational evi-dence found at the Kings' house site, seem to represent the materi-als and supplies necessary for a basic existence and also a few lux-uries such as clay pipes for tobacco-smoking. Evidence of firearms and some alcoholic beverage bottles was found at the possible slave quarters site.

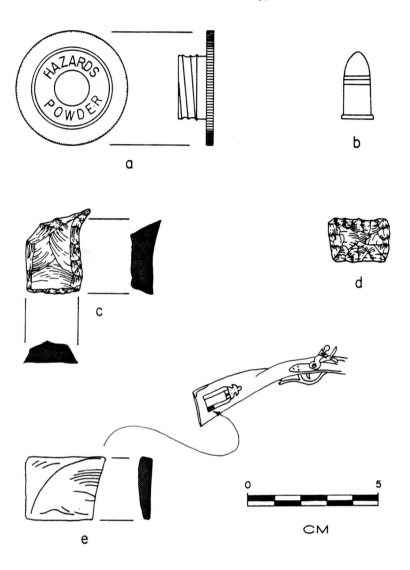

FIG. 7.12   *Firearm-related items from the King Place, 41LK202 and 41LK31/32, on the Lower Frio River, Live Oak County.* a, zinc powder container cover; b, .41 caliber rimfire short cartridge for Remington Derringer; c, possible gun flint or strike-a-light (made from local flint); d, pistol flint; e, brass patch box cover. (From Fox 1982:Fig. 26. Courtesy Center for Archaeological Research, The University of Texas at San Antonio. Drawings by D. E. Fox.)

Taken together, the archeological evidence of the King homestead complex is a fine example of the first stages in the development of the cattle industry at a time, before the range was fenced off in the early 1880's, when people leased cattle instead of pastureland. And assuming that the Kings were descendants of Southern planters or farmers, their occupation of the Lower Frio River Valley fits well into the general pattern of frontier settlement in Texas suggested by Fehrenbach (1968:297):

. . . hunter-trader-trapper on the far frontier; hunter-farmer behind him through a large yeoman belt; then the planters, forging their own kind of civilized existence in the rear. The towns, most of which were minor ports or river stations or mere crossroads settlements, supported this settlement when and where they could.

About six miles to the east of the Kings' place was the growing community of Oakville. Some 12 miles to the west, up the Frio River, were the frontier cattlemen of Yarbrough Bend. Further west was Dog Town and the Laredo-San Antonio Road and beyond it the vast expanse of unsettled wilderness.

The frontier environment of southern Texas also is reflected by one of the cemeteries located and researched during the archeological investigation of the proposed Choke Canyon Reservoir area. Two headstones side-by-side at a single rock-covered grave on a remote hilltop near the Frio River Valley mark the remains of victims of the Taylor-Sutton Feud which left bodies scattered across southern Texas after the Civil War (Everett 1981:48). The feud involved the Taylor family and their friends, who were cattle ranching in DeWitt County, and members of the Sutton family and their associates, who some say were thieves (Day 1937) and others claim were authorized by the post-war government to hunt down Confederate renegades and troublemakers (Rose 1880). The fact of the matter is that times were hard after the Civil War. Confederates returned home to find their property under different ownership. Greed and fraud were prevalent, especially on the lawless frontier.

Martin Luther Taylor operated a ranch near that of his father-in-law, David Morris, somewhere north of Yarbrough Bend. Supposedly they had moved there with their wives to avoid the feud. Apparently in 1869, several members of the Sutton gang tracked down Taylor and Morris at their homesteads, kidnapped them and, once they were away from witnesses, murdered the two defenseless captives and left their bodies to rot where they fell. According to local legend, a posse found the corpses and buried them near the road between Dog Town (by then called Tilden) and Oakville. Some of the legend is borne out by the location of the grave, near where Texas Highway 72 used to run before it was re-routed around the area to be inundated by the Choke Canyon lake. Census records listed Taylor's and Morris' wives as living together with no male companions in 1870 (U.S. Department of Interior).

Because the grave was in the area to be covered by the lake, the burials were exhumed and reinterred at a new cemetery plot. On hand when a mortician and his crew undertook the authorized removal of the burials were bureaucrats from the U.S. Bureau of Reclamation, responsible for construction of the lake, and also representatives of the Taylor family and archeologists from the Center for Archaeological Research of The University of Texas at San Antonio. Unfortunately, the undertaker was in a hurry and all the archeologists could do was observe the mechanical excavations and record what they saw (A. Fox n.d.).

The graves were marked by two cast concrete headstones inscribed with Morris' and Taylor's names and the date 1869. The headstones had been broken and later mended and set at the edge of a layer of sandstone slabs, or cairn, which covered the grave. Some of the slabs of the cairn turned out to be fragments of even older sandstone grave markers that had been broken and probably had been replaced with the concrete ones.

The bones of the two individuals were encountered less than two and one-half feet below the ground surface. Portions of the skeletons that the archeologists were given time to examine were apparently those of males, one a rather robust man and the other probably slighter and younger. It was evident that they had both been buried "with their boots on." Artifacts observed included buttons, one of which was a U.S. military button, a clasp knife, a U.S. dime, a two-piece military buckle, and some fragments of shirt and coat fabric that had been preserved by salts from the deteriorating metal artifacts. No guns or bullets were seen, although careful examination of the grave fill was not allowed, but it was apparent that the men had been buried in a simple, shallow grave without any sort of coffin. The fact that nothing had been taken

FIG. 7.13 *The Taylor-Morris grave site on a lonely hillside overlooking the Frio River, McMullen County.* (Courtesy Center for Archaeological Research, The University of Texas at San Antonio.)

from the pockets of the dead men indicated that their corpses were in an advanced state of decay when they were found and quickly buried.

Pioneer Strongholds

When the Anglo-American colonists arrived in Texas, they inherited an Indian problem that had a long history of development during the years of Spanish Colonial and Mexican Texas. There were "civilized" Texas aborigines who wanted a place to live peacefully, but there were thousands of other Indians who waged war on scattered, unprotected frontier settlements. With no real assistance from their Mexican government, the first Anglo-American colonists organized militia and made treaties to deal with the Indian inhabitants of the regions they settled in.

The policy toward Indians set by Sam Houston, first president of the Republic of Texas, was one of peace and trade, coupled of course with a strong frontier defense against Indian harassment. However, the Republic's next president, Mirabeau Lamar, was set on complete extermination of the Indians, which resulted in a great deal of bloodshed. Although it did secure the core areas of settlement and opened new areas further west, Lamar's policy contributed greatly to the Republic's indebtedness and helped to weaken its financial structure. Houston reinstituted a policy of peace instead of war during his second presidential term and helped to work out treaties between the non-Indians of the Republic and most of the major Texas Indian tribes.

The whole Indian relations situation became confused when Texas became a state and the federal government and its military assumed control of Indian affairs. As the frontier pushed westward into the Indians' territories, settlers continued to find it necessary to defend their farmsteads, ranches, and small, scattered frontier communities against the threat of Indian raids.

Numerous blockhouses and fortified settlements were built in early American Texas, but many of the earliest pioneer strongholds were abandoned by the time Texas became a state. The sites of others built before and after 1845 have been obliterated by the development of towns and cities and by agricultural and industrial activities that have altered the landscape. Some of the sites of early blockhouse forts and fortified settlements have been found, and some are being preserved as historic places. Few pioneer strongholds have been investigated archeologically.

Some time during the first half of the nineteenth century, a large fortified adobe structure, later known as Fort Leaton, was constructed on the north side of the Rio Grande a couple of miles downstream from present-day Presidio. The State of Texas erected stone monuments there in 1936 to proclaim the adobe ruins as the location of a mission established in the late seventeenth century and a presidio established during the late eighteenth century. The Works Progress Administration dug there and made measured drawings of the ruins in 1940. Several rooms within the complex were archeologically excavated by students from Illinois State University in 1969 (Jelks 1969). Additional excavations were conducted by an archeologist from the Texas Parks and Wildlife Department in 1971 and 1973 after Fort Leaton became a State Historic Site (Ing and Kegley 1971; Knox *et al.* 1974; Ing and Roberson 1974).

Given the desert setting of the Fort Leaton ruins and its appearance as a maze of adobe walls situated on an elevated area overlooking the Rio Grande, it is no wonder that it has been interpreted, without serious investigation, as an ancient Spanish Colonial hacienda complex. Lending to this interpretation are the accounts of the La Junta area nearby, where the Rio Conchos from Mexico meets the Rio Grande. Here Cabeza de Vaca and other Spaniards visited the Jumano Indians in the sixteenth century, Mission del Apostal Santiago was established in 1683–1684, and a Spanish presidio, El Fortín de San José, was established in 1773. However, despite its ancient, weathered appearance and its location in relation to La Junta and Presidio, thorough archeological investigations at the Fort Leaton ruins have found no evidence of any occupation earlier than the 1820's, and the site probably was not occupied until the mid-nineteenth century.

Nor was Fort Leaton constructed as a military fort. Historical records indicate that it was first occupied by a man named Juan Bustillos in the 1840's, who sold it and some adjacent farmland to an American farmer, trader, and veteran of the Mexican War named Ben Leaton in 1848. Leaton and his family maintained and expanded the adobe structure and occupied it as a residence and trading post. After 1851, when Leaton died, his wife, Juana Pedraza, and her new husband, John Hall, lived at Fort Leaton until the early 1860's, when it became the property of John Burgess. The Burgess family managed the place and made numerous alterations to it. The adobe building complex, enclosed in an adobe wall, and its associated adobe chapel building nearby, were abandoned in 1927, although it was used later as a temporary residence for a family of migrant farm workers and as a livestock pen.

The very nature of Fort Leaton as a picturesque, Spanish-looking feature and the legends about it have encouraged excavations by historically-minded investigators, resulting in considerable disturbance to the archeological deposits within and outside the ruins. By 1971 most of the more than 30 rooms of the Fort Leaton complex had been excavated or disturbed by previous investigations, and archeological work had to be concentrated outside the main building complex in an area thought to contain, among other features, a corral.

The 1971 investigations found the remains of a variety of previously undiscovered features, including eight rooms, a cobble-paved drainage ditch, a strange room of unknown function with a cobble-paved trough running through it, evidence of a brush ar-

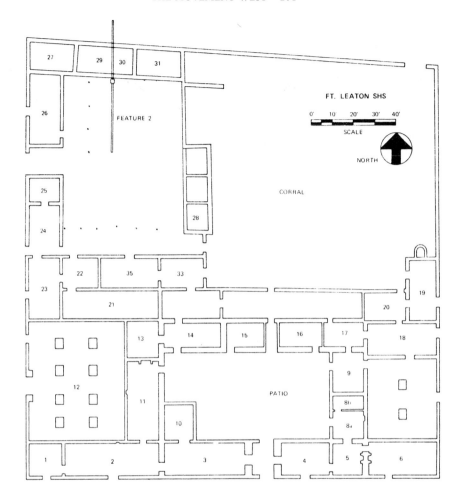

FIG. 7.14   *Plan of the ruins of Fort Leaton, Presidio County.* (From Ing and Roberson 1974: Fig. 2. Courtesy Texas Parks and Wildlife Department.)

bor or *ramada*, the corral, various living floors, the north outer wall of the building complex, 54 postholes, and about 450 feet of adobe walls which enclosed the newly-discovered rooms. In one of the less disturbed areas investigated, some of the earliest evidence of Fort Leaton's occupation was found, including five copper coins with dates ranging from 1833 to 1855 and bearing the inscription "Estado Soberano De Chihuahua" (Soverign State of Chihuahua). Also found were sherds of British-made edged, sponged, and transfer-printed white earthenware pottery, typical of the first half of the nineteenth century, and a large number of nineteenth-century Mexican and possibly Indian pottery sherds.

Although the ages of individual artifacts suggest that the ruins could have been occupied as early as the 1820's or the 1830's, the range of the dates of the evidence, and the overall appearance of the artifact collection when compared to artifact collections from other nineteenth-century sites, seems to indicate that the adobe complex actually was occupied from the 1840's until the 1920's. This coincides with the historical records of the occupation of Fort Leaton by the Bustillos, Leaton, and Burgess families. Besides the typical nineteenth-century building hardware, household garbage, and other kinds of artifacts, the further evidence of nineteenth-century cartridges, British-made ink bottles and pottery, and the Mexican-made pottery and coins support the historical accounts that Fort Leaton had been a trading post on the Chihuahua Trail linking American settlements to the north and east with Mexican trade centers south of the Rio Grande.

The archeological investigations in 1969 found that the adobe walls probably had been constructed in three major building phases. Excavations in 1973 at the chapel structure located about

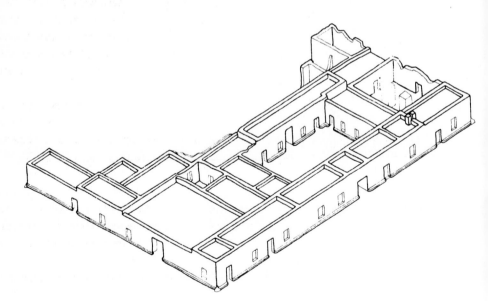

FIG. 7.15 *Isometric view of Fort Leaton, as the adobe ruins looked in 1936.* (Courtesy Texas Parks and Wildlife Department.)

150 feet northeast of the fort complex found that the small adobe structure, which contained at least two plaster-coated adobe floors and a Burgess family headstone, was probably built by the Burgess family in the 1920's.

In recent years, an intensive investigation has been carried on by archeologists of the Panhandle-Plains Museum at Canyon, and by members of the Panhandle-Plains Historical Society and others interested in their heritage, at the site of Adobe Walls, a frontier stronghold in the Texas Panhandle (Billy Harrison, personal communication, October, 1982). Originally Adobe Walls was built in the early 1840's as a trading post on the Canadian River. The adobe wall fortifications enclosed an area about 80 feet square. Abandoned because the southern Plains was one of the last hunting grounds of the American Indians and was not safe for American frontier settlement, the adobe ruins became a landmark for buffalo hunters and traders on the Plains during the mid-nineteenth century. In 1864, when Kit Carson led a U.S. Army expedition against the winter quarters of the Comanche and Kiowa, he used the ruins as a defensive position and held off attacks by large numbers of Indians.

In the spring of 1874, a fortified buffalo-hunter's settlement grew up not far from the original Adobe Walls. The second Adobe Walls contained at least four businesses, including two stores and a saloon. The community thrived until June, 1874, when several hundred Comanche, Cheyenne, and Kiowa Indians attacked. The 28 men and one woman of the Adobe Walls settlement gathered in the saloon and repelled several attacks. By the fifth day, hunters in the vicinity heard of the situation and joined the besieged defenders. The Indians rode away frustrated.

After this, the second battle of Adobe Walls, the area was abandoned. The settlement was set afire soon afterward, probably by the Indians who were struggling to subsist on what the foreigners had left of their buffalo herds. Soon the last Indians were moved to reservations and the Adobe Walls site became just another part of the landscape of large cattle ranches at the turn of the century. But always remembered as an early pioneer stronghold on the frontier, Adobe Walls became the property of the Panhandle-Plains Historical Society in 1924 and since then has been protected as an important historical site.

In 1974, one century after the last battle of Adobe Walls, the Panhandle-Plains Museum adopted a long-range plan for the investigation and preservation of the site. One of the primary goals was to determine which of the dozen written tales of the 1874 site could be verified. Work was begun in 1975 and still is being carried on today.

Historical research has located copies of several accounts of the Adobe Walls stronghold, the 1874 battle, and the various people who lived, visited, and fought there. The accounts range from a work by the wife of pioneer Billy Dixon, who was one of the participants in the battle and later became the owner of the Adobe Walls site (Dixon 1914, 1927), to more recent, less reliable, and more embellished stories and magazine articles. The researchers report that they have found an interesting account by the famous Comanche chief Quanah Parker in an interview reported by General Hugh Scott. The analysis of the various accounts should make fascinating reading when it is published as part of the Panhandle-Plains Historical Museum's forthcoming report on the investigations at Adobe Walls.

The actual field investigation began with a thorough surface survey of the Adobe Walls site that found chipped stone tools and pottery, worked bone and shell artifacts, glass beads, and other evidence of probable Indian occupation on the site area in prehistoric and historic times. Controlled excavations uncovered traces of various parts of the Adobe Walls stronghold, including Hanrahan's Saloon, the Meyers and Leonard Mess Hall and Store, the Rath and Wright Store and associated outbuildings, O'Keefe's Blacksmith Shop, and other features, such as corrals and even a horse burial.

A large collection of 1870's artifacts was recovered from the Adobe Walls site, including windowpane fragments, personal items such as shoe parts, beads, buttons, tobacco pipes, conchas and mirror fragments, various tools, harness and wagon parts, horse, mule, and ox shoes, rifle parts and accessories, flint and iron arrow points, musket balls, bullets, buckshot, cartridge cases and percussion caps, buffalo, deer, antelope, duck, fish, rabbit, and turkey bones, chinaberry seeds, coffee beans, corn cobs, peas, peach and plum pits, fragments of colanders, crocks, food grinders, kettles, coffee mills, dutch ovens and wood stoves, silverware, ironstone "china" and glassware fragments, marbles and coins,

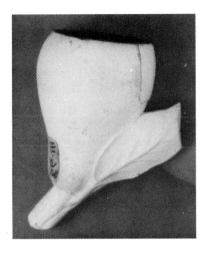

FIG. 7.16   *Two clay tobacco pipes, typical of the 1860's and 1870's, found at the site of Hanrahan's Saloon at Adobe Walls, Canadian River Valley, Hutchinson County.* (Courtesy Panhandle-Plains Historical Museum.)

and even oyster shells and buffalo hair. This rich, carefully re-covered sample of archeological evidence, when analyzed in the context of the various historical accounts, should provide a wonderfully-detailed picture of what life and warfare were like on the Panhandle-Plains frontier.

Sheep and Cattle Ranches on the Panhandle-Plains

Settlement of the Panhandle-Plains of Texas began much later than the settlement of the eastern half of the State. It occurred in the 1870's, after the Adobe Walls stronghold was abandoned, and after the Comanche and the Kiowa were removed to Oklahoma by the U.S. Army and the commercial slaughter of the buffalo by Anglo-American hunters left the Llano Estacado deserted.

The first settlers did not come from the east. Instead they were sheepherders, or *pastores*, from New Mexico. Sheep were introduced into the Southwest by Spanish explorers and colonists during the sixteenth and seventeenth centuries. The Indians of the region realized the benefits of raising sheep, and by the 1880's it was common for New Mexican families to have flocks of as many as a quarter of a million (Beck 1962:256–257).

The Panhandle-Plains became open for use as grazing land at

a time when the New Mexico ranges were overgrazed. *Pastores* quickly moved into the unclaimed area and established wide-ranging grazing circuits in the Cimarron, Canadian, and Red river valleys where potable water and grass were sufficient to sustain large flocks of sheep. But the *pastor* settlement of the Panhandle-Plains lasted only about a decade. Anglo-American cattlemen also were attracted to the new open rangelands and quickly established their claim to the land, constantly harassing the *pastores* and eventually forcing them out.

An archeological survey has found several *pastor* settlements, or *plazas*, on the Llano Estacado, usually in areas near springs that would supply dependable sources of water for household use, gardening, and livestock (Taylor 1980). In some areas, *acequias* were constructed to carry water to the *plazas*. The houses were constructed with thick walls of sandstone, if available, or other materials such as adobe brick made from the clayey soils of the area. The walls were plastered with clay and were usually whitewashed. Flat roofs were constructed of several layers of wood and dirt. Floors were made of packed earth covered with a smooth layer of sand and clay. Each room had a corner fireplace and each household usually had an outdoor adobe oven, or *horno*.

The *pastor* occupation sites found during the archeological survey occurred as multi-structure and single-structure habitations, as well as an assortment of miscellaneous archeological sites with stone enclosures and unidentified stone structures. Multi-structure habitations include the ruins of houses, outbuildings, and livestock pens, *acequias* in some cases, and other structural features. Some of the larger complexes have the remains of several family household structures arranged like small towns. Other, smaller sites probably were occupied seasonally by individual families as they migrated with their flocks across the Plains.

The *plazas* vary in the degree to which they have been preserved or have been disturbed by twentieth-century land uses, relic collecting, and vandalism. Some *plaza* houses and corrals have been maintained and are still used as ranch structures. Others have been neglected, buried by wind-blown sand, or destroyed. Historical research and interviews with long-term residents of the Panhandle-Plains have provided a considerable amount of information concerning the histories of many individual *plaza* sites, including the names of their inhabitants in some cases and the time periods during which they were occupied. Information obtained by combined archeological and historical investigation is helping to detail the history of the development of New Mexican settlement of the Texas Panhandle-Plains and the displacement of the *pastores* by Anglo-American cattlemen on the late nineteenth-century frontier.

An interesting archeological site on the Texas Panhandle-Plains was investigated in 1978 and 1979. Legend held that the remote site, known as the Soda Lake Ruins, was of Spanish-Mexican origin and served as a base camp for *comancheros* while they roamed about the Plains hunting buffalo and trading with the Comanche (Guffee 1980). The legend had its basis in the long history of the *comancheros*, who began during the Spanish Colonial Period as buffalo hunters, or *ciboleros*, and peaceful traders, and later found it profitable to barter gunpowder, lead, firearms, and whiskey with the Comanche in exchange for cattle, horses, and Anglo-American captives (Kenner 1969). The site also could have been used by the *pastores* who moved onto the Panhandle-Plains as far south as Blackwater Draw and the Soda Lake area. Indeed, the first *pastores* may have been *comancheros* or their descendants, who were already familiar with the locations of water sources and suitable habitation areas on the Plains.

FIG. 7.17   *Artist's reconstruction of the early ranch headquarters at Soda Lake in the sand hills of Lamb County on the Texas Panhandle-Plains.* (From Guffee 1980:Cover. Courtesy Llano Estacado Museum, Plainview. Drawing by Jack Thompson.)

The Soda Lake Ruins consist of three clusters of caliche rock walls covered with sand and, nearby, several possible hand-dug wells in a massive outcrop of caliche bedrock. Located in an area of sand dunes, the ruins complex is situated in a large "blow-out" which has been deflated by wind erosion. The site's name comes from its proximity to a deep *playa* or natural depression located less than a mile away on the Llano Estacado.

An old resident of the Soda Lake area recalled that his two brothers camped at the ruins each autumn between 1900 and 1912 with their herds of sheep. At that time the structures of the Soda Lake site were in an advanced state of decay. The archeological excavations placed within the ruins found that the roofs of the rectangular structures had been constructed of layers of wood and clay and that they had floors of smoothed layers of sand. As the structures began to deteriorate, the roofs fell in, followed by the inward collapse of the upper portions of the caliche rock walls, and later during the dust bowl era of the 1930's, the remnants of the walls caught the drifting sand and helped to give the ruins a mysterious, ancient appearance.

The structures investigated included a probable dwelling, consisting of a rectangular living room with a fireplace and an attached caliche rock addition. Nearby was a circular rock corral about 40 feet in diameter with two attached storage and work rooms separated from each other by a partition wall of caliche rock masonry. Artifact accumulations found outside the walls of the habitation structure indicated that what household garbage the occupants did not leave on the floor was simply tossed out the door of the house. Fewer artifacts were found at the corral and in its attached rooms, but this limited quantity and the kinds of artifacts found there would be expected at a storage and maintenance area for ranching activities.

The evidence recovered during the archeological investigation of the Soda Lake Ruins indicated that the caliche rock structures were not constructed and occupied by *comancheros* or *pastores*, but instead by late nineteenth-century Anglo-American ranchers. The

FIG. 7.18 *Floor plan of Structure II, the household and workshop at the Soda Lake ruins in the sand hills of Lamb County on the Texas Panhandle-Plains.* (From Guffee 1980: Fig. 2. Courtesy Llano Estacado Museum, Plainview.)

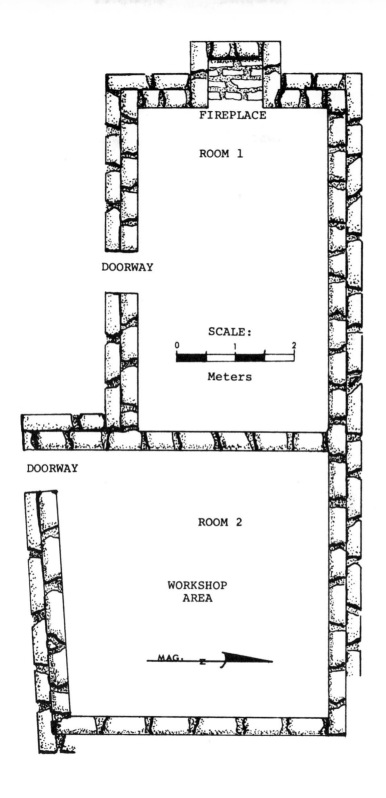

FIREPLACE

ROOM 1

DOORWAY

SCALE:

0   1   2

Meters

DOORWAY

ROOM 2

WORKSHOP
AREA

MAG.

buildings were too massive and well arranged to have been constructed by migratory hunters, rustlers, or bandits. The corral was more appropriately designed for penning sheep or goats than for holding cattle. The buildings were constructed in English measurements and the great majority of the artifacts found are Anglo-American in origin and include an assortment of things that would fit an Anglo-American ranching occupation. The evidence included poker chips, a shirt stud, safety pins, a guitar string, metal trademarks from chewing-tobacco pouches, wagon parts, harness trappings, bridle parts, a variety of late nineteenth-century and early twentieth-century rifle and pistol cartridges, and the bones of sheep, chickens, and possibly those of a milk cow.

The investigations concluded that the original occupants of the Soda Lake structures probably were members of a single Anglo-American family who attempted to establish a homestead based on sheepherding and gardening until the first dry years forced them to leave the area. The site probably was occupied later, in the early twentieth century, as a temporary campsite until it fell into ruin and was covered by sand. It has served to stimulate the imaginations of passersby ever since.

One archeological site on the Panhandle-Plains has been thoroughly investigated archeologically which was occupied by *pastores* during the 1870's and the 1880's and may have been used as a base camp for *ciboleros* or *comancheros* in the 1860's. The Merrell-Taylor Village Site, located in northeastern Floyd County, consisted of the ruins of three dugouts in the stream terrace of Quitaque Creek, and another located about one quarter of a mile up the creek. The site also contained remains of refuse dumps and an irrigation ditch that carried water to the *plaza* from a dam on the creek.

In 1972, one of the dugouts was destroyed and the other three were disturbed by a relic collector. When the owner of the land on which the site was located began disturbing the area as part of the operation and maintenance of his ranch and the total destruction of the archeological site area was imminent, intensive archeological salvage investigations were undertaken by the Llano Estacado Museum (Guffee 1976).

The excavations revealed that the dugouts were constructed to a depth of about four feet into the terrace slope and probably

FIG. 7.19 *Artist's reconstruction of the Merrell-Taylor Village Site on Quita-que Creek, Floyd County, on the Texas Panhandle-Plains.* (From Guffee 1976:Cover. Courtesy Llano Estacado Museum, Plainview. Drawing by Jack Thompson.)

had super-structures of cottonwood logs with roofs of poles and branches covered with buffalo hides. The dugouts of the main *plaza* complex were located about 18 feet apart and apparently were laid out in Spanish-Mexican dimensions. They were about 18 feet long and 13 feet wide with entrance passageways, corner fireplaces, and water traps dug across the intersection of the passageway and the main dugout room.

A large number of artifacts was found during the Museum excavations in 1974 and 1975 at the Merrell-Taylor Village. *Cibolero* occupation is suggested by the large numbers of buffalo bones found and by a Spanish lance blade of the type used for buffalo hunting by the *ciboleros.* The bones of sheep, deer, and turkey were also found. Most of the materials recovered, however, are indicative of *pastores* occupations that focused upon sheepherding and gardening. Most of the artifacts dated from the 1870's and the 1880's. A variety of post-Civil War rifle and pistol cartridge cases were found, along with the remains of three rifles and a Civil War model 1861 .44 caliber Remington Army pistol.

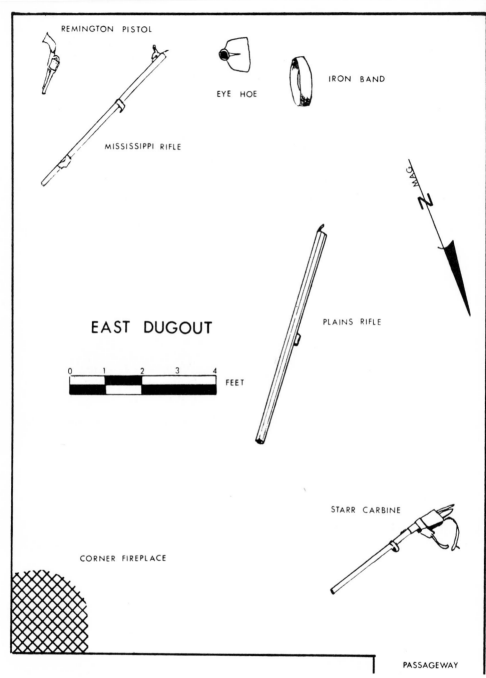

REMINGTON PISTOL

EYE HOE

IRON BAND

MISSISSIPPI RIFLE

MAG. N

EAST DUGOUT

PLAINS RIFLE

0 1 2 3 4
FEET

STARR CARBINE

CORNER FIREPLACE

PASSAGEWAY

FIG. 7.20 *Plan of one of the dugouts at the Merrell-Taylor Village Site on Quitaque Creek, Floyd County, on the Texas Panhandle-Plains.* (From Guffee 1976: Fig. 3. Courtesy Llano Estacado Museum, Plainview.)

The artifact collection also included square-cut nails and other hardware, harness trappings, sharpening stones, a hoe and other simple agricultural implements, harmonica parts, buttons and other clothing fasteners including some from U.S. military uniforms, and other artifacts reflecting a frontier hunting, sheep ranching, and gardening occupation. Careful excavation of the dugout ruins found that the structures probably began to deteriorate shortly after Anglo-American ranchers arrived in the area and the New Mexican inhabitants abandoned the *plaza* site. Fortunately, Llano Estacado Museum archeologists managed to salvage a sample of the evidence of one of the first settlements of the Texas Panhandle-Plains before the archeological site was destroyed by modern land uses.

VIII

European Farmsteads

BY 1860 THE SETTLED AREAS west of the Brazos River were becoming culturally and economically different from the Southern style occupations of Anglo-American planters and Afro-American slaves in the eastern part of the State. On the coastal plain, Anglo-American planters, farmers, pioneers, and the few Hispanic-Texans who remained after the Revolution and survived the social pressures of the Republic were joined by groups of European immigrants who were prompted by economic and political pressures to leave their German-ruled homelands (Meinig 1969:50–56). Families of German immigrants settled a large area of the frontier in central Texas, far in advance of Anglo-American settlement.

Although there were a few German settlers in Mexican Texas during the early nineteenth century, it was not until later that literature advertising Texas attracted large numbers of European immigrants to the Republic and to the new State. An Alsatian colony led by Henry Castro established itself in 1844 on the hostile frontier below the Balcones Escarpment in the Medina River Valley west of San Antonio. Between 1844 and 1846, an organization of wealthy, titled Germans, known as the Society for the Protection of German Immigrants in Texas, sponsored the settlement of a large area of the central Texas Hill Country (Fehrenbach 1968: 291–293). They established a coastal port of entry called Carlshafen, or Indianola, and settled New Braunfels as a way station into the frontier. Soon another community, known as Fredericksburg, was established on the Upper Pedernales River, on the very western edge of frontier settlement.

Many families of Germans and other Europeans settled farmsteads on their way inland from the coast. Others moved into the already established towns, such as Victoria and San Antonio. From the new German towns of New Braunfels and Fredericksburg, families spread out through the bottomlands along the major rivers and then up the tributary valleys in the central Texas Hill Country. Following a lull during the Civil War, immigration re-

sumed and German frontier settlement reached all the way westward to the Llano and San Saba rivers and southwestward to the
Balcones Escarpment northwest of San Antonio.

Although they adapted to the same environments and were
dependent upon the same markets of the United States and Western Europe as other Texas settlers, the German immigrants maintained much of their cultural identity while becoming Texans. At
first they adopted the architecture of the Anglo-American pioneers and other technological elements already well adapted to the
frontier. But as soon as their farmsteads were established, they returned to more traditional, Old World styles of building construction and attempted to reinstitute many of their European customs
(Jordan 1966:199–200).

By the time of the Civil War, there was quite a contrast between the Anglo-American landscape, with its mixture of back-
woods settlements, sprawling plantations, hundreds of slaves,
cash crops of corn, sugarcane and cotton, and large areas of unused lands, and that of the rural German farmsteads of central
Texas and the coastal plain, which were family-operated, smaller
and more intensively used, and much more diversified in agricultural production. Only toward the end of the nineteenth century did later generations of German families begin to build frame
houses in the more typically American style. Their lifeway became a blend of adopted and imported traits, so that by the twentieth century German-Texans differed from their countrymen
back in Europe as well as from Anglo-American Texans (Jordan
1966:192).

Of the variety and large numbers of European immigrants to
the new state of Texas, the Germans have received the most attention from historians and archeologists. The stability of rural German settlement, based upon the stability of the family as the basic
social and economic unit (Flach 1974:6, 51), is reflected by the
sturdy, enduring presence of German farm complexes in the Hill
Country and on the coastal plain. The antiquity, integrity, and architectural distinctiveness of these mid- to late nineteenth-century
sites has attracted public interest and has encouraged several archeological investigations. Some archeological, architectural, and
historical studies have focused on sites of German settlement in
the Hill Country and others have been done at German farmsteads
on the coastal plain.

FIG. 8.2 *Artist's reconstruction of a German immigrant farmstead in the central Texas Hill Country, LBJ State Park, Gillespie County.* (From Tunnell and Jensen 1969:Frontispiece. Courtesy Texas Historical Commission. Drawing by Gene Mobley.)

The German Hill Country

In 1968 preliminary investigations were conducted at German farmsteads in LBJ State Park on the Pedernales River east of Fredericksburg (Tunnell and Jensen 1969). The park area's landscape is typical of Hill Country German settlement areas, with log cabins, stone houses, log barns, rock fences, well houses, smokehouses, and livestock corrals. The historical and archeological research found that other typical German occupational features were a part of the settlement pattern of the park area, such as storage cellars for vegetables and wine, hand-dug wells, a one-room schoolhouse, a limekiln where mortar was made, and a small family cemetery.

The archeological investigations concentrated on two farmsteads, the Behrens' Cabin and the Sauer Homesite. Fieldwork at another, earlier homestead, known as the Danz Place, was limited to site mapping and intensive surface inspection because of limited funding for the project. The three farmsteads were located on a land grant issued by the Republic of Texas in 1838 which was not occupied until around 1860 when it was acquired by a German immigrant named Casper Danz who built his home there and sold parts of his property to other German families. John Sauer bought his parcel from Danz in 1869. Henry Behrens bought his in 1872.

The investigations found that the first major buildings at each homestead were log cabins that had a one-room design or were built as two rooms separated by a dog-run, like the pioneer dwellings that the Anglo-American settlers found to be adaptable to the frontier. As the German families established themselves, these temporary households were replaced by more substantial structures of stone and wood construction, with cellars and with associated wells, fences, yards, and outbuildings arranged more in the traditional style of their farms back in Europe. From around the structural features and from trash disposal areas, an interesting collection of artifacts was recovered that reflects the household and agricultural activities carried on at the farmsteads from the mid-nineteenth century to the mid-twentieth century. Buried architectural information was recovered by the archeological studies, such as the ways in which the foundations were laid for different kinds of structures, the more or less standard dimensions of different structural elements, and the methods of construction of cellars, wells, and outbuildings.

Another series of archeological investigations was carried out in 1977 at a U.S. military reservation known as Camp Bullis in the rugged hills of the Balcones Escarpment north of San Antonio. Sites of several rural farmsteads were found that had been occupied by families of German immigrants and their descendants during overlapping time periods ranging from the mid-nineteenth century until the area was purchased by the government, parcel by parcel, between 1906 and 1941 (Gerstle, Kelly, and Assad 1978:257–301). The sites were not excavated, but were mapped and photographed in detail. Their histories were researched and samples of their occupational evidence were collected from the surface and analyzed so that the age and significance of each site could be de-

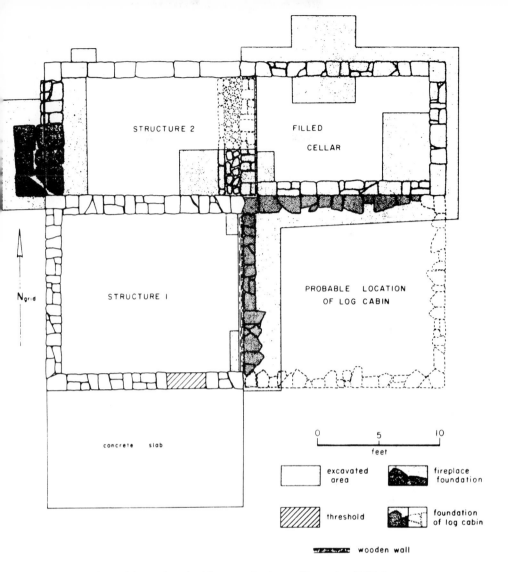

STRUCTURE 2

FILLED

CELLAR

N grid

STRUCTURE 1

PROBABLE LOCATION
OF LOG CABIN

concrete slab

0   5   10

feet

excavated
area

fireplace
foundation

threshold

foundation
of log cabin

wooden wall

FIG. 8.3 *Plan of the earliest buildings at the Sauer Homesite, LBJ State
Park, Gillespie County.* (From Tunnell and Jensen 1969: Fig. 26. Courtesy
Texas Historical Commission.)

termined and the important sites can be preserved. Unfortunately,
almost all of the structures already had been destroyed or removed
and much of their archeological remains had been disturbed before
the investigation commenced.

The farmsteads were marked by foundations of limestone
blocks and associated features such as cisterns, walkways, out-

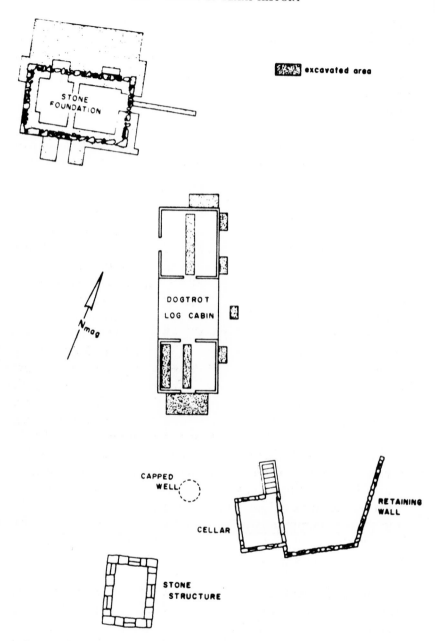

FIG. 8.4 *Plan map of the Behrens Homesite, LBJ State Park, Gillespie County.* (From Tunnel and Jensen 1969: Fig. 13. Courtesy Texas Historical Commission.)

building foundations, and fence rows. They were situated overlooking farm and pasturelands along the stream drainages that form the headwaters of Salado Creek in the southern part of the military reservation and the lowlands of the Cibolo Creek Valley which forms the northern boundary of the government land. The most substantial ruin in the study area was the remains of the only house with walls constructed completely of stone. Built into the base of a steep hillside near a spring, the site was known as Comanche Springs, as plotted on maps and referred to in early land records.

Although most of the construction materials and the artifacts found in and around the massive stone ruins appeared to date no earlier than the late nineteenth century, sherds of edged ware and banded slip, or mocha, ware that date from before the Civil War were found in association with some scattered stone foundation remains for a wooden structure that was located a short distance out from the base of the hill. Interestingly enough, the historical research found that the land around Comanche Springs was purchased by John O. Meusebach in 1847. Meusebach (actually Otfried Hans, Freiherr von Meusebach) was the adaptable German businessman who led much of the German immigration into central Texas in the 1840's (King 1967; Fehrenbach 1968:293–294). After resigning his position as Commissioner-General for the Society for the Protection of German Immigrants in Texas, Meusebach lived at Comanche Springs until the beginning of the Civil War, when he moved to Fredericksburg. Afterward the land was owned by various people. It came into the possession of the Schasse family in 1881, when the stone structure probably was built and after which Meusebach's old homestead probably was torn down. The large stone structure apparently was dismantled or blown up by the military after it purchased the property in 1906 and began to use it for military exercises.

One of the westernmost frontier German farmsteads in the central Texas Hill Country was settled sometime around 1855 by an immigrant named Louis Martin and his family. The settlement area, which later became known as Hedwig's Hill, was located near the Llano River, not far from Fort Mason, a U.S. Army outpost established in 1851 to protect Texas settlers from hostile Indians. Martin arrived in Fredericksburg in the mid-1840's and opened a store there. He became the first sheriff of Gillespie County in 1848 and was trading with military personnel and Indians on the frontier by 1851.

After Martin settled on the Llano River, his dog-run log cabin became the first post office in Mason County. In the 1860's he had business dealings with F. Groos and Company of San Antonio and hauled freight across the frontier to various places, including Mexico. The frontiersman's life ended on a trip to Eagle Pass, when thieves—or possibly a group of Confederate renegades angered by Martin's anti-slavery leanings—hanged him, and later stopped by his Llano River farmstead and informed his family of their deed. By 1867, Martin's settlement came into the possession of another German immigrant named John Keller, a blacksmith by trade, who established a store there that had the only beer cellar for miles on the frontier and on the first road from San Antonio to El Paso.

Martin's cabin, Keller's store, and associated farmstead buildings were investigated in 1971 in coordination with a restoration project that involved the relocation of historic ranch headquarters buildings to an area where they can be preserved and exhibited next to the Museum at Texas Tech University in Lubbock (Dragonwagon n.d.). When the archeological investigation began, the log house already had been removed and only its foundation and wooden flooring remained. When the floor planks were removed, a large assortment of artifacts was found, including buttons, coins, cartridges, and other items small enough to have fallen through the cracks between the floor boards. Architectural information was recovered concerning the foundation of the house, an attached shed, and the chimneys which stood at each end of the dog-run structure. Keller's store was a rectangular sandstone masonry building which the excavation found to have had an original dirt floor and later sand and plaster floor surfaces. The excavation also unearthed the cellar, with its stone retaining walls and steps leading into the small, shallow enclosure. Garbage disposal areas, or middens, also were investigated, which contained broken pieces of household "china," fragments of glass food and medicine containers, military buttons, and other discarded materials.

The artifact collection from the Martin-Keller complex at Hedwig's Hill included a variety of objects which were manufactured as early as the 1820's. Pottery types included pre-Civil War

FIG. 8.5   *The Louis Martin dog-run, Hedwig's Hill, Mason County, after the superstructure and floor planks were removed to Lubbock, Texas, exposing the sleeper/joists and foundation stones that supported the frontier house from the 1850's until 1971.* (Courtesy Texas Historical Commission.)

FIG. 8.6   *Assorted clothing fasteners from the Martin-Keller Complex, Hedwig's Hill, Mason County.* (Courtesy Texas Historical Commission.)

British-made edgewares, hand-painted wares, sponged and spatter wares, post-Civil War undecorated white ironstone wares, and early twentieth-century decaled and colored-glaze wares, as well as sherds from stoneware crockery and hard porcelain vessels dating from the nineteenth and twentieth centuries. Hundreds of fragments of bottle glass and fruit jars were found, as well as an assortment of deteriorated metal containers. Along with this household garbage, an assortment of hardware, tools, harness trappings, and agricultural implements was found. Personal items

FIG. 8.7 *A green glass alcoholic beverage bottle and a stoneware pottery ginger beer bottle dating from the 1860's, found at the Martin-Keller Complex, Hedwig's Hill, Mason County.* (Courtesy Texas Historical Commission.)

found included metal, glass, porcelain, bone, and shell buttons, marbles, a comb, a bone toothbrush handle, a straight razor, a hairpin, ceramic doll parts, toy dishes, a watch chain, slate pencils, a penknife, the reed from a harmonica, a ceramic tobacco-pipe fragment, and jewelry, including glass beads of various shapes and colors, an earring, a stone finger ring, and a shell inlay. Several coins were recovered, including pennies and nickels dating from 1857 to 1911 and a 2-½-dollar gold piece dated 1861.

Immigrant Settlements on the Coastal Plain

Prompted by plans for the construction of a power plant and related facilities, three nineteenth-century immigrant farmsteads were archeologically and historically investigated in an area known as the Biegel Settlement near La Grange on the coastal plain (Carter and Ragsdale 1976). According to the historical accounts, the settlers were from various central European states but evidently shared many German cultural patterns. The land on which the community developed was given as a Mexican title to Joseph Biegel in 1832 as part of Austin's Colony. At that time the owners of the lands adjoining Biegel's league were Anglo-Americans, but by the Civil War several European immigrant families had become Biegel's neighbors.

The archeological investigations were hampered by time and funding limits, by the legal requirements that determined the objectives of the study, by the disturbed condition of the sites that were to be investigated, and by the construction activities that went on while the archeological field work was being done. Fortunately, the investigators managed to recover a good bit of historical information. They recorded architectural details and collected samples of artifacts that can be compared to collections from other historic sites of the period from the mid-nineteenth century to the present.

At the Biegel Settlement, the Legler Site was recorded as the remains of a rectangular log cabin with mounds of earth nearby. The log structure was originally constructed of hewn logs, dovetailed to fit into each other at the corners of the building. The lower timbers rested on foundation stones and the tongue-and-groove flooring was made of unfinished (full-size) 1-inch by 6-inch planks fastened down with square-cut and wire nails. The rafters for the roof rested on wooden plates that were fastened with wooden pegs to the logs beneath. The roof was constructed of corrugated metal sheathing, which covered layers of shingles that had been an earlier roof. The large timbers in the structure had notches and cuts in them that were not related to the construction of the building, reflecting the conservation and reuse of lumber from earlier structures.

Test excavations were placed into the low mound nearest the log structure and found only a thin deposit of the kinds of debris which, confined mostly to the surface of the mound, would be expected to occur beneath the floor of a more or less weatherproof structure. The mound was evidently a remnant of the original ground surface that was preserved from the erosion that deflated the surrounding area. Clearing of the surface of the mound did not find any foundation stones but did locate a drip line where rainwater had eroded a narrow, shallow line beneath the eave of the roof along one side of the building. The relationship of the mound and the drip line to the standing log structure indicated that both probably were the rooms of a dog-run with a breezeway separating the two rectangular enclosures. The absence of household items and the abundance of agricultural implements, hardware, construction materials, automobile parts, and harness trappings showed that the structure served as a barn, garage, and other purposes as an outbuilding. Although the historical records showed that the site area was occupied from before 1850 until 1975, the majority of the artifacts found at the dog-run date from around the turn of the century, possibly indicating that the structure was built at that time with materials salvaged from other, perhaps much older structures in the site area.

Another farmstead, the Biegel-December Site, was reported to have been occupied first by Joseph Biegel and his wife beginning around 1850. It consisted of a log house of dovetailed hewn timbers that was enlarged with later additions of more modern frame construction. The family cemetery was located on a hill to the southwest of the house. Because the site was not in immediate danger of being destroyed and because of time limits placed on the field work, the archeological investigation focused on recording the site plan and excavation of test units to recover information about the construction of the foundations. Only a few artifacts were found.

The third archeological investigation at the Biegel Settlement took place at the Polasek Site which was first occupied by Edward Gentner as a farmstead in 1850. When Gentner died in 1854, an inventory of his holdings was recorded (Carter and Ragsdale 1976:84). It listed 20 acres of cultivated land, 81 acres of uncultivated land, a double-pen house with a gallery (probably a dog-run log structure), a kitchen, a cellar, a smokehouse, a cotton house and a hog pen (possibly another dog-run), a horse stable and corn crib with a passage (probably another dog-run), various tools, furniture, and other items.

A German cabinetmaker named Helmut Kroll bought the Gentner place in 1861 and made a number of changes to the buildings. He also established a general store, a pickle factory, and a

FIG. 8.8 *The dismantling of the "pickle factory" at the Polasek Site near La Grange, in the Biegel Settlement, Fayette County.* Note the dovetail corner notching that held the hewn timbers in place. (Courtesy Texas Archeological Research Laboratory, The University of Texas at Austin.)

commercial distillery there. The property was owned by other families in later years and the farm and the store remained in operation until 1975 when the Lower Colorado River Authority purchased the area for the construction of a power plant.

When the Polasek Site was first visited by an archeological survey team in 1974, it was a working farmstead reminiscent of farmsteads in eastern Europe (Jackson and Skelton 1975). It consisted of Mr. Polasek's house with various outbuildings around a barnyard behind it. But before the more thorough archeological investigations could be carried out in 1975, the standing structures had been removed from the site. Further disturbance occurred when a backhoe trenching machine was used to search for the grave of a Kroll family child reportedly buried near the kitchen of the old house. And more destruction took place while the investigators worked to salvage information from what was left of the farmstead. For reasons unknown, a bulldozer operator destroyed about 2,700 square feet of the Kroll Store area with his machine. Some of the foundations and buried evidence of the various structures remained. Some evidence of the pickle factory, the dog-run house, and other features was found, along with nineteenth- and twentieth-century artifacts. But little more than scattered bits of architectural and archeological information could be recovered.

In 1977, archeological and historical investigations were carried out at a German settlement on Coleto Creek near Victoria where another electrical generating plant and its associated water supply reservoir were to be constructed (Fox and Livingston 1979). This investigation focused on an old family landholding where two farmsteads and a family cemetery were located.

The earliest homesite was occupied from the early 1850's until about 1882 by a German immigrant named Carl Steiner and his family. Judging from the historical accounts, the Steiners were from a well-educated, German upper-class background and had to adapt quickly to a rural frontier lifestyle. By 1860, according to census records, they owned horses, milk cows, oxen, cattle, and swine. They grew Indian corn and Irish potatoes, made butter, and produced large quantities of wine from the native mustang grapes that grow in the Coleto Creek area. They sold and traded many of their products, particularly Carl Steiner's wine which evidently was well known in many parts of Texas and was exported to markets outside the State.

Carl Steiner died of yellow fever in Victoria in 1867. His wife died sometime later and was the first to be buried in the cemetery near the family house on the Coleto. Shortly before they died, the Steiners transferred ownership of the farm to their daughter, Minna, perhaps as a dowry. In the same year she married Friedrich Schob, another German immigrant, who was known as Friedrich Schob de Leon when he was listed on the 1860 census as a laborer on the Steiner farm. Between 1880 and 1882 they built a large two-story house of sandstone blocks that were quarried from an outcrop on the banks of the Coleto near the old farmstead. The new home was passed on to their descendants until 1977 when the property was purchased by the Guadalupe-Blanco River Authority for construction of a power-plant reservoir.

When the archeological investigations began, the original Steiner farmstead was completely overgrown by trees, grapevines, and underbrush. As the site was cleared, the sandstone rocks of the foundations for the house and a hand-dug, stone-lined well were found. The family cemetery was located up a gradual slope about 85 feet to the east of the house foundation. From family tradition and from historical and archeological evidence, the investigators were able to postulate that a low mound of earth and sandstone rocks about 20 feet northwest of the house foundation probably was the location of the kitchen. Down the slope toward the Coleto were the foundation remains of what probably was the smoke-house. Further down the slope, on the bluff overlooking the creek, the sandstone outcrop was found where the stone probably was quarried for the Steiner building foundation and for the later Schob house.

Excavations verified the location of the kitchen. Numerous food bones and other refuse that would be expected to occur at a food storage and preparation area were found in association with alignments of stones that apparently had supported a wooden structure measuring about 13 feet by 16 feet. The foundation area apparently was filled with debris when the kitchen building was torn down or relocated. A layer of clay capped the surface of the low mound, reflecting the meticulous way in which the abandoned farmstead was cleaned up.

Down the slope from the house site area, about 35 feet from the probable kitchen foundation, was a rectangular line of sandstone rocks that had supported a wooden structure measuring about 7 feet by 8 feet. Very few artifacts were found in association with the foundation remains—as might be expected if the structure was a typical smokehouse with airtight walls and a simple dirt floor.

The historical accounts indicated that the Steiner house was a one-story frame structure. Its general layout became recognizable after the brush was cleared away and careful excavations exposed alignments of sandstone blocks and rubble. Square-cut nails and other artifacts found along the rows of stones and the ways in which the stones were set in place showed that they had formed the foundations for a simple rectangular house with a porch on the southeast side to catch the prevailing breezes. The house probably was about 16 feet wide and 24 feet long, with the porch approximately 9 feet by 24 feet.

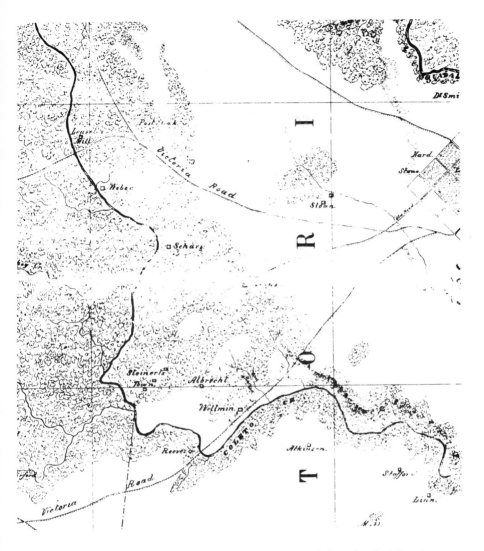

FIG. 8.9 *Map showing the "Steiner's Town" area on Coleto Creek, Victoria County, taken from a Confederate topographic map dated 1864.* (From Fox and Livingston 1979:Fig. 2. Courtesy Center for Archaeological Research, The University of Texas at San Antonio.)

The stone foundation of a fireplace and its chimney was located on the eastern end of the house foundation and filled postholes were found in that area which probably were dug for scaffolding used in the chimney's construction. Within the eastern part of the house foundation was a depression that once was a cellar. This was filled in with rubble and other debris from the structure and with late nineteenth- and twentieth-century trash. The fill de-

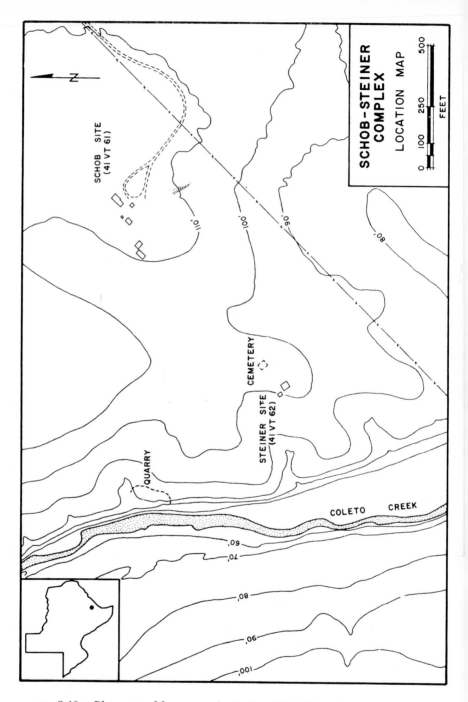

FIG. 8.10 *Plan map of features at the Steiner-Schob Complex, Victoria County.* (From Fox and Livingston 1979: Fig. 15. Courtesy Center for Archaeological Research, The University of Texas at San Antonio.)

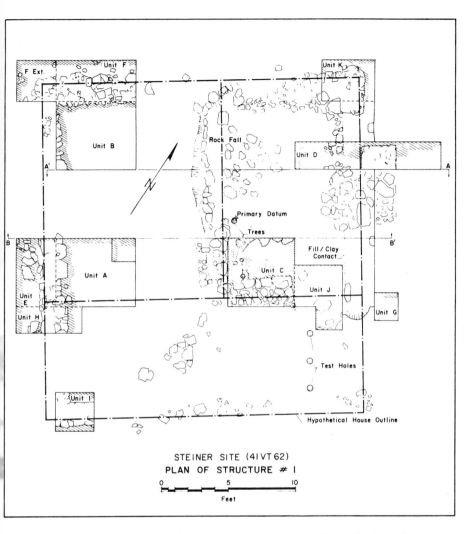

FIG. 8.11   *The foundations of Steiner's House, as exposed by archeological excavations, Victoria County.* (From Fox and Livingston 1979: Fig. 25. Courtesy Center for Archaeological Research, The University of Texas at San Antonio.)

posits near the bottom of the cellar contained fragments of broken wine bottles, sherds from a crockery jug, and pieces of a canning jar from the nineteenth century. These materials, along with metal hardware and a German coin dated 1844 found in the lower soil layer, indicated that it was deposited while the cellar was in use and perhaps shortly after its abandonment. The enclosure probably measured about 9 feet by 13 feet and there apparently was less than 6½ feet of space between the floor of the cellar and the bottoms of the wooden joists that supported the floor of the house above it.

In comparison to the simple frame house on a low stone foundation at the mid-nineteenth-century Steiner farmstead, the Schob house of the late nineteenth century was a large two-story rectangular structure made of sandstone blocks quarried from the banks of the Coleto. The house plan consisted of two rooms situated side by side on each floor and a large attic space that formed a third floor. The overall dimensions of the house were about 33 feet by 20 feet. Like the Steiner house, the Schob house was oriented toward the southeast. But instead of a fireplace, the Schob house was heated with wood stoves that vented through a flue built into the stone crosswall separating the rooms of the house and then up a chimney. A wooden kitchen wing was attached to the northwest corner of the house. Surrounding the building was a grassy yard, shaded by large anaqua trees and enclosed by a wire fence. A stone-lined well was located in the yard. Several late nineteenth-century and twentieth-century outbuildings stood in the southwestern portion of the farmstead.

The goal of the archeological and historical investigations was to reconstruct the layout of the Schob farmstead as it was first built in the late nineteenth century. Details were recorded concerning the dimensions and methods of construction of the various structures. An attempt was made to find the location of the first kitchen, which reportedly stood separate from the house until it was damaged by a hurricane in 1886 and then was moved over and attached to the house. Because of disturbance to the area where the original kitchen was supposed to have been, no architectural remains could be found; but signs of a drip line and artifact concentrations were uncovered that indicated the frame structure probably stood about 20 feet away from the house.

Family tradition held that after Schob completed the careful construction of the stone house in 1882, the structures from the old Steiner place were moved up to serve as outbuildings for the new farmstead. Close inspection of the Schob structures seemed to verify this. The smokehouse, which later became a guinea hen house at the Schob farm, appeared to have been constructed of mid-nineteenth-century materials and fit the general dimensions of the postulated smokehouse foundation back at the Steiner place.

FIG. 8.12   *The Schob House, Victoria County.* (Courtesy Center for Archaeological Research, The University of Texas at San Antonio.)

The remains of an old double corncrib at the Schob farmstead was constructed in the typical dog-run plan of old dovetailed hewn timbers and probably came from the Steiner place, although time limits did not allow for a search for archeological evidence of this structure in the Steiner site area. The inspection of the kitchen attached to the Schob house found that much of its framework was constructed of hewn timbers, some of which appeared to have been taken from earlier structures. Of course, family tradition explained that the kitchen had moved over from its 1880's location, but it is possible that many of the timbers, if not all of them, had been recycled from the framework of the kitchen at the Steiner place.

The most interesting relocated structure was the wooden barn at the Schob farm. Although the wooden walls were of late nineteenth-century construction, the structure of the barn was found to be composed of hewn timbers, each notched and pegged into place to form a framework of studs, plates, braces, joists, and rafters. Although the frame had been altered to have a barn door

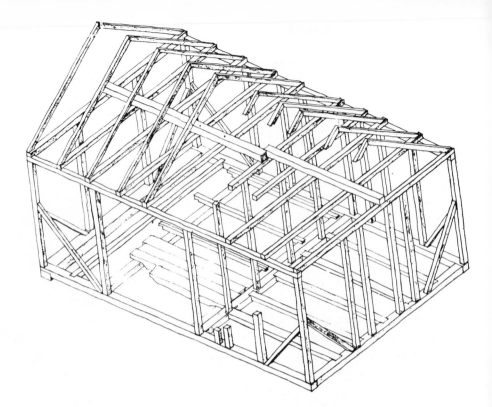

FIG. 8.13 *Isometric drawing of the framing elements of the Schob barn, once the frame of the Steiner House, Victoria County.* (From Fox and Livingston 1979:Fig. 6. Courtesy Center for Archaeological Research, The University of Texas at San Antonio.)

opening in one side and it had a twentieth-century roof and other renovations, the plan of the barn and that of the foundation walls of the Steiner house compared so closely that there is little doubt that the frame of the barn originally was the frame of the Steiner house. Even the size of the smaller of the two rooms of the barn's framework matched the area that would have covered the cellar beneath the eastern end of the Steiner house.

The information recovered by the archeological and historical investigations at the Steiner-Schob Complex was compared with the evidence reported from the earlier archeological studies at LBJ State Park and the Biegel Settlement (Fox and Livingston 1979:75–77). Some features noted at the Biegel Settlement corresponded to those found at the Steiner-Schob Complex, such as hewn log building construction with dovetailed corner notching and the reuse of structures and structural materials. However, the settlement at the LBJ State Park seemed to compare more closely, perhaps because building stone and other construction materials occur naturally in the Victoria and the Fredericksburg areas and not in the La Grange area, but possibly because the LBJ State Park and the Steiner-Schob settlements were inhabited by German immigrants who remained relatively isolated from the influences of peoples of other backgrounds, while the people of the Biegel Settlement were a more international group surrounded by an Anglo-American cultural environment.

The sherds of ceramic vessels found at the Steiner-Schob Complex occurred in the usual pattern for the period from the mid-nineteenth century through the twentieth century, beginning with the decorated British-made pearl wares of the period before the Civil War, followed by the plain white ironstone wares of the late nineteenth century, and then by decaled wares and plain white earthenwares with molded decorations common in the early twentieth century. In one important way, though, the ceramics from this German family settlement were different from those found at the sites of Anglo-American settlements of the same time periods. The difference was in the length of time that certain ceramic wares were used. Although the occupation of the Schob farm dated after 1880, sherds of typically pre-Civil War decorated British-made wares were found there that were of the same decorative patterns as those found at the earlier Steiner house site, suggesting that the dishes acquired by the Steiner family before the Civil War were still in use, perhaps as cherished heirlooms, or at least well cared for, by the Schobs in the late nineteenth century. This archeological evidence and the architectural evidence of the reuse of structures and building materials reflects the frugality and the importance of family tradition to German settlers in Texas.

The glass vessel fragments found at the Steiner-Schob Complex did not provide special information, although the large number of fragments of handmade olive green wine bottles from Steiner's house site fits his reputation as a winemaker. Much of the metal hardware from the Steiner house site, such as door and window latches, was hand-wrought, probably by a local blacksmith. It was simple, durable, and functional, and not very different from the hardware used during the previous two centuries. In contrast, the door latches, lock plates, and other hardware at the Schob house were more like the mass-produced varieties advertised in the Montgomery Ward catalogue for 1895 (1969). This change in the shape and nature of manufacture of building materials reflects the increased availability of manufactured goods corresponding to the increased industrialization of America and the integration of Texans into the American socioeconomic system toward the end of the nineteenth century.

IX

Battlegrounds, Forts, and Other Military Sites

JUST AS THE SPANISH presidios greatly influenced the demography and other characteristics of the civil settlements of the Spanish borderlands, warfare, the presence of military forces, and the markets they create have played important roles in Texas' social, political, and economic development. Ever since Mexican Texas became independent from Spain and the Republic of Texas became independent from Mexico, Texans have taken measures to defend themselves and their State's social and economic integrity against outside forces—military and otherwise.

Conflicts between Texans and Mexicans did not end with the Battle of San Jacinto or even with the Treaty of Guadalupe Hidalgo formally ending the Mexican War. Mexican bandits terrorized the southern border settlements as late as the early twentieth century. The conflict and the threat of conflict between Texans and Indians that slowed the westward expansion of early American Texas continued until the last warring Indians were removed in the late nineteenth century. The Texas Rangers evolved during the first half of the nineteenth century as policing agents who fought both Indians and Mexicans on the frontier. They and other Texans joined the Confederacy to defend states' rights against the outside pressures toward industrialization. U.S. military bases and outposts were occupied on the frontier and along the border as a show of force and to provide for defense before, during, and after the Civil War.

Battlefields of the Mexican War

After the Battle of San Jacinto, Mexico argued that Texas, particularly the area between the Nueces River and the Rio Grande, was still a part of her territory. When it was apparent that Texas would become a state in the Union, U.S. President Polk sent General Zachary Taylor and an army of U.S. troops as a show of

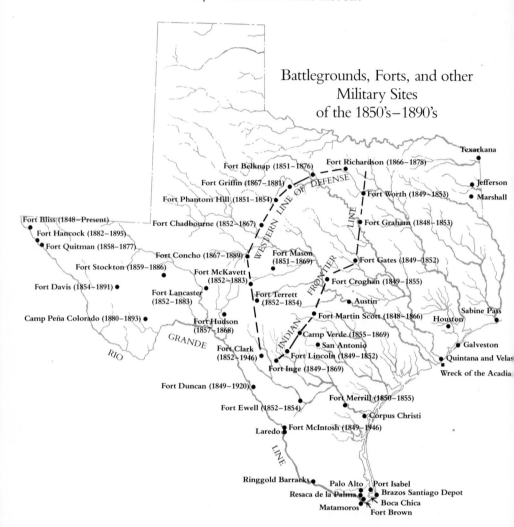

FIG. 9.1   *Battlegrounds, forts, and other military sites of the second half of the nineteenth century.*

force to influence negotiations with Mexico concerning territoriality (Fehrenbach 1968:270–272).

Taylor arrived at Corpus Christi at the mouth of the Nueces River in July 1845 and established a military supply depot there. When it was obvious that the Mexican government would not negotiate, Taylor was ordered to move to the Rio Grande in April 1846. He established a depot at Port Isabel a few miles up the coast

FIG. 9.2   *Theodore Gentilz's "Bagdad, Mexico (Boca del Rio Grande)"*
shows how the lower Texas Gulf Coast looked at about the time of the Mex-
ican War. (Courtesy Library of the Daughters of the Republic of Texas at
the Alamo, San Antonio.)

from the mouth of the Rio Grande where a natural deep-water
pass at Brazos Santiago was navigable for ocean-going supply
ships. Then he placed a detachment under the command of Major
Jacob Brown directly across the Rio Grande from Matamoros.

The anger of landowners living in Matamoros who held title
to large areas of land north of the river pressured Mexican General
Mariano Arista into sending several hundred of his cavalrymen
and lancers across the river. On April 24, 1846, some of these
Mexican military forces caught a patrol of U.S. Army dragoons in
a trap. Then Arista began a siege and bombardment of Major
Brown's breastworks with part of the Mexican forces and positioned his main body of troops to lie in wait for Taylor's forces
when they came to relieve Brown.

Taylor's army, which included several Texas volunteers, encountered the Mexican emplacements on May 8 at a place called
Palo Alto on the coastal plain about eight miles north of Brown's
fortifications. The U.S. forces numbered about 2,300 men with a
supply train of between 200 and 400 wagons (Frost 1850; Peck
1970; Smith and Judah 1968). The Mexican forces numbered more
than 4,000 (Nevin 1978; Ramsey 1970). As the Americans ad-

vanced, the Mexican artillery batteries opened fire. The superior American artillery returned fire and inflicted heavy losses. Other maneuvers drove the Mexicans into retreat. The battle, which lasted only a couple of hours, left about six Americans dead and 40 wounded. The Mexican casualties were estimated to have been about 200 killed and 200 wounded. The American artillery fired some 3,000 rounds during the battle, while the Mexican artillery fired only about 650 rounds. According to a military observer:

In passing over the battleground of the former day, the terrible effects of our artillery were visible in the heaped-up masses of dead bodies disfigured with ghastly wounds and distained with blood—in dead horses scattered along the route of the retreating cavalry—, and in the fragments of arms, military accoutrements, and clothing strewed over the field in admirable confusion (Brooks 1849:137–138).

The Mexican force made its retreat and began establishing new defensive positions at an old river channel or oxbow lake, known as Resaca de la Palma, about five miles south of the Palo Alto battlefield and about three and one-half miles north of Major Brown's defenses on the Rio Grande. The Americans allowed the Mexicans to retreat while they erected earthworks for the protection of their wagon train and prepared to pursue Arista's army. The next day, the Americans overtook the Mexican positions at Resaca de la Palma. The Mexican forces were badly mauled by Taylor's army and fell back in disorder across the Rio Grande. When Taylor's forces reached the besieged breastworks on the river, the Americans were holding their own. Major Brown was mortally wounded during the battle, and later a fort named after him was established where the city of Brownsville is located today.

FIG. 9.3   *Sketch maps of the Port Isabel–Brownsville area in 1846 and 1847.* A. Re-drawn from map by J. H. Eaton, 3rd Infantry, in Taylor's Official Report of 1846 and reprinted in Smith and Judah 1968, showing the road between Port Isabel and Matamoros (Fort Brown) and the locations of the Battle of Palo Alto (May 8, 1846) and the Battle of Resaca de la Palma (May 9, 1846). B. Drawn from map done under instructions from Col. J. J. Abert, Corps of Engineers, by Lt. J. D. Webster and T. E. Mullowny, Esq., and reproduced in Baxter and Killen 1976, showing the locations of the battles of Palo Alto and Resaca de la Palma in 1847. (From Bond 1978:Fig. 4. Courtesy Cultural Resources Laboratory, Texas A&M University.)

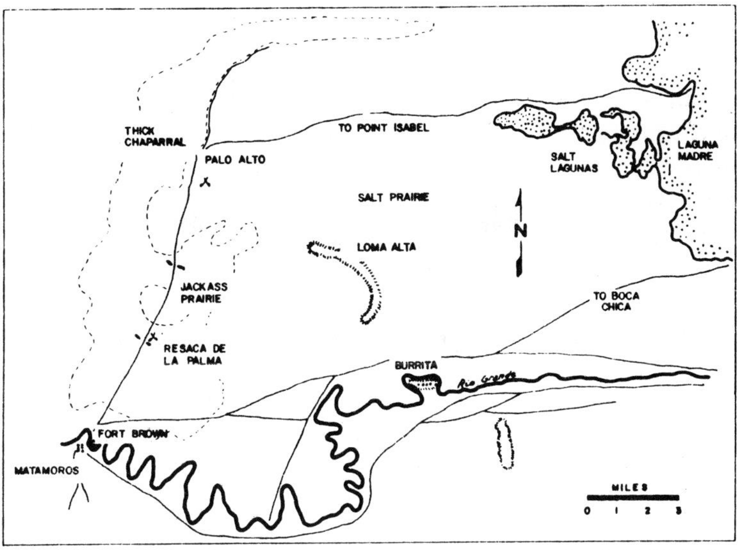
THICK CHAPARRAL
TO POINT ISABEL
PALO ALTO
SALT PRAIRIE
SALT LAGUNAS
LAGUNA MADRE
N
LOMA ALTA
JACKASS PRAIRIE
TO BOCA CHICA
RESACA DE LA PALMA
BURRITA
Rio Grande
FORT BROWN
MATAMOROS
MILES
0 1 2 3

A

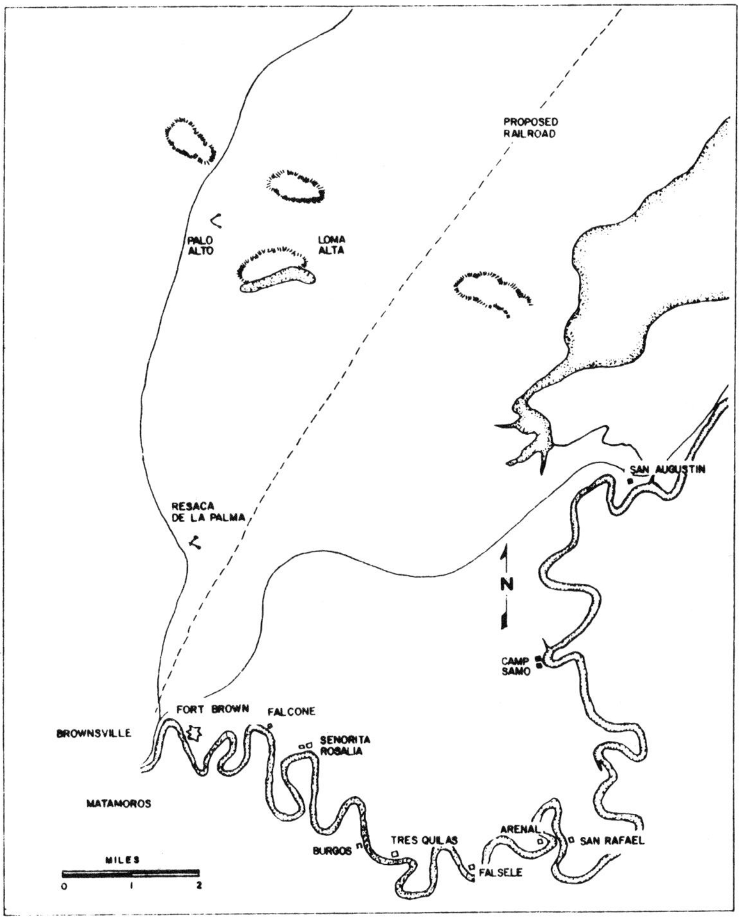
PROPOSED RAILROAD
PALO ALTO
LOMA ALTA
SAN AUGUSTIN
RESACA DE LA PALMA
N
CAMP SAMO
FORT BROWN
FALCONE
BROWNSVILLE
SENORITA ROSALIA
MATAMOROS
ARENAL
SAN RAFAEL
TRES QUILAS
BURGOS
FALSELE
MILES
0 1 2

B

During the two years of war that followed the battles of Palo Alto and Resaca de la Palma, there was considerable movement of troops and military supplies across the Lower Rio Grande Valley. Roadways became established and privately-owned steamboats were used to transport men and supplies from the coastal depot at Brazos Santiago to outposts up the river. But the rest of the actual warfare was waged on Mexican soil. As a result of the war, settlement along the north bank of the Rio Grande, although predominantly Hispanic in population, became dominated by Americans like steamboat captains Richard King and Mifflin Kenedy who managed to acquire huge areas of old Spanish-Mexican landholdings and developed immense ranches in the 1850's (Fehrenbach 1968:288–290).

In 1979, archeologists from Texas A&M University conducted an investigation to locate the Palo Alto battlefield where the Mexican and American artilleries duelled on May 8, 1846, and to assess the archeological potential of the battleground site (Bond 1979). The investigation was sponsored by the National Park Service to obtain information needed for acquisition and preservation of the Mexican War site. The area studied is located in Cameron County in agricultural land and pastureland north of Brownsville and south of the community of Los Fresnos. During the more than 130 years since the battle, land use in the area has altered the landscape to such an extent that the precise location of the battlefield and the battle lines of the opposing armies were unknown and it was difficult to compare 1840's maps of the battleground, roads, and other features with what the area looks like today. It was hoped that archeological evidence could be found to help delineate the boundaries of the Palo Alto battlefield.

The 1979 investigation involved historical background research, a proton magnetometer survey, systematic prospecting with metal detectors, and a thorough visual inspection of the general area. Preliminary archeological studies conducted prior to 1979 along a proposed new railroad found historical and archeological evidence to suggest that the battle had occurred in an area near a topographic feature called Loma Alta Lake, on the northern edge of present-day Brownsville (Shafer 1974; Baxter and Killen 1976). But re-examination of small lead balls used as part of the evidence that this was the battlefield disclosed that they were from the shells of 1897-model guns fired during target practice by the

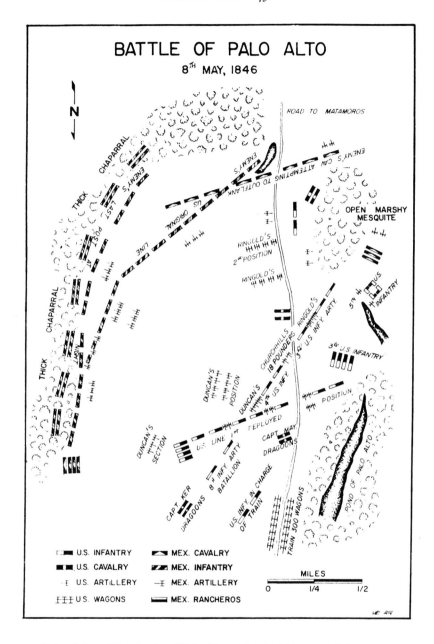

FIG. 9.4   *Map of the Battle of Palo Alto, May 8, 1846, copied from a map printed in Brooks 1849.* Note that the map is oriented with north toward the bottom. (From Bond 1979: Fig. 6. Courtesy Cultural Resources Laboratory, Texas A&M University.)

U.S. Army in the early twentieth century, instead of cannister or grapeshot from the 1846 battle. And historical accounts that came to light after the preliminary archeological investigations suggested that the actual Battle of Palo Alto occurred to the north and northwest of Loma Alta Lake.

The 1979 investigation had more historical information, as well as the data gained by the earlier studies, on which to base its research design. During the remote sensing and visual inspection of the suspected battlefield site, 131 artifacts were found, most of which were modern "contamination" such as foil wrappers, beverage containers, some modern shotgun shells and pistol and rifle cartridge cases, and more evidence of the U.S. Army's use of the general area as a target range in the early 1900's. A few artifacts of prehistoric Indian occupation also were found. Only 20 artifacts

FIG. 9.5   *The remains of some of the individuals recovered from a mass grave disturbed as the result of a real estate development of the Resaca de la Palma Battlefield, Cameron County.* (Courtesy Texas Archeological Research Laboratory, The University of Texas at Austin. Photo by M. B. Collins.)

could be identified as being directly related to the battle of 1846 at Palo Alto.

During the investigation, the archeologists met several relic collectors who reported finding cannonballs and other military artifacts in the area. Unfortunately, the collectors kept no records of the precise locations from which their artifacts were taken, and so their collections' relationship to the battle could not be verified and the artifacts were useless for locating the limits of the battleground or the more precise locations of the battle lines.

The 20 battle-related artifacts found during the 1979 investigation included lead balls and other parts from artillery shrapnel shells, iron cannon shot, a part of a Brown Bess musket, copper and brass cannister or grapeshot, lead musket balls and other American and Mexican ordnance, brass buckles, and other military objects documented as having been used during the battle. These artifacts, and their distribution with respect to each other and to topographic features, enabled the investigators to confidently define the limits of the battlefield as described in the historical accounts. It includes an irregularly-shaped area of *resacas*, depressions, rises, open country and chaparral that has been altered significantly by twentieth-century land use. The positions of the artifacts enabled the archeologists to suggest the locations of the actual battle lines, and those hypotheses can be further refined with additional archeological and historical research of the Palo Alto battlefield site.

In 1967, a team of anthropology students from the University of Texas at Austin excavated a mass grave that was discovered by earthmoving activities in construction of a subdivision near a *resaca* on the northern outskirts of Brownsville (Collins, Hester, and Ellezy n.d.; Hester 1978). The historical accounts indicated that the Mexican dead from the Battle of Resaca de la Palma, May 9, 1846, were interred in mass graves on the day after the battle. The grave accidentally uncovered by the construction was located in the appropriate area described in historical accounts and probably marked the battlefield site. The skeletons of several individuals were found, along with canteens, shirt and trouser buttons, buckles, musket balls, and other military artifacts.

Laboratory analysis determined that a total of 37 and possibly 38 individuals were represented by the bones recovered during the archeological work (Wesolowsky 1982). Many of the skeletal remains had been damaged or destroyed by the environmental conditions of the grave site and by the machinery that disturbed it. Only three skeletons were complete. Of the 13 skulls recovered, only three were complete enough for their anthropomorphic characteristics to be studied. Age and sex could be estimated based on the characteristics of the skeletons and parts of skeletons of 28 individuals. The range of ages is what would be expected for a military sample. One individual was in his late teens, 12 were between 18 and 30 years of age, and 14 could be generally classified as adult. These 27 skeletons had characteristics which indicated that they probably were males. The bones of the twenty-eighth skeleton had characteristics of a 21-year-old female, although it is not uncommon for males in human populations to have gracile, or more delicate than normal, bones.

The height of the individuals who were buried at Resaca de la Palma could be established from the skeletal remains. The statures ranged from 5 feet 3 inches to 5 feet 8¼ inches, based on measurements of the bones of 19 individuals. The soldiers represented by the sample averaged about 5 feet 5 inches tall, which may seem somewhat shorter than would be expected for American soldiers but may be about right for a nineteenth-century Mexican army including a large number of Mexican Indians. It would have been possible to estimate stature from other bones recovered from the mass grave, but because many of the leg and arm bones were found separate from the rest of their skeletons, they were not included in order to avoid the possibility of counting the bones of a single individual more than once.

Several instances of pathology (abnormal characteristics observable in the bones) were found during the study of the skeletal remains, but only two cases could be identified confidently as having been the result of battle wounds. A fragment of the right humerus, or upper arm bone, of one individual had an unhealed cut in it which apparently was caused by an edged weapon. The location of the cut mark on the back of the elbow joint may be where the soldier was struck as he raised his arm across his face to ward off the blow of a saber. The right tibia, or shinbone, of another skeleton had a lead projectile embedded in it just below the knee joint. The projectile, probably a musket ball or grapeshot, had been flattened by its impact with the bone. It was firmly embedded and the fractures radiating from it were unhealed, indicating that the soldier died not long after he was shot in the leg.

The other instances of pathology could not be identified definitely as battle wounds. Several of the skulls were crushed, but this damage might have happened before death or as the result of the pressure of the soil during the more than 120 years that the skulls were buried. The incomplete skeletons could have been the result of dismemberment from gunshots, artillery fire, blows struck with edged weapons, or even animals feeding on the bodies, but instances of traumatic amputation could not be demonstrated by the skeletal analysis.

Civil War Sites

Secession did not occur all at once over the slavery issue, but as the result of a much more complicated crisis that had been brewing for some time during the mid-nineteenth century. The real conflicts were between the pressures toward social and economic integration with the industrializing states of the North and the totally different, more conservative system of values of the South, still agrarian economically and based upon individual and states' rights. The people of the South, including most Texans, refused to be subjugated by outside forces of any kind, especially those that would remove state sovereignty, Constitutional property rights, and other basic privileges already well established as part of Texas society by the mid-nineteenth century (Fehrenbach 1968:327–329).

Even though Texas was geographically on the southwestern margin of the War Between the States, several fortified defensive installations were placed along the borders and some Civil War battles were fought on the edges of Texas. And, although there were few large-scale industries and manufacturers in Texas at the beginning of the war, the state government, the Confederate Army, private enterprises, and individual family households made every effort to supply their troops with military materials necessary to carry on the war and to provide the everyday necessities that no longer were available through normal trade networks. There was a tremendous drain on the resources of Texas, but the state's greatest commitment and her greatest loss were the thousands of men who died in various Civil War battles, most of which took place outside of Texas and east of the Mississippi.

Unfortunately, only a few Civil War military sites have been preserved and fewer have been archeologically investigated. The Sabine Pass battleground is now a State Historic Park located on the Texas side of the natural channel at the mouth of the Sabine River. In 1861, an earthwork fort was built by Texas state troops on the shoreline to command navigation of the pass. When the Confederate Army became concerned with the defense of the pass, plans were drawn up for a new earthwork to be constructed about a mile from the Texas fort. In September, 1862, the old fort was shelled by U.S. Navy ships. It was abandoned and the construction of the new fort was hurried along. It was almost finished when the Battle of Sabine Pass took place in September, 1863.

A large federal invasion fleet assembled off the coast from the pass on September 7. The fleet included gunboats and several transports carrying about 5,000 infantry and artillery to be used to take control of areas farther inland in Texas. Thousands of other federal troops were preparing to board Union transport ships in New Orleans to reinforce the invasion. In command of the Confederate earthworks at Sabine Pass was Lieutenant Dick Dowling, with 42 fellow-Irishmen, who manned the fort's artillery, and five other officers. Dowling's company had only six cannons.

The assault began in the afternoon of September 8, when four Union gunboats steamed up the pass and began firing at the fort. Dowling's artillery quickly silenced the two lead gunboats and, because the shoreline at the fort was the only feasible landing area, the embarrassed Union fleet had to return to New Orleans. The federal force lost two warships with 13 heavy guns. Twenty-four Union soldiers were killed or wounded, 37 were unaccounted for, and 315 were captured. None of the Texas defenders were killed or wounded. Confederate forces constructed and manned two other forts at Sabine Pass but neither saw action during the war and little remains of them today.

Archeological investigations were conducted at the Sabine Pass Battleground State Historic Park in 1972, 1973, and 1974 to verify the location of the Confederate fort and to search for evidence of its occupation (Holtzapple and Roberson 1976). Although several different maps dating to the 1860's leave little doubt that the park encompasses the fort site, the excavation of several machine-dug and hand-controlled test units placed in various parts of the park found no evidence of the earthworks or artifacts definitely related to the Civil War period. This lack of evidence may be the result of a long history of disturbance to the area which began as early as 1875 with channel-dredging activities conducted by the U.S. Army Corps of Engineers.

Before several Southern states had seceded from the Union, President Lincoln ordered a blockade of the coastline from the Virginia capes to the mouth of the Rio Grande. Actually, the federal government did not have enough ships to enforce the blockade at the beginning of the Civil War. Accelerated ship-building quickly increased its effectiveness. Of course, the Confederacy, without the industrial capability to build warships, had an even less effective navy and encouraged privateering by merchant ships and other privately-owned vessels which were armed and flew the Confederate flag. As the blockade was strengthened, it became more difficult to obtain necessities in the South, and blockade-running became more profitable than privateering. The blockade-running business came to be controlled primarily by British seamen and British ships, but merchant ships of various countries participated. Neutral ports like Halifax (Nova Scotia), Nassau (Bahamas), Havana (Cuba), Vera Cruz and Matamoros (Mexico) boomed as bases for these enterprises that traded special hard-to-get articles for Southern cotton.

Blockade-running became so profitable that some entrepreneurs ordered the manufacture of speedy, efficient side-wheeler steamships, especially designed as blockade-runners. One of these, completed in July of 1864, was the *Acadia*, which was owned by two Canadians (Hole 1974). Built in a Canadian shipyard and registered in Montreal, the *Acadia* set sail for Nassau with a party of "pirates" on board in December of 1864. After making port at Nassau, she sailed to Havana and then to Vera Cruz. There she took on more cargo and dropped off her notorious passengers, who proceeded overland to the Pacific and raided maritime shipping. From Vera Cruz, the *Acadia* sailed cautiously to the Texas coast, where, on the night of February 5, 1865, her captain attempted to make the run for the port at Velasco at the mouth of the Brazos River. Lost in the fog without a pilot, the *Acadia* ran aground. The next morning a federal blockader patrolling the coastline out of the range of Confederate shore batteries, happened upon the stranded, defenseless side-wheeler and opened fire on her. Confederate troops managed to salvage most of the cargo before the shelling started. The *Galveston Weekly News* on Wednesday, February 22, 1865, reported the auction the previous day of the cargo from the *Acadia*. Among the goods, which sold at rather exorbitant prices, were various kinds of fabric, handkerchiefs, clothing, buttons, stationery, tools, canned fruits, coffee, and quinine.

The lookout mast and other parts of the wreck of the *Acadia* were visible for a long time after the Civil War, protruding out of the water about 300 yards offshore in about 15 feet of surf. The wreck was not often visited by treasure hunters because of the heavy surf, strong currents, and turbid waters. On several occasions during the 1960's when the weather was right, a dentist and amateur underwater archeologist named Wendel E. Pierce swam out to the wreck in his scuba gear. First he estimated the dimensions and other details of the wreck, much of which he had to do by feel because of the murky water and his poor eyesight. He found the wreck to be more than 160 feet long, constructed of heavy wood timbers reinforced with iron rods and sheathed with lead and brass. The vessel was flat bottomed, able to navigate in shallow waters. By this time its wreck had sunk three feet into the clay bottom of the bay.

Dr. Pierce found the ship's boiler, rusted metal engine parts, steam pipes and paddle wheels, and some of the coal that was used to fire her engines. He recovered a crate-load of marble door knobs, cast-iron locks, brass keys, door latches, and other building hardware. He even managed to bring ashore one of the ship's fancy copper and lead commodes and a variety of other artifacts. His most ambitious project was to saw off the bow of the steamer so that it could be hung on a museum wall in Houston, but he died before he could complete the endeavor.

After Dr. Pierce's death, Dr. Frank Hole, an archeologist at Rice University, prepared a report (1974) on the history of the *Acadia* and the materials recovered from her wreck, based on the field notes and historical research that Dr. Pierce had compiled. This information, and details that can be recovered by more properly controlled archeological investigations of Civil War shipwrecks, will help us to reconstruct the history of blockade-running along the Gulf coast that was so important to the economy of Civil War Texas.

Another military site on the Texas coast is the Brazos Santiago Depot located on the extreme northern end of Brazos Island at Brazos Santiago Pass, near Port Isabel. The natural harbor at Brazos Santiago was used as early as 1523 as a stopover by Spanish ships (Hall and Grombacher 1974). In 1820, Spain established a port there and trade—legal and illegal—increased between New Orleans and Mexican settlements along the Lower Rio Grande (Graf 1942). The pass and the harbor at Brazos Santiago were the scene of brief military encounters and blockades involving American, Texas, Mexican, and French ships during the 1830's (Pierce 1917:22–23).

A storm completely destroyed the settlement on Brazos Island in 1837 and when General Zachary Taylor established an American military supply depot there in 1846, Port Isabel was a small village of thatched cottages. Confederate troops were stationed at Brazos Santiago in 1861. But a Union force landed at Brazos Island in November 1863 and invaded the Lower Rio Grande Valley. Confederate forces and Texas Rangers under the command of John Salmon (Rip) Ford forced a large army of federal troops out of the area and onto Brazos Island during the Battle of Palmito Ranch on May 13, 1865. Occurring more than a month after Lee surrendered to Grant at Appomattox, Ford's victory at Palmito Ranch turned out to be the last battle of the Civil War (Thompson 1965:87–88; Fehrenbach 1968:389–392). The Brazos Santiago Depot was destroyed by a storm in 1867 and covered by sand after abandonment. But another depot was established on the southern end of Brazos Santiago, which continued to serve as a supply point until the early 1880's when the pass separating Brazos Island from the mainland silted up, destroying the natural harbor.

Archeologists rushed to Brazos Santiago in 1967 after Hurricane Beulah exposed a large part of the Mexican War and Civil War occupations of the depot area. Much of the area was photographed and mapped and a large collection of artifacts was collected, including wine bottles, china dishes, rusted metal objects, and an interesting assortment of leather boots, shoes, and hats that had been preserved by the saltwater environment for more than a century. Unfortunately, relic hunters robbed the exposed area of many of the artifacts. Neither time nor funds were available for an intensive archeological investigation and as yet a report on the salvage work at Brazos Santiago has not been published. Sand again accumulated on the island and obscured all traces of the military site.

An archeological survey conducted in 1973 found that sand and mud, or "spoil," dredged from the coastal areas near Brazos Santiago Pass had been placed on part of the depot site (Hall and Grombacher 1974). The surveyors recommended that no additional spoil areas be established on the historically sensitive area, although the continuing use of the spoil reservoir already there probably would not harm the archeological deposits of the Brazos Santiago Depot. After Hurricane Allen struck the southern Texas coast in 1980, archeologists from the Texas Historical Commission salvaged another collection of artifacts from the depot site after relic collectors had already made off with large numbers of the items from the Mexican War and Civil War occupations. (Boggs n.d.). A study of the glass and ceramic artifacts recovered from the site by the Texas Historical Commission currently is being done as a master's thesis project by a graduate student from The University of Texas at Austin (Cynthia Banks, personal communication, September, 1982). Fortunately, during this hurricane the spoil banks helped to protect portions of the depot from weather damage and from the relic hunters. The Brazos Santiago Depot site was listed in the National Register of Historic Places in 1971 and should therefore receive protection.

After Vicksburg had fallen and control of the Mississippi River was lost to Union forces in 1863, the Trans-Mississippi Department's connections with the rest of the Confederacy were severed, and Texas and the other states of the Department had to become self-sustaining and self-reliant (Parks 1954:311). Galveston on the coast and Marshall in northeastern Texas became fortified cities.

Marshall became the site of the principal powder mill and headquarters for the chiefs of ordnance, conscription, quartermaster, subsistence, and medical bureaus of the Department, as well as the capitol-in-exile of the state of Missouri (Roney 1962:55). The Marshall powder mill produced tons of gun powder, rifles, rifle parts, bayonets, other small arms, and other military hardware. Because of this, Marshall was one of the targets of a federal campaign involving a fleet of gunboats and an army that attempted to

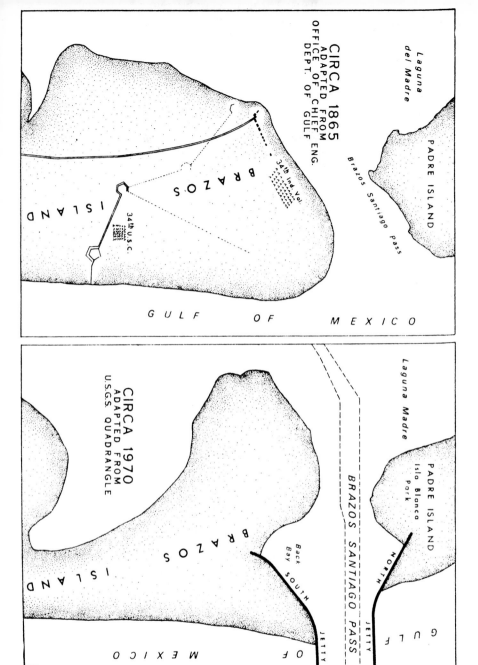

FIG. 9.6 *Maps of the north end of Brazos Island in 1865 and in 1970, showing changes in shape of the island in relation to the locations of military facilities there.* (From Hall and Grombacher 1974: Fig. 3. Courtesy Texas Archeological Survey, The University of Texas at Austin. Drawing by M. L. Freeman.)

invade Texas by way of the Red River in April, 1864. The Union forces, under the command of General N.P. Banks who failed to capture Sabine Pass seven months before, were defeated at the Battle of Mansfield in northwestern Louisiana and the Marshall powder mill continued to operate until the end of the War.

Shortly after the end of the War was announced in Texas, most of the Confederate officials in Marshall fled to Mexico with General Shelby of San Antonio; federal troops moved in to occupy Marshall. Tons of powder were still stored at the mill's powder magazine. On August 28, 1865, an explosion occurred that severely burned four soldiers, two of whom died the next day. After the disaster the mill was dismantled. Most of the reusable brick was "robbed" from the masonry structures of the mill complex. Although some of the frame structures remained standing until the turn of the century, the area was looted for scrap metal and Civil War artifacts in the 1920's and the 1930's. Later, parts of the powder mill site became a popular picnic area, a dump ground, and a saw mill. By 1970, the archeological site had become pastureland with an open lowland meadow along a creek and a hillside covered with a mixed pine and hardwood forest. The only visible signs of the powder mill complex were earthen embankments from some of the defensive gun emplacements, traces of brick and hematite sandstone foundations, and a section of a creek that was rechanneled as part of the development of the powder mill during the Civil War.

In 1971, archeologists with the Texas Highway Department began to investigate alternative routes for a new highway loop to be constructed around the north side of the city of Marshall. The investigations were done to recover information with which to recommend a route that would be the least destructive to the Marshall Powder Mill site.

An initial archeological reconnaissance and limited testing of the right-of-way areas found man-made alterations in the landscape, accumulations of brick rubble, and artifacts which enabled recommendations to be made for intensive archeological testing. The next phase of investigations, including a program of machine-dug and hand-controlled excavations, was conducted in 1972 and found the foundation remains of several structures built during the Civil War, as well as metal, ceramic, and glass artifacts—definite evidence of the occupational and industrial activities that took

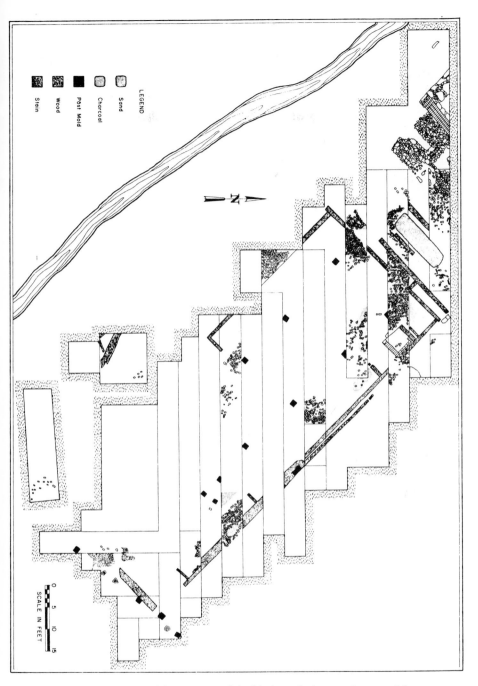

LEGEND

Sand
Wood
Post Mold
Charcoal
Stain

N

SCALE IN FEET
0 5 10 15

FIG. 9.7 *Plan map of the remains of the blacksmith shop at the site of the Marshall Powder Mill, Harrison County.* (From Luke 1978:Fig. 10. Courtesy Texas Department of Highways and Public Transportation.)

FIG. 9.8 *View of the archeological remains of the blacksmith shop at the Marshall Powder Mill, Harrison County, looking northwest.* Note brick foundation remains and nails marking location of wooden structural elements. (From Luke 1978:Fig. 20. Courtesy Texas Department of Highways and Public Transportation.)

place at the powder mill complex (Weir 1973). Also located were features that appeared to have been a defensive earthwork and a well. At least eight of 12 features found during the test investigations were located within the highway route that was selected, but the route was chosen because it was obvious that alternative routes would disturb an even greater number of significant archeological features.

The largest structural feature found within the selected right-of-way was thought to be the main mill, not only because of its size but because a large depression in its center was interpreted as being the crater caused by the explosion that occurred in 1865. Also interesting, the archeological evidence suggested that the complex had been much more than just a powder mill. The historical accounts indicate that gunsmiths and machine shops, foundries, and other military industrial facilities were located there (Albaugh 1958:38).

Once the highway route was chosen and the Texas Antiquities Committee agreed with the selection, the Texas Highway Department proceeded to acquire the right-of-way and its archeologists undertook the total recovery of the archeological resources that would be destroyed by the highway construction (Luke 1978). The remains of different structures were uncovered and their architecture was reflected by massive brick and hematite sandstone foundation walls, by lines of stained soil and square-cut nails where wooden walls once stood, by the discolored spots in the soil where postholes had been dug, and by other features. Much of the investigation concentrated on the remains of what probably was a blacksmith shop, where ash, iron scrap, the foundations of brick forges, and other evidence was found.

The wide assortment of metal items produced at the Marshall Powder Mill was reflected by the artifacts recovered. The blacksmith shop was evidently used in the manufacture of wagon parts, harness trappings, and other gear, and in the alteration, or modernization, of old Kentucky flintlock rifles so that they could be fired with percussion caps instead of gunflints. Bullet molds, chains, horseshoes, nuts, bolts, and other hardware, leather knives, axes, adzes, and other tools were found, as well as fragments of green glass wine and whiskey bottles of the shape typical of the Civil War period.

Frontier Forts

Although the people of Texas tended to resent any sort of federal interference in Texan affairs, the federal government was convenient for certain expensive and difficult situations, such as the operation of postal and diplomatic services, the construction and maintenance of harbors, roads, and other civil engineering, and the guarantee of defense against outside forces (Fehrenbach 1968:275–278). The U.S. government assumed responsibility for protecting settlement on the frontier when Texas was annexed in 1845. The need for military outposts was growing rapidly by this time (Taniguchi, *et al.* 1968). The number of settlers in Texas grew from about 135,000 in 1845 to more than 212,000 in 1850. Indian problems on the frontier, the international boundary dispute with Mexico, and the need to maintain supply depots and communication routes all encouraged the establishment of several U.S. military forts before and after the Civil War.

The first line of federal forts, known in Washington as the Indian Frontier Line, consisted of seven outposts established beginning in 1849. The line ran roughly from north-central Texas to the Rio Grande through the middle of the state and included Forts Worth, Martin Scott, Inge, Graham, Croghan, Lincoln, and Gates. A Rio Grande Line of outposts developed between the time of the Mexican War and the Civil War and included Fort Brown near the mouth of the Rio Grande and Fort Bliss at El Paso, with Ringgold Barracks and Forts McIntosh, Duncan, and Quitman in between.

The frontier changed rapidly during the mid-nineteenth century and the forts of the first line of defense quickly outlived their usefulness. The development of a new Western Line of Defense began in 1851 as a series of outposts running from present-day Jacksboro in north-central Texas to Brackettville in southwestern Texas. Most of the Western Line was established by 1856 but three other forts were added to it after the Civil War. The line included Forts Belknap, Richardson, Merrill, Griffin, Terrett, Phantom Hill, Concho, McKavett, Clark, Chadbourne, and Camp Cooper. In addition to the three lines of military posts, there were several miscellaneous forts scattered across the frontier in west-central and western Texas. These included Forts Mason, Davis, Stockton, Lancaster, and Camp Verde.

All of the frontier outposts actually were planned military

communities and cantonments rather than forts. They were not blockhouses and were not fortified against attack, although they usually were strategically placed and manned so as to discourage attacks—and none of the Texas forts ever were attacked by more than a few Indians. Some were large, rigorously arranged complexes of sturdy officers' quarters, enlisted men's barracks, quartermaster's stores, hospitals, powder magazines, bakeries, blacksmith's shops, and other facilities. Other outposts were smaller and much less substantially constructed. Fort structures were usually built with the materials available in the vicinity of the outposts, such as stone in the central Texas area and Mexican brick and adobe along the Rio Grande. Frame and picket (upright log) construction were used for most structures at the outposts. Buildings often were thrown up using more temporary materials, with the intention of making them more durable later.

Most of the earlier frontier military forts were abandoned during the Civil War. Afterward, these and new forts were occupied until Indian troubles ceased. The more isolated posts fell into ruin. Others were maintained as military posts into the twentieth century, particularly those in strategic places and those where towns grew up.

Historians and archeologists have researched all of the Texas frontier forts. The sites of some have been almost completely destroyed by relic collectors and by twentieth-century land uses. Several others have become State Historic Parks. Government reports, plans, and other records document the organization, personnel, and operation of the forts and provide some sketchy information about the military lifestyle on the frontier. Archeological investigation has become an important means of verifying this documentation and obtaining specific information about fort layouts and architecture. Most archeological work has been oriented toward recovering the details necessary for historic site restoration, but more recent investigations have begun to search for evidence of what life was like at the Texas frontier forts.

Recently, concerned citizens of the Uvalde area have begun the historical and archeological investigation and the preservation of Fort Inge, one of the forts of the Indian Frontier Line (Nelson 1981). The site of Fort Inge was neglected until after much of it was bulldozed in 1961. Finally, several local amateur archeologists

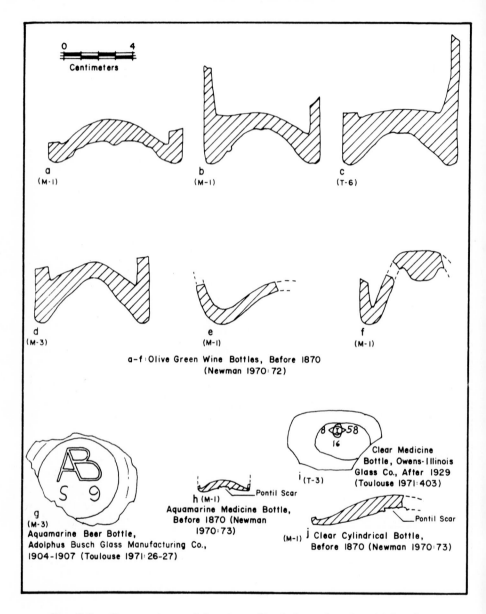

FIG. 9.9 *Cross sections and drawings of bottle bases from Fort McIntosh, Laredo, Webb County.* (From Fox 1979: Fig. 11. Courtesy Center for Archaeological Research, The University of Texas at San Antonio.)

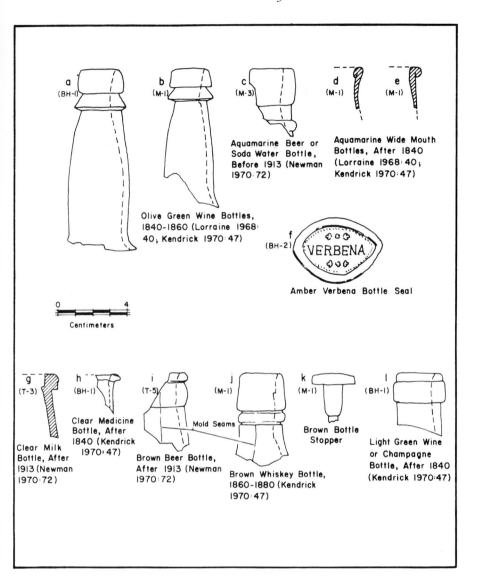

FIG. 9.10 *Drawings and cross sections of bottle necks and rims from Fort McIntosh, Laredo, Webb County.* (From Fox 1979: Fig. 12. Courtesy Center for Archaeological Research, The University of Texas at San Antonio.)

FIG. 9.11   *Some of the stone chimneys at the site of Fort Phantom Hill, Jones County.* (Courtesy Texas Historical Commission.)

and historians sponsored by the Uvalde County Historical Commission got the financial support with which to undertake preliminary archeological studies to determine the extent of the bulldozer damage, to locate structural features, and to evaluate the archeological potential of the fort site. The investigators also did a great deal of historical research and located several accounts documenting the occupation of Fort Inge and events that took place in the area before, during, and after the fort's existence as a military outpost.

The site's location has been known since the Spanish Colonial Period for a prominent hill, or pilot knob, nearby which juts above the prairie south of the Balcones Escarpment. This distinctive basalitic rock formation is evidence of volcanic activity that took place millions of years ago. The hill became a lookout and a point of reference for travellers through the area. The fort was established in 1849 on the bank of the Leona River at the foot of the pilot knob. It was named for Lieutenant Zebulon M. P. Inge who died at the Battle of Resaca de la Palma.

Tents probably were used by the first soldiers stationed at

Inge. In 1856, when Robert E. Lee visited the post, Fort Inge consisted of about a dozen buildings of various sizes arranged around a parade ground. The buildings were of *jacal* (log, stick, and mud construction) and of logs and stone, and were whitewashed and neatly kept. In the 1850's, the post had officers' quarters, a commissary building, a hospital, company quarters, a guard house, stables, a bakery, and probably other structures. The 1850 census lists officers and their families, enlisted men, musicians, herdsmen, a guide, a clerk, laundresses, a blacksmith, and others who were part of the community of Fort Inge. Across the Leona River from the fort was an encampment of Texas Rangers, laborers, herdsmen, farmers, and a stone mason. The post was temporarily abandoned several times. Confederate troops were stationed there during the Civil War. Federal troops returned in 1866 and Fort Inge remained in operation until its final abandonment as a U.S. military outpost in 1869.

Texas Rangers continued to use the fort site as an encampment off and on as late as the 1880's. In the 1870's, local farmers constructed a dam and an irrigation system on the Leona River using materials taken from the ruins of the fort structures. A huge flood devastated the area in 1895. Throughout the twentieth century the fort site has undergone continued disturbance. Until the importance of preserving the archeological deposits of Fort Inge was realized, unmanaged public use of the site as a county park resulted in additional damage.

FIG. 9.12 *Drawing of Fort Inge as it looked in 1867.* (From Nelson 1981: Fig. 18. Courtesy Uvalde County Historical Commission.)

The 1981 archeological investigations discovered foundation remains of several buildings and portions of a low stone wall that was built around the fort complex sometime shortly before or after the Civil War. Even though the investigation found that the fort site has been thoroughly disturbed, a large sample of military artifacts was recovered and several archeologically-sensitive areas were identified which can be preserved so that further historical and archeological research may still be able to reconstruct more of the history of this—one of the earliest U.S. military forts on the Texas frontier.

Fort McIntosh in present-day Laredo is an example of a frontier fort of the Rio Grande Line that has received preliminary archeological investigations. Officially established as Camp Crawford on March 3, 1849, and renamed on January 7, 1850, Fort McIntosh consisted mainly of tents during the first couple of years (Thompson 1974:165–166). By July, 1853, six frame two-story structures had been constructed (Crimmins 1950:204) and by November, 1853, 14 more frame structures had been added (National Archives 1853).

Like the other U.S. Army outposts on the Texas frontier, McIntosh was not a true fort, but by 1856 a defensive earthwork of the type known as a star fort had been constructed near the cantonment area. At that time, Fort McIntosh was occupied by four companies of infantry, two companies of mounted rifles, and one company of artillery (Crimmins 1939:228–239). The post was abandoned in March, 1859, and 30 of its buildings were put up for sale at public auction. But in February, 1860, Fort McIntosh was reoccupied because of Juan Cortina's raiding along the Rio Grande. Then it was abandoned again at the beginning of the Civil War.

After the war, the fort again was occupied and the construction of an entirely new post was begun. By 1875 Fort McIntosh had several stone, adobe, and wooden structures including a guardhouse, storehouses, stables, a hospital, corrals, officers' quarters, a blacksmith's shop, laundresses' quarters, and a small headquarters building (Conway 1963:571; U.S. Army Corps of Engineers 1876: 202–203). The fort continued to be improved with newer more permanently-built structures of brick beginning in the 1880's. Fort McIntosh was built up during World Wars I and II and then was officially closed as a U.S. military base in 1946. Today it is the campus of Laredo Junior College and Laredo State University.

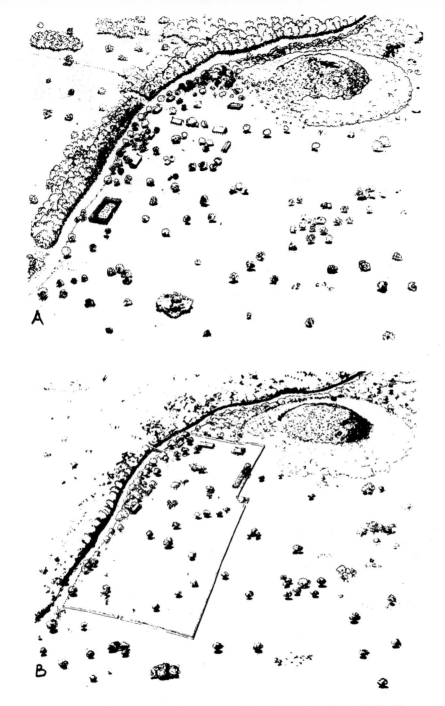

FIG. 9.13 *Bird's-eye views of Fort Inge, (A) in 1853 and (B) in 1867.* (From Nelson 1981:Fig. 26 and Fig. 27. Courtesy Uvalde County Historical Commission. Drawings by G. S. Nelson.)

In 1977, short-term archeological investigations were conducted at Fort McIntosh by archeologists from the Center for Archaeological Research, The University of Texas at San Antonio, and volunteers from the Laredo Junior College and University and the Webb County Archeological Society (Ivey, Medlin, and Eaton 1977; D. Fox 1979). The purpose of the investigations was to determine what archeological resources would be disturbed by a series of modifications proposed for the fort site. Initial surveys of the surface of the proposed construction areas found concentrations of artifacts dating from both the pre–Civil War and the post–Civil War forts, but limited subsurface testing found no evidence of the structures or preserved archeological deposits dating from the early fort. Because of the many decades of alteration of the fort grounds, it was feared that most, if not all, traces of the early fort had been obliterated by later construction episodes and related modifications to the fort site as it gradually became a part of the growing urban area of the city of Laredo.

But the initial test excavations did find evidence to suggest that thick layers of silt had been deposited on parts of the fort site by floods that have occurred since the time of the Civil War, and that remains of the early Fort McIntosh could be buried and not recognizable from surface inspection or by limited shallow subsurface testing. Intensive historical research was done in order to develop a map showing where traces of the earlier and later fort structures would be expected to occur. The archeologists were able to predict that in an area where a complex of tennis courts was proposed to be constructed evidence of the sutler's store might be found where a storekeeper was allowed to sell various provisions to the military men stationed at the post before the Civil War.

In an open area located away from the modern standing structures of the campus, in an area that had been the post garden in the late nineteenth century and where part of the athletic complex was proposed in the 1970's, archeological excavations found evidence of the pre–Civil War occupation of Fort McIntosh. But it was not so much in the form of structural remains as in the kinds and amounts of mid-nineteenth-century artifacts found concentrated in one particular spot.

The pre–Civil war dates of the artifact sample recovered by the test excavations and the relatively large proportions of food-, medicine-, and beverage-related materials indicated that the artifact concentration may have been the remains of the sutler's store. A large number of wine and other alcoholic beverage bottles, some fragments of clay tobacco pipes, and other kinds of artifacts that would be expected to occur in the area of such a business were found there. These findings enabled the investigators to predict that other evidence of pre-Civil War Fort McIntosh may be buried and preserved beneath flood deposits in undeveloped parts of the fort site, and recommendations were made that any necessary earth-moving activities proposed for those areas should be preceded by careful archeological investigation. More recent short-term archeological investigations of Fort McIntosh have come to the same conclusion (Alton K. Briggs, personal communication, October, 1982).

Most Texas frontier-fort archeology has been done at military posts of the Western Line of Defense. These sites are some of the better preserved and architecturally more impressive forts and many of them are now State Historic Parks. As with the other Texas frontier forts, most of the archeological research at outposts of the Western Line has focused on the retrieval of architectural information, the assessment of the condition of archeological deposits, and the definition of spacial limits of archeological and architectural features. Because of these research orientations, the results of most of the archeological investigations are rather technical, but important information recovered has been reported from investigations at Fort McKavett State Historic Site at the headwaters of the San Saba River in Menard County (Texas Parks and Wildlife Department 1977), at Fort Richardson State Historic Park at some natural springs near Jacksboro between Fort Worth and Wichita Falls (Dickson 1976; Westbury 1976), and at Fort Griffin State Historic Park on the Brazos River near Albany in Shackelford County (Olds 1969; A. Fox 1973, 1976).

Fort Griffin was first established as Camp Wilson in July, 1867, and was renamed in February, 1868, when it was moved from the bottomland along the Brazos up onto a nearby plateau (Rister 1956; Graham 1968). Arranged around an open parade ground, the post structures included tent barracks, huts, officers' quarters, and a commandant's residence—which was a log cabin that had been moved from a neighboring ranch. Except for the cabin, the first buildings at Griffin were of temporary picket con-

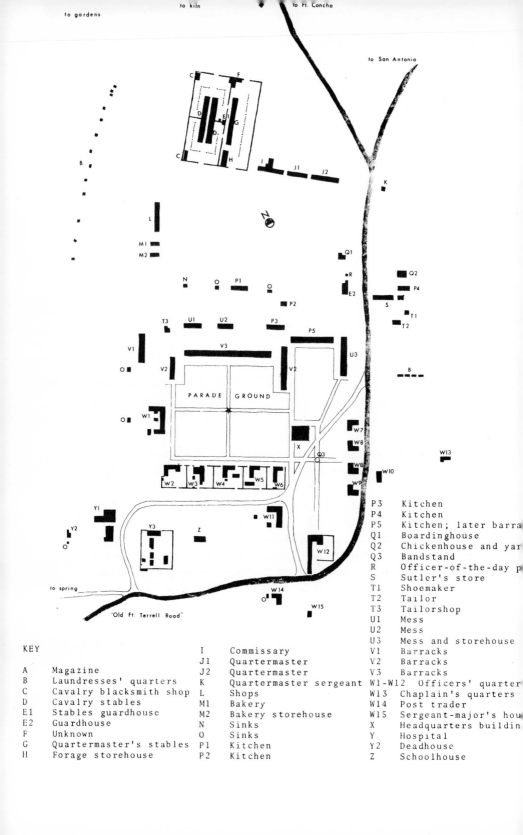

to gardens

to kiln   to Ft. Concho

to San Antonio

N

PARADE GROUND

to spring

"Old Ft. Terrell Road"

P3   Kitchen
P4   Kitchen
P5   Kitchen; later barra
Q1   Boardinghouse
Q2   Chickenhouse and yar
Q3   Bandstand
R   Officer-of-the-day p
S   Sutler's store
T1   Shoemaker
T2   Tailor
T3   Tailorshop
U1   Mess
U2   Mess
U3   Mess and storehouse
V1   Barracks
V2   Barracks
V3   Barracks
W1-W12 Officers' quarter
W13   Chaplain's quarters
W14   Post trader
W15   Sergeant-major's hou
X   Headquarters buildin
Y   Hospital
Y2   Deadhouse
Z   Schoolhouse

KEY

A   Magazine
B   Laundresses' quarters
C   Cavalry blacksmith shop
D   Cavalry stables
E1   Stables guardhouse
E2   Guardhouse
F   Unknown
G   Quartermaster's stables
H   Forage storehouse

I   Commissary
J1   Quartermaster
J2   Quartermaster
K   Quartermaster sergeant
L   Shops
M1   Bakery
M2   Bakery storehouse
N   Sinks
O   Sinks
P1   Kitchen
P2   Kitchen

struction with walls of vertical logs hastily erected in trenches and covered with roofs of sod or canvas. After a sawmill was brought in from the military depot at San Antonio, the picket buildings were gradually replaced with more substantial structures of rough-sawn lumber. The board walls were chinked and plastered, and most of the buildings had shingle roofs. The Army intended to construct even more permanent stone structures. Some masonry buildings were completed, but most of the frame and plaster structures remained until the fort was abandoned in 1881.

In the 1870's, Fort Griffin was similar to other frontier military outposts and had series of barracks, officers' quarters, headquarters buildings, a post library, a school and chapel complex, blacksmith and carpenter's shops, a powder magazine, sheds and stables, and other military buildings, as well as laundresses' quarters and a sutler's store (Graham 1968:18). After the post was abandoned, many of the structures fell into decay. In 1905 not many of its landmarks remained (Biggers 1974:131). Some of the more substantial structures were still standing. The stone adjutant's office was being occupied as a ranch residence. The old stone magazine was serving as a barn.

From the time Fort Griffin was abandoned, it was of interest to historians, journalists, architects, and archeologists. In the early 1940's, a crew of the Civilian Conservation Corps spent more than a year excavating the fort site (Beard n.d.). In the 1960's, brush-clearing of the method known as chaining (one of the most destructive to archeological sites) eliminated or scattered most of the architectural features that were there in the 1940's. This disturbance to the fort was confirmed by archeological investigations carried out in 1969, 1971, and 1973 by the Texas Parks and Wildlife Department. Following these preliminary investigations, an archeological project was funded in 1976 to accurately map and permanently mark the historic features of the fort that had been or could be relocated, including the gravel pathways and the corners of the buildings of enlisted men's huts and mess hall complex, the pathways and building corners of three groups of officers' quar-

FIG. 9.14 *Plan map of Fort McKavett, Menard County.* (From Taniguchi *et al.* 1968:Fig. 1. Courtesy Texas Parks and Wildlife Department. Prepared by the School of Architecture, The University of Texas at Austin.)

FIG. 9.15   Old photograph of Fort McKavett in the 1890's, a few years after it was abandoned as a frontier military post. (Courtesy Texas Parks and Wildlife Department.)

ters, foundation remains of other buildings on one end of the parade ground, and the grave plots of a civilian cemetery at the fort site (A. Fox 1976).

One of the more interesting areas studied at Fort Griffin was the civilian cemetery, located not far from the fort's military cemetery but apparently not related to it. When the archeologists began to clear away the brush and weeds, it looked like a typical small family plot, similar to hundreds of other nineteenth-century cemeteries scattered throughout Texas. But when the clearing and mapping were completed, more than 50 graves and possible graves had been plotted. More were marked with simple tombstones, others by mounds of rock, and some were only recognizable as depressions in the ground surface. A few were covered by carefully constructed rock crypts, or cairns.

On the low mound of earth that covered one grave, rodent burrows had exposed more than 2,000 glass trade beads of various shapes and colors, two shell hair ornaments with traces of vermillion paint on them, six metal bells of the "hawk" type commonly found as Indian trade goods, a spherical brass button, coffin nails, wood screws, and a few fragments of human bone. Among the possible explanations for this grave is that it was the burial of an Indian who died away from his home and his people, or a trapper or trader who preferred to wear Indian clothing, or perhaps the Indian wife of a local man. The historical accounts and archeological information gathered suggest that the cemetery was the "boot hill" associated with the town of Fort Griffin that grew

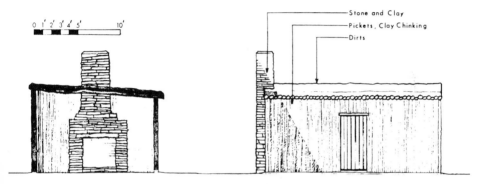

TEMPORARY PICKET COTTAGE

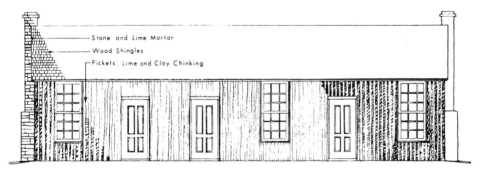

PERMANENT PICKET COTTAGE

FIG. 9.16 *Architectural details of picket buildings constructed at frontier forts.* Types of construction probably varied from fort to fort, depending upon locally available materials. (From Taniguchi *et al.* 1968. Courtesy Texas Parks and Wildlife Department. Prepared by the School of Architecture, The University of Texas at Austin.)

up around the military outpost. The history of Fort Griffin indicates that there was a need for a cemetery for the gunfighters, transients, and other riffraff of the frontier community, which had been referred to as the "Sodom of the Plains" (Metz 1966:48). One description of the town states that in a 12-year period 35 men had been killed "publicly," eight or ten others had been found dead, and 12 more had been shot or strung-up by law enforcement officers and vigilantes (Rister 1956:146).

By the 1850's, the basic pattern of military outposts had been created for defense against the Indians on the frontier. But the gold strike in California encouraged a rapid westward migration of settlers that necessitated more protection for travellers and supplies moving along the road from San Antonio to El Paso. One of the military outposts that were established to meet this need was Fort Lancaster, located on Live Oak Creek near the Pecos River crossing.

Established in August, 1856, Lancaster consisted of temporary picket and adobe structures and Turnley Portable Cottages, which were prefabricated wooden buildings designed for use by troops in Texas, New Mexico, and Arizona (Tanaguchi, *et al.* 1968; Francell 1969:60; Black 1974:5–6). In 1857, most of the fort's personnel still were living in temporary quarters, but the more permanent structures required by Army regulations were under construction. Stone and adobe buildings housed the officer's quarters, mess halls, and company kitchens. Although the soldiers had problems finding construction materials on the remote West Texas frontier, by 1860 most of Lancaster's 27 buildings had been constructed of stone and adobe bricks, some thatched and others shingled. But then the fort was abandoned by U.S. Army troops when the federal military bases in Texas were surrendered at the beginning of the Civil War.

A garrison of Confederate troops occupied Fort Lancaster during the first year of the War. After the War, the post was used sporadically as a U.S. military substation until it was finally abandoned in 1875. During the late nineteenth century, Lancaster's buildings fell into ruin and by 1912 only a few partial walls, a chimney, and wall foundations were visible on the rugged, rocky landscape of creosote and mesquite bushes, yuccas, cacti, and burro grass of Trans-Pecos Texas. The fort site was deeded to

FIG. 9.17. *Historic photograph of Fort Richardson in the 1870's, showing picket officers' quarters buildings.* (Courtesy Texas Parks and Wildlife Department.)

Crockett County in 1965 and in 1968 it was donated to the Texas Parks and Wildlife Department.

A series of archeological investigations of the Fort Lancaster ruins began in 1966, when archeologists from Southern Methodist University searched for architectural details and other archeological information which could be used in the development of the fort site as a historic park (Hays and Jelks 1966). At that time, the visible remains of the fort consisted of the heaps of stone and adobe rubble from 29 buildings, a limekiln dug into the ground, a cemetery, and several trash dumps. In addition to the larger, historically-documented structures, several masonry ruins were discovered which turned out to be the foundations for latrines. The archeological investigation focused on a masonry barracks ruin, but small test excavations were placed in four other ruins. Three of the latrines were excavated which yielded an interesting assortment of bottles, dishes, tools, and other artifacts that had been used and discarded by the occupants of the frontier outpost.

Various details of the architectural and occupational history of the stone barracks and other buildings were recovered during the 1966 excavations that could be used in an authentic reconstruction of the structures. The investigations found that the structures studied had been burned. The evidence indicated that the barracks building had a roof of sacahuisti thatch when it burned, although an 1860 map of the fort refers to the structure as having a shingle roof. Either the 1860 map was in error or the shingles were replaced with thatch after the map was drawn. One of the two rooms of the stone barracks ruin apparently was reoccupied temporarily after the building burned, possibly when the military outpost was used after the Civil War. Some of the fallen debris from the fire was cleared, an adobe floor and an adobe partition wall were added, and the old passageway between the two original rooms was sealed with adobe bricks. In the late nineteenth century, settlers in the area tore down the structure's walls to get building stones, leaving only piles of rubble and the lower portions of the walls.

In the 1970's a series of archeological investigations were conducted at Fort Lancaster by archeologists working with the Texas Parks and Wildlife Department (Clark 1972; Lorrain n.d.; Black 1974). Again, the studies were done to recover architectural information, but samples of artifacts were recovered that helped detail the occupational histories of the different fort structures investigated and the activities that took place in them. Artifacts such as military uniform buttons and ornaments, percussion caps and other firearm-related items, and numerous fragments of liquor, wine, and patent medicine bottles were typically found in enlisted men's barracks. From the ruins of an officer's quarters building, artifacts were recovered that indicated food preparation and dining and the storage and mending of men's and women's clothing took place in one room, while pipe-smoking, cleaning, and servicing of firearms, and other male-associated activities were restricted to the other room of the building (Black 1974:119–120).

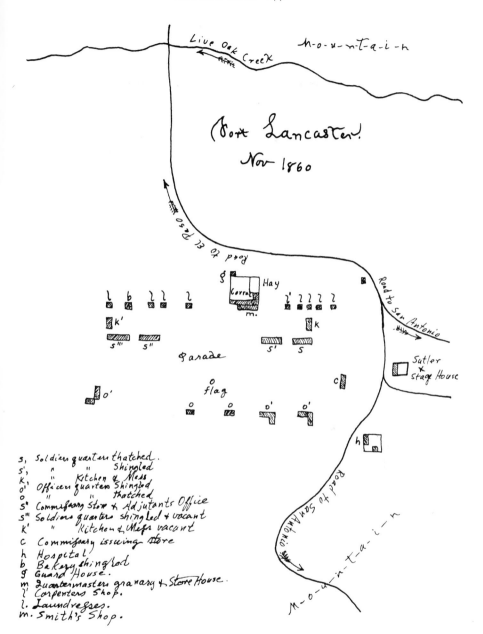

FIG. 9.18   *Sketch map of Fort Lancaster, Crockett County, made in 1860, traced from copy of the original in the U.S. National Archives. (From Hays and Jelks 1966: Fig. 1. Courtesy Texas Historical Commission.)*

FIG. 9.19   *The ruins of Fort Lancaster, Crockett County.* (From Hays and Jelks 1966: Frontispiece. Courtesy Texas Historical Commission. Drawing by Gene Mobley.)

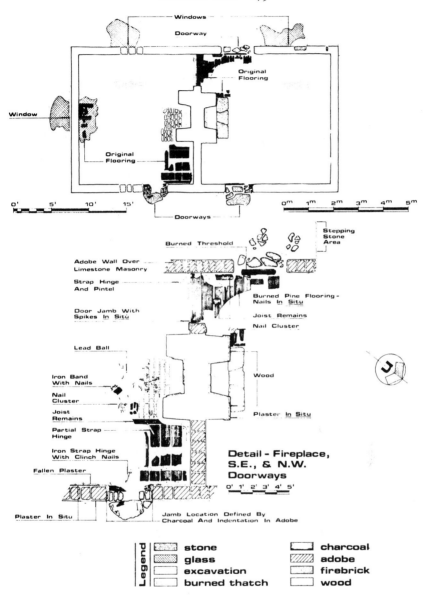

Bldg. 9   Officers' Quarters

FIG. 9.20   *Plan of architectural and archeological features at one of the ruins, Fort Lancaster, Crockett County.* (From Black 1974:Fig. 23. Courtesy Texas Parks and Wildlife Department.)

Besides the larger and better-known Texas frontier forts of the second half of the nineteenth century, there were also sub-posts created to fill in the spaces between forts, particularly in the more remote, untamed areas. Probably because of their remote locations and because they are not as well known, the historic sites of the sub-posts of the Army's frontier defense system have not attracted as much destruction by vandals and relic hunters as have the major fort sites. An excellent example is the site of Camp Peña Colorado, which was one of the last U.S. Army outposts established on the Texas frontier and which provided the focus for a civilian settlement that grew to become the present-day town of Marathon (Guffee 1976).

Camp Peña Colorado was established in August of 1879, during the last years of the Army's war with the Apache, to provide

FIG. 9.21 *Map of military roads of western, or Trans-Pecos, Texas, in the 1880's.* (From Guffee 1976: Fig. 3. Courtesy E. J. Guffee.)

labor forces and protection for the construction of a new military road which led southeastward from Fort Davis toward Del Rio on the Rio Grande. Following this route, the Galveston, Harrisburg, and San Antonio Railroad was built three years later to meet the Southern Pacific as its construction moved eastward from California. Peña Colorado Creek provided the only reliable water source between Fort Stockton and the Rio Grande.

As with some of the other frontier forts, the Peña Colorado military reservation occupied land that was leased from private landowners. Isolated as it was from civilization, the sub-post's structures had to be built with local materials. An Army company commander described what Camp Peña Colorado looked like in July, 1880:

> We found there several soldier-made mud and stone huts, roofed with mud and grass and the rainy season was just beginning. We repaired and completed these buildings the best we could . . . The men were housed in two long narrow huts, facing two others in which Lieutenant Augur and I lived. The officers' quarters were of one room each. We roofed over the four walls of a structure of stone on the third side of the square, and used it as a storehouse (Crane 1923:106).

Because the Army companies stationed at the sub-post were rotated frequently and because the soldiers' labor often was diverted to the construction of the road and patrolling the frontier, it was several years before permanent stone and wood buildings replaced the tents, lean-tos, and rock huts that were the original Camp Peña Colorado.

But as isolated and temporary as the sub-post was, Camp Peña Colorado outlived its mother posts. Fort Stockton was abandoned in 1886 and Fort Davis in 1891. After the final removal of the Apache from the Trans-Pecos area in the 1880's, the soldiers of Camp Peña Colorado became the principal law enforcement officers between the railroad and the Rio Grande, where the vastness of the country made it possible for bandits, smugglers, and outlaws to elude capture. Some of the Seminole Negro Indian scouts who rendered service with federal troops in western Texas spent time at Camp Peña Colorado in the 1880's (Leckie 1967:238). Finally, on February 10, 1893, the sub-post was abandoned.

When historian and archeologist Eddie Guffee studied the site of Camp Peña Colorado in the 1960's and the 1970's, he found that

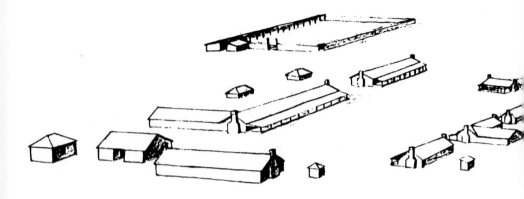

FIG. 9.22 *Reconstruction of the appearance of Camp Peña Colorado, Brewster County, in 1892.* (From Guffee 1976: Fig. 9. Courtesy E. J. Guffee.)

the post had been occupied by ranchers and their families since it was abandoned as a military outpost (Guffee 1976:117–125). Some of the original post structures had become residences and ranch buildings. One resident of the post site in the 1970's was a ranch manager and the grandson of a Seminole Negro Indian scout. He lived in the only one of the three officers' quarters remaining on one side of the old parade ground. The stone hospital was still standing. Portions of the post corral were intact, and even though the other post buildings had collapsed or been torn down, their positions were marked by stone foundations, rubble, and artifacts.

The ruins of Camp Peña Colorado have not been archeologically excavated, but Guffee conducted a detailed survey of the surface of the site and carefully collected samples of artifacts, some of which were manufactured during the Civil War. The densities of different types of artifacts and their spacial relationships to structural features made it possible to identify specific activity areas and the functions of different post building ruins. For example, a concentration of cannon friction primers on the southern edge of the site marked the position of the three-inch field rifle that one of the post commanders managed to procure in 1888.

The most common artifacts found were cartridge cases, most of which were caliber .45-.55 for use in the model 1873 Springfield single-shot carbine, but also included shell cases from various sorts of small-arms ammunition produced throughout the last quarter of the nineteenth century. Also found on the surface of the historic site were metal canteens, brass cavalry spurs, military buttons, and even a metal field safe. The remains of various post features were located, including the administration building, the guard house, the mess hall, enlisted men's barracks, and latrines. On the edges of the site were the remains of the post cemeteries for black and for white soldiers, the dump ground, the target range, and the ruins of the saloon that was of so much concern to the commanding officers when it was in operation, off and on, in 1889 and 1890.

The Texas forts are valuable as cultural resources for the comparative information they contain. Architectural information and artifact samples can be associated with specific functions and time periods at fort sites and can be used as comparative data for the identification and interpretation of non-military frontier homesteads and settlements of the same approximate time periods. Methods of stone, frame, canvas, picket, and adobe construction employed at the forts were adapted to local conditions and sometimes involved civilian labor and expertise. Food, household, and personal goods and other necessities were procured from many of the same depots and markets that supplied other frontier communities.

The assemblage of material culture of Texas forts includes the typical ceramic, glass, and metal of the period from about 1850 to the 1880's. Brightly-decorated, British-made, white paste earthenwares, characteristic of pre-Civil War occupation, include edged, hand-painted, transfer-printed, and blue flown wares. Other decorated types such as mocha, or banded, wares and sponged wares probably were used before and for a short time after the Civil War. After about 1860, the market became flooded with undecorated ironstone china, the most common ceramic wares at the forts. Sherds of porcelain and stoneware crockery vessels also occur. Occasional sherds of Mexican-made tin-enameled and lead-glazed pottery are found at fort sites near the Mexican border.

Bottle glass at the forts is indicative of the period just before and after the invention of the snap case which superseded the use of the pontil in the manufacture of glass bottles. Except for an occasional free-blown vessel, most bottles from the forts have molded bases and bodies and hand-finished necks and rims. Numerous cylindrical and lettered-panel bottles represent the popularity of patent medicines during and after the Civil War.

Square nails, agate-ware door knobs, hinges, locks and windowpane glass are common at frontier forts. Personal items include clay tobacco pipes of various forms, coins, clothing fasteners, pen knives, pins, and thimbles. Harness trappings and stove parts also are common. The military nature of the outposts is reflected in the layout of structures and their standardized nature of construction, by uniform buttons and insignia, by military bridle parts, and by weapon-related items such as lead balls, percussion caps, and cartridge cases dating from the second half of the nineteenth century.

Each kind of artifact is indicative of details about fort construction, the function of different post structures, the way the inhabitants dressed and what they ate. The relative frequencies at which various characteristic kinds of artifacts occur reflect the life styles at the frontier military outposts. Perhaps the most easily recognizable pastime of the soldiers is indicated by the large quantity and variety of alcoholic beverage bottles found at every fort site. At Fort McIntosh in 1856, Colonel J. K. F. Mansfield observed (Crimmins 1939:237):

There is a sutler at this post, and as at other posts is permitted to sell ardent spirits. The regulations forbid the sutler to sell ardent spirits, but the disregard of it, is excused on the ground that others would hover around in the vicinity of the post and sell liquor to the men, and that it was better for them to obtain it of the sutler. The regulation should either be rescinded or enforced. Beer, cheap wine or cider would be a very good substitute for strong drink and no doubt satisfy all the wants of the men who have been brought up to drink habitually.

There probably was some variation in the quality of accommodations at a frontier fort based upon rank. Officers, of course, had more comfortable quarters and probably greater access to finer things than the enlisted men. But post personnel as a community encountered hostile Indians and desperados and endured bad weather and other discomforts of life in desolate places. The documentary records and the archeological evidence seem to indicate that the soldiers at Texas' frontier forts lived a routine of daily activities, boredom, and booze.

X

Early Industries
and Factories

By THE MID-NINETEENTH CENTURY, the Texas cotton industry was established and the cattle industry began its development. They became the means by which the young Texas Empire reached out to tap the markets in the industrializing regions of the United States and the already industrialized nations of Europe. After the Civil War, the state's population continued to grow, the ranching industry boomed, and the frontier pushed westward.

But while Texans were recovering from the War and the Texan way of life was being carried into new territories, the state was being invaded by powerful interests that sought to remove state sovereignty over politics, economics, and social organization. The railroads came in, as did waves of immigrants who settled the vacant and unused lands and moved into the growing urban areas. Soon the state's varied natural resources and growing labor markets became accessible to exploitation from the outside. By the late nineteenth century, the cotton and cattle kingdoms of Texas were made tributary to American industrialized society (Fehrenbach 1968:603; Meinig 1969:63–64).

Before the War and the railroads, many of the staple foods, livestock, construction materials, and other basic commodities necessary to sustain the settlement of Texas were processed or manufactured for local and regional markets by small-scale household and community industries. The distance separating Texas from the industrial centers of the western world and the pressing need for basic subsistence goods on the frontier demanded a great deal of self-sufficiency in early Texas settlements. The development of local industries also was encouraged by the high cost of imported goods. Several small-scale processing and manufacturing operations were a part of Spanish Colonial settlement in Texas and were reinstituted during the frontier settlement of American Texas, such as grain- and flour-milling, salt-mining, sugar-

FIG. 10.1 *Industrial and urban sites, 1860's–1880's.*

refining, and the production of lime mortar, bricks, and other building materials. While these local industries increased in number and were technologically improved, home-based production of wine, beer, furniture, pottery, and other commodities also became an established part of the predominantly rural, agrarian economy of antebellum Texas.

The Civil War weakened ties between Texas and the industrial centers of the western world that had supplied many of the goods necessary for the early growth and development of the Republic (Webb 1964:8–13). Most of Texas' home-based and community-based industrial operations had to be geared up, expanded, and adapted during the War for the manufacture and processing of the goods needed to maintain daily life and for military supplies to support the Confederate war effort.

The poverty and environmental destruction in the South that resulted from the Civil War encouraged the movement of large numbers of Anglo-American immigrants into Texas' growing towns and cities (Jordan 1966:75). With this growth of large, concentrated labor markets, combined with the development of the railroads as the ultimate in efficient and reliable transportation, and with the arrival of new sources of power and new methods of production, the setting was created for the establishment of the first full-scale urban-industrial complexes in the last part of the nineteenth century. Most home- and community-based industries were abandoned by then because they could not compete with large-scale, highly capitalized industrial operations that produced less expensive goods in much larger quantities and could distribute their products rapidly to a wide variety of markets.

Arrival of the telegraph and telephone allowed the separation of transportation and communication; it became possible to operate widespread businesses from a central location. Rural areas ceased to be self-sufficient and became more and more closely tied to urban centers as agricultural production became specialized for urban markets and, in exchange, goods mass-produced by urban industries were distributed throughout the countryside.

Economic Change in Rural Areas

The historical development of rural economies is being studied historically and archeologically in the Upper Trinity River Basin of north-central Texas. The pattern there advanced from settlement based upon cash crop farming, cotton plantations, and a reliance on river navigation before the Civil War, to tenant farming, lumbering, and the establishment of railroad transportation in the late nineteenth century, and then to an agribusiness period of urban growth, automotive transportation, mining and beef and hay production in the twentieth century (Richner and Lee 1976, 1977; Richner and Bagot 1978; Guderjan 1981; Skinner 1982). By the end of the nineteenth century, Dallas and the other cities of the Grand Prairie became intertwined with the markets of the North; as urban and industrial centers they began to rival Houston and Galveston, which already were growing rapidly because of their early links by rail and by sea to the expanding markets of the industrialized northeastern United States and Europe (Meinig 1969:74–76).

The history and archeology of the Lower Frio River Valley present a story of change in rural South Texas economies which have been based upon cattle-ranching since the 1850's, when the area was first settled (Lynn, Fox, and O'Malley 1977; Everett 1981; Bandy 1981; A. Fox n.d.a). Immigration from south of the Rio Grande reinforced Hispanic ranching traditions and influenced the development of various characteristics of South Texas culture. A sheep and wool industry grew up in southern Texas during the 1870's, but it soon ended because of overgrazing and the accompanying infestation of the rangelands with brush and predators. During the 1880's, the open range was being fenced with barbed wire. The great cattle drives ceased and the settlement pattern in southern Texas became one of large family-owned cattle ranches and small towns with increasing Hispanic populations, usually dominated politically and economically by Anglo-Americans.

But since the beginning of settlement of the Lower Frio River Valley in the mid-nineteenth century, community closeness provided for most of the needs of individual community members, regardless of ethnic background, religion, or socioeconomic status. This community self-sufficiency, which was necessary for *physical* survival during the nineteenth century, became necessary for *cultural* survival during the twentieth century as powerful private and public corporations, with their lakes, strip mines, super highways, and petroleum recovery operations, began to open huge holes in the brush and expose the distinctive communities of South Texas to rapid integration into American industrialized society.

Transportation

With continued westward settlement after the Civil War and the beginnings of urbanization and industrialization of the settled areas of Texas, railroads were extended into traditionally agricultural areas and across remote frontier regions. San Antonio was

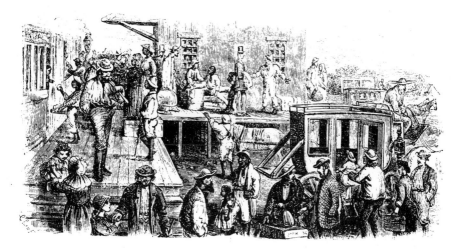

FIG. 10.2   *J. W. Champney's drawing of a railroad depot in Texas in 1874, crowded with "negros, immigrants, tourists, and speculators."* (From King 1974.)

connected to the growing network of railroads in the late 1870's. By 1881, Laredo became a major market on the railway systems that linked Mexico and Texas (Fehrenbach 1968:604–605; Wilkinson 1975:362–379). The idea of building a railroad to bring California closer to the eastern United States was considered as early as the 1840's by the U.S. Congress but was put aside during the Civil War. The first transcontinental railroad was completed in Utah in 1869. After the new southern transcontinental was joined in Texas in 1883, the state became permanently tied to the rest of America and traditional territorial relationships were rearranged.

The construction of the Southern Pacific Railroad across western and southwestern Texas was accomplished by laborers of various nationalities, including a large work force of Chinese immigrants. Over-population, natural disasters, and political strife in China combined with economic opportunities in California to encourage the emigration of large numbers of Chinese peoples during the 1850's and the 1860's. Although many of them found employment and established businesses in the growing cities and towns, hundreds of Chinese immigrants were put to work as laborers in the mines and on the railroads in the West.

Beginning in 1969, an anthropology student from The University of Texas at Austin undertook an intensive historical and

FIG. 10.3   *Theodore Gentilz's "San Francisco de la Espada," showing the ruins of San Antonio's Mission Espada in the mid-nineteenth century.* Oxcarts like the one pictured here were the principal form of freight transportation in southern Texas until the railroads arrived after the Civil War. (Courtesy Library of the Daughters of the Republic of Texas at the Alamo, San Antonio.)

archeological investigation of two camps that were occupied in 1882 by Chinese and Anglo-American railroad workers on the Southern Pacific in southwestern Texas (Briggs 1974). One habitation area was located near Langtry on the Stockton Plateau west of the Pecos River, near the old roadbed of the Langtry Cut-Off that was abandoned in 1925. The other campsite was about 16 miles down the line, across the Pecos on the Edwards Plateau, and presumably was related to the construction of the Upper Rio Grande

Tunnel Number One, which was abandoned after the Pecos River Viaduct was completed in 1892. Most of the archeological field-work. involved careful mapping of topographic and architectural features, and controlled, systematic collection of samples of artifacts that were exposed on the arid, rocky surfaces of the railroad camps.

Tent outlines, ruins of stone masonry and half-dugout structures, hearths, and artifact concentrations were the typical occupational features found at the railroad camps. Except for the remains of blacksmith's shops located away from the main living areas, little evidence of activity was found that was directly associated with the railroad construction. The artifacts sampled represented the domestic activities of more than 500 temporary residents at the Langtry Camp and more than 240 at the Upper Rio Grande Tunnel Number One Camp. The patterning in which certain kinds of occupational features and artifacts occurred marked the arrangement of various activity areas within the camps and reflected the consideration that was given to site drainage and prevailing wind patterns in planning the locations of living quarters, fire hearths, livestock pens, and other facilities.

The segregation of Anglo-Americans and Chinese into different camps was observable in the kinds and amounts of American- and European-made artifacts found at the Upper Rio Grande Tunnel Number One Camp versus the numbers of Chinese-made objects and materials and occupational features adapted to characteristically Chinese uses at the Langtry Camp. The Anglo-American occupation areas were identifiable by firearm-related artifacts, by collections of predominantly American- and European-made ceramic tablewares, and by the predictable frequency of occurrence of other typically American artifacts. Imported Chinese goods, such as eating and cooking utensils, preserving jars, and opium vapor inhaler bowls, were found as evidence of the maintenance of culturally traditional diet, medicines, and drug use. But other artifacts indicated that the Chinese workers had adopted European clothing, carried their belongings in carpetbags, and consumed various kinds of American foodstuffs and beverages.

The study of the Anglo-American campsite found the remains of habitation areas where tents and half-dugouts were located, many of which apparently were occupied by family groups.

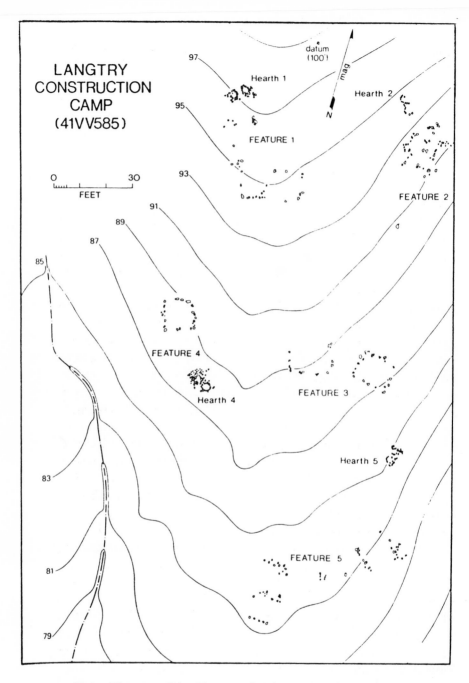

FIG. 10.4 *Plan map of the Chinese railroad camp near the Rio Grande in Val Verde County.* (From Briggs 1974: Fig. 8. Courtesy Lone Star Archeological Services.)

Also found were business activity areas where a restaurant-saloon, an administration building, a hotel, a general store, and a possible infirmary were located, and the locations of a blacksmith's forge and livestock pens. The spacial arrangement of features and artifacts at the Chinese campsite reflected a denser, more orderly residential pattern in which the workers lived in separate groups, each with its own special staff hired to meet the domestic needs such as cooking, laundry, and housekeeping. The distribution of archeological materials indicated that the Chinese camp was much more neatly kept than the Anglo-American campsite.

Despite the ethnic differences observable between the two railroad camps, similarities were found in the evidence of general kinds of maintenance activities that took place and the rates at which artifacts occurred that represented each maintenance activity. Artifacts related to food supply and food preparation comprised as much as one-half of the artifact collections from each campsite. Hardware related to the construction and maintenance of shelters and equipment comprised the next largest category, followed by medicine and drugs, then clothing, water supply, and so on. Regardless of ethnic differences in the ways each camp was occupied, the major objective of both settlement systems was to subsist as comfortably as possible in a harsh, desolate environment.

Other historic sites of Texas' developing transportation networks that were necessary for industrialization and urbanization have been preserved, although few of them have been studied archeologically. Bridges, fords, and other sorts of early highway crossings have been found during historical and archeological surveys in various parts of the state.

Preliminary archeological studies were incorporated into the planning for the recent development of a public park in downtown Waco, where the first suspension bridge ever built in Texas still spans the Brazos River (D. Fox 1979). The bridge was built in 1870, when Waco was beginning its recovery from the Civil War and the booming cattle industry replaced the cash crop production of slave plantations as the basis of the area's commerce. It was the longest suspension bridge in the world in those days, and being the only bridge across the Brazos, it channelled movement along the Chisholm Trail and other overland routes into Waco. The bridge, with its long roadway suspended from a system of thick

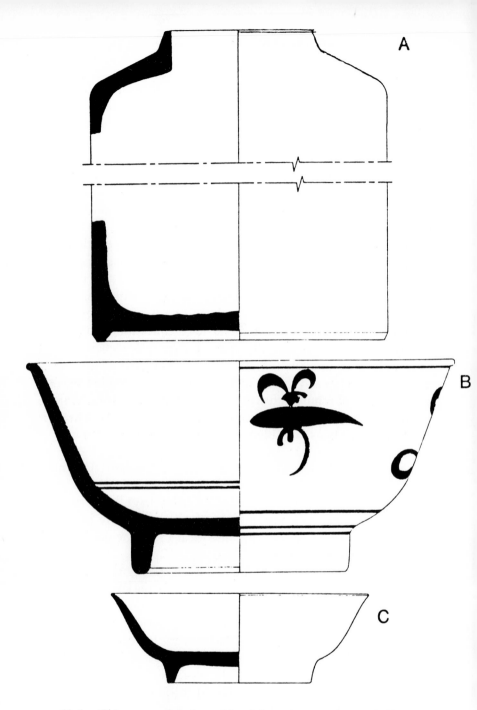

FIG. 10.5 *Chinese porcelain jar and bowl forms (cross sections and side views), found at the Chinese railroad camps of Val Verde County.* (From Briggs 1974: Fig. 11. Courtesy Lone Star Archeological Services.)

wire cables secured at massive brick anchor houses on each shoreline, must have amazed visitors to the growing frontier city.

Archeological test excavations found that fill deposits around
various ·parts of the structural complex on both river banks contain material evidence that can be used to help document the construction and maintenance of the bridge and the urban development of the neighborhood around it. For example, the excavations
found wall footings for a brick structure that was attached to one
of the cable anchor houses. Household artifacts found in soil layers
that accumulated while the building was standing indicated that
it may have been occupied as the living quarters of the bridge's
tollkeeper.

Construction Materials

Lumbering and lumber-milling reached maturity as a major
industry in Texas after the railroads penetrated the pineywoods of
eastern Texas in the 1880's. Of course, lumbering on a local scale
was carried on long before that, where logs and milled lumber
were needed for the construction of frontier farmsteads and town
buildings (Easton 1947). Sawmills became important attachments
to water-powered gristmills before and after the Civil War.

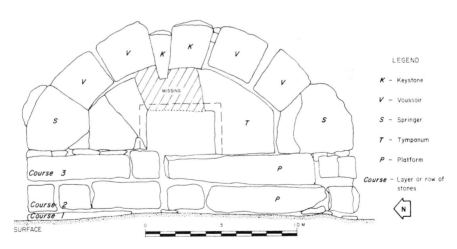

FIG. 10.6   *Details of a baking oven used by railroad construction workers east
of the Pecos River in Val Verde County in the 1880's.* (From Patterson
1980:Fig. 9. Courtesy Texas Department of Highways and Public
Transportation.)

FIG. 10.7 *The Waco Suspension Bridge, Waco.* (Courtesy Center for Archaeological Research, The University of Texas at San Antonio.)

In the Wallisville Lake area on the Lower Trinity River in southeastern Texas, the site of the turn-of-the-century Cummings Lumber Mill has been investigated archeologically (Fox, Day, and Highley 1980:142–149). The construction of a roadway in recent years destroyed most of the remains of the boarding houses and other structures associated with the mill complex. But the brick mill foundations, a mounded dump area of ashes, charcoal, and rusted metal, brick wall ruins of various structures, and foundations for the steam boiler that powered the sawmill have been located and mapped so that they can be preserved for future study of the early Texas lumber industry. In the Sabine National Forest in deep eastern Texas, a study has been made of the earthworks for an early railroad tramway that was a part of logging operations between 1890 and the 1920's (Skinner 1979).

The manufacture of other sorts of building materials began as small-scale industries in Spanish Colonial Texas and developed again on the early nineteenth-century frontier. Limekilns were common local features in settlement areas where limestone and the fuel to burn it were readily available. Limekilns usually are found as bell-shaped chambers, lined with stone masonry and built into creek banks. This left the lower parts of the kilns easily accessible and their fires could be fuelled to maintain the intense heat necessary to break down the limestone piled inside. A series of Spanish Colonial Period limekilns of this sort have been found in the river bank near Mission Espada in San Antonio (A. Fox 1970; Killen and Scurlock n.d.).

A variety of limekilns dating from the nineteenth century and the early twentieth century have been found in creek banks in the Hill Country of central Texas. Many of them are located in rural settlement areas where they could be shared as needed by different families or as community endeavors (Malone and Fox n.d.). An interesting limekiln site that deviates from the usual pattern has been investigated in northern Bexar County (A. Fox n.d.b). Instead of one or two small separate kiln features built into a creek bank, this industrial complex consisted of three large stone-lined chambers that had been dug into the bedrock on the top of a hill. An associated chamber, with steps leading down into it, provided access to the lower parts of the kilns so that their fires could be stoked and the burned lime and ash could be removed. The kiln chambers were much larger than usual, indicating that the complex may have been a commercial operation. Railroad rails were used for the grates that supported the limestone in the kilns. The rails had been deformed by the intense heat of the furnaces.

Like lumbering and mortar production, brick-making was an early Texas industry that developed in response to urbanization's demand for building materials. Brickyards and brick kilns have been found in various areas where the right clays occurred and the fuel was available to burn it, and where transportation networks brought markets within reach, such as along the bayous east of the Houston-Galveston area.

One 1870's brickyard, the Almeras Brick Works in the Lower Trinity River area, has received preliminary archeological investigation (Fox, Day, and Highley 1980:157–161). Test excavations placed in the ruins of one of the Almeras kilns found that the structure was about 35 feet square and had massive walls of hand-formed bricks. A large depression a short distance away probably

FIG. 10.8 *Documenting a lime kiln in the Texas Hill Country.* (Courtesy Texas Historical Commission.)

was a cistern used to store water for the brick-making operation. Intensely burned spots found near the brickyard features may mark areas where charcoal was manufactured as another commercial product of the brickyard. The bricks and charcoal probably were transported on barges and other sorts of watercraft to the growing metropolitan areas down the coastline.

Closer to Houston and Galveston, nineteenth-century brickyards have been found as large complexes of massive ruins of brick kilns, huge open cisterns, and associated brick foundations that look like ancient Mayan ruins covered with pine needles and vines in the forest along the banks of Cedar Bayou (Cartier and Hole 1972; Whitsett and Fox n.d.). Some historical accounts have been found that document how these industrial complexes were operated. The commercial brick-making process progressed in

FIG. 10.9   *The ruins of the Denton Lime Kilns, northern Bexar County.*
(Courtesy Center for Archaeological Research, The University of Texas
at San Antonio.)

stages from mixing the clay with a horse- or mule-drawn "mud
mill" in a molding pit, to the hand-forming, drying, and stock-
piling of unburned bricks. Then the bricks were stacked in a special
way within the kiln chamber and fired for several days; the kiln's
temperature was gradually increased at first, then the intensity of
the heat maintained for a certain period, and finally the furnace and
its contents were allowed to cool before the finished bricks were
removed and stockpiled for shipment.

Scattered brick-making areas also have been found in other
parts of the coastal plain. The possible site of an 1830's Mexican
brick kiln referred to in the historical accounts as El Banco Colorado was recorded on a red clay bluff on the Lavaca River where
Palmetto Bend Reservoir has been constructed (Mallouf, Fox, and

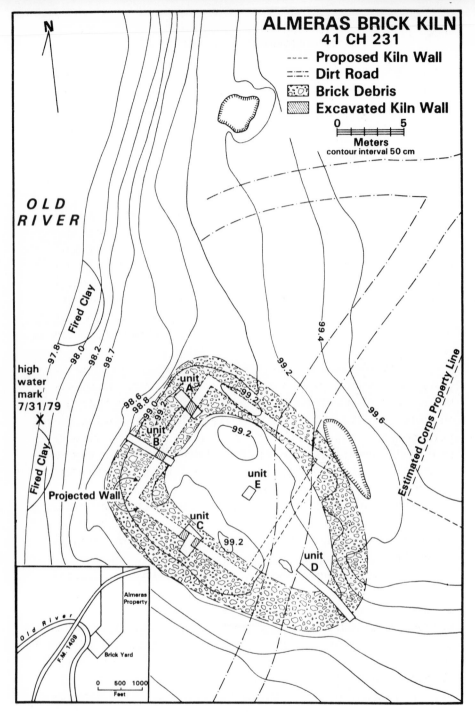

FIG. 10.10   *Plan of the site of the Almeras Brick Yard, Chambers County.*
(From Fox, Day, and Highley 1980: Fig. 51. Courtesy Center for Archaeological Research, The University of Texas at San Antonio.)

Briggs 1973:154–156). Some abandoned early twentieth-century circular, dome-shaped brick kilns are still standing near Giddings, east of Austin (Malone and Fox n.d.), and there probably are other kiln sites in other areas where lignite coal was available for use as fuel for firing bricks.

Mining and Mineral Extraction

One of the first industrial developments considered by the Spanish. in Texas was the mining of the province's mineral resources, and ever since, there have been successful and unsuccessful attempts to extract various minerals from Texas' geological resource areas. Various mines have operated in the more ancient rock formations of western Texas and the Llano Uplift area of central Texas, and several old mines and mining communities have been recorded as historic sites of early mining operations in those regions.

Lignite mining, which has become a major industry in recent years and is overtaking thousands of acres of land on the coastal plain, had its beginnings during the settlement of parts of central and eastern Texas in the first half of the nineteenth century. Reports of lignite deposits in Texas were published in France as early as 1819 (Stenzel 1946:197) and in 1867 a formal survey of lignite resources in certain areas of Texas was undertaken by the state government (Buckley 1874). More than 150 lignite mining operations have existed in at least 35 Texas counties since then (Fisher 1963:8). The discovery of oil near Beaumont in 1901 distracted investors away from the lignite industry for a while, but it continued to develop.

The critical demand for energy supplies for America in recent years has created the economic impetus for further development of the lignite mining industry. Archeological surveys of newly proposed strip-mining areas near Rockdale and near Athens have located several early shaft-type lignite mining sites and related communities and have gathered a considerable amount of historical background information concerning the development of this important-again Texas industry (Betancourt and Lynn 1977; Guderjan 1981). This information not only can be used to help detail and interpret the history of the lignite industry; it also can be used to study the effects that extensive modern earthmoving operations

will have on the social, economic, and natural environments surrounding the large rural areas of uplands and lowlands that the
strip-mining eventually will be permitted to destroy.

Besides mining and the manufacture of building materials
from timber, clay, and limestone, other commodites were produced through the early industrial exploitation of Texas' natural
resources. The value of salt deposits was recognized early in the
Spanish Colonial Period and by Indians for thousands of years before that. Archeological investigations have been conducted by
archeologists from Southern Methodist University in 1969 at the
Neches Saline, a natural salt flat, or saline prairie, and commercial
salt manufacturing area that now is under Lake Palestine (Skinner
1971). Salt was produced from the Neches Saline in large quantities
between 1820 and 1870, particularly during the Civil War.

Eight salt-rendering furnace sites were located during the investigation. One of them was completely excavated. It was built
into the gradual slope at the edge of the salt flat and was composed
of a long, narrow, stone-lined trench, or flue, that was designed to
carry the intense heat from a firebox on the lower end of the furnace to the chimney at the other end. The flue was covered with
boiler plates on which the water was evaporated from the brine
extracted from a well near the furnace. Large cast-iron kettles
probably were placed along the flue in the early years of the industry's development until they eventually were replaced by more
efficient salt pans.

Pottery Making

Trench kilns also were used as ovens for firing crockery storage containers in the nineteenth century and the early twentieth
century. The flue was covered on these groundhog-type kilns to
maintain a controlled atmosphere of intense heat around the pottery vessels carefully stacked inside it (Greer 1977a).

Excavations were carried out in the early 1970's in Montgomery County at Kirbee Kiln, an unusually long groundhog kiln that

FIG. 10.11 *Plan and cross section of salt evaporator at the Neches Saline,
Smith County.* (From Skinner 1971:Fig. 9. Courtesy Texas Historical
Commission.)

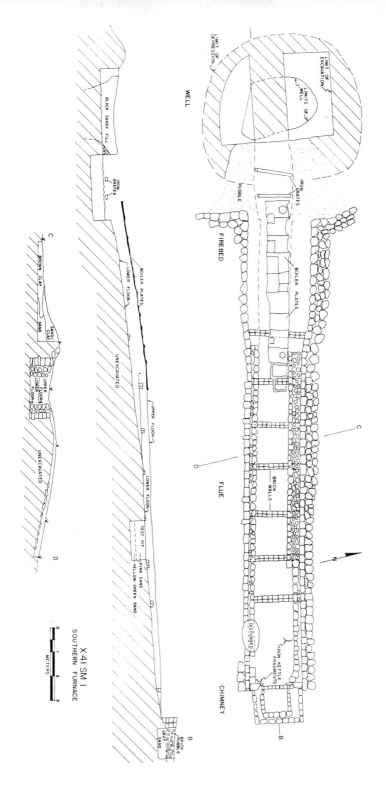

X 41 SM 1
SOUTHERN FURNACE

WELL

FIREBED

FLUE

CHIMNEY

LIMIT OF DEPRESSION

LIMIT OF EXCAVATION

LIMITS OF WELL

BLACK SANDY FILL

IRON GRATES

IRON GRATES

RUBBLE

BOILER PLATES

BOILER PLATES

BRICK WALLS

DISTURBED

IRON KETTLE FRAGMENTS

BRICK RUBBLE

GRAY SAND

BOILER PLATES

LOWER FLOOR

UPPER FLOOR

UNEXCAVATED

LOWER FLOOR

TEST PIT

PINK SAND

YELLOW-GREEN SAND

BROWN CLAY

SANDY CLAY

SAND

UPPER FLOOR

LOWER FLOOR

UNEXCAVATED

0   1   2   3
METERS

C

D

B

N

was in operation during the decade before the Civil War (Malone, Greer, and Simons 1979). An analysis of samples of hundreds of fragments of discarded crockery vessels collected from waster piles near the kiln found that this early commercial pottery factory produced a limited variety of utilitarian stoneware of typically Southern styles, conforming to the tradition of stoneware production that had been evolving for some time in the Old South. The principal Kirbee vessel forms were jugs, storage jars, large bowls, chamber pots (portable urinals), and pitchers. This crockery was wheel-thrown (fashioned by hand on a potter's wheel). It was waterproofed with vitreous green and gray alkaline glazes produced intentionally as an effect of the intense heat of the kiln on coatings of specially prepared slips (mixtures of water, clay, and ashes) applied to the walls of the unfired pottery vessels.

Kirbee was one of only a few such stoneware potteries that are known to have been in operation in Texas in the mid-nineteenth century. Another early one, the Abraham Babcock Pottery Manufactory, was afforded preliminary study as part of the investigation of the Palmetto Bend Reservoir area of Jackson County (Greer 1977b). This factory was unique because around 1860 it produced earthenware (instead of stoneware) pottery with lead glazes rather than alkaline glazes. Lead glaze is a type of impervious coating commonly found on earthenwares produced in Mexico. But lead-glazed earthenwares also were produced at early American stoneware potteries in the eastern United States.

Further west on the coastal plain, the archeological remains of three commercial stoneware manufacturing operations currently are being studied at the community of Capote near Seguin in Wilson County (Brachner 1982). The first industrial operation was established there in 1857 by J. M. Wilson, a Presbyterian minister, shortly after he moved to Texas from the South with his family and some 20 slaves. The pottery operated until 1869, when Wilson sold his remaining interest in the business to a potter named M. J. Durham who already had been working at the site. Durham promptly moved the operation to a new location nearby.

A stone-lined well, the ruins of a groundhog-type kiln, and a huge waster pile of discarded stoneware sherds mark the place where for twelve years the minister's slaves labored to produce an apparently enormous amount of crockery to meet the demand for food storage vessels in mid-nineteenth-century frontier Texas. In

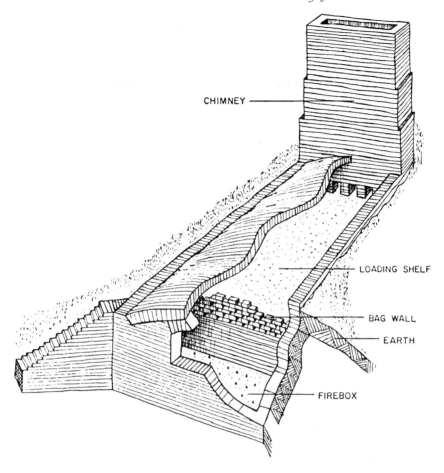

FIG. 10.12   *Schematic view of a typical groundhog kiln.* (From Malone, Greer, and Simons 1979:Fig. 1. Reprinted from Northeast Historical Archeology, Vol. 6, Nos. 1 and 2. Courtesy Texas Historical Commission.)

general, the remains of the pottery-making operation are typical of traditional Southern alkaline-glazed stoneware production. But salt-glazed sherds were found associated with the alkaline-glazed sherds in the waster piles, and drops of salt glaze on some alkaline-glazed sherds indicate that both types were being fired in the same kiln. Salt glazes were not customary in the antebellum South, but were more characteristic of pottery-making in the North.

Historical research found that besides Durham, who had moved to Texas from South Carolina, two other immigrant potters—a white man named Isaac Suttles from Ohio and a black man named John Chandler from South Carolina—may have been working at the Reverend J. M. Wilson's pottery business before Emancipation. Implications are that Durham, Suttles, and Chandler may have trained Wilson's slaves and that Suttles probably introduced the technique of salt-glazing to the pottery manufacturing operation.

The census for 1870 listed three black potters who were working in the area. Hirum, James, and Wallace Wilson, who probably had been the minister's slaves before Emancipation, started their own pottery factory soon after Durham took over the original pottery operation. The site of the H. Wilson & Company Pottery was located further off the main road than the J. M. Wilson and the M. J. Durham potteries and was marked by the remains of a smaller groundhog kiln and two associated waster piles of salt-glazed stoneware sherds. Studies of the broken vessels have shown that the free black potters produced a line of fine quality stoneware that was similar in many ways to the products of the first pottery operation. But almost all of their products were salt-glazed and exhibited creative innovations like unusual-shaped handles and storage vessels designed with special stoneware lids. Further studies of the Wilson potteries and other stoneware manufacturing sites will learn more about the transition from slave-potter to free-potter and more about the integration of Texas' small-scale industries into the greater American socioeconomic system during the late nineteenth century.

Sugar-Refining

Trench-type furnaces have been used as simple facilities for refining sugar and molasses, although they usually were not as long as those for pottery and often were built up off the ground for easier access, since more attention had to be paid to processing the syrup in the pan covering the flue. The earliest known archeological site of such a sugar refinery in Texas is at Mission San José in San Antonio. The refinery complex may have been in operation as early as 1755 and evidently was used throughout the rest of the eighteenth century for producing sugar from cane cultivated in the hacienda's irrigated fields.

According to the historical accounts and some bits of archeo-

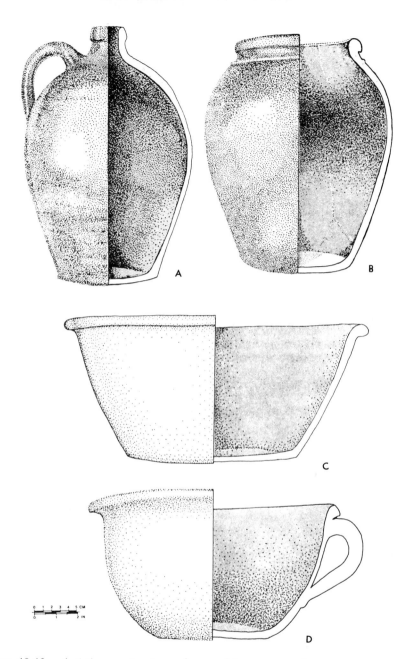

FIG. 10.13 *Artist's reconstructions of some of the more popular stoneware vessel forms produced in the mid-nineteenth century at the Kirbee Pottery, Montgomery County. A, one-gallon jug; B, one-gallon storage jar (larger sizes were also produced); C, two-gallon bowl; D, chamber pot. (From Malone, Greer, and Simons 1979: Figures 15, 16, 17, and 21. Courtesy Texas Historical Commission. Drawings by Sharon Roos.)*

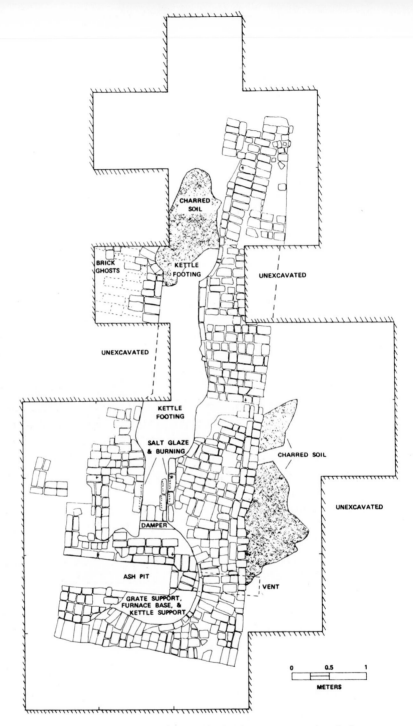

FIG. 10.14 *Plan of the ruins of the Sutherland sugar evaporator, Jackson County.* (From Freeman and Fawcett 1980: Fig. 14. Courtesy Texas Archeological Survey, The University of Texas at Austin.)

logical evidence, the refinery, or *ingenio*, at San José was arranged under a cane roof (Clark 1976). The cane was crushed in a milling area. The juice extracted by the mill works was collected and transferred to vats or large cauldrons covering the flue of the furnace, or *payla*, where it was cooked to an almost caramelized state, then cooled and poured into cone-shaped molds where the sugar would harden to form *piloncillo*. Toward the end of the eighteenth century, a water-powered mill replaced the hand-crushing of sugarcane at Mission San José.

Surviving examples of nineteenth- and twentieth-century sugar and sorghum mills and refineries located in Hays, Kendall, and Jasper counties, Texas, and in Nuevo León, Mexico, have been compared to the *ingenio* at San José (Clark 1976). Despite some technological improvements in later years and some minor variations in the layout of the components of small-scale refineries, the basic process remained virtually unchanged and still is in use today for the production of sugar and molasses in rural areas of the United States (Wigginton 1975:424–436).

Historians have traced the development of sugar-refining and its spread from Venice to the rest of Europe and then to the Caribbean Islands by the early seventeenth century, and finally to the United States in the second half of the eighteenth century (Deerr 1950). Experimental sugarcane cultivation began in Louisiana in the last quarter of the eighteenth century and may have been introduced by emigrants from Santo Domingo (Sitterton 1953). As sugar-refining became a successful enterprise in Louisiana in the 1820's, its influence spread into Texas, where planters began to experiment with sugar production along the coast. By the time of the Revolution, several sugar refineries were in operation in Austin's and DeWitt's colonies (Curlee 1932:174–177). Farming methods and refining processes improved in the 1840's and shipments of sugar to Galveston merchants increased from 213 hogsheads (approximately 1,000 pounds each) in 1846 to 11,023 in 1852 (Webb 1952:684).

Sugarcane cultivation and sugar-refining probably was centered in the old Anglo-American settlement areas of present-day Wharton, Colorado, Fort Bend, and Brazoria counties; but the industry evidently extended into other areas by the time it reached its peak in the early 1850's. Frederick Olmsted (1978:244–245), who travelled through Texas in 1854, mentioned how well crops of sugarcane were growing in the Lower Guadalupe River Valley above Victoria and in the area around Seguin. Cold weather in 1856, a severe drought in 1859, and a bad frost in 1860 severely reduced sugarcane production. The Civil War removed the slave labor that made possible the success of the antebellum sugar industry.

At the turn of the century, sugarcane growing again became an important agricultural pursuit in the same areas of the coastal plain that had been the "sugar bowl" half a century before, and sugarcane also became an important crop in the Lower Rio Grande Valley. But the only refinery in Texas was at Sugar Land, in Fort Bend County, and by the 1920's, what little sugarcane that was being grown was used for syrup-making on a local scale, and the refinery at Sugar Land came to rely on the West Indies for its raw material.

Previously mentioned in the discussion of archeological evidence of frontier settlement of American Texas, the remains of sugar refineries have been found at several old plantation sites on the coastal plain. Few of these early industrial sites have been investigated, although the early Texas sugar industry is attracting the attention of a growing number of archeologists. Unfortunately, many early sugar mill sites in the coastal area have been destroyed by hurricanes and other natural processes; many others have been disturbed by man's activities, such as the 1850's Hawkinsville steam-powered mill site on Caney Creek in Matagorda County, which has been robbed of its bricks for reuse as building materials (Fritz 1975). Fortunately, examples of a couple of early sugar refineries are being preserved, such as the one at the Varner-Hogg Plantation State Historic Park in Brazoria County (Historic Engineering Site Survey 1975). The remains of other early refineries may still be discovered at other nineteenth-century historic sites on the coastal plain.

The archeological investigations at the disturbed site of the Sutherland Plantation on the Navidad River in the Palmetto Bend Reservoir area of Jackson County uncovered one of the best documented early sugar refineries that has been studied so far in the old Anglo-American settlement areas near the coast (Freeman and Fawcett 1980). Records left by George Sutherland's neighbor and relative, John Sutherland Menefee, detail his experiments with sugar-refining in 1843, apparently after Sutherland began his sugar experiments. Menefee even brought in an experienced sugarmaker from Barbados in the West Indies to advise him on methods to produce sugar of higher quality than was being produced in frontier settlement areas. Sutherland may also have had similar expertise on hand when he began his sugar-refining operation.

Summarizing the process, the conversion of sugarcane to sugar began with milling, in which the juice was pressed with a roller mill, probably animal-powered in Sutherland's and Menefee's operations. From the mill, the juice was collected and transferred to a juice box, or clarifier, to which lime was added. After it was allowed to settle, the juice was drawn off into the first of a series, or batterie, of kettles on the cooker, or evaporator. The kettles were graduated in size and were arranged along the flue of the evaporator, which was shaped much like the trench kilns used for processing salt at the Neches Saline and like the groundhog kilns used for firing pottery. Cement was used to enclose the spaces around the kettles to keep the heat inside the flue and beneath the batterie. The first and largest kettle, called the grande, was positioned nearest the chimney of the evaporator. As the juice approached the boiling point in this kettle, lime was added as necessary to control the thickness and turbidity of the mixture. A flow of juice from the clarifier to the first kettle was maintained so that, as it was filled and cooked to the proper extent, the juice was decanted into the next kettle, and then the next, until it filled the batterie kettle that was situated over the most intense heat of the furnace itself. After transfer to a cooling trough, the syrup went to a drawing room where the molasses was allowed to drain out into a storage compartment, or cistern, leaving the brown sugar to be removed and dealt with as the finished product.

The archeological remains of the evaporator found at the Sutherland Plantation site was first thought to be the ruin of one of Sutherland's slave cabins until it was noted as an anomaly during a magnetometer survey of an area of the plantation located away from the main residential headquarters area. After machinery removed the overburden of soil covering the feature, careful hand-excavation exposed the brick ruins of Sutherland's early 1840's evaporator.

The feature was about 24 feet long and was oriented north-south, with the furnace on the south end. Although the chimney area had been destroyed, the furnace and much of the long, narrow flue of the evaporator were relatively well preserved. The footings for three of the four kettles along the flue were built into the tops of the thick, low brick walls that formed the structure. Charred soil and burned bricks were evidence of the intense heat that moved through the flue beneath the kettles. The furnace was a circular chamber, or firebox, containing an iron grate on which the fire was built. The ashes fell through the grate and into an ash pit below. An air vent was built into the massive brick walls of the fire pit, opposite the ash pit, to allow air to enter and fuel the fire. The rim around the top of the furnace chamber supported the last in the series of kettles along the evaporator. A damper built across the opening between the firebox and the flue regulated the heat transferred beneath the batterie of kettles as it was drawn along the flue and up through the chimney.

Ash, charcoal, and rubble found outside the walls of the furnace represented several firing episodes that took place during the operation of Sutherland's evaporator. A brick shelf around the furnace area and the distribution of nails and spikes found outside the structure probably were evidence of a wooden superstructure that housed the evaporator. The mill used to crush the juice from the sugarcane probably was located nearby, up the slope, in an area accessible to the fields where the cane was cultivated. Although artifacts were not found that could be used to date the sugar refinery precisely, the archeological remains of the evaporator fit the historical description of early nineteenth-century refineries, and there is little doubt that Sutherland's refinery represents one of the earliest attempts in the development of the sugar industry in American Texas.

Milling

The industrial milling of grains began in Texas in the mission haciendas, where a labor force of Indians ground corn, wheat, and other food grains by hand with stone implements much like those that had been used by their prehistoric ancestors for thousands of years. By the end of the Spanish Colonial Period, Mission San José in San Antonio had a gristmill that was powered by water supplied by the mission's *acequia* (Clark 1976; 1978). Several hand-operated and mule- or horse-driven mills were in use by 1826 in the Anglo-American settlement areas. By the beginning of statehood, water-propelled and steam-powered gristmills were in operation in several parts of American Texas. Before the Civil War, flour- and grist-milling became the top-ranking industry in Texas and continued to be important throughout the rest of the nineteenth century. However, by the mid-twentieth century, custom milling for community markets became a thing of the past, as the Texas milling industry came to be controlled by big business corporations (Webb 1952:199–200).

Some nineteenth-century mills have been studied in Texas and a few of them are being preserved as historic places. Most other early mill sites have been neglected or destroyed, such as Anderson's Mill in the hills of Travis County northwest of Austin. Built by a Pennsylvanian named Thomas Anderson after he arrived in Texas in 1859, the gristmill was ordered to be used as a gunpowder mill for the Confederate cause by the Texas State Military Board in 1863. The mill was used extensively for grinding corn after the war, and in the 1870's Anderson also began ginning cotton there.

An old sketch shows that the mill was powered by a large, vertically-mounted waterwheel, as compared to most other early Texas mills which had horizontally-mounted turbines. Only piles of rubble and some remnants of stone foundation walls of the mill

FIG. 10.15 *Sketch of Anderson's Mill, Travis County, as it looked in the 1860's.* (From Durrenberger 1965: Fig. 2. Courtesy Texas Archeological Society.)

structure remained after the Lower Colorado River Authority completed preparation of the low-lying areas along Cypress Creek to be inundated by the rising waters of Lake Travis in the 1940's. Members of the University of Texas Archeological Society investigated the site of Anderson's mill and farm complex in the 1960's (Durrenberger 1965), but not much information could be recovered from the mill ruins. The investigation did manage to salvage some samples of artifacts and some architectural details from the ruins of Anderson's homestead, located on the hillside near the mill site, before the area was completely overtaken by Austin's urban sprawl.

Since the construction of San José's gristmill in the 1790's, as many as 16 water-powered mills for grinding grain, milling gunpowder, ginning cotton, and generating electricity have operated along the Upper San Antonio River between San Pedro Springs and Mission San Juan Capistrano (McDowell n.d.: 1–3; Scurlock, Benavides, Isham, and Clark 1976:56–57). Most of these are in ruins or have been destroyed. Some of the mill sites are located along San Antonio's Mission Parkway and may be preserved.

Three gristmills were established by a German-Texan named Hilmer Guenther after he arrived in San Antonio in 1859. Earlier, he had built one of the first mills in the Fredericksburg area. The sites of his first two mills on the San Antonio River are now the location of Pioneer Flour Mills, an important twentieth-century San Antonio industry developed by members of the Guenther family. The ruin of Guenther's upper mill, which was established in 1868 in the old King William area of San Antonio, recently has been removed stone by stone so that when the U.S. Army Corps of Engineers completes its channelization of a section of the river, the mill can be reconstructed on its original site (Flynn, Fox, and Cox n.d.).

In 1852, the *Texas State Gazette* announced the opening of Thomas F. McKinney's "elegant flouring mill" on Onion Creek, a few miles south of Austin. According to the advertisement, up until that time all flour used in "Western" Texas had to be imported from the North. Archeological excavations conducted at the limestone masonry mill ruins in 1974 by members of the Texas Archeological Society and Texas Parks and Wildlife Department personnel traced the walls of the mill structure and determined that the

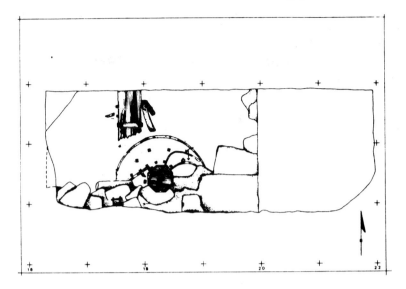

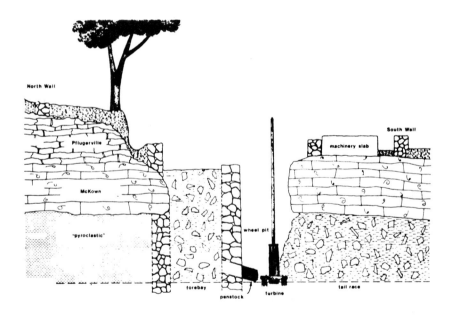

FIG. 10.16 *Plan of the wheel pit and cross section of the mill works at the ruins of McKinney's Mill on Onion Creek, Travis County.* (From McEachern and Ralph 1981: Figs. 3 and 4. Courtesy Texas Archeological Society.)

mill was of the type with a horizontally-mounted turbine. A fore-bay, or water storage compartment, was used to retain a certain volume of water entering the mill so that a constant head of water pressure could be released from it and directed toward the turbine in the adjoining wheel pit (McEachern and Ralph 1981). Also found were traces of the millrace, or head race, which channelled water from the millpond on Onion Creek to the forebay, and evidence of the tailrace that carried the water discharged from the wheel pit back into the creek. Only the machinery slab and the lower portions of the stone walls remained of what had been the work rooms of the superstructure that stood above the forebay and the wheel pit.

An assortment of metal hardware, such as nails, spikes, bolts, nuts, and pins, was found in the fill archeologically excavated from the mill ruins, as were fragments of windowpanes, fragments of bottles primarily of the types used for alcoholic beverages, and a few rifle and pistol cartridges. Also found were a

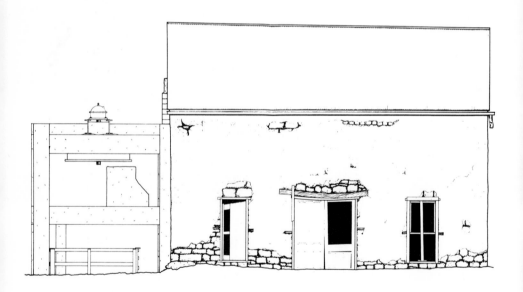

FIG. 10.17 *Elevation of the Haass-Quintle Mill, Landmark Inn State Historic Site, Castroville, Medina County.* (From Texas Parks and Wildlife Department 1976. Courtesy Texas Parks and Wildlife Department.)

monkey wrench, a mill pick, a leather knife and some other tools, and machinery parts, such as an adjusting lever from the mill's turbine and the pinion gear, rack gear, and a portion of the shaft which operated together in the drive train that transferred the power from the turbine to the machinery of the milling area above. Several other machinery parts that were expected to be found were missing, indicating that most of the salvageable equipment was removed from McKinney's mill after it was destroyed by a flood on Onion Creek in 1869.

Another early Texas mill that is being preserved by the Texas Parks and Wildlife Department is part of the Landmark Inn State Historic Park in the 1840's Alsatian colonial town of Castroville. The Haass-Quintle Mill, with its two-story, stone masonry mill building, underground millrace, tailrace, and wood and stone dam across the Medina River, was built in 1854 next door to John Vance's Hotel. Soon after it was established, a cotton gin was added to the gristmill. The operation was purchased in 1876 by Joseph Courand and his son, who expanded the milling business and bought out Vance's Hotel by 1899. During its history, the Haass-Quintle Mill complex included not only a gristmill and a cotton gin, but also had a lumber-drying kiln, a lumber mill and a roller mill. In 1925, the mill was converted into an electric generating plant.

Archeological investigations of the mill ruins in 1975 found evidence of the historical development of the industrial complex, such as in the turbine pit, which was renovated and remodelled several times (Texas Parks and Wildlife Department 1976). Portions of the horizontally-mounted turbine and flywheel of the mill works were found, as was a floor drain that facilitated the cleaning of the wheel pit. Architectural and mechanical details were recorded as a result of the archeological investigations of the various interrelated components of the mill complex. In comparison to most of the other water-powered mills studied in Texas that had horizontally-mounted turbines, the Haass-Quintle Mill apparently did not have a forebay and was powered by the force of a stream of water channelled directly from the constant level lake on the Medina through the millrace into the turbine pit. Perhaps a forebay was necessary to assure a constant flow of water to millworks whose water supplies were more variable, like McKinney's Mill which was dependent upon the flow in Onion Creek and Mission San José's mill which was dependent upon the flow of water in the mission *acequia*.

Breweries

Wine- and beer-making were important small-scale industries in mid-nineteenth-century Texas. Besides the home wineries and breweries previously mentioned, such as Carl Steiner's household winery at his farmstead near Coleto Creek on the coastal plain and beer cellars at German farmsteads in the central Texas Hill Country, several breweries became prosperous on a larger scale by the time of the Civil War, serving local and even regional markets (Dugas 1955).

The Eighth U.S. Census listed 11 breweries in Texas in 1860. Except for those at El Paso and Nacogdoches, the breweries served areas that were settled predominantly by German immigrants. Between 1870 and 1880, the brewing industry reached its peak in Texas and then began a rapid decline. Reflecting the centralization of industry in Texas during the late nineteenth century, the traditionally local-market breweries found it more and more difficult to compete with well-financed, technologically-advanced competitors who used pasteurization and artificial methods of refrigeration and could ship their products rapidly by rail to markets nationwide (Spratt 1955). While the number of local Texas breweries continued to decline, the volume of Texas-brewed beer actually increased. But this was due to the early mass-production of San Antonio's Lone Star Brewery, established in 1883 and 1884 as the first large, mechanized commercial brewery in the State.

The development and decline of the early Texas brewing industry is exemplified by the history of Kreische's Brewery, which now is a State Historic Site near La Grange. Heinrich L. Kreische practiced his profession as a stone mason after he arrived in Texas from Germany in 1846. But during the 1860's he established a brewery that was the third largest in Texas (Texas Parks and Wildlife Department 1980). Kreische retailed his product at a beer garden near his homestead and at a beer hall in La Grange. After his death in 1882, the brewery fell into disrepair and by 1890 his sons listed their occupations as farm laborers instead of brewers.

When Kreische's Brewery was investigated by archeologists

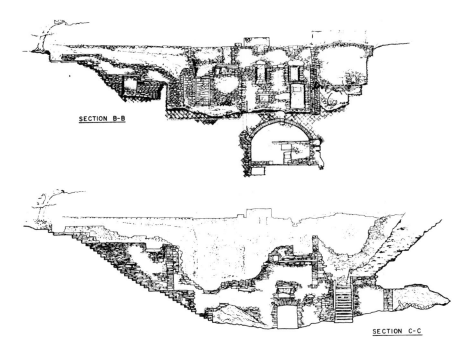

SECTION B-B

SECTION C-C

FIG. 10.18   *Cross sections of the ruins of the Kreische Brewery near La Grange, Fayette County.* (From Texas Parks and Wildlife Department 1980:A-40. Courtesy Texas Parks and Wildlife Department. Drawings by M. Conrad and M. Ragsdale.)

from the Texas Parks and Wildlife Department in the late 1970's, it was a ruin of partial stone walls and piles of soil and stone rubble. But architectural information was recovered that enabled the investigators to reconstruct the brewery complex and its beer-making operations. Kreische's Brewery had been a three-story, stone masonry structure of vaulted rooms with intermediate levels and walkways that provided access to the industrial equipment, storage, and loading areas. It was intentionally built into a spring-fed upland creek, where the stream flow could be retained in a holding pond and filtered through stone-lined tanks before being piped to a cistern chamber and then distributed beneath the brewery. A series of strategically-positioned, vertical ventilation shafts drew air up through the fermentation and aging rooms from the water system below it. With this elaborate evaporative cooling system, Kreische could maintain the temperatures of his brewing areas

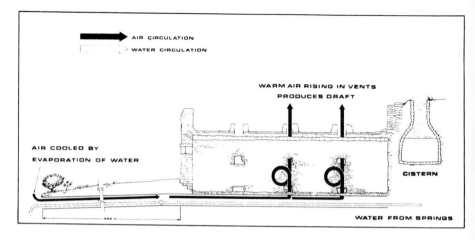

FIG. 10.19   *The cooling system at the Kreische Brewery near La Grange, Fayette County.* (From Texas Parks and Wildlife Department 1980:Fig. 12. Courtesy Texas Parks and Wildlife Department.)

within the range from 40 degrees to 65 degrees Fahrenheit necessary for the proper yeast fermentation. This enabled him to begin his brewing operations early in the fall and continue them into the late spring.

Also studied was the brewery's kiln, which dried the malt and also may have been used for drying the dregs from the brewing operations to make livestock feed. The malting room contained a firebox, a heat radiating flue and its chimney, a perforated malting floor where the malt could be dried by the heat rising from below it, and even a special opening that allowed access for maintenance of the kiln. The malt-milling area also was found, where the grain was ground in a horse-powered mill. Also reconstructed on paper were the brewery's storage chambers, stairways, landings, and other architectural features, each with its own function as part of the industrial complex.

Except for the garbage left by picnickers after the brewery began to fall into ruin, the artifacts recovered during the archeological excavations were related primarily to the industrial operation. The number of artifacts found was small in comparison with the quantity and variety of archeological evidence that usually appears at sites of household occupations and other places where there was much more variation in the kinds and intensity of occupational activity. Artifacts related to the industrial activities at Kreische's Brewery include such things as barrel hoops, bushings from the bungs used as stoppers in wooden kegs, a skimmer made of perforated sheet metal, and part of a brass saccharimeter scale used in calculating the amount of sugar added during the preparation of the mixtures fermented and aged to make beer.

Urban Manufacturing Sites

Established as part of urban development, Texas' early urban industrial complexes either have evolved into modern industries on their present sites or have been covered over or obliterated by later development, and few early urban manufacturing sites have been studied archeologically. As part of historical and archeological research conducted in advance of the construction of the Paseo del Rio—a scenic route between Alamo Plaza and San Antonio's River Walk—machinery slabs, drainage systems, and other structural remains of an 1870's ice factory have been found that happened to survive twentieth-century urban development (Fox and Ivey 1979; Ivey and Fox n.d.).

In another part of downtown San Antonio, the historic site of Menger's Soap Works has been studied (Ivey n.d.). Prussian immigrants Johann Simon Nicolas Menger and his wife arrived in Texas in 1846. They lived in New Braunfels for a couple of years and then moved to San Antonio, where Menger practiced his profession as a music teacher and then became involved in business interests. He entered into a partnership with a vinegar brewer in 1850 and purchased a soap-making operation in 1851. A flood severely damaged the soap works in 1859 and Menger moved his factory to a new location in the western part of downtown San Antonio where water could be channelled a short distance from the San Pedro *acequia* to the industrial operation.

The new factory, constructed in 1861 and 1862, was expanded and modernized several times by Menger, then by his sons after they took over the soap works in 1882, and later by his grandson who ran it from 1897 until around 1911, when the business was closed down. The building was used as a mattress factory for a while, and by the late 1940's it had become an auto repair and storage business. Still owned by the Menger family, the basic stone shell of the old soap works complex was converted into apartments in 1950. The neighborhood around it was razed after 1970 as part of an urban renewal program and the old building became a refuge for vagrants.

The basic, stone soap works building is still standing today and is listed in the National Register of Historic Places. In 1979, historical and archeological investigations were conducted in conjunction with plans for the renovation of the surviving structure (Ivey n.d.). The documentary history of the soap works was researched and the actual soap-making procedure carried out in the 1880's was reconstructed. It involved the processing of oils from vegetal matter and from tons of animal fats, tallow, suet, and other discards acquired from local slaughterhouses and butcher shops, and continued with the methodical rendering down of clean fats in a steam boiler works. Then pigments, perfumes, and other aesthetic additives were mixed into the soap before it was molded, pressed, and otherwise shaped; finally it was packaged and labelled to be sold under brand names such as Extra Olive, Magnolia, and Extra German.

The actual archeological excavations were confined primarily to the engine and boiler room of the old Menger Soap Works, where a patchwork of structural remains showed the repeated expansion and renovation of the facilities. Remains of the tall brick chimney and other traces of the original factory were identified, as were structural alterations that took place around 1881, 1897, and during the conversion of the building into an apartment house in 1950. Also uncovered were portions of the old basement wall of the oil room where the fats and suet were processed, the possible remains of a stone-lined ditch that channelled water into the soap works from the San Pedro *acequia*, and an early drain that carried away the fluids discarded during the rendering process.

Because of the numerous alterations of the structural complex, the artifacts found during the preliminary excavations could not be associated with specific events or activities that took place at the soap works. Most of the artifacts found were evidently brought into the structure with loads of fill material, trash, and debris deposited during the remodelling of the structure in 1950. But architectural evidence of the structural development of the historic urban manufacturing site is contained within the walls of the old building, and undisturbed areas outside the building can be preserved which contain the archeological evidence of the history of the Menger Soap Works.

FIG. 10.20   *One of the buildings of the Menger Soap Works, San Antonio.*
(Courtesy Center for Archaeological Research, The University of Texas
at San Antonio.)

The coastal ports became the most prominent early trade centers for cotton, sugar, cattle, and other products of Texas' agrarian
economy before the Civil War (Jordan 1966:68). The railroads
reached out after the war to tap the previously inaccessible markets, and much of Texas' commerce became focused upon the
early urban industrial centers of Houston—the early hub of the
transportation networks—and Galveston—the major seaport and
international trade center (Meinig 1969:59–61, 71–74).

Galveston's population grew from about 14,000 in 1870 to
22,000 in 1880 (Fehrenbach 1968:601), and after the city received
government funding for the construction of a deepwater port
(Ziegler 1938;108), it continued to boom as the principal market
where Texas' agricultural products were exchanged for a huge
volume of mass-produced, inexpensive, and exotic trade goods.
The city expanded, even while much of America suffered a great
economic depression in the 1890's, and hundreds of American and
European immigrants moved through the port of entry. Some

managed to make their fortunes in Galveston. Most others failed in their business ventures, as in the case of Nottingham, an industrial town that was planned around the establishment of a lace-curtain and mosquito-netting factory on Galveston Island in the early 1890's.

Named after the lace-making city in England, Nottingham was located in an isolated, undeveloped part of Galveston Island, near a railroad line that carried tourists to a popular picnic area called Lafitte's Grove. In 1978, students from the Anthropology Department of Rice University conducted historical and archeological investigations at the Nottingham townsite, where previous visits to the area found brick foundations of the curtain and netting factory (Anderson 1980).

A composite map was put together on which the streets of the town and the railway through it—as shown on an 1892 plat of the townsite—could be verified as lines evident on a 1930 aerial photograph. The actual fieldwork involved the excavation of the factory ruin and adjacent structural features. Most of the archeological materials recovered were pieces of broken windowpanes, bricks, mortar, and asphalt. The archeologists took some low-level aerial photos of the townsite that showed a depression located in an area across the street from the factory in the 1890's. Test excavations found this feature to be a trash pit that dated to the time the factory was in operation. The dump contained a large assortment of ceramic sherds and glass fragments, as well as metal artifacts like tin containers and utensils, a wick-adjustment device from a kerosene lamp, table knives, and building hardware.

The collection of ceramic artifacts recovered from the trash pit included sherds from earthenware and stoneware utility vessels and tablewares, and also a few sherds of porcelain china. All of the dishes and containers represented by the sherds were of the types produced during the late nineteenth century. Very little of the pottery was decorated, which is typical of ceramic wares of the period and contrasts with brightly-decorated British pottery found at pre-Civil War household occupation sites in Texas. Of the 20 sherds found with makers marks on them, 14 were the trademarks of American potteries, reflecting the increase in the proportion of pottery supplied by American manufacturers after the Civil War. Also found was a white pottery doll, which had been discarded after its legs were broken off, and a porcelain holder for a tobacco

FIG. 10.21 *Photograph of a rendering of the Nottingham Lace Curtain Factory on Galveston Island, 1890's, from a blueprint on file at the Rosenberg Library in Galveston.* (Verbal descriptions and newspaper accounts indicate that this is a fairly accurate picture of what the factory looked like. (Courtesy Texas Anderson, Houston, the Houston Archaeological Society, and the Department of Anthropology, Rice University.)

pipe of the old-world type popular around the turn of the century, which had a cherrywood stem, cork fittings, a porcelain bowl or furnace, with a hinged metal lid and a tasseled silk cord.

Glassware included fragments of beer, soft drink, wine, whiskey, and bitters bottles, and fragments of a glass bowl, a goblet, mugs, a drinking glass, a chandelier finial, eyeglass lenses, medicine stirrers, white glass buttons, and a piece of a white glass shade for a kerosene lamp—all of which are typical of the late nineteenth century (Wetzel n.d.). The bottle fragments were from the kinds of containers produced after the crown cap (like modern-day soda-water bottle tops) was introduced in 1892 and after the semi-

FIG. 10.22 *Some of the Nottingham Lace Curtain Factory foundations exposed by archeological excavations on Galveston Island.* Judging from the lack of occupational evidence found in the thin layers of soil covering the foundations, the factory was in operation for only a short while in the late nineteenth century, and after the 1900 hurricane there was no occupation of the factory area. (Courtesy Texas Anderson, Houston, the Houston Archaeological Society, and the Department of Anthropology, Rice University.)

automatic bottle-making machine had been invented (around 1880). Many of the bottle necks found at the trash dump were of the type produced during the 1890's on which the mold seams extend up the length of the neck almost all the way to the rim. The Owens fully-automatic bottle-making machine, invented in 1899, led to the mass-production of bottles, particularly after about 1910. On these entirely machine-made bottles, the mold seams extend all the way up the neck and over the lip of the rim (Kendrick 1963; McKearin and McKearin 1950, 1971; Toulouse 1971).

Taken together, the artifact collection dates to the period corresponding to the construction and operation of the lace factory in the 1890's. Historical research found an 1892 newspaper article reporting that a boardinghouse had been completed for the factory's construction workers and that the framework was completed for a restaurant and beer hall. During the 1890's, the Joseph Labadie store in Nottingham ran ads in a Galveston newspaper announcing the sale of the kinds of goods that match the inventory of artifacts found in the trash pit, including cheap crockery, plain white hotel china, lanterns, flower vases and flowerpots, and tin wares. The Labadie family also sold groceries and in 1899 advertised furnished rooms for rent. Apparently, the dump was part of the occupation of a boardinghouse or restaurant that operated near the lace factory, until Nottingham was devastated by the hurricane that ravaged Galveston Island in 1900.

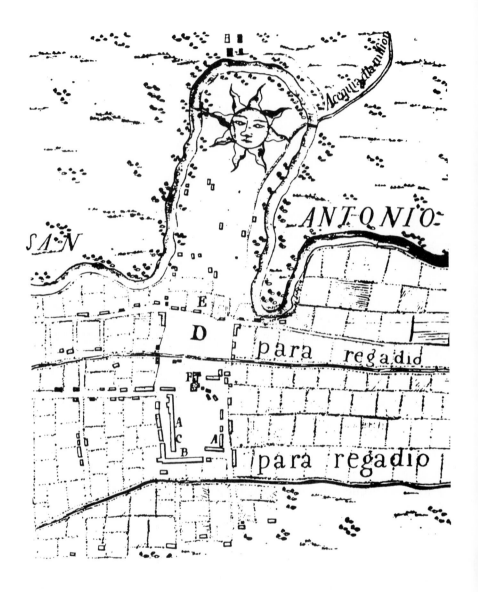

FIG. 11.1 *The Villa and the Presidio of San Antonio in 1767, copied from a map drawn by Joseph de Urrutia.* A. Casa del Presidio. B. Casa del Capitán (the "Governor's Palace"). C. Cuerpo de Guardia. D. Plaza de la Villa (Main Plaza). E. Casas Reales. F. Iglesia (the San Fernando Church). (From Fox 1977: Fig. 1. Courtesy Center for Archaeological Research, The University of Texas at San Antonio.)

XI

Urban Texas

By THE MID-NINETEENTH CENTURY, the interrelated processes of urbanization and industrialization were well underway in the northeastern United States (Williamson 1965). The activities related to the territorial expansion necessary for the continued growth and development of America's urban and industrial system of social and economic organization began to reach into the South and even into developing areas west of the Mississippi. The Civil War effectively eliminated the resistance that had been shown by the peoples of these traditionally agrarian socioeconomic systems.

By the 1880's, the various widely-scattered markets of the United States had been attached to the transportation networks provided by the railroads, and urban growth proceeded at an unprecedented rate (Gilmore 1953; McKelvey 1963). Ten years later, most of Texas' frontier areas had been settled and even much of the state's unused land was being developed. Since then, the prevailing trend in population distribution and redistribution has focused on urban centers which exercise control over large metropolitan areas around them, including tributary towns, villages, and suburban residential areas.

Although concerned citizens of Texas cities have been careful to protect the more architecturally distinctive and historically well-known buildings and neighborhoods of their communities, only in recent years have they begun to realize the contributions that archeology can make to the management and interpretation of their historic places. Only a few historic sites dating from the second half of the nineteenth century have been investigated archeologically in scattered Texas cities, and almost all of these historical and archeological studies have been preliminary assessments of protected historic properties and recovery operations designed to salvage information from historic places that have been badly damaged or doomed to destruction. But a surprising amount of evidence has been recovered by archeological test excavations on the properties around historic buildings and also from short-term investigations of old urban areas where there are no visible, above-ground historic remains.

As preliminary as these introductory studies have been, they have provided new details about historical trends in building construction, architectural styles, and property use in different urban areas, and also some new information about the development of water distribution, energy supply and waste disposal systems, and other components of the public service infrastructure that has been an important part of urban growth. Also observable archeologically are the historical roots of the distinctive urban lifestyles that characterize different Texas cities and old established neighborhoods within them.

Downtown San Antonio

Previous discussion of the archeology of Spanish Colonial and Mexican Texas already has shown how combined archeological and historical investigations have helped to reconstruct the urban history of San Antonio. Alamo Plaza and the bustling downtown area around it have been found to contain a complexity of archeological deposits representing more than a century of life in Spanish Colonial mission and civil communities, evidence of the famous revolutionary battle and—on top of that—fill layers, foundation remains, and various kinds of debris that have accumulated during the last century and a half of urban development (Fox, Bass, and Hester 1976; Fox and Ivey 1979; Ivey and Fox n.d.). In contrast, archeological test excavations at the Spanish Governor's Palace have found very little evidence of the more than 250 years of life there because construction activities during the nineteenth and twentieth centuries, including those associated with the development of the property as a historic park, have thoroughly disturbed a large part of the Governor's Palace site (A. Fox 1977).

By 1873, architectural alteration of the Spanish Colonial church of the Villa de San Fernando, across Military Plaza from the Governor's Palace, created the San Fernando Cathedral in the growing downtown urban area of post-Civil War San Antonio. The San Fernando Cathedral itself is an interesting artifact of San Antonio's urban development. When archeologists studied it in the 1970's (Fox, Scurlock, and Clark 1977), the cathedral was com-

FIG. 11.2   *Activity at Military Plaza, downtown San Antonio, in the early 1870's.* (From King 1974. Drawing by J. W. Champney.)

posed of three principal architectural units. The main portion of the original stone Spanish Colonial church, including its apse, transept, and part of its original nave, was almost completely hidden from view. The eastern side of the old church and the cemetery in front of it were covered by the larger nineteenth-century, brick cathedral nave, its tall Gothic facade and twin bell towers rising above the sidewalk along the edge of Main Plaza. A two-story rectory of cut limestone constructed in the 1930's completely surrounded the north, east, and south walls of the Spanish Colonial church so that only the vaulted roof and its lantern dome were exposed to view and this only from the upper floor windows of the multi-story office buildings that dwarf the cathedral building today. Recently, the rectory has been removed to expose the back of the 250-year-old Colonial church so that it looks much like it did

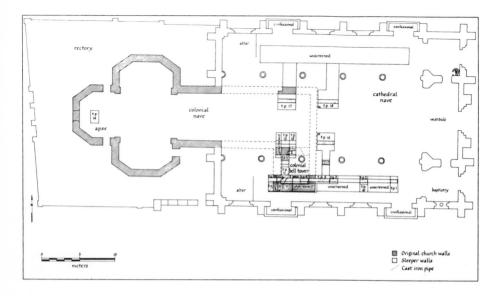

FIG. 11.3 *Plan of the San Fernando Cathedral, showing the Spanish Colonial church walls that remain and those that were torn down to ground level to make room for the addition of the 1860's cathedral nave.* (From Fox, Scurlock, and Clark 1977:Fig. 8. Courtesy Texas Historical Commission.)

when it stood as the central, most prominent building between the two open plazas of eighteenth-century Villa de San Fernando and early nineteenth-century San Antonio de Bexar.

In 1977, an archeological investigation was conducted at the historic Gresser House, a nineteenth-century, one-story, four-room stone structure located in the old La Villita neighborhood of downtown San Antonio (Ivey 1978a). The study was designed to recover as much information as possible from a small area of foundation remains that was exposed in the 1960's by the demolition of a small brick attachment to the Gresser House. Unfortunately, before the archeologists arrived, this area on the corner of South Presa and Nueva streets had been thoroughly disturbed by the demolition of the brick structure, by subsequent clearing and scraping with heavy machinery, and by more recent trenching for the construction of new cinder-block walls and the installation of gas and water lines. But careful examination of the stratigraphy exposed by the disturbances, searches through county archives,

study of various other historical accounts, and some controlled
test excavations gathered enough information with which to reconstruct the history of the street corner next to the Gresser
House.

The two adjacent city lots on which the Gresser House is located originally were acquired by a retired Spanish soldier named
Miguel Buentello and a civilian named Ignacio Villaseñor in 1818,
when new regulations caused squatters who had established small
farmsteads in the area to petition for legal title to the land they occupied. Villaseñor sold his tract to another retired soldier named
José Casas later in 1818. Casas acquired Buentello's lot sometime
after a flood devastated the neighborhood in 1819. The area may
have been abandoned for a while after that, but in 1861, when
Casas' widow sold the lots to a German immigrant named Louis
Gresser and his wife, the Casas' house was part of the property
transferred.

FIG. 11.4   *Looking across Main Plaza toward the San Fernando Church,
downtown San Antonio, in the 1850's.* (Courtesy Catholic Archives of San
Antonio.)

FIG. 11.5 *The nineteenth-century Gothic facade of the San Fernando Cathedral, San Antonio, in 1975.* (From Fox, Scurlock, and Clark 1977: Fig. 14. Courtesy Texas Historical Commission.)

The Casas House, which may have been built on the site of Buentello's residence, was a two-room structure with an associated kitchen. It had a thatched roof and walls constructed of upright posts bound together with rawhide strips, chinked and plastered with mud and whitewashed. This method of construction, called *chamacuero* or *palisado*, was common in the San Antonio area

FIG. 11.6   *Rear view of the San Fernando Cathedral, San Antonio, showing the dome of the eighteenth-century Spanish Colonial church, surrounded by the nineteenth-century cathedral nave and the twentieth-century rectory.* (From Fox, Scurlock, and Clark 1977:Fig. 13. Courtesy Texas Historical Commission.)

during the eighteenth and early nineteenth centuries. The shaped-stone Gresser House that remains today was added sometime after 1861 to the north wall of the smaller Casas House, which stood on the street corner until the 1920's when it apparently burned. In its place, a small brick structure was attached to the Gresser House. It was used as a store before it was torn down in the 1960's and the construction work began that exposed the archeological evidence of the successive urban residential occupations that took place there throughout the nineteenth century.

The Gresser House also has been called the Gresser-Hays House because tradition insists that the famous Texas Ranger Colonel John Coffee Hays occupied the place. Hays, who came to Texas and settled in San Antonio in the late 1830's, was a surveyor by profession and was employed by the Republic to survey the frontier. He became captain of a company of Rangers in 1840,

a

b

FIG. 11.7 *Two views of the Gresser House, La Villita, San Antonio.* A, the Gresser House in 1928, when the Casas House was still standing at the end of it; B, south wall of the Gresser House during renovations in the 1970's, after the brick structure that replaced the Casas House had been removed. The outline of the Casas House roof, marked by the line between the plaster and the exposed masonry, is visible below the flat roof line of the brick structure. (From Ivey 1978: Fig. 8. Courtesy Center for Archaeological Research, The University of Texas at San Antonio.)

fought Indians at Enchanted Rock and Bandera Pass, participated in the Battle of Plum Creek and the Battle of Salado, and then fought in the Mexican War. He led an expedition to look for a suitable overland route from San Antonio through El Paso to Chihuahua, spending several days at Fort Leaton in 1848. Then during the gold rush, he went off to California, where he served as sheriff of San Francisco County and laid out the City of Oakland (Webb 1952:628, 789). Jack Hays was an illustrious character, to say the least, and it is understandable that townspeople would like to say he once occupied their favorite historic places. But the archeological and historical investigation of the Gresser House found that, unless Hays and his bride happened to rent the Casas House for a while in the 1840's, the famous Texas Ranger probably lived in his own house on his own property, located a few hundred feet away in an area that today is a parking lot (Ivey 1978a:29).

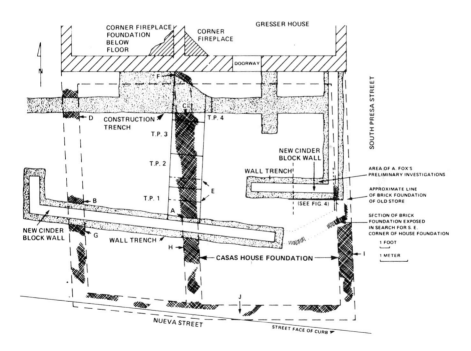

FIG. 11.8   *Plan of architectural features, construction areas, and archeological excavations at the Gresser House, on the corner of South Presa and Nueva streets, San Antonio. (From Ivey 1978:Fig. 3. Courtesy Center for Archaeological Research, The University of Texas at San Antonio.)*

Although the Casas House has been destroyed and its site badly disturbed, another archeological and historical assessment has found that at least one other early nineteenth-century residential property in La Villita is relatively well preserved (Fox, Valdez, and Bobbitt 1978). Located only half a block away from the Gresser House on Nueva Street, the Dolores Aldrete House property consists of three old city lots on which a *palisado* house is still standing that probably was constructed in the early nineteenth century when Buentello and Villaseñor were living down the street. Also on the property is a mid-nineteenth-century, two-room caliche-block structure, known as the Caile House, with more recent brick and frame additions. Other structures dating from the late nineteenth and early twentieth centuries extend across the back of the property. Limited archeological test excavations recovered artifacts that reflect changes in the function of the historic site from an early nineteenth-century residence to a twentieth-century commercial property. Fortunately, the Dolores Aldrete House site is owned by San Antonians who are aware of the significance of the archeological deposits there, as well as the importance of the architectural features, and the historic site can be preserved as a resource of information about the cultural heritage of early urban San Antonio's La Villita barrio.

Investigations in the Arciniega Street area, on the southern edge of La Villita near Hemisfair Plaza, have found the remains of several residential structures, irrigation ditches that were a part of San Antonio's 250-year-old *acequia* system, a trash dump full of late nineteenth-century household artifacts, a latrine, and other architectural and archeological features (Katz 1978). One of the more interesting features found in the Arciniega Street area was a cistern about seven feet deep, roughly rectangular in outline, and partially lined with stone masonry. It had been dug into the caliche bedrock that underlies the neighborhood. Attached to it was another, shallower rectangular pit that may have been used as a cooling chamber. Early twentieth-century bottles and other household garbage were found in the 20-inch-deep soil layer that covered the original late nineteenth-century ground surface of the cistern area. Below this, loose brown soil, pockets of ash, and artifacts filled the subterranean enclosure. The nature of the deposits at the bottom of the cistern indicated that it contained water when its use as a trash pit began.

FIG. 11.9 *The Dolores Aldrete, or "Palisado" House (early nineteenth century), in the La Villita neighborhood, San Antonio.* (From Fox, Valdez, and Bobbitt 1978:Fig. 3b. Courtesy Center for Archaeological Research, The University of Texas at San Antonio.)

A wide assortment of late nineteenth-century household artifacts was recovered from the cistern and its associated chamber, including various food, medicine, and beverage bottles, glass jars, tumblers, goblets, pitchers and bowls, earthenware, porcelain, and crockery dishes and containers, metal stove parts, cooking and eating utensils. Metal parts from harnesses, tools, and other objects were found in the cistern fill as evidence of other activities of the residential occupation. During her analysis of the artifacts, Anne Fox found that several mold-made drugstore bottles in the collection were some of the most helpful artifacts for the precise dating of the filling of the cistern feature (Katz 1978:41–72). It was common practice in the late nineteenth century for druggists and soda-water bottlers to have the names of their firms embossed on their bottles. Using old city business directories, Fox compiled a chart correlating the time periods when the various firms were in operation with the names on the bottles. From this she was able to conclude that the cistern was filled between 1899 and 1905, perhaps when public water distribution was installed that removed the need for individual household water storage facilities.

FIG. 11.10   *The Caile House (mid-nineteenth century) in the La Villita neighborhood, San Antonio.* (From Fox, Valdez, and Bobbitt 1978: Fig. 3a. Courtesy Center for Archaeological Research, The University of Texas at San Antonio.)

The animal bones recovered from the cistern provided some information about the inhabitants of one old residential property in the Arciniega Street area. A large number and wide assortment of bones from small birds, fish, wild turkey, and rabbits suggested that at least one of the occupants of the lot above the cistern was a hunter and fisherman. The quantity of chicken bones found indicated that poultry was readily available; perhaps chickens were raised in the backyard. Beef was a common meat item on the family table, judging from the number of sawed bones and the variety of cuts of meat they represented. Rats apparently were a nuisance and probably thrived in the damp, dark cistern and in the air spaces under the buildings on the lot above it.

In 1978, the Bexar County Commissioner's Court authorized an archeological investigation of a parking lot area where an annex building was proposed to be constructed not far from the Bexar County Courthouse in downtown San Antonio (A. Fox n.d.). Historical research found that the project area was once part of an eighteenth-century and early nineteenth-century neighborhood designated by Spanish city planners as Barrio del Sur—the district, or ward, south of Main and Military plazas in early San Antonio.

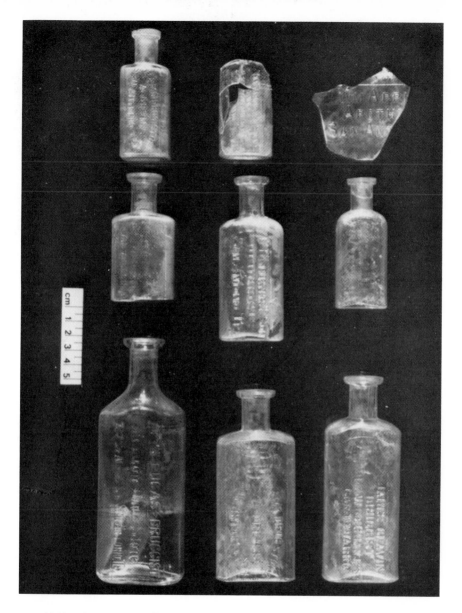

FIG. 11.11 *Late nineteenth-century drugstore bottles from a cistern in the Arciniega Street area, near La Villita, San Antonio.* (From Katz 1978: Fig. 31. Courtesy Center for Archaeological Research, The University of Texas at San Antonio.)

Actually, the first houses in the neighborhood were concentrated in a row facing the plazas and by the mid-nineteenth century only a few structures had been built south of there, where the courthouse annex was to be constructed. By 1873, however, rows of adobe houses had been built along the streets of the Barrio del Sur.

Test trenches were excavated in the areas where the locations of the nineteenth-century adobe buildings could be predicted based upon the historical accounts. Structural remains and occupational debris were found on three of the old city lots on West Nueva Street which were evidence of the habitation of the project area between about 1850 and the 1920's. A section of the San Pedro *acequia* also was located. On one lot, the cut limestone foundations of an 1860's house and its associated kitchen building were found. The historical records indicated that this was the late nineteenth-century and early twentieth-century residence of Dr. Charles A. R. Campbell, who became known worldwide for his successful experiments with the cultivation of colonies of bats to control mosquito populations and thereby help eradicate malaria. The archeological excavations happened to uncover a group of metal plates stashed

FIG. 11.12   *Theodore Gentilz's picture of his home, a rather typical residential neighborhood scene in mid-nineteenth-century San Antonio.* (Courtesy Library of the Daughters of the Republic of Texas at the Alamo, San Antonio.)

under the house which were used in the printing of Dr. Campbell's book, entitled *Bats, Mosquitoes and Dollars* (1925).

On another old city lot in the courthouse annex site, the archeological excavations found mid-nineteenth-century stone rubble foundations of a house and kitchen which apparently were consumed by fire in the early twentieth century. On the neighboring lot, cut limestone foundations were found that had been badly disturbed by later construction activities, but evidently were the remains of buildings constructed in the mid-nineteenth century which became the residential property of John Dullnig and his family in 1879. In the early 1900's, Dullnig opened a grocery store in the old house on the front of the lot and moved his family to the building on the back of the property.

The section of the old Spanish Colonial water supply ditch known as the San Pedro *acequia* that was found in the courthouse annex project area was in relatively good condition, although one of its walls had been completely robbed of its lining of limestone blocks that was added in the nineteenth century when the *acequia* system was repaired and reopened for use by the growing San Antonio community. The historical records indicate that the flow of water through the ditch was not stopped until 1906. When the *acequias* were in operation, it was customary for the residents who used them to clean the ditches once a year, and several sections of different *acequias* studied in the San Antonio area have been found to be devoid of artifacts because they had been cleaned out. But residents of the Barrio del Sur apparently were not very meticulous about cleaning their section of the San Pedro *acequia*. The archeological excavations found fragments of mid-nineteenth-century dishes, and even some sherds of eighteenth-century Mexican-made pottery, in the mud on the bottom of the stone-lined ditch. The fill above contained late nineteenth- and early twentieth-century trash and construction debris that was thrown in when the *acequia* was no longer in use.

Several other urban historic sites have been studied archeologically in the San Antonio area. Investigations at the Wulff House (Clark 1974a) and at the foundations of the Mayer House (Ivey 1978b) in the King William Historic District have assessed the archeological potential of those neighboring properties and made recommendations for their management as parts of the late nineteenth-century neighborhood of stately homes on the south-

FIG. 11.13 *The Old Ursuline Convent, San Antonio, in the 1870's.* (From King 1974. Drawing by J. W. Champney.)

ern edge of downtown San Antonio. Short-term investigations also have been conducted at the Old Ursuline Academy, established in the 1850's by Catholic nuns as a school for girls (Clark 1974b; Katz 1977; Jones n.d.). Information was recovered with which to assess the archeological potential of the school buildings and grounds.

Excavation of a cistern beneath an old commercial building in downtown San Antonio recovered bottles and other refuse from a period of about 20 years after the Civil War (McGraw and Valdez n.d.). Like other cisterns that were common architectural features under nineteenth-century urban buildings, the cistern at Rio Rita was a time capsule containing evidence of the late nineteenth-century use of the commercial space above it. Chinaware, eating utensils, and a large assortment of liquor bottles represent the occupation of a hotel establishment. A variety of lenses and fragments of lenses for eyeglasses in various stages of manufacture represent the operations of an optician's office during the late nineteenth century.

In 1974 and 1975, archeologists investigated an old dump ground in the path of the construction for the McAllister Freeway through the northern edge of downtown San Antonio (Clark n.d.). Judging from the datable artifacts found, the dump was located on the outskirts of town when it was in use at the turn of the century. A variety of glass, ceramic, and metal artifacts were recovered, many of which apparently were the household refuse of German San Antonians who made up a large segment of the city's growing population in the late nineteenth century. Some of the bowls and plates found were labelled with German names, and the large number of tobacco pipes recovered from the dump reflect a habit common to the German-Texans.

FIG. 11.14 *A family at a German beer garden at San Pedro Springs, San Antonio, in the 1870's.* (From King 1974. Drawing by J. W. Champney.)

A Laredo Barrio

Investigations in downtown Laredo have found a considerable amount of archeological and architectural information about an urban Mexican-American barrio, most of which was levelled for the construction of Interstate Highway 35 through the center of the city to the International Bridge (Clark and Juarez n.d.; Cox 1982). Several downtown lots and a plaza comprising more than four city blocks were studied shortly after many of the structures on them had been demolished. Various standing buildings, foundation remains, cisterns, and other architectural features were recorded in detail and various building sites, trash pits, and other features were investigated archeologically.

Four basic architectural phases were recognized, beginning with the earliest period of historic occupation of the barrio from the 1840's to the 1870's, when the most common buildings were small, simple stone dwellings of the vernacular style of the border area. With the arrival of the railroad in 1881, downtown Laredo underwent rapid growth and development, as was exemplified by larger residences constructed of local brick and stone in Italianate, Romanesque, Victorian, and other architectural styles of the late nineteenth century. Next came a Mexican Revolution phase dating from about 1910 until the 1930's, when simple board and batten "peon" houses were the most common new buildings constructed. This phase was followed by the construction of twentieth-century American urban residential and commercial buildings and the maintenance and modernization of older structures.

The archeological investigation of the urban Laredo barrio recovered some occupational evidence and land use information that can be compared with archeological evidence found at historic sites in San Antonio and other parts of Texas (John Clark, personal communication, September, 1982). Although the methods and materials used in the construction of the mid-nineteenth-century residences in the Laredo barrio are somewhat different from those in San Antonio neighborhoods of about the same time period, there are similarities in the ways residential properties were occupied. In the early urban areas of both San Antonio and Laredo, the dwellings were small in comparison to later-day houses and the general pattern of property use was for the house to be situated on the very front of the lot. The patio in the rear of the barrio residence was an important household activity area. If they

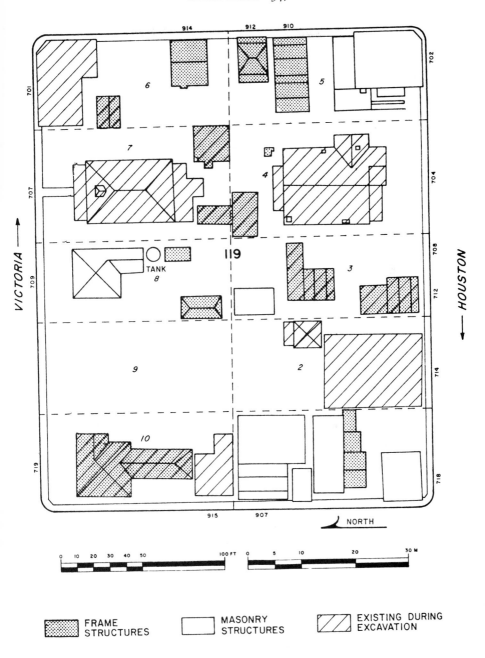

FIG. 11.15   *Plan of one of the city blocks (119) investigated in Laredo.* (From Clark and Juarez n.d. Courtesy Texas Department of Highways and Public Transportation.)

could afford to, families in the Laredo barrio built walls to protect the privacy of their yards. Waste disposal areas (refuse pits and outhouses) usually were located on the very back of the urban residential property, which probably was a common pattern in various nineteenth-century urban neighborhoods and contrasts with rural homesteads whose residents often disposed of trash in the most convenient manner—often simply tossing it out the doors and windows of their houses.

The kinds of artifacts and the frequencies with which they occurred at the residential sites of the Laredo barrio can be compared with the archeological evidence recovered from household occupation sites in other parts of Texas. As might be expected, Mexican-made pottery vessels occur more commonly along the Mexican border than they do at sites further north. But the traditional, colorful, tin-enameled majolica wares (produced in Mexico during the Spanish Colonial Period and still being produced today) were not common in the Laredo barrio. In all of the hundreds of pottery sherds collected during the investigations, no sherds of eighteenth-century majolica vessels were found which might be expected to occur as the remains of family heirlooms or special tablewares. Nineteenth-century British and American ceramics comprised the greatest proportion of tablewares and may have been much less expensive or easier to come by than fine decorative majolica dishes. The Mexican pottery types, which amounted to as much as 20 percent of the pottery sampled from the nineteenth-century Laredo barrio, were primarily lead-glazed wares. Perhaps they were inexpensive and easy to obtain, but lead-glazed pottery also was important culturally as the pottery used to prepare traditional kinds of foods; they can be compared and contrasted with stoneware and metal utilitarian vessels which are found more commonly at nineteenth-century urban and rural households north of the border that were occupied by peoples of different cultural heritages.

Other comparisons of kinds and amounts of material evidence point to differences between ethnic and socioeconomic backgrounds of the late-nineteenth-century residents of Laredo and other parts of Texas. Wine bottles, instead of whiskey and beer bottles, were found in the Laredo neighborhood and cough remedy bottles were very common, perhaps because these "medicines" were a relatively inexpensive and socially acceptable source

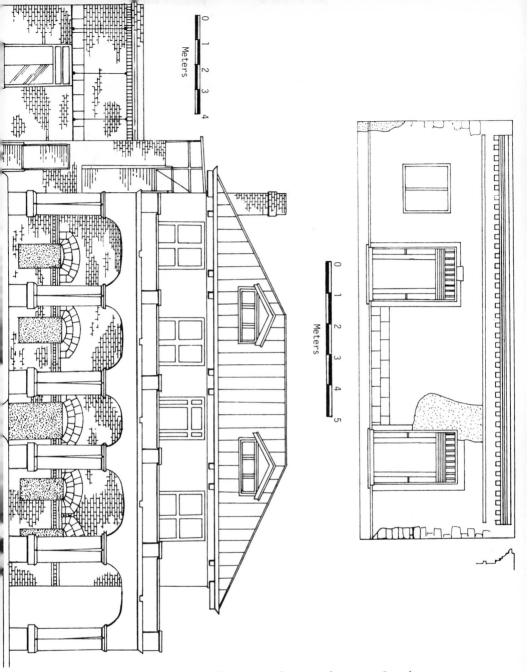

FIG. 11.16 *Architectural styles of houses in a barrio in downtown Laredo.*
A. Mid-nineteenth-century Mexican vernacular. B. Late nineteenth-century architecture, after the arrival of the railroad. (From Clark and Juarez n.d. Courtesy Texas Department of Highways and Public Transportation.)

of alcohol. Tobacco pipes occur very infrequently in the Laredo barrio, probably not so much because tobacco or pipes were hard to come by, but because tobacco was consumed in cigarettes instead of special paraphernalia like the decorative clay pipes commonly found at sites that were occupied by Anglo-American and European Texans.

Austin

For several years after its creation on March 2, 1836, the revolutionary government of the Republic of Texas was moved from one Anglo-American colonial settlement to another on the coastal plain. A permanent location was selected in 1839 and an orderly arrangement of streets and lots was laid out for the capital city of Waterloo on the banks of the Colorado River at the foot of the Balcones Escarpment. Positioned on the very edge of the frontier, however, the new capital site was exposed to attacks by hostile Indians and was haphazardly settled. In 1842, when Mexican forces took control of San Antonio and other old Hispanic towns of the Department of Bexar, the government of the Republic was moved to Houston temporarily, and then to Washington-on-the-Brazos where it originally began. Finally, by the time Texas was annexed to the United States, the town of Austin began its development as the permanent capital city, located on the very spot where Waterloo had been planned (Brown n.d.; Barkley 1963).

Austin did not become a city as early and did not grow as rapidly as most of the other early urban areas of Texas, and many of the capital city's early public and commercial buildings have been refurbished and reoccupied as Austin developed around them. A variety of nineteenth-century stone, brick, and frame buildings were being preserved and maintained through use as residences, businesses, professional offices, governmental offices, and museums. But Austin's urbanization has increased at an incredible rate in recent years, corresponding to the expansion of its governmental complexes, academic institutions, and private industries. The resulting alteration of the landscape has encouraged Austinites to pay more attention to protection of their cultural and environmental resources from the destructive and contaminating effects of urban development and urban sprawl.

FIG. 11.17 *The State Capitol in Austin in the early 1870's.* (From King 1974. Drawing by J. W. Champney.)

Some of Austin's early government buildings have been investigated archeologically. As mentioned in the discussion of the study of the historic sites of the Texas Republic, archeological excavations have been used to determine the exact location of the original kitchen built in 1841 and 1842 as part of the residential headquarters of the French foreign minister in Austin (Olds 1967). But the French Legation had its day long before Austin began its urban growth in the second half of the nineteenth century. '

Historical and archeological investigations have been conducted at the site of the temporary state capitol that was constructed after the old stone capitol burned and while the present-day capitol building was being erected between 1883 and 1888 (Moore *et al.* 1972). After 1888, the temporary building, which was located across 12th Street from the present-day capitol grounds, was used for school classroom space and for other purposes until it burned down in 1899 (Willoughby 1981). The archeological investigations were undertaken in the early 1970's, when the parking lot area where the temporary capitol once stood was being considered as the possible site for a new office building for the Texas State Department of Highways and Public Transportation.

Historical research found a variety of records pertaining to the temporary capitol, including architectural plans and drawings and the contract documents for the building's construction. Ar-

FIG. 11.18 *Front elevation of the Temporary Capitol of Texas, 1883–1888, Austin.* (From Moore *et al.* 1972: Cover. Courtesy Texas Department of Highways and Public Transportation.)

cheological excavations exposed the grid pattern of stone foundations that supported the building and also found the remains of a drainage system, walkways, and a large, bell-shaped, brick-lined underground cistern that stored rainwater draining from the roof of the building. Much of the stone used in the temporary capitol apparently was robbed from the ruins of the previous capitol building. The architectural remains uncovered by the archeological excavations indicated that the temporary building was not constructed with the craftsmanship implied in the government contract documents which authorized the construction. Evidence of cutting corners was found and the measurements of several parts of the building's foundations did not match those in the construction plans and drawings.

Thousands of artifacts were found in the fill layers of the building site, including household occupational debris like ceramic tablewares, glass beverage and food containers and metal utensils, firearm-related items such as cartridges, and personal items like clothing fasteners and a few coins. Most dated from about 1883 and 1899 when the building was standing, but some artifacts from the 1850's and the 1860's and others from the first years of the twentieth century also were found. As yet this collection has not been studied for the purpose of detailing the various actual uses of the temporary capitol site and the events that took place there as part of the urban growth of Austin in the second half of the nineteenth century.

In 1971 and 1972, intensive archeological and historical investigations were conducted at the Carrington House, a large two-story stone house that was built in the 1850's and has survived to become the headquarters of the Texas Historical Commission (Roberson 1974). Located only a few blocks from the state capitol, the house was built for a wealthy Austin businessman named L. D. Carrington and his family. It was one of several prominent Austin Chalk limestone structures constructed during the decade before the Civil War, including the Governor's Mansion, one of Austin's first state capitol buildings, the General Land Office Building, and the Austin City Jail. Carrington's house probably was built by some of the same craftsmen who created these historic places at the time when Austin had a population of less than 3,000. The house was spacious for its day and may have been the largest residence in the city. In contrast to the architecturally-ornate Victorian houses of the late nineteenth century, the stark, sturdy appearance and uncluttered lines of the Carrington House reflect the austerity of the mid-nineteenth-century architecture in central Texas. The original plan, with its breezeway separating the kitchen from the rest of the rooms on the lower floor, is reminiscent of the dog-runs of frontier Texas.

The stone house and its associated structures were occupied by the Carringtons, their boarders, and their servants until 1870, when Carrington sold his city residence and moved to the small town of Buda south of Austin. Afterward, the Carrington House served as a residence for other Austin families, as an eye, ear, and throat clinic, and as a boarding house.

Archival research has found several old photographs taken from the dome of the capitol that document the development of the neighborhood around the Carrington House since the late nineteenth century. Specific occupations were difficult to identify archeologically, although information was recovered concerning the times at which alterations were made to the various parts of the Carrington House, and some evidence of its associated outbuildings was recovered. The brick-lined, bell-shaped underground cistern near the back porch of the house compared closely to the cistern found at the site of Austin's temporary capitol (Moore *et al.* 1972:19, 72, 134). The most important archeological find was a large collection of occupational debris recovered from the dry, dusty space beneath the wooden floor of the kitchen wing. Dating from a relatively narrow time span, the collection provides a comparative sample that can be used to help identify dates and activities represented by artifacts found at other archeological sites of the late nineteenth century and the early twentieth century.

Most of the Carrington artifacts evidently date from around the turn of the century, when the first major renovations of the building took place. Included in this assortment of Victorian period artifacts was a variety of construction materials (complete with a lumber company receipt), door and window hardware, wallpaper fragments, glass lamp globe and lamp chimney fragments, early electric and gas fixtures, furniture hardware, tableware and kitchen utensils, stove parts, food and beverage containers, medicine bottles, and various personal goods, such as buttons and other clothing fasteners and ornaments, toys, thimbles, and firearm-related items.

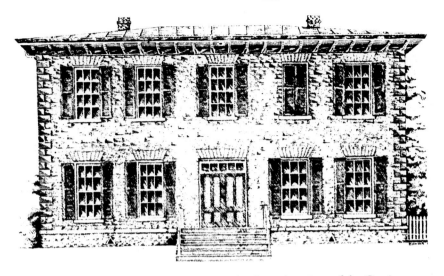

FIG. 11.19 *The limestone masonry facade, front elevation, of the Carrington House, constructed in the 1850's and now the offices of the Texas Historical Commission, Austin.* (From Roberson 1974: Cover. Courtesy Texas Historical Commission. Drawing by Edwina Traverso.)

More recent archeological investigations have been conducted in a part of downtown Austin known as the Sixth Street Historic District, which is recognized for its Richardson-Romanesque Driskill Hotel, two of Austin's first skyscrapers, the 1878 Renaissance Revival Post Office and Federal Building, Victorian commercial buildings, and other early urban structures. The area investigated was Block 61, a parking lot scheduled to become the Grant Building and Plaza, designed to blend in architecturally with the rest of the old urban area east of Congress Avenue (Briggs 1981).

Background research pieced together the written history of the parking lot area. The alignments of some old building foundations were visible as cracks and bumps in the asphalt pavement. But once the earthmoving for the project was underway, most of the investigation consisted of construction monitoring and emergency recovery operations instead of well-planned archeological excavations. Even so, an interesting collection of artifacts was recovered and structural remains were recorded that reflect the development of the urban area from the days of the Republic and early statehood—when the area was residential and Sixth Street

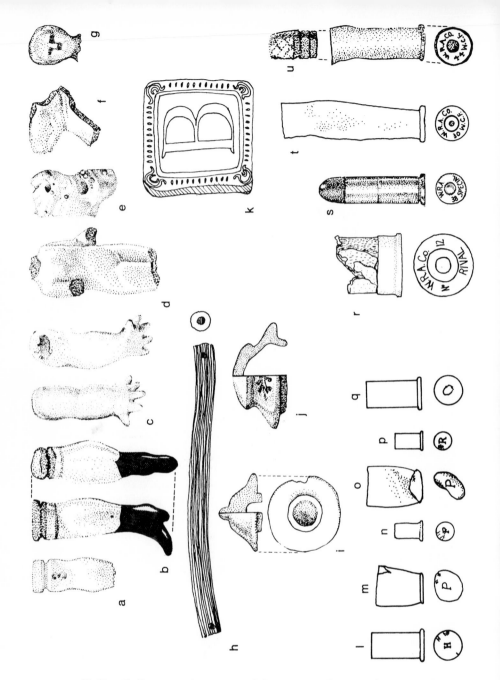

FIG. 11.20 *Doll parts, other toys, and firearm cartridge cases from the Carrington House, Austin.* a–g, porcelain doll parts; h, celluloid tube; i–j, porcelain toy teapot lids; k, wooden toy block; l–u, cartridge cases. (From Roberson 1974 : Fig. 62. Courtesy Texas Historical Commission. Drawings by Nola Montgomery.)

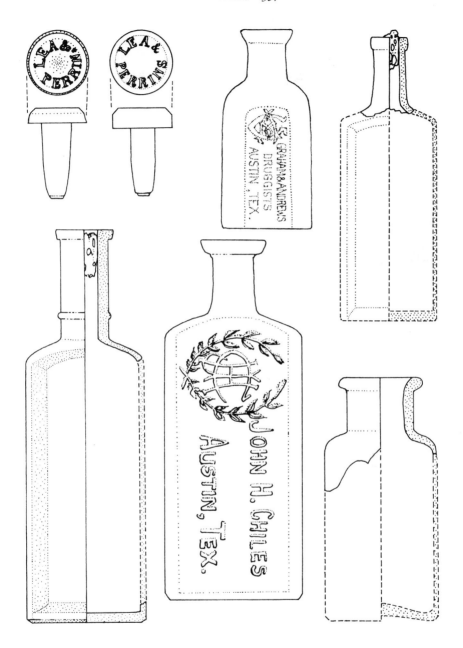

FIG. 11.21   *Glass bottles and glass bottle stoppers from the Carrington House, Austin.* (From Roberson 1974: Fig. 57. Courtesy Texas Historical Commission. Drawings by Nola Montgomery.)

was East Pecan—to the end of the nineteenth century, when the area began to be subdivided and built up into a series of commercial buildings.

A cistern and the remains of a firebox and an ash pit that happened to survive later development were the archeological evidence of a residential site that was first occupied in the 1840's and 1850's. Apparently the household structure changed several times from its beginnings as a dog-run cabin to a Greek Revival building complex, until finally all structures on Block 61 were razed in the 1890's for the construction of a planing mill and lumberyard. Certain kinds of artifacts indicated that the residents of the household occupation site included children and one member of the family may have been a war veteran and perhaps was a printer by trade. The archeological remains reflected the urban, rather than rural, context of the residential occupation. The family's furniture was factory-made and their meats were purchased from a local butcher shop. Many of their seasonings and other supplies came from the Northeast and from Europe.

Judging from the kinds of artifacts found and the frequencies with which they occurred in the collection, the nineteenth-century Austinites living on East Pecan Street did not indulge in very much alcohol consumption, but they did consume a lot of tobacco. The firebox from the residential occupation probably was used as a privy during the late nineteenth century. Associated with it were several bottles for certain brands of alcohol evidently preferred by one of the workers at the lumber mill.

Massive building foundations dating to the turn of the century represented the period of maximum urban commercial development of Block 61. As urbanization took over, the area no longer was a worthwhile location for a lumberyard. And even though the early twentieth-century commercial buildings had their heyday, the outward growth of the Austin community resulted in deterioration of the downtown business district as the primary focus of commerce. By 1957, the structures on Block 61 had been razed for the parking lot.

In recent years, there has been a revitalization of the Sixth Street neighborhood. If archeological studies are a part of this, when Pecan Street–Sixth Street passes on to the next stage of urban development, the material evidence of its history will be preserved.

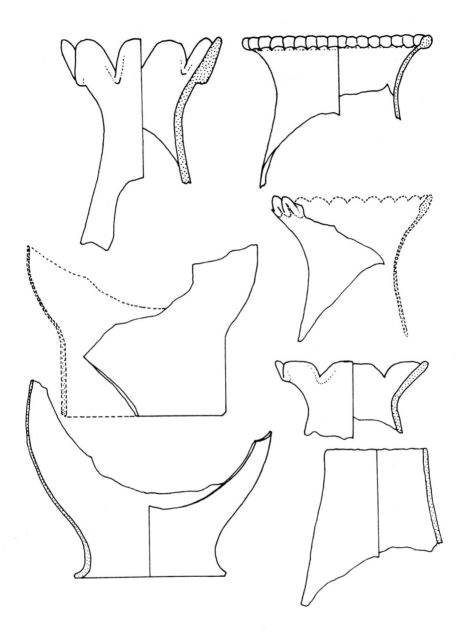

FIG. 11.22 *Clear glass lamp chimney fragments from the Carrington House, Austin.* (From Roberson 1974: Fig. 36. Courtesy Texas Historical Commission. Drawings by Nola Montgomery.)

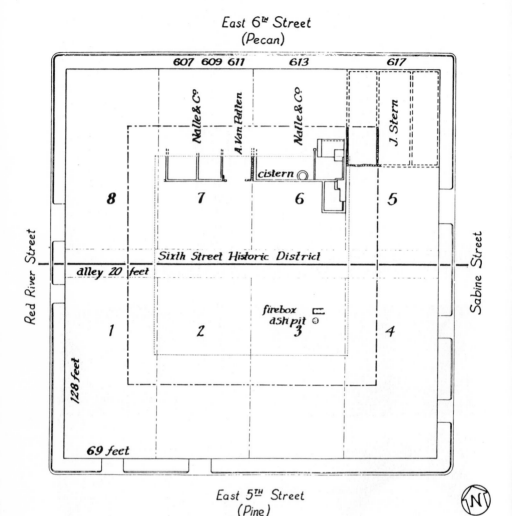

FIG. 11.23 *Grant Building and Plaza project area, plan of Block 61, downtown Austin.* (From Briggs 1981: Fig. 21. Courtesy Crow-Austin, No. 5, and Lone Star Archeological Services.)

Galveston

In another early urban area of Texas, recent investigations have recovered archeological, historical, and architectural evidence of the development of an elite residence that was built more

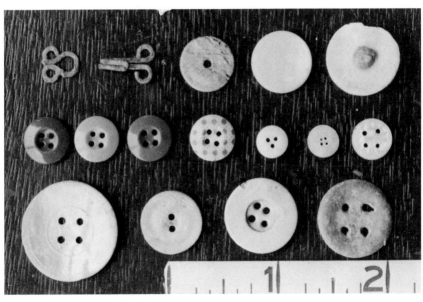

FIG. 11.24 *Metal, glass, shell, bone, and plastic buttons, and a hook-and-eye from the Grant Building and Plaza, downtown Austin.* (From Briggs 1981: Figs. 28 and 29. Courtesy Crow–Austin, No. 5, and Lone Star Archeological Services.)

FIG. 11.25   *Galveston's elegant Ashton Villa, built in 1859, as it looked at about the turn of the century.* (Courtesy Texas Anderson, Houston, the Houston Archaeological Society, and the Department of Anthropology, Rice University.)

than 120 years ago and withstood a 12-foot tidal wave in 1900 which left 5,000 or more people dead and the city of Galveston in ruins (Anderson 1982; n.d.). Ashton Villa was built in 1859 by Jones Moreau Brown, who left New York as an apprentice brick mason of 16 and arrived in the Republic of Texas in 1843, when the city of Galveston was less than a decade old. Brown's success grew as quickly as Galveston's did during the second half of the nineteenth century. He became involved in various aspects of the city's urban development, running a large wholesale hardware business and a construction business, besides being president of the First National Bank, president of the first electric company, vice president of the first gas company, a purchasing agent for the Confederacy, and holding executive posts in the waterworks, a railroad line, a wharf company, and other enterprises.

The family residence he built in 1859 was designed in the latest Italianate style, with some classic conservative elements.

After Brown died at Christmas, 1895, his eldest daughter took charge of Ashton Villa, directing the construction of a large addition to the house and altering its classic architectural appearance to fit the Victorian style of the day. Learning from the disastrous effects of the 1900 hurricane and tidal wave, the people of Galveston constructed a seawall and brought in sand dredged up from the bay to raise the ground level of the island. Although the massive brick structures of Ashton Villa could not be jacked up like the many frame structures in the city, fill was deposited over the site area. In 1929, the property was sold to the Shriners, who tore down the villa's kitchen and servants' quarters building, the con-

FIG. 11.26   A gold and burgundy banded porcelain spittoon from the privy vault at Ashton Villa, Galveston. (Courtesy Texas Anderson, Houston, the Houston Archaeological Society, and the Department of Anthropology, Rice University.)

servatory, and the family dining hall, and altered several other parts of the building complex. Since 1970, the historic site has been maintained as a museum administered by the Galveston Historical Foundation.

Investigations in 1980 and 1981 at Ashton Villa by Rice University archeologists and members of the Houston Archaeological Society involved an intensive survey of the visible architectural features, research of the abundant archival materials about the extravagant public lives of the Brown family, and archeological test excavations in various parts of the historic property. Beneath the layers of sand that have preserved the grounds of the villa since the turn of the century, the archeological excavations uncovered curbed driveways and walkways of handmade brick, laid in graceful herringbone patterns, and even a brick-lined privy vault in the stableyard of the urban estate.

In contrast to most nineteenth-century urban and rural resi-

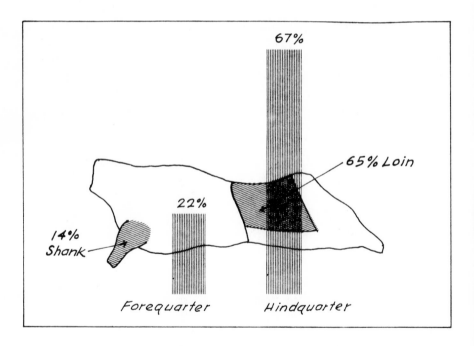

FIG. 11.27 *Chart of beef cuts represented by bones from the privy vault at Ashton Villa, Galveston.* (Courtesy Texas Anderson, Houston, the Houston Archaeological Society, and the Department of Anthropology, Rice University.)

dences, Ashton Villa had running water and gas lights from the time it was constructed. Wood and copper cisterns in the attic fed the baths of the house and an enormous cistern under the kitchen supplied water for other uses. While most family residences of the period show simple, functional arrangement of rooms and out-buildings, Mr. Brown's site-plan for Ashton Villa was architec-turally (and culturally) balanced in every detail, including the loca-tion of the servants' privy near the stables, hidden from view by the stableyard wall.

The archeological excavations found the brick-lined privy vault full of household garbage which shows that the Browns' life-style was very different indeed from those of other late nineteenth-century urban families. Besides glass bottles that once contained wine, beer, ale and Udolpho Wolfe's Aromatic Schnapps, the privy contained bottles of Pond Lily Wash (a facial astringent) and French perfumes. Numerous glass medicine bottles were found, as was a free-blown glass syringe which possibly was used by Mr. Brown during his losing struggle with cancer. Most of the ceramic vessels found in the privy were European porcelain, much of it finely decorated. This is in contrast to the much less expensive Eu-ropean and American earthenwares, which are the most common types of china found at other urban residential sites. A large num-ber of food bones were found. Many of them were from cuts of beef, primarily from the most expensive parts, including Porter-house, T-bone, and sirloin steaks that averaged more than an inch thick. The bones of turkey, chicken, pork, mutton, crab, and fish also were found in the privy fill. Obviously, the Brown family ate very well.

XII

Preserving the Evidence
of Texas History

THE URBANIZATION and industrialization of Texas has been responsible for the development of a modern, progressive state whose people take great pride in their cultural integrity and their cultural heritage. But urbanization and industrialization also have caused the destruction and disturbance of much of the material evidence of Texas history. The Texas Historical Commission estimates that 5,000 to 7,000 archeological sites and historic properties are damaged or destroyed in Texas each year (Mallouf et al. 1981:ix). The Texas Historical Foundation estimates that the number is greater than 10,000.

Probably more than one third, and possibly as many as 60 percent, of the prehistoric and historic archeological sites in Texas have been badly damaged or destroyed by urban and industrial expansion, by strip mining and agricultural activities, by the construction of highways, pipelines, and lakes, and by vandalism (Texas Historical Commission 1973:62). Probably less than one percent of the archeological sites in Texas have been properly recorded and investigated, and most of this work has focused on prehistoric rather than historic sites.

Fortunately, heritage-minded citizens and conscientious developers and industrialists have recognized the importance of many well-known historic landmarks and a variety of historically and architecturally distinctive buildings have been preserved in Texas cities, towns, and rural areas. Serious amateur and professional historians and archeologists have organized into local, regional, statewide, and national societies for the preservation of our cultural resources and the recovery of archeological information from historic sites in the path of destruction. These societies and other concerned individuals and groups have supported the enactment of historic preservation and antiquities laws that have helped to protect historic sites and provide for the identification and careful management of historical and archeological resources on public lands and in the path of publicly-sponsored construction activities.

Unfortunately, the importance of the archeological contexts of historic places often has not been recognized. Most people have not been shown that the archeological deposits beneath and around standing structures often contain architectural information which can be used in the authentic reconstruction, restoration, or renovation of historic buildings. Fewer Texans know that the archeological components of historic sites often contain the only real material evidence of how and when the historic places were occupied. Some people simply do not care, particularly those who fear that the existence of potentially significant historical and archeological resources might hold up their construction activities or otherwise affect their development plans.

Although historical archeology is a relatively new field of study, it has become not only a part of historic preservation, but also a part of the public service of cultural resource management in Texas, as society has begun to realize the irreplaceable nature and scientific value of historical archeological remains. Historical archeology is attracting more and more archeologists, historians, planners, developers, and private citizens from various walks of life. The increasing amount of historical archeological research in Texas is rapidly accumulating a substantial body of comparative information that is contributing to the study of Texas history and can enhance studies in cultural geography and anthropology.

Recognizing this as a new area of popular interest that can be controlled, several influential scholars in anthropology and history already have begun to promote their own patented research designs, which they assert will stimulate more imaginative research and lead to more anthropologically and historically meaningful results. But many Texans who are involved in historical archeology know that standardized methods and politically-motivated research designs could stifle innovation and encourage stagnation of the discipline; they can also expose historical archeology to management by government agencies who control the purse strings for much of the cultural resource management and by professional organizations that inadvertently seek to manage vocational archeologists' behavior as much as they work to manage cultural resources (D. Fox 1980). Avocational archeologists in Texas and the professional archeologists who work with them will continue to foster the growth of the discipline of historical archeology by

demonstrating to the public how this research can enrich our understanding of modern social, economic, and political institutions.

There are many research questions about Texas history that have yet to be approached through archeological investigation. A variety of historic sites have not been investigated because of problems in obtaining legal access to them, because of limited funds available to finance the work, because of potential political repercussions and, often, simply because of lack of interest among vocational and avocational archeologists. Public interest in archeology and history can encourage the preservation and investigation of significant historic sites, but archeologists are leery about publicizing the existence and locations of many sites for fear of exposing them to relic hunters, developers, and others who might damage or destroy them.

Archeological investigation of the Indians of Texas is being coordinated with detailed studies of the descriptive accounts left by the early Europeans who explored Texas in the sixteenth and seventeenth centuries (Campbell 1972, 1975, 1977). Archeologists have begun to compare the cultural remains of historic Indians, like those found in the Spanish Colonial missions, with prehistoric archeological evidence so that the peoples of the Late Prehistoric Period can be identified and their acculturation can be studied (Fox 1979; Hester 1980:164). More and more archeological investigations at historic Indian sites in Texas will help to reconstruct the culture histories of the different groups of people who inhabited Texas at the beginning of written history and help to detail the ways in which the original human cultures of Texas disappeared by the end of the nineteenth century.

Because the value of archeological investigations as part of the reconstruction and interpretation of Texas history only now is being realized, archeological studies of most Spanish Colonial sites in Texas have been preliminary in scope. There has not been enough public and financial support for well-designed, intensive investigations, even though archeological studies have helped to verify the locations of Spanish Colonial settlements, and occupational features within settlements, and have recovered information about the material things of life in eighteenth-century Texas. Historical archeology has much more to offer the accurate, detailed reconstruction of Spanish Colonial history and our understanding of how a mixture of Spanish military, settler, and acculturated Indian, or *Ladino*, elements adapted to the frontier and evolved into the Mexican society that the Anglo-American settlers encountered in the early nineteenth century.

The archeological evidence of early nineteenth-century Texas has been studied, primarily, through emergency recovery, or salvage, operations at historic shrines, like the Alamo and the birthplaces and homesteads of Texas heroes. And yet there are archeological sites of hundreds more who did not figure as prominently in the history books but were, nevertheless, very much a part of Anglo-American colonization, the Revolution, and the Republic. One of the most difficult topics to study historically is the integration of the diversity of peoples who became Texans in the first half of the nineteenth century. Besides Anglo-American immigrants from different cultural backgrounds, Afro-Americans, Mexicans, and immigrants of a variety of European nationalities had become Texans by the time of the Civil War. Most of these people left no written records of their lives and their contributions to the development of Texas. But their histories are preserved in archeological sites and can be reconstructed from the material things they left behind.

Archeologists have only begun to scratch the surface of historic sites of early American Texas. Plantations and rural estates, civil strongholds and military encampments, river crossings and inns, shipwrecks, and even actual town sites have been found in many parts of eastern Texas, on the coastal plain, and along the edge of the Edwards Plateau. Many of the more easily recognizable historic sites are located on public lands and are protected and managed as parts of public parks and as designated historic sites, like stately homes and old public buildings, battlefields of the Mexican War and the Civil War, and frontier forts of the nineteenth century. But many other important historic archeological sites are not as well known and are not protected. Historical archeology has not yet been done in some of Texas' largest, fastest-growing metropolitan areas.

Historical archeologists are learning new ways to recover information from historic sites, including those where no structures remain, and ways to prospect for submerged and buried sites and occupational features within them. They are learning how to use various kinds of ceramic, glass, and metal artifacts to assign precise dates to periods of construction and occupation, to determine the nature of different occupations, the activities that took place and the ethnic backgrounds of the occupants, and to study the relationships between settlement patterns, environmental conditions, transportation, and trade networks. The range of historic sites being investigated has been extended to include early Texas industries and factories. Some recent studies have focused on historic cemeteries, not by excavating them, of course, but through the analysis of information on tombstones, which can be used to study genealogical relationships, population make-up, and social organization within communities (Rutenberg 1981).

In recent years, the Texas Historical Commission has begun to develop a Texas Heritage Conservation Plan designed to help concerned government agencies, public groups, and individuals make effective, practical decisions about how to manage our historical and archeological resources. The Texas Historical Foundation is creating an Archeology Bank as an endowment fund to encourage a variety of activities dealing with the protection and preservation of historic sites, ranging from educational programs and academic research to archeological surveys and full-scale archeological investigations. Vocational and avocational archeologists will continue to find, protect, and investigate the cultural resources of Texas history and prehistory.

The Texas Archeological Society has more than 1,000 members now, and continues to grow, along with regional and local organizations across the state. But all Texans should learn to think of themselves as stewards of the past, and we all must be sure that we do not condone or perpetrate thoughtless and unnecessary destruction of our irreplaceable cultural resources—the only real, lasting, material evidence of Texas history.

Recommended Readings

T RACES OF TEXAS HISTORY focuses primarily on the archeological evidence that has been recovered and history as it has been studied archeologically in Texas. Although I have tried to place the findings of historical archeology within the context of written Texas history and folklore, there are several published sources which give a much broader historical background and present a variety of different perspectives of Texas history. There also are some good general works on Texas prehistory, archeological methods and theory, and other topics related to historical archeology in Texas.

Anne A. Fox suggested most of the following sources and I have added a few. There are many other studies of community, county, family, and state history. But the following Recommended Readings should give the reader a well-rounded familiarity with the body of knowledge within which historical archeology is done in Texas. Thomas R. Hester's book *Digging Into South Texas Prehistory* (1980) contains lists of journals and monograph series that deal with archeology in Texas. The offices of the Texas Historical Commission have information about antiquities and preservation legislation, the programs of state and federal agencies, colleges and universities, archeological societies, historical organizations, and museums.

On second listing, brief title is followed by a number in **boldface** type, referring to chapter list where full reference appears.

I Prehistoric and Historical Archeology in Texas

Deetz, J. 1977. *In Small Things Forgotten: The Archeology of American Life*. Anchor Press, New York.

Ferguson, L. (editor). 1977. Historical Archaeology and the Importance of Material Things. *The Society for Historical Archaeology, Special Publication Series*, No. 2.

Hester, T. R. 1980. *Digging Into South Texas Prehistory*. Corona Publishing Company, San Antonio.

Hume, I. N. 1969. *Historical Archaeology*. Alfred A. Knopf, Inc., New York. (1975 edition, W. W. Norton and Company, Inc., New York.)

Hume, I. N. 1970. *A Guide to Artifacts of Colonial America*. Alfred A. Knopf, Inc., New York.

Jelks, E. B., E. M. Davis, and H. B. Sturgis (editors). 1960. Review of Texas Archeology. *Bulletin of the Texas Archeological Society*, Vol. 29.

Newcomb, W. W., Jr., and F. Kirkland. 1967. *The Rock Art of Texas Indians*. University of Texas Press, Austin.

Schuyler, R. L. (editor). 1978. *Historical Archaeology: A Guide to Substantive and Theoretical Contributions*. Baywood Publishing Company, Inc., Farmingdale, New York.

Suhm, D. A., and E. B. Jelks. 1962. Handbook of Texas Archeology: Type Descriptions. *Texas Archeological Society, Special Publication*, No. 1.

Suhm, D. A., A. D. Krieger, and E. B. Jelks. 1954. Handbook of Texas Archeology. *Bulletin of the Texas Archeological Society*, Vol. 25.

Willey, G. R., and J. Sabloff. 1974. *A History of American Archaeology* (Reprinted 1980). W. H. Freeman and Company, San Francisco.

II Texas at the Beginning of Written History

Hester, T. R. 1980. *Digging Into South Texas Prehistory*. **I**

Inglis, J. M. 1964. A History of Vegetation on the Rio Grande Plain. *Texas Parks and Wildlife Department, Bulletin*, No. 45.

John, E. A. H. 1975. *Storms Brewed In Other Men's Worlds*. Texas A&M University Press, College Station.

Newcomb, W. W., Jr. 1961. *The Indians of Texas, from Prehistoric to Modern Times*. University of Texas Press, Austin.

Story, D. A. (editor). 1982. The Deshazo Site, Nacogdoches County, Texas. Vol. 1. *Texas Antiquities Committee, Permit Series*, No. 7.

Wallace, E., and E. A. Hoebel. 1952. *The Comanches: Lords of the Plains*. University of Oklahoma Press, Norman.

Weniger, D. *Texas As It Was*. To be published by University of Texas Press, Austin.

III The First Europeans

Bolton, H. E. (editor). 1959. *Spanish Exploration in the Southwest: 1542–1706*. 1916 reprint. Barnes and Noble, New York.

Hodge, F. W., and T. H. Lewis (editors). 1953. *Spanish Explorers in the Southern United States, 1528–1543: Original Narratives of Early American History*. 1907 reprint. Barnes and Noble, New York.

Joutel, H. 1962. *A Journal of La Salle's Last Voyage*. 1714 reprint. Corinth Books, New York.

McDonald, D., and J. B. Arnold III. 1979. Documentary Sources for the Wreck of the New Spain Fleet of 1554. *Texas Antiquities Committee Publication*, No. 8.

Olds, D. L. 1976. Texas Legacy from the Gulf: A Report of Sixteenth Century Shipwreck Materials Recovered from the Texas Tidelands. *Texas Memorial Museum, Miscellaneous Papers*, No. 5. *Texas Antiquities Committee Publication*, No. 2.

Weddle, R. S. 1973. *Wilderness Manhunt: The Search for LaSalle*. University of Texas Press, Austin.

IV Remains of the Spanish Colonial Empire

Bolton, H. E. 1970. *Texas in the Middle Eighteenth Century*. University of Texas Press, Austin.

Habig, M. A. 1968. *The Alamo Chain of Mis-*

sions. Franciscan Herald Press, Chicago.

John, E. A. H. 1975. *Storms Brewed in Other Men's Worlds.* **II**

Weddle, R. S. 1964. *The San Saba Mission: Spanish Pivot in Texas.* University of Texas Press, Austin.

Weddle, R. S. 1968. *San Juan Bautista: Gateway to Spanish Texas.* University of Texas Press, Austin.

Weddle, R. S., and R. S. Thonhoff 1976. *Drama and Conflict.* Madrona Press, Austin.

V   Sites of Mexican Texas, the Revolution, and the Republic

Almaraz, F. D., Jr. 1971. *Tragic Cavalier: Governor Manuel Salcedo of Texas, 1808–1813.* University of Texas Press, Austin.

Garrett, J. K. 1939. *Green Flag Over Texas.* Cordova Press, Inc., New York.

Gray, R. S. (editor). 1975. *A Visit to Texas in 1831.* Cordovan Press, Houston.

Green, R. M. (editor). 1921. *Memoirs of Mary A. Maverick, San Antonio's First American Woman.* Alamo Printing Company, San Antonio.

Hogan, W. R. 1975. *The Texas Republic: A Social and Economic History.* University of Texas Press, Austin.

Pierce, G. S. 1969. *Texas Under Arms: The Camps, Posts, Forts, and Military Towns of the Republic of Texas.* Encino Press, Austin.

Weber D. J. 1982. *The Mexican Frontier, 1821–1846: American Southwest Under Mexico.* University of New Mexico Press, Albuquerque.

VI   The Settlement of American Texas

Barker, E. C. 1969. *The Life of Stephen F. Austin, Founder of Texas, 1793–1836.* Cokesbury Press, 1926. Reprinted by University of Texas Press, Austin.

Hollon, W. E., and R. L. Butler (editors). 1956. *William Bollaert's Texas.* University of Oklahoma Press, Norman.

Jordan, T. G. 1981. *Trails to Texas: Southern Roots of Western Cattle Ranching.* Univer-

sity of Nebraska Press, Lincoln.

Latham, F. S. 1971. *Travels in the Republic of Texas, 1842.* Encino Press, Austin.

Olmsted, F. L. 1978. *A Journey Through Texas: Or, A Saddle Trip on the Southwestern Frontier.* University of Texas Press, Austin.

Sibley, M. M. 1967. *Travelers in Texas, 1761–1860.* University of Texas Press, Austin.

VII   The Movement West

Dobie, J. F. 1929. *A Vaquero of the Brush Country.* Little, Brown and Company, Inc., New York. Reprinted by University of Texas Press, Austin, 1981.

Flanagan, S. 1974. *Trailing the Longhorns.* Madrona Press, Austin.

Jenkins, J. H., III (editor). 1973. *Recollections of Early Texas: The Memoirs of John Holland Jenkins.* University of Texas Press, Austin.

Kenner, C. L. 1969. *A History of New Mexican–Plains Indian Relations.* University of Oklahoma Press, Norman.

Lehmann, V. W. 1969. *Forgotten Legions: Sheep in the Rio Grande Plain of Texas.* The Western Press, University of Texas at El Paso.

Matthews, S. R. 1958. *Interwoven: A Pioneer Chronicle.* Hertzog, El Paso.

Scott, F. J. 1966. *Historical Heritage of the Rio Grande.* Texian Press, Waco.

VIII   European Farmsteads

Baker, T. L. 1979. *The First Polish Americans.* Texas A&M University Press, College Station.

Hebert, R. B. 1981. *The Forgotten Colony: San Patricio de Hibernia.* Eakin Press, Burnet.

Jordan, T. G. 1966. *German Seed in Texas Soil: Immigrant Farmers in Nineteenth-Century Texas.* University of Texas Press, Austin.

Newcomb, W. W., Jr. 1978. *Friedrich Richard Petri, German Artist on the Texas Frontier.* University of Texas Press, Austin.

Oberste, W. H. 1953. *Texas Irish Empresarios*

and Their Colonies. Von-Boeckmann–Jones, Austin.

IX Battlegrounds, Forts, and Other Military Sites

Kerby, R. L. 1972. *Kirby Smith's Confederacy, The Trans-Mississippi South, 1863–1865.* Columbia University Press, New York.

Leckie, W. H. 1967. *The Buffalo Soldiers: A Narrative of the Negro Cavalry in the West.* University of Oklahoma Press, Norman.

Pierce, G. S. 1969. *Texas Under Arms.* **V**

Rister, C. C. 1956. *Fort Griffin on the Texas Frontier.* University of Oklahoma Press, Norman.

Whitman, S. E. 1962. *The Troopers: An Informal History of the Plains Cavalry, 1865–1890.* Hastings House, New York.

X Early Industries and Factories

Jackson, A. T. 1971. *Mills of Yesteryear.* Texas Western Press, University of Texas at El Paso.

Jordan, T. G. 1981. *Trails to Texas.* **VI**

King, E. 1974. *An Eyewitness Account of Conditions in Post-Reconstruction Texas.* With Illustrations by J. W. Champney. 1874 reprint. Cordovan Press, Houston.

San Antonio Museum Association. 1973. *Early Texas Furniture and Decorative Arts.* Trinity University Press, San Antonio.

Spratt, J. S. 1955. *The Road to Spindle Top: Economic Change in Texas, 1875–1901.* Southern Methodist University Press, Dallas.

Taylor, L. 1975. *Texas Furniture: The Cabinetmakers and Their Work, 1840–1880.* University of Texas Press, Austin.

XI Urban Texas

Barkley, M. S. 1963. *History of Travis County and Austin, 1839–1899.* The Steck Company, Austin.

Everett, D. E. 1975. *San Antonio: The Flavor of Its Past.* Trinity University Press, San Antonio.

Haynes, C. W. 1974. *Galveston: History of the Island and the City.* Jenkins Garrett Press, Austin.

McKelvey, B. 1963. *The Urbanization of America, 1860–1915.* Rutgers University Press, New Brunswick.

Steinfeldt, C. 1979. *San Antonio Was, Seen Through a Magic Lantern.* San Antonio Museum Association, San Antonio.

Wilkinson, J. B. 1975. *Laredo and the Rio Grande Frontier.* Jenkins Publishing Company, Austin.

Willoughby, L. 1981. *Austin: A Historical Portrait.* Donning Company, Norfolk, Virginia.

XII Preserving the Evidence of Texas History

Hester, T. R. 1980. *Digging Into South Texas Prehistory.* **I**

Jordan, T. G. 1982. *Texas Graveyards: A Cultural Legacy.* University of Texas Press, Austin.

McGimsey, C. R., III. 1972. *Public Archaeology.* Seminar Press, New York.

Texas Historical Commission. 1973. *Historic Preservation in Texas: The Comprehensive Statewide Historic Preservation Plan for Texas* (2 volumes). Published jointly by the Texas Historical Commission and the Office of Archeology and Historic Preservation, U.S. Department of the Interior.

References Cited

On second citation, brief title is followed by a number in **bold-face** type, referring to chapter notes where full listing appears.

Introduction

Deetz, J. 1967. *Invitation to Archaeology*. Natural History Press, New York.

Hester, T. R. 1980. *Digging into South Texas Prehistory*. Corona Publishing Company, San Antonio.

Hester, T. R., R. F. Heizer, and J. A. Graham. 1975. *Field Methods in Archaeology* (6th edition). Mayfield Publishing Company, Palo Alto.

Hole, R., and R. F. Heizer. 1973. *An Introduction to Prehistoric Archaeology* (3rd edition). Holt, Rinehart and Winston, New York.

Hume, I. N. 1969. *Historical Archaeology*. Alfred A. Knopf, Inc., New York (1975 edition, W. W. Norton and Company, Inc., New York).

———. 1970. *A Guide to Artifacts of Colonial America*. Alfred A. Knopf, Inc., New York.

I Prehistoric and Historical Archeology in Texas

Bandelier, A. F. 1892. Final Report of Investigations Among the Indians of the Southwestern United States Carried on Mainly in the Years from 1880 to 1885. *Papers of the Archaeological Institute of America, American Series*.

Bond, C. L. 1978. Three Archeological Sites at Hoxie Bridge, Williamson County, Texas. *Anthropology Laboratory, Texas A&M University, Report*, No. 43.

Cook, H. J. 1927. New Geological and Paleontological Evidence Bearing on the Antiquity of Mankind in America. *Natural History*, Vol. 27, pp. 240–247.

Cotter, J. L. 1958. Symposium on Role of Ar-chaeology in Historical Research. Reprinted in *Historical Archaeology: A Guide to Substantive and Theoretical Contributions*, edited by R. L. Schuyler. Baywood Publishing Company, Inc., Farmingdale, New York.

Davis, E. M. 1979. The First Quarter Century of the Texas Archeological Society. *Bulletin of the Texas Archeological Society*, Vol. 50, pp. 159–194.

Dollar, C. 1968. Some Thoughts on Theory and Method in Historical Archaeology. *The Conference on Historic Site Archaeology*, Vol. 2, No. 2, pp. 3–30.

Fewkes, J. W. 1902. Pueblo Settlements near El Paso, Texas. *American Anthropologist*, Vol. 4, pp. 57–75.

Fontana, B. L. 1965. On the Meaning of Historic Sites Archaeology. *American Antiquity*, Vol. 31, No. 1, pp. 61–65.

Fox, A. A., and K. Livingston. 1979. Historical, Architectural and Archaeological Investigations at the Steiner-Schob Complex, Victoria County, Texas. *Center for Archaeological Research, The University of Texas at San Antonio, Archaeological Survey Report*, No. 52.

Freeman, M. D., and W. B. Fawcett, Jr. 1980. The Antebellum Period in the Stephen F. Austin Colony: Historical and Archeological Research in the Palmetto Bend Reservoir Area, Jackson County, Texas. Part I: The Sutherland Plantation and the Alabama Settlement: A Study in Cluster Migration (by Freeman), Part II: Archeological Investigations at Historic Sites (by Fawcett). *Texas Archeological Survey, The University of Texas at Austin, Research Report*, No. 70, *Palmetto Bend Reservoir Series*, Vol. 5.

Gilmore, K. 1969. The San Xavier Missions:

A Study in Historical Site Identification. *State Building Commission, Archeological Program, Report*, No. 16.

———. 1973. The Keeran Site: The Probable Site of La Salle's Fort St. Louis in Texas. *Office of the State Archeologist, Texas Historical Commission, Report*, No. 24.

Griffin, J. W. 1958. End Products of Historic Sites Archaeology. Reprinted in *Historical Archaeology: A Guide to Substantive and Theoretical Contributions*, edited by R. L. Schuyler. Baywood Publishing Company, Inc., Farmingdale, New York.

Harrington, J. C. 1955. Archaeology as an Auxiliary Science to American History. *American Anthropologist*, Vol. 57, No. 6, pp. 1121–1130.

Hester, T. R. 1980. *Digging Into South Texas Prehistory*. **Intro**

Hosmer, C. B. 1978. The Broadening View of the Historical Preservation Movement. In *Material Culture and the Study of American Life*, edited by I. M. G. Quimby. W. W. Norton and Company, Inc., New York.

House, K. D. 1978. Texas Archeology: Essays Honoring R. King Harris. *Institute for the Study of Earth and Man, Reports on Investigations*, No. 3.

Hume, I. N. 1969. *Historical Archaeology*. **Intro**

———. 1978. Material Culture with the Dirt on It: A Virginia Perspective. In *Material Culture and the Study of American Life*, edited by I. M. G. Quimby. W. W. Norton and Company, Inc., New York.

Humphreys, G., and W. Singleton. 1978. Historic Archeology in Texas. In Texas Archeology: Essays Honoring R. King Harris, edited by Kurt D. House. *Institute for the Study of Earth and Man, Reports of Investigations*, No. 3.

Jelks, E. B., E. M. Davis, and H. B. Sturgis (editors). 1960. A Review of Texas Archeology. *Bulletin of the Texas Archeological Society*, Vol. 29.

Kirkland, F., and W. W. Newcomb, Jr. 1967. *The Rock Art of Texas Indians*. (With paintings by Kirkland, text by Newcomb.) University of Texas Press, Austin.

Mallery, G. 1886. Pictographs of the North American Indians: A Preliminary Paper. *Annual Report of the Bureau of American Ethnology*. Vol. 4, pp. 2–256.

Moir, R. W. 1982. Sheet Refuse: An Indicator of Past Lifeways. Chapter 12 in Settlement of the Prairie Margin: Archaeology of the Richland Creek Reservoir, Navarro and Freeman Counties, Texas, 1980–81, by M. Raab and others. *Archaeology Research Program, Southern Methodist University, Archaeological Monographs*, No. 1.

Moore, C. B. 1912. Some Aboriginal Sites on Red River. *Journal of the Academy of Natural Sciences of Philadelphia*, Vol. 14, pp. 1–163.

Pearce, J. E. 1919. Indian Mounds and Other Relics of Indian Life in Texas. *American Anthropologist*, Vol. 21, pp. 223–234.

Prewitt, E. R. 1981. Cultural Chronology in Central Texas. *Bulletin of the Texas Archeological Society*, Vol. 52, pp. 65–89.

Quimby, I. M. G. (editor). 1978. *Material Culture and the Study of American Life*. W. W. Norton and Company, Inc., New York.

Raab, M., and others. Sheet Refuse: An Indicator of Past Lifeways. Chapter 12 in Settlement of the Prairie Margin: Archaeology of the Richland Creek Reservoir, Navarro and Freeman Counties, Texas, 1980–81. *Archaeology Research Program, Southern Methodist University, Archaeological Monographs*, No. 1.

Russell, C. P. 1967. *Firearms, Traps, and Tools of the Mountain Men*. Alfred A. Knopf, Inc., New York.

Schuyler, R. L. (editor). 1978. *Historical Archaeology: A Guide to Substantive and Theoretical Contributions*. Baywood Publishing Company, Inc., Farmingdale, New York.

Schuyler, R. L. 1980. Book Review: Research Strategies in Historical Archeology, edited by S. South, 1977, Academic Press, New York. *American Anthropologist*, Vol. 82, pp. 200–202.

Simons, H. 1981. Index: Bulletin of the Texas Archeological Society, Vols. 1–50. *Bulletin of the Texas Archeological Society*, Vol. 52, pp. 237–312.

South, S. 1977a. *Method and Theory in Historical Archaeology*. Academic Press, New York.

————. 1977b *Research Strategies in Historical Archeology*. Academic Press, New York.

Suhm, D. A., A. Krieger, and E. B. Jelks. 1954. An Introductory Handbook of Texas Archeology. *Bulletin of the Texas Archeological Society*, Vol. 25.

Walker, I. C. 1974. Binford, Science and History: The Probabilistic Variability of Explicated Epistemology and Nomothetic Paradigms in Historical Archaeology. *The Conference on Historic Site Archaeology*, Vol. 7, pp. 159–214.

Wendorf, F. 1978. The Changing Roles of Amateurs and Professionals in Texas Archeology. In Texas Archeology: Essays Honoring R. King Harris, edited by K. D. House. *Institute for the Study of Earth and Man, Reports on Investigations*, No. 3, pp. 7–14.

Woodward, A. 1937. The Study of Historic Archaeology in America. *Boletín Bibliográfico de Antropología Americana*, Vol. 1, pp. 101–103. Reprinted in *Historical Archaeology: A Guide to Substantive and Theoretical Contributions*, edited by R. L. Schuyler, 1978. Baywood Publishing Company, Inc., Farmingdale, New York.

Word, J. H. 1979. Historical Perspective: A History of the Texas Archeological Society and the Establishment of a State Archeologist. *Bulletin of the Texas Archeological Society*, Vol. 50, pp. 153–158.

Young, A. 1841. *Chronicles of the Pilgrim Fathers*. Boston.

II Texas at the Beginning of Written History

Bell, R. E., E. B. Jelks, and W. W. Newcomb, Jr. (assemblers). 1967. A Pilot Study of Wichita Indian Archaeology and Ethnohistory. National Science Foundation Report, Washington, D.C.

Berlandier, J. L. 1969. *The Indians of Texas in 1830*. Edited and annotated by John C. Ewers. Smithsonian Institution, Washington, D.C.

Bolton, H. E. (editor). 1959. *Spanish Exploration in the Southwest: 1542–1706*. 1916 reprint. Barnes and Noble, New York.

Cambell, T. N. 1973. Systematized Ethnohistory and Prehistoric Culture Sequences in Texas. *Bulletin of the Texas Archeologi-cal Society*, Vol. 43, pp. 1–11.

————. 1975. The Payaya Indians of Southern Texas. *Southern Texas Archaeological Association, Special Publication*, No. 1.

————. 1977. Ethnic Identities of Extinct Coahuiltecan Populations: Case of the Juanca Indians. *The Pearce-Sellards Series*, No. 26, Texas Memorial Museum, Austin.

Chevalier, F. 1966. *Land and Society in Colonial Mexico: The Great Hacienda*. University of California Press, Berkeley.

Corbin, J. E., A. Kalina, and T. C. Alex. 1980. Mission Dolores de los Ais: Archaeological Investigations at an Early Spanish Colonial Mission, San Augustine County, Texas. *Papers in Anthropology*, No. 2, Stephen F. Austin State University, Nacogdoches.

Davis, E. M. (editor). 1961. Proceedings of the Fifth Conference on Caddoan Archeology. *Bulletin of the Texas Archeological Society*, Vol. 31, pp. 77–143.

Donoghue, D. 1936. Coronado, Oñate and Quivira. *Preliminary Studies of the Texas Catholic Historical Society*, Vol. 3, No. 3. Reprinted in An Ethnohistorical Survey of Texas Indians by L. L. M. Skeels, *Texas Historical Survey Committee, Archeological Report*, No. 22, pp. 74–82.

Doran, G. H., and R. M. Malina. 1974. Skeletal Material from the Cogdell Burial in Floyd County, Texas. *Bulletin of the Texas Archeological Society*, Vol. 46, pp. 65–67.

Duffield, L. F., and E. B. Jelks. 1961. The Pearson Site: A Historic Indian Site in Iron Bridge Reservoir, Rains County, Texas. *Archaeology Series*, No. 4, Department of Anthropology, The University of Texas at Austin.

Fehrenbach, T. R. 1968. *Lone Star: A History of Texas and the Texans*. MacMillan Company, New York.

Foik, P. J. (translator). 1933. Capitán don Domingo Ramón's Diary of His Expedition into Texas in 1716. *Preliminary Studies of the Texas Catholic Historical Society*, Vol. 2, No. 5.

Forrestal, P. P. (translator). 1935. Peña's Diary of the Aguayo Expedition. *Preliminary*

Studies of the Texas Catholic Historical Society, Vol. 2, No. 7.

Fox, A. A., F. A. Bass, and T. R. Hester. 1976. The Archaeology and History of Alamo· Plaza. *Center for Archaeological Research, The University of Texas at San Antonio, Archaeological Survey Report,* No. 16.

Fox, D. E. 1979. The Lithic Artifacts of Indians at the Spanish Colonial Missions, San Antonio, Texas. *Center for Archaeological Research, The University of Texas at San Antonio, Special Report,* No. 8.

————. 1980. The Material Evidence of Texas History. *Bulletin of the Texas Archeological Society,* Vol. 51, pp. 271–287.

Gatschet, A. S. 1891. The Karankawa Indians, the Coast People of Texas. *Archaeological and Ethnological Papers of the Peabody Museum,* Vol. 1, No. 2.

Gregory, H. F. 1980. Excavations: 1979. Presidio de Nuestra Sñra. del Pilar de los Adaes. Report submitted to the Division of State Parks, Louisiana State Department of Culture, Recreation and Tourism.

Harris, R. K., and I. M. Harris. 1961. Spanish Fort: A Historic Trade Site. *The Record,* Vol. 16, No. 1.

Harris, R. K., I. M. Harris, J. C. Blaine, and J. Blaine. 1965. A Preliminary Archeological and Documentary Study of the Womack Site, Lamar County, Texas. *Bulletin of the Texas Archeological Society,* Vol. 36, pp. 287–364.

Hester, T. R. 1980. *Digging Into South Texas Prehistory.* **Intro**

Hodge, F. W. (editor). 1907. Handbook of American Indians North of Mexico. *Bureau of American Ethnology, Bulletin,* No. 30, Parts 1 and 2. Washington, D.C.

Hodge, F. W., and T. H. Lewis (editors). 1953. *Spanish Explorers in the Southern United States, 1528–1543: Original Narratives of Early American History.* 1907 reprint. Barnes and Noble, New York.

Hoijer, H. 1946. Tonkawa. *Vicking Fund Publications in Anthropology,* No. 6, pp. 239–311.

Hsu, D. P. 1969. The Arthur Patterson Site: A Mid-Nineteenth Century Site, San Jacinto County, Texas. *State Building Commission and Texas Water Development Board, Archeological Survey Report,* No. 5.

Hughes, J. T., P. S. Willey, and B. R. Harrison. 1978. The San Pit Site. In Archeology of MacKenzie Reservoir, by J. T. Hughes and P. S. Willey. *Office of the State Archeologist, Texas Historical Commission, Archeological Survey Report,* No. 24, pp. 233–253.

Humphreys, G., and W. Singleton. 1978. Historic Archeology in Texas. **I**

Inglis, J. M. 1964. A History of Vegetation on the Rio Grande Plain. *Texas Parks and Wildlife Bulletin,* No. 45.

Jelks, E. B. (editor). 1967. The Gilbert Site: A Norteño Focus Site in Northeastern Texas. *Bulletin of the Texas Archeological Society,* Vol. 37 (for 1966).

Jelks, E. B. 1970. The Stansbury Site (41-39B1-1). In Archeological Investigations in the Whitney Reservoir Area, Central Texas, edited by R. L. Stephenson. *Bulletin of the Texas Archeological Society,* Vol. 41, pp. 58–111.

Jelks, E. B., E. M. Davis, and H. F. Sturgis (editors). 1960. A Review of Texas Archeology. **I**

John, E. A. H. 1975. *Storms Brewed in Other Men's Worlds.* Texas A&M University Press, College Station.

Johnson, E., V. T. Holliday, M. J. Kaczor, and R. Stuckenrath. 1977. The Garza Occupation at the Lubbock Lake Site. *Bulletin of the Texas Archeological Society,* Vol. 48, pp. 83–109.

Jones, B. C. 1968. The Kinsloe Focus: A Study of Seven Historic Caddoan Sites in Northeast Texas. Master's thesis. The University of Oklahoma, Norman.

Jones, W. K. 1969. Notes on the History and Material Culture of the Tonkawa Indians. *Smithsonian Contributions to Anthropology,* Vol. 2, No. 5.

Kelley, D. 1971. The Tonkawas. In *Indian Tribes of Texas,* by D. H. Winfrey and others, pp. 151–168. Texian Press, Waco.

Krieger, A. D. 1961. The Travels of Alvar Nuñez Cabeza de Vaca in Texas and Mexico, 1534–1536. In *Homenaje a Pablo Martinez del Rio en el XXV Aniversario de* la Edición de los Orígenes Americanos, the Instituto National de Antropología y Historia, pp. 459–474. Reprinted in An Ethnohistorical Survey of Texas Indians, by L. L. M. Skeels, *Texas Historical Survey Committee, Archeological Report,* No. 22, pp. 57–73.

Marcy, R. B. 1874. *Thirty Years of Army Life on the Border.* Harper and Brothers, New York.

Marriott, A. L. 1945. *The Ten Grandmothers.* Norman.

Marsh, R. H., Martin and Jacobson (editors). 1974. *The Alabama-Coushatta.* Garland Press, New York.

McReynolds, R. L. 1982. An Iron Projectile from Gillespie County, Texas. *La Tierra,* Vol. 9, No. 2, pp. 30–32.

Mooney, J. 1898. Calendar History of the Kiowa Indians. *Bureau of American Ethnology, Annual Report,* Vol. 17, Part I.

Neighbors, K. L. 1973. Tonkawa Scouts and Guides. *West Texas Historical Association Yearbook,* Vol. 69, pp. 90–113.

Newcomb, W. W., Jr. 1955. An Historic Burial from Yellowhouse Canyon, Lubbock County. *Bulletin of the Texas Archeological Society,* Vol. 26, pp. 186–199.

———. 1961. *The Indians of Texas, from Prehistoric to Modern Times.* University of Texas Press, Austin.

Newcomb, W. W., Jr., and W. T. Field. 1967. An Ethnohistoric Investigation of the Wichita Indians in the Southern Plains. In R. E. Bell, E. B. Jelks, and W. W. Newcomb, Jr., *A Pilot Study of Wichita Indian Archaeology and Ethnohistory,* pp. 240–331. *National Science Foundation Report,* Washington, D.C.

Parsons, M. L. 1967. Archeological Investigations in Crosby and Dickens Counties, Texas, During the Winter, 1966–1967. *State Building Commission, Archeological Program, Report,* No. 7.

Peebles, R. 1968. Westward Migration of the Alabama-Coushatta. Master's thesis. Sam Houston State University, Huntsville.

Prewitt, E. R. 1975. Bayou Loco: Investigations and Speculations. Paper presented at the Caddo Conference, Texas A&M University, College Station.

———. 1982. The 1982 TAS Field School, Rowe Valley, Texas. *Texas Archeology, The Newsletter of the Texas Archeological Society,* Vol. 26, No. 3, p. 205.

Prewitt, E. R., J. W. Clark, Jr., and D. S. Dibble. 1972. An Assessment of the Archeological and Historical Resources of the Bayou Loco Reservoir Area, Nacogdoches County, Texas. *Texas Archeological Survey,* The University of Texas at Austin, Research Report, No. 11.

Richardson, J. 1940. Law and Status Among the Kiowa Indians. *Monograph of the American Ethnological Society,* Vol. 1.

Schuetz, M. K. 1969. The History and Archeology of Mission San Juan Capistrano, San Antonio, Texas. Vol. 2 (of two volumes): Description of the Artifacts and Ethno-History of the Coahuiltecan Indians. *State Building Commission, Archeological Program, Report,* No. 11.

Sibley, M. M. 1967. *Travelers in Texas, 1761–1860.* University of Texas Press, Austin.

Sjoberg, A. F. 1953a. The Culture of the Tonkawa, A Texas Indian Tribe. *Texas Journal of Science,* Vol. 5, pp. 280–304.

———. 1953b. Lipan Apache Culture in Historical Perspective. *Southwestern Journal of Anthropology,* Vol. 9, pp. 76–98.

Skeels, L. L. M. 1972. An Ethnohistorical Survey of Texas Indians. *Texas Historical Survey Committee, Archeological Report,* No. 22.

Stephenson, R. L. 1947. Archeology Survey of Whitney Basin: A Preliminary Report. *Bulletin of the Texas Archeological and Paleontological Society,* Vol. 18, pp. 129–142.

Stephenson, R. L. (editor). 1970. Archeological Investigations in the Whitney Reservoir Area, Central Texas. *Bulletin of the Texas Archeological Society,* Vol. 41, pp. 37–286.

Story, D. A. (editor). 1982. The Deshazo Site, Nacogdoches County, Texas. Volume 1: The Site, Its Setting, Investigation, Cultural Features, Artifacts of Non-Native Manufacture, and Subsistence Remains. *Texas Antiquities Committee, Permit Series,* No. 7.

Swanton, J. R. (editor). 1942. Source Material on the History and Ethnology of the

Caddo Indians. *Bureau of American Ethnology, Bulletin*, No. 132. Smithsonian Institution, Washington, D.C.

Wallace, E., and E. A. Hoebel. 1952. *The Comanches: Lords of the South Plains.* University of Oklahoma Press, Norman.

Webb, C. H. 1960. A Review of Northeast Texas Archeology. In Review of Texas Archeology, edited by E. B. Jelks, E. M. Davis, and H. F. Sturgis. *Bulletin of the Texas Archeological Society*, Vol. 29, pp. 35–62.

Weniger, D. n.d. Texas as It Was. To be published by University of Texas Press, Austin.

Willey, P. S., B. R. Harrison, and J. T. Hughes. 1978. The San Pit Site. In Archeology of MacKenzie Reservoir, by J. T. Hughes and P. S. Willey. *Office of the State Archeologist, Texas Historical Commission, Archeological Survey Report*, No. 24, pp. 233–253.

Williams, S. 1961. Historic Sites in the Caddoan Area. In Proceedings of the Fifth Conference on Caddoan Archeology, edited by E. M. Davis. *Bulletin of the Texas Archeological Society*, Vol. 31, pp. 78–143.

Winfrey, D. H., and others. 1971. *Indian Tribes of Texas.* Texian Press, Waco.

Witte, A. H. 1938. Spanish Fort: An Historic Wichita Site. *Bulletin of the Texas Archeological and Paleontological Society*, Vol. 10, pp. 234–244.

Word, J. H., and A. A. Fox. 1975. The Cogdell Burial in Floyd County, Texas. *Bulletin of the Texas Archeological Society*, Vol. 46, pp. 1–63.

III   The First Europeans

American State Papers. 1832. Class I: Foreign Relations, Vol. II, and Class II: Indian Affairs, Vol. 1. Gales and Seaton, Washington, D.C.

Arnold, J. B. III., 1976. An Underwater Archeological Magnetometer Survey and Site Test Excavation Project Off Padre Island, Texas. *Texas Antiquities Committee Publication*, No. 3.

Arnold, J. B. III, (editor). 1978a. Beneath the Waters of Time: The Proceedings of the Ninth Conference on Underwater Archaeology. *Texas Antiquities Committee Publication*, No. 6.

Arnold, J. B., III. 1978b. 1977 Underwater Site Test Excavations Off Padre Island, Texas. *Texas Antiquities Committee Publication*, No. 5.

Arnold, J. B. III, and R. S. Weddle. 1979. *The Nautical Archeology of Padre Island: The Spanish Shipwrecks of 1554.* Academic Press, New York.

Bolton, H. E. 1914. *Athanase de Mézières and the Louisiana-Texas Frontier, 1768–1780.* Arthur H. Clark Company, Cleveland.

———. 1924. The Location of La Salle's Colony on the Gulf of Mexico. *Southwestern Historical Quarterly*, Vol. 27, No. 3, pp. 171–189. Reprinted from *The Mississippi Valley Historical Review*, Vol. 2, No. 2, 1915.

———. 1959. *Spanish Exploration.* **II**

Briggs, A. K. 1971. *Archeological Resources of the Texas Coastal Lowlands and Littoral.* Texas Historical Survey Committee and Texas Water Development Board, Austin.

Butler, C. T., Jr. 1948. A West Texas Rock Shelter. Master's thesis. The University of Texas at Austin.

Chelf, C. 1946. Grooved Clubs from a Peat Bog in Texas. *Bulletin of the Texas Archeological and Paleontological Society*, Vol. 17, pp. 42–47.

Clausen, C. J., and J. B. Arnold III. 1976. The Magnetometer and Underwater Archaeology: Magnetic Delineation of Individual Shipwreck Sites, A New Control Technique. *The International Journal of Nautical Archaeology and Underwater Exploration*, Vol. 5, No. 2, pp. 159–169.

Cole, E. W. 1946. La Salle in Texas. *Southwestern Historical Quarterly*, Vol. 49, No. 4, pp. 473–500.

Corbin, J. E., A. Kalina, and T. C. Alex. 1980. Mission Dolores de los Ais. **II**

Dávila Padilla, A. 1596. *History and Discourse Concerning the Founding of the Province of Santiago, Mexico, by the Order of Preachers, by Means of the Lives of Its Outstanding Men and the Notable Events of New Spain.* Pedro Madrigals, Madrid. Translation No. 28 in Documentary Sources for the

Wreck of the New Spain Fleet of 1554, by D. McDonald and J. B. Arnold III. *Texas Antiquities Committee Publication*, No. 8, pp. 227–238.

Donoghue, D. 1936. Coronado, Oñate and Quivira. **II**

Forrestal, P. P. (translator). 1935. Peña's Diary. **II**

Fox, A. A., D. W. Day, and L. Highley. 1980. Archaeological and Historical Investigations at Wallisville Lake, Chambers and Liberty Counties, Texas. *Center for Archaeological Research, The University of Texas at San Antonio, Archaeological Survey Report*, No. 90.

Gilmore, K. 1973. The Keeran Site. **I**

Hallenbeck, C. 1940. *The Journey and Route of Alvar Nuñez Cabeza de Vaca.* Arthur H. Clark Company, Glendale.

Hamilton, D. 1976. Conservation of Metal Objects from Underwater Sites: A Study in Methods. *Texas Antiquities Committee Publication*, No. 1.

Hays, T. R., and E. Herrin. 1970. Padre Island Project. Unpublished report to the Texas Antiquities Committee on file at the Texas Historical Commission, Austin.

Hester, T. R. 1980. *Digging into South Texas Prehistory.* **Intro**

Hodge, F. W., and T. H. Lewis (editors). 1953. *Spanish Explorers.* **II**

Joutel, H. 1962. *A Journal of La Salle's Last Voyage.* 1714 Reprint. Corinth Books, New York.

Kelley, J. C. 1952. Factors Involved in the Abandonment of Certain Peripheral Southwestern Settlements. *American Anthropologist*, Vol. 54, No. 3, pp. 356–387.

Krieger, A. D. 1961. Travels of Cabeza de Vaca. **II**

McDonald, D., and J. B. Arnold III. 1979. Documentary Sources for the Wreck of the New Spain Fleet of 1554. *Texas Antiquities Committee Publication*, No. 8.

Miroir, M. P., R. K. Harris, J. C. Blaine, and J. McVay. 1973. Benard de la Harpe and the Nassonite Post. With the collaboration of D. C. Book, F. Cigainero, R. McVay, J. B. Raffaelli, and P. E. Schoen. *Bulletin of the Texas Archeological Society*, Vol. 44, pp. 113–167.

Olds, D. L. 1976. Texas Legacy from the Gulf: A Report of Sixteenth Century Shipwreck Materials Recovered from the Texas Tidelands. *Texas Memorial Museum, Miscellaneous Papers*, No. 5, *Texas Antiquities Committee Publication*, No. 2.

Scurlock, D. 1974. An Assessment of the Archeological Resources of Padre Island National Seashore, Texas. *Office of the State Archeologist, Texas Historical Commission*, Special Report, No. 11.

Skeels, L. L. M. 1972. An Ethnohistorical Survey of Texas Indians. **II**

Smith, R. A. (translator and annotator). 1958. Account of the Journey of Benard de la Harpe: Discovery Made by Him of Several Nations Situated in the West. *Southwestern Historical Quarterly*, Vol. 62, No. 2, pp. 246–259.

Taylor, H. C., Jr. 1949. The Archaeology of the Area About the Mouth of the Pecos. Master's thesis. The University of Texas at Austin.

———. 1960. Archeological Notes on the Route of Cabeza de Vaca. *Bulletin of the Texas Archeological Society*, Vol. 31, pp. 273–290.

Tunnell, C., and J. R. Ambler. 1967. Archeological Excavations at Presidio San Agustín de Ahumada. *State Building Commission, Archeological Program, Report*, No. 6.

Weddle, R. S. 1973. *Wilderness Manhunt.* University of Texas Press, Austin.

IV Remains of the Spanish Colonial Empire

Adams, R. E. W. 1975. Archaeology and Ethnohistory of the Gateway Area, Middle Rio Grande of Texas: Report of the 1975 Investigations. With contributions by J. D. Eaton, R. E. W. Adams, T. R. Hester, J. P. Nunley, and F. D. Almaraz, Jr. Preliminary Report submitted to National Endowment for the Humanities by The University of Texas at San Antonio.

———. 1976. The Archaeology and Ethnohistory of the Gateway Area, Middle Rio Grande of Texas: Report of the 1976 Investigations. With contributions by

R. E. W. Adams, F. D. Almaraz, Jr., B. Davidson, J. D. Eaton, A. A. Fox, T. R. Hester, J. P. Nunley, and F. Valdez, Jr. Preliminary Report submitted to National Endowment for the Humanities by The University of Texas at San Antonio.

Adams, R. E. W., and T. R. Hester. 1973. Letter to Dr. Fred Wendorf, Chairman, Texas Antiquities Committee, Concerning Completion of Excavations at Mission San Antonio de Valero, November 26.

Almaraz, F. D., Jr. 1979. Crossroad of Empire: The Church and State on the Rio Grande Frontier of Coahuila and Texas, 1700–1821. *Archaeology and History of the San Juan Bautista Mission Area, Coahuila and Texas, Report*, No. 1. Center for Archaeological Research, The University of Texas at San Antonio.

Bolton, H. E. 1915. *Texas in the Middle Eighteenth Century*. 1962 Edition. Russell and Russell, New York.

———. 1960. *The Mission as a Frontier Institution in the Spanish-American Colonies*. 1917 Reprint. Academic Reprints, El Paso.

Campbell, T. N. 1979. Ethnohistoric Notes on Indian Groups Associated with Three Spanish Missions at Guerrero, Coahuila. *Archaeology and History of the San Juan Bautista Mission Area, Coahuila and Texas, Report*, No. 3. Center for Archaeological Research, The University of Texas at San Antonio.

Casteñeda, C. E. 1936. The Mission Era: The Winning of Texas, 1693–1731. *Our Catholic Heritage in Texas*, Vol. II. Von Beckmann–Jones Company, Austin.

Chabot, F. C. 1937. *With the Makers of San Antonio*. Artes Gráficas Press, San Antonio.

Clark, J. W., Jr. 1976. The Sugar Industry at Mission San José y San Miguel de Aguayo. *Bulletin of the Texas Archaeological Society*, Vol. 47, pp. 245–260.

———. 1978. Mission San José y San Miguel de Aguayo: Archeological Investigation, December, 1974. *Office of the State Archeologist, Texas Historical Commission, Report*, No. 29.

———. 1980. Sa Reina Norteña: History and Archeology of San José Mission. *La Tierra*, Vol. 7, No. 1, pp. 3–15.

Clark, J. W., Jr., and E. R. Prewitt. 1979. Archeological Test Excavations in Areas to be Affected by a Proposed French Drain West of the Granary, Mission San José State Historic Site (41BX3), Bexar County, Texas. *Reports on Investigations*, No. 3. Prewitt and Associates, Inc., Austin.

Cook, P. J. 1980. A Review of the History and Archaeology of Mission Concepción. *La Tierra*, Vol. 7, No. 3, pp. 3–16.

———. 1981. A Review of the History and Archaeology of Mission San Lorenzo, Real County, Southern Texas. *La Tierra*, Vol. 8, No. 3, pp. 3–15.

Corbin, J. E., A. Kalina, and T. C. Alex. 1980. Mission Dolores de los Ais. **2**

Corner, W. 1890. *San Antonio de Bexar: A Guide and History*. Bainbridge and Corner, San Antonio.

Fox, A. A. 1977a. Archaeological Observations at Alamo Plaza. Unpublished report on file at the Center for Archaeological Research, The University of Texas at San Antonio.

———. 1977b. The Archaeology and History of the Spanish Governor's Palace Park. *Center for Archaeological Research, The University of Texas at San Antonio, Archaeological Survey Report*, No. 31.

———. 1978. Archaeological Investigations of Portions of the San Pedro and Alazan Acequias in San Antonio, Texas. *Center for Archaeological Research, The University of Texas at San Antonio, Archaeological Survey Report*, No. 49.

———. n.d. Archaeological Investigations at Mission Concepción and Mission Parkway, Part II (of 2 parts): Mission Parkway Survey. *Center for Archaeological Research, The University of Texas at San Antonio, Archaeological Survey Report*, No. 114. In preparation.

Fox, A. A., F. A. Bass, and T. R. Hester. 1976. Alamo Plaza. **II**

Fox, A. A., D. W. Day, and L. Highley. 1980. Wallisville Lake. **III**

Fox, A. A., and T. R. Hester. 1976. Archaeological Test Excavations at Mission San Francisco de la Espada. *Center for Archae-*

ological Research, The University of Texas at San Antonio, Archaeological Survey Report, No. 22.

Fox, A. A., and J. E. Ivey. n.d. Archaeological and Historical Investigations at Alamo Historical Park, San Antonio, Texas. Center for Archaeological Research, The University of Texas at San Antonio, Archaeological Survey Report, No. 120. In preparation.

Fox, D. E. 1970. Archeological Salvage at Mission San José, December 1969, April and August 1970. Report prepared by the Texas Historical Survey Committee, Austin.

Fox, D. E., D. Scurlock, and J. W. Clark, Jr. 1977. Archeological Excavations at San Fernando Cathedral, San Antonio, Texas: A Preliminary Report. Office of the State Archeologist, Texas Historical Commission, Special Report, No. 22.

Frkuska, A. J., Jr. 1981. Archaeological Investigations of the San Pedro Acequia, San Antonio, Texas. Center for Archaeological Research, The University of Texas at San Antonio, Archaeological Survey Report, No. 103.

Gilmore, K. 1967. A Documentary and Archeological Investigation of Presidio San Luis de las Amarillas and Mission Santa Cruz de San Sabá, Menard County, Texas: A Preliminary Report. State Building Commission, Archeological Program, Report, No. 9.

———. 1969. San Xavier Mission. **I**

———. 1973. The Keeran Site. **I**

———. 1974. Mission Rosario, Archeological Investigations. Parts 1 and 2 (for 1973 and 1974). Historic Sites and Restoration Branch, Park Division, Texas Parks and Wildlife Department, Archeological Report, No. 14.

———. 1982. So Shall We Reap: The San Xavier Missions. La Tierra, Vol. 9, No. 1, pp. 3–10.

Greer, J. W. 1967. A Description of the Stratigraphy, Features and Artifacts from an Archeological Excavation at the Alamo. State Building Commission, Archeological Program, Report, No. 3.

Gregory, H. F. 1980. Excavations: 1979, Presidio de Nuestra Sñra. del Pilar de los Adaes. **II**

Habig, M. A. 1968. The Alamo Chain of Missions. Franciscan Herald Press, Chicago.

Hatcher, M. A. 1905. The Municipal Government of San Fernando de Béxar, 1730–1800. Southwestern Historical Quarterly, Vol. 8, No. 4, pp. 277–352.

Holmes, W. H. 1962. The Acequias of San Antonio. Master's thesis. St. Mary's University, San Antonio.

Ivey, J. E. 1981. A Reexamination of the Site of Presidio San Sabá. La Tierra, Vol. 8, No. 4, pp. 3–11.

———. n.d. Archaeological Investigations at Mission Concepción and Mission Parkway, Part I (of 2 parts): Excavations at Mission Concepción. Center for Archaeological Research, The University of Texas at San Antonio, Archaeological Survey Report, No. 114. In preparation.

Ivey, J. E., and A. A. Fox. 1981. Archaeological Survey and Testing at Rancho de las Cabras, Wilson County, Texas. Center for Archaeological Research, The University of Texas at San Antonio, Archaeological Survey Report, No. 104.

Kress, M. K. (translator). 1932. Diary of a Visit of Inspection of the Texas Missions Made by Fray Gaspar José de Solís in the Years 1767–68. Southwestern Historical Quarterly, Vol. 35, No. 1, pp. 28–76.

Minor, J. E., and M. L. Steinberg. 1968. A Brief on the Acequias of San Antonio. The San Antonio Branch, American Society of Civil Engineers.

Moorhead, M. L. 1975. The Presidio: Bastion of the Spanish Borderlands. University of Oklahoma Press, Norman.

Olsen, S. C., and C. Tunnell. 1975. Mission Concepción. Archeological Completion Report Series, No. 5. Division of Grants, Office of Archeology and Historic Preservation, National Park Service, Department of Interior, Washington, D.C.

Saenz de Gumiel, Juan Joseph. 1772. Ynventario de la Espada. Unpublished manuscript, Old Spanish Missions Historical Research Library, Zacatecas and Celaya microfilm, Roll 13: Fr. 1338–1374, December 15, 1772.

Schuetz, M. K. 1966. Historic Background of the Mission San Antonio de Valero. State Building Commission, Archeological Program, Report, No. 1.

——. 1968. The History and Archeology of Mission San Juan Capistrano, San Antonio, Texas. Vol. I: Historical Documentation and Description of the Structures. *State Building Commission, Archeological Program, Report,* No. 10.

——. 1969. San Juan Capistrano. **II**

——. 1970. Excavation of a Section of the Acequia Madre in Bexar County, Texas, and Archeological Investigations at Mission San José in April, 1968. *Texas Historical Survey Committee, Archeological Program, Report,* No. 19.

——. 1973. Archeological Investigations at Mission San Antonio de Valero, The Second Patio. Unpublished manuscript, Office of the State Archeologist, Texas Historical Commission, Austin.

——. 1974. The Dating of the Chapel at Mission San Juan Capistrano, San Antonio, Texas. *Office of the State Archeologist, Texas Historical Commission, Special Report,* No. 12.

Scurlock, D., A. Benavides, Jr., D. Isham, and J. W. Clark, Jr. 1976. An Archeological and Historical Survey of the Proposed Mission Parkway, San Antonio, Texas. *Office of the State Archeologist, Texas Historical Commission, Archeological Survey Report,* No. 17.

Scurlock, D., and D. E. Fox. 1977. An Archeological Investigation of Mission Concepción, San Antonio, Texas. *Office of the State Archeologist, Texas Historical Commission, Report,* No. 28.

Scurlock, D., and T. P. Powers, Jr. 1975. Interim Report for Mission Concepción (Archeological Investigations), San Antonio, Bexar County, Texas. *Office of the State Archeologist, Texas Historical Commission, Special Report,* No. 7.

Smith, H. P. 1931. Old and New San Antonio. *Architectural Progress,* Vol. 5, No. 7.

Smith, H. P., Jr. 1980. Espada Mission: Research and Restoration. *La Tierra,* Vol. 7, No. 2, pp. 3–18.

Sorrow, W. M. 1972. Archeological Salvage Excavations at the Alamo (Mission San Antonio de Valero), 1970. *Texas Archeological Salvage Project, The University of Texas at Austin, Research Report,* No. 4.

Tunnell, C. 1966. A Description of Enameled

Earthenware from an Archeological Excavation at Mission San Antonio de Valero (the Alamo). *State Building Commission, Archeological Program, Report,* No. 2.

Tunnell, C., and J. R. Ambler. 1967. Presidio San Agustín de Ahumada. **III**

Tunnell, C., and W. W. Newcomb, Jr. 1969. A Lipan Apache Mission: San Lorenzo de la Cruz, 1762–1771. *Bulletin of the Texas Memorial Museum,* Vol. 14.

Valdez, F., Jr., and J. D. Eaton, 1979. Preliminary Archaeological Survey of Part of the San Pedro Acequia, San Antonio, Texas. *Center for Archaeological Research, The University of Texas at San Antonio, Archaeological Survey Report,* No. 85.

Weddle, R. S. 1964. *The San Sabá Missions: Spanish Pivot in Texas.* University of Texas Press, Austin.

——. 1968. *San Juan Bautista, Gateway to Spanish Texas.* University of Texas Press, Austin.

V Sites of Mexican Texas, the Revolution, and the Republic

Almaraz, F. D., Jr. 1971. *Tragic Cavalier: Governor Manuel Salcedo of Texas, 1808–1813.* University of Texas Press, Austin.

Barker, E. C. 1969. *The Life of Stephen F. Austin, Founder of Texas, 1793–1836.* Cokesbury Press 1926. Reprinted by the University of Texas Press, Austin.

Baxter, E. P., and J. E. Ippolito. 1976. An Archeological Survey of the Freeport, Texas, Hurricane Flood Protection Project, Brazoria County, Texas. *Anthropology Laboratory, Texas A&M University, Report,* No. 22.

Butler, B. 1974. Letter to A. A. Fox reporting the results of skeletal analysis of Blue Wing Road Burial, January 18. On file at the Center for Archaeological Research, The University of Texas at San Antonio.

Crosby, H. A. 1977. Architecture of Texana, 1831–1883. *Texas Archeological Survey, The University of Texas at Austin, Research Report,* No. 57 *(Palmetto Bend Reservoir Series,* No. 2).

Davis, E. M., and J. E. Corbin. 1967. Archeological Investigations at Washington-on-the-Brazos State Park in 1966. *State Building Commission, Archeological Program, Report,* No. 5.

Deiss, R. W. 1981. The Development and Application of a Chronology for American Glass. *Midwestern Archeological Research Center*, Illinois State University, Normal.

Eaton, J. D. 1980. Excavations at the Alamo Shrine (Mission San Antonio de Valero). *Center for Archaeological Research, The University of Texas at San Antonio, Special Report*, No. 10.

Fehrenbach, T. R. 1968. *Lone Star.* **II**

Fontana, B. L., and J. C. Greenleaf. 1962. Johnny Ward's Ranch: A Study in Historic Archaeology. *Kiva*, Vol. 28, Nos. 1 and 2.

Fox, A. A. n.d. The Blue Wing Road Burial (41BX34). Field Notes on file, Center for Archaeological Research, The University of Texas at San Antonio.

Fox, A. A., F. A. Bass, and T. R. Hester. 1976. Alamo Plaza. **II**

Fox, A. A., D. W. Day, and L. Highley. 1980. Wallisville Lake. **III**

Fox, A. A., and J. E. Ivey. n.d. Alamo Historical Park. **IV**

Fox, A. A., J. E. Ivey, and J. C. Markey. 1982. Cultural Resource Survey, Freeport Harbor, Texas (45 Foot) Navigation Improvement Project, Brazoria County, Texas. *Center for Archaeological Research, The University of Texas at San Antonio, Archaeological Survey Report*, No. 107.

Fox, D. E., R. J. Mallouf, N. O'Malley, and W. M. Sorrow. 1974. Archeological Resources of the Proposed Cuero I Reservoir, DeWitt and Gonzales Counties, Texas. *Texas Historical Commission and Texas Water Development Board, Archeological Survey Report*, No. 12.

Fox, D. E., F. Valdez, Jr., and L. O. Bobbitt. 1978. An Archaeological Assessment of the Dolores Aldrete House Property, San Antonio, Texas. *Center for Archaeological Research, The University of Texas at San Antonio, Archaeological Survey Report*, No. 58.

Fox, D. E., W. H. Whitsett, and C. J. Jurgens. 1981. An Archeological Reconnaissance at City of Round Rock, Williamson County, Texas. Unpublished report prepared for the Construction Grants and Water Quality Planning Division, Texas Department of Water Resources, Austin.

Freeman, M. D., and W. B. Fawcett, Jr. 1980. Stephen F. Austin Colony. **I**

Godden, G. A. 1964. *Encyclopaedia of British Pottery and Porcelain Marks.* Crown Publishers (Bonanza Books), New York.

———. 1967. *An Illustrated Encyclopaedia of British Pottery and Porcelain.* Crown Publishers, New York.

Greaser, A., and P. H. Greaser. 1967. *Homespun Ceramics.* Third Edition, Enlarged. A-B-E Printing Company, Allentown.

Gulick, C. A., Jr., and W. Allen (editors). 1924. The Papers of Mirabeau Buonaparte Lamar, Vol. IV, Part II (of 6 volumes). 1973 Reprint, edited from the original papers of the Texas State Library. AMS Press, New York.

Hole, F. 1980. Letter to A. A. Fox concerning results of investigations at Quintana, November 13. On file at the Center for Archaeological Research, The University of Texas at San Antonio.

Hume, I. N. 1970. *A Guide to Artifacts of Colonial America.* **Intro**

Ing, J. D. 1976. Fort Lipantitlan State Historic Site, Nueces County, Texas, Archeological Testing—1974. *Texas Parks and Wildlife Department, Historic Sites and Restoration Branch, Archeological Report*, No. 16.

Ivey, J. E., and A. A. Fox. n.d. Excavations at the Paseo del Rio, San Antonio, Texas. Center for Archaeological Research, The University of Texas at San Antonio, manuscript in preparation.

Jackson, M. F. 1977. Texana: Excavations at a Nineteenth Century Inland Coastal Town, Jackson County, Texas. *Texas Archeological Survey, The University of Texas at Austin, Research Report*, No. 57.

Katz, P. R. 1978. Archaeological and Historical Investigations in the Arciniega Street Area, Downtown San Antonio, Texas. *Center for Archaeological Research, The University of Texas at San Antonio, Archaeological Survey Report*, No. 61.

Kendrick, G. 1970. *The Antique Bottle Collector.* Third Edition. Edwards Brothers, Ann Arbor.

Lorrain, D. 1968. An Archeologist's Guide to Nineteenth Century American Glass. *Annual Publication of the Society for Histor-*

ical Archaeology, Vol. 2.

Lorrain, D., and M. K. Jackson. n.d. Archeological Investigations at Washington-on-the-Brazos. Unpublished manuscript on file, Texas Historical Commission, Austin.

Luckett, B. n.d. Report of the Impossibility of the Stable Remains in NCB 155, Lot 26, Being Originally a Spanish Fort. Unpublished manuscript on file, Texas Historical Commission, Austin.

Lynn, W. M. n.d. Draft Technical Report of Archeological Survey and Excavation on Quintana Island, Texas. Unpublished manuscript on file, Texas Historical Commission, Austin.

Mallouf, R. J., D. E. Fox, and A. K. Briggs. 1973. An Assessment of the Cultural Resources of Palmetto Bend Reservoir, Jackson County, Texas. *Texas Historical Commission and Texas Water Development Board, Archeological Survey Report*, No. 11.

Mankowitz, W., and R. G. Haggar. 1975. *The Concise Encyclopedia of English Pottery and Porcelain.* Hawthorn Books, Inc., New York.

Meinig, D. W. 1969. *Imperial Texas: An Interpretive Essay in Cultural Geography.* University of Texas Press, Austin.

Menchaca, A. 1937. Memoirs. *Yanaguana Society Publications*, Vol. II. San Antonio.

Nelson, L. H. 1968. Nail Chronology as an Aid to Dating Old Buildings. American Association for State and Local History Technical Leaflet 48. *History News*, Vol. 24, No. 11.

Newman, T. S. 1970. A Dating Key for Post-Eighteenth Century Bottles. *Historical Archaeology* 1970. (Annual Publication of the Society of Historical Archaeology, Vol. 4).

Olds, D. L. 1967. The French Legation Kitchen. Report of Investigations, prepared for the Daughters of the Republic of Texas. Texas Archaeological Research Laboratory, The University of Texas at Austin.

Parsons, M. L., J. E. Corbin, and C. D. Tunnell. n.d. A Preliminary Report on Archeological Investigations at Washington-on-the-Brazos, 1964. Unpublished manuscript on file, Texas Archaeological Research Laboratory, The University of Texas at Austin.

Pierce, G. S. 1969. *Texas Under Arms: The Camps, Posts and Military Towns of the Republic of Texas, 1836–1846.* The Encino Press, Austin.

Santos, R. G. 1967. The Quartel de San Antonio de Béxar. *Texana*, Vol. 5, No. 3, pp. 187–203.

Scarbrough, C. S. 1976. *Land of Good Water.* Williamson County Sun Publishers, Georgetown.

Schuetz, M. K. n.d. Archeology of the Quartel. Unpublished manuscript on file, Texas Historical Commission, Austin.

Scurlock, D., and D. E. Fox. 1977. Mission Concepción. **IV**

Texas Parks and Wildlife Department. 1977. *Preservation Plan and Program for Washington-on-the-Brazos State Historical Park, Washington County, Texas.* Texas Parks and Wildlife Department, Historic Sites and Restoration Branch.

Webb, W. P. (editor). 1952. *The Handbook of Texas* (2 Volumes). Texas State Historical Association, Austin.

Yoakum, H. 1856. *History of Texas From Its First Settlement in 1685 to Its Annexation to the United States in 1846* (2 Volumes). Redfield, New Jersey.

VI   The Settlement of American Texas

Arnold, J. B., III. 1974. A Magnetometer Survey of the Nineteenth Century Steamboat "Black Cloud." *Bulletin of the Texas Archeological Society*, Vol. 45, pp. 225–230.

Bornhorst, J. 1971. Plantation Settlement in the Brazos River Valley, 1820–1860. Master's thesis, Texas A&M University, College Station.

Bowman, B. 1966. *This Was East Texas: Anthology of Ghost Towns.* Angelina Free Press, Diboll.

Brooks, R., and B. J. Baskin. 1976. Archeological Investigation of the Barn at the Admiral Nimitz Center, Fredericksburg, Texas. *Office of the State Archeologist, Texas Historical Commission, Special Report*, No. 19.

Burnett, R. E. 1981. *Archeological Testing,*

Fanthorp Inn State Historic Site, 41GM79, Grimes County, Texas. Texas Parks and Wildlife Department, Historic Sites and Restoration Branch, Austin.

Carlson, S. B. 1982. The Economic Development of an East Central Texas Rancher. Paper presented at the 53rd Annual Meeting of the Texas Archeological Society, October 29–31, College Station.

Clark, J. W., Jr. 1980. The Woodlands: Archeological Investigations at the Sam Houston Home, Huntsville, Walker County, Texas. *Reports on Investigations,* No. 4. Prewitt and Associates, Inc., Austin.

Collier, G. L. 1982. Evolution of Cultural Patterns in East Texas. In *Texana II: Cultural Heritage of the Plantation South* (Proceedings of a public humanities conference for the exploration of antebellum Texas and slavery), edited by C. Volz, pp. 7–12. Texas Historical Commission, Austin.

Crouch, D. J. 1982. *Varner-Hogg Plantation State Historical Park, Brazoria County, Texas, Archeological Investigations, 1979–1981.* With contribution by Dr. C. A. Brandimarte. Historic Sites and Restoration Branch, Texas Parks and Wildlife Department.

Curlee, A. 1932. A Study of Texas Slave Plantations, 1822 to 1865. Ph.D. dissertation, The University of Texas at Austin.

Fehrenbach, T. R. 1968. *Lone Star.* **II**

Fox, A. A., D. W. Day, and L. Highley. 1980. Wallisville Lake. **III**

Fox, D. E., R. J. Mallouf, N. O'Malley, and W. M. Sorrow. 1974. Cuero I Reservoir. **IV**

Freeman, M. D., and W. B. Fawcett, Jr. 1980. Stephen F. Austin Colony. **I**

Hollon, W. E., and R. L. Butler (editors). 1956. *William Bollaert's Texas.* University of Oklahoma Press, Norman.

Jackson, J. M. 1982. Archeological Investigations of Slave Plantations. In *Texana II: Cultural Heritage of the Plantation South* (Proceedings of a public humanities conference for the exploration of antebellum Texas and slavery), edited by C. Volz, pp. 51–57. Texas Historical Commission, Austin.

Jensen, H. P., Jr. 1969. Archeological Excavations at James S. Hogg Birthplace, Rusk, Texas. *State Building Commission, Archeological Program, Report,* No. 14.

Jordan, T. G. 1964. The Imprint of the Upper and Lower South on Mid-Nineteenth Century Texas. *Annals of the Association of American Geographers,* Vol. 57 (December), pp. 667–690.

———. 1969. The Origin of Anglo-American Cattle Ranching in Texas: A Documentation of Diffusion from the Lower South. *Economic Geography,* Vol. 45, No. 1, pp. 63–87.

Kniffen, F. 1965. Folk Housing: Key to Diffusion. *Annals of the Association of American Geographers,* Vol. 55 (December), pp. 549–577.

Meinig, D. W. 1969. *Imperial Texas.* **V**

Newton, M. 1974. Cultural Preadaptation and the Upland South. In *Geoscience and Man,* edited by B. F. Perkins, Vol. V: *Man and Cultural Heritage Papers in Honor of Fred B. Kniffen,* edited by H. J. Walker and W. G. Haag. The School of Geoscience, Louisiana State University, Baton Rouge.

Olmsted, F. L. 1978. *A Journey Through Texas: Or, A Saddle Trip on the Southwestern Frontier.* University of Texas Press, Austin.

Otto, J. S. 1977. Artifacts and Status Differences—A Comparison of Ceramics from Planter, Overseer, and Slave Sites on an Antebellum Plantation. In *Research Strategies in Historic Archaeology,* edited by Stanley South. Academic Press, New York.

Pevey, J. C. 1981. The Sam Houston Home, 41WY46, Huntsville, Walker County, Texas: 1980–1981 Archeological Investigations and Monitoring. *Prewitt and Associates, Inc., Reports of Investigations,* No. 12, Austin.

Puryear, P. A., and N. Winfield, Jr. 1976. *Sandbars and Sternwheelers: Steam Navigation on the Brazos.* Texas A&M University Press, College Station.

Richner, J. J., and J. T. Bagot (assemblers). 1978. *A Reconnaissance Survey of the Trinity River Basin, 1976–1977.* With contributions by M. Chaffin-Lohse, M. Johnston,

D. McGregor, R. Moore, J. Newman, and C. Shaw. Archaeology Research Program, Department of Anthropology, Southern Methodist University, Dallas.

Simons, H. (editor) n.d. The Gaines–McGown Site: Archeological Investigations and Related Research. With contributions by G. H. Greer, J. M. Malone, H. Simons, and Office of the State Archeologist staff. Manuscript in preparation, Texas Historical Commission, Austin.

Smith-Savage, S., and J. D. Ing. 1982. Fanthorp Inn: A Case Study of Historic Site Development (Part 1). *Texas Association of Museums Quarterly*, Vol. 7, No. 6, pp. 13–14.

South, S. A. 1964. Some Notes on Bricks. *Florida Anthropologist*, Vol. 17, No. 2, pp. 67–74.

South, S. A. (editor). 1977. *Method and Theory in Historical Archaeology*. Academic Press, New York.

Texas Archeological Survey. 1974. The Historic and Prehistoric Archeological Resources of the Seadock Area. *Texas Archeological Survey, The University of Texas at Austin, Technical Bulletin*, No. 5.

Texas Parks and Wildlife Department. 1976. *Preservation Plan and Program for Landmark Inn State Historical Site, Medina County, Texas*. Texas Parks and Wildlife Department, Historic Sites and Restoration Branch, Austin.

Texas Parks and Wildlife Department. n.d. Preservation Plan and Program for Varner-Hogg Plantation State Historical Site. Texas Parks and Wildlife Department, Historic Sites and Restoration Branch, Austin. Unpublished manuscript subject to approval.

Webb, W. P. (editor). 1952. *Handbook of Texas*. **V**

VII The Movement West

Bandy, P. A. 1981. Historical Archaeological Resources of the Choke Canyon Reservoir Area in McMullen and Live Oak Counties, Texas. (1 of 2 parts). *Center for Archaeological Research, The University of Texas at San Antonio, Choke Canyon Series*, Vol. 2, pp. 76–190.

Beck, W. A. 1962. *New Mexico: A History of Four Centuries*. University of Oklahoma Press, Norman.

Bender, A. B. 1933. Opening Routes Across West Texas, 1848–1850. *Southwestern Historical Quarterly*, Vol. 37.

Day, J. H. 1937. *The Sutton Taylor Feud*. Sid Murray and Son Printers, San Antonio.

Dixon, O. K. 1914. *Life and Adventures of "Billy" Dixon of Adobe Walls, Texas, Panhandle*. Co-Operative Publishing Company, Guthrie.

———. 1927. *Life of "Billy" Dixon, Plainsman, Scout and Pioneer*. P. L. Turner Company, Dallas.

Everett, D. 1981. Historical Resources of the Choke Canyon Reservoir Area in McMullen and Live Oak Counties, Texas. (1 of 2 parts). *Center for Archaeological Research, The University of Texas at San Antonio, Choke Canyon Series*, Vol. 2, pp. xiii–64.

Fehrenbach, T. R. 1968. *Lone Star*. **II**

Fox, A. A. 1979. Archaeological and Historical Investigations at 41BX180, Walker Ranch, San Antonio, Texas. Phase I. *Center for Archaeological Research, The University of Texas at San Antonio, Archaeological Survey Report*, No. 83.

———. n.d. Observations of the removal of the Morris and Taylor burials, 41MC6. Field notes on file, Center for Archaeological Research, The University of Texas at San Antonio.

Fox, A. A., and W. Cox. n.d. Archaeological and Historical Investigations at Walker Ranch, San Antonio, Texas. Phase II. Center for Archaeological Research, The University of Texas at San Antonio, manuscript in preparation.

Fox, D. E. 1982. Excavations at Sites 41LK31/32 and 41LK202 in the Choke Canyon Reservoir, South Texas. Part II: Historic Investigations. *Center for Archaeological Research, The University of Texas at San Antonio, Choke Canyon Series*, Vol. 8, pp. 91–132.

Franz, J. B. 1952. The Mercantile House of McKinney and Williams, Underwriters of the Texas Revolution. *Bulletin of the Business Historical Society*, Vol. 26, pp. 3–20.

Guffee, E. J. 1976. *The Merrell-Taylor Village Site: An Archeological Investigation of Pre-Anglo, Spanish-Mexican Occupation on Quitaque Creek in Floyd County, Texas.* Archeological Research Laboratory, Llano Estacado Museum, Wayland Baptist College, Plainview.

———. 1980. *The Soda Lake Ruins: An Archeological Investigation of Anglo Occupation in the Sandhills of Lamb County, Texas.* Archeological Research Laboratory, Llano Estacado Museum, Wayland Baptist College, Plainview.

Hendricks, S. B. 1919. The Somervell Expedition to the Rio Grande, 1842. *Southwestern Historical Quarterly,* Vol. 23.

Hollen, W. E., and R. L. Butler (editors). 1956. *William Bollaert's Texas.* **VI**

Hudson, W. R., Jr., W. M. Lynn, and D. Scurlock. 1974. Walker Ranch, An Archeological Reconnaissance and Excavations in Northern Bexar County, Texas. *Office of the State Archeologist, Texas Historical Commission, Report,* No. 57.

Ing, J. D., and G. Kegley. 1971. *Archeological Investigations at Fort Leaton Historic Site, Presidio County, Texas, Spring, 1971.* Texas Parks and Wildlife Department, Historic Sites and Restoration Branch, Austin.

Ing, J. D., and W. Roberson. 1974. Fort Leaton State Historic Site: Summary of Archeological Investigations, and Excavation of Chapel, 1973. *Historic Sites and Restoration Branch, Texas Parks and Wildlife Department, Archeological Report,* No. 15.

Jelks, E. B. 1969. Archeological Excavations at Fort Leaton State Park. Report Prepared for the Texas Parks and Wildlife Department, Austin.

Kenner, C. L. 1969. *A History of New Mexican–Plains Indian Relations.* University of Oklahoma Press, Norman.

Knox, O., *et al.* 1974. *Preservation Plan and Program for Fort Leaton State Historical Site, Presidio County, Texas.* Texas Parks and Wildlife Department, Historic Sites and Restoration Branch, Austin.

Lynn, W. M., D. E. Fox, and N. O'Malley. 1977. Cultural Resources Survey of Choke Canyon Reservoir, Live Oak and McMullen Counties, Texas. *Office of the State Archeologist, Texas Historical Commission, Archeological Survey Report,* No. 20.

McEachern, M., and R. W. Ralph. 1980. Archeological Investigations at the Thomas F. McKinney Homestead, Travis County, Texas: An Experiment in Historic Archeology, Part I. *Bulletin of the Texas Archeological Society,* Vol. 51, pp. 5–127.

———. 1981. Archeological Investigations of the Thomas F. McKinney Homestead, Travis County, Texas: An Experiment in Historic Archeology, Part II. *Bulletin of the Texas Archeological Society,* Vol. 52, pp. 5–63.

Meinig, D. W. 1969. *Imperial Texas.* **V**

Ralph, R. W., and M. McEachern. 1974. *TAS Field School 1974.* Speleo Press, Austin.

Richner, J. J., and T. R. Lee. 1976. Cultural Resources at Tennessee Colony Lake. *Archaeology Research Program, Southern Methodist University, Research Report,* No. 87.

———. 1977. Archaeological and Ethnohistorical Survey at Tennessee Colony Lake 1975. *Archaeology Research Program, Southern Methodist University, Research Report,* No. 104.

Rose, V. 1880. *The Texas Vendetta: The Sutton-Taylor Feud.* J. J. Little and Company, New York. Reprint by Frontier Press, Houston, 1956.

Scott, F. J. 1966. *Historical Heritage of the Rio Grande.* Texian Press, Waco.

Scurlock, D., and W. R. Hudson, Jr. 1973. An Archeological Investigation of Walker Ranch. *Office of the State Archeologist, Texas Historical Commission, Special Report,* No. 9.

Taylor, A. J. 1980. *A Survey of New Mexican "Pastores" in the Texas Panhandle-Plains, 1876–1886.* Texas Historical Foundation, Austin.

U.S. Department of Interior. 1870. The Ninth Census, 1870. Returns of Schedule One, Population. Manuscript in microfilm, Southwest Collection, Texas Tech University, Lubbock.

Victoria Sesquicentennial, Inc. 1974. *The Victoria Sesquicentennial "Scrapbook" 1824–*

1974. Advocate Printing, Inc., Victoria.

Webb, W. P. (editor). 1952. *Handbook of Texas.* **V**

Whitsett, W. H., and D. E. Fox. n.d. Cultural Resources of Lower Onion Creek. Unpublished manuscript prepared for the Construction Grants and Water Quality Planning Division, Texas Department of Water Resources, Austin.

VIII European Farmsteads

Carter, E. S., and C. S. Ragsdale. 1976. Biegel Settlement: Historic Sites Research, Fayette Power Project. Fayette County, Texas. *Texas Archeological Survey, The University of Texas at Austin, Research Report,* No. 59.

Dragonwagon, n.d. Archeological Investigations at Hedwig's Hill, Mason County, Texas. Report prepared for the Ranch Headquarters Association, The Museum of Texas Tech University. Unpublished manuscript on file, Texas Historical Commission, Austin.

Fehrenbach, T. R. 1968. *Lone Star.* **II**

Flach, V. 1974. *A Yankee in German America: Texas Hill Country.* Naylor, San Antonio.

Fox, A. A., and K. Livingston. 1979. Steiner-Schob Complex. **I**

Gerstle, A., T. C. Kelly, and C. Assad. 1978. The Fort Sam Houston Project: An Archaeological and Historical Assessment. With contributions by P. Dering, A. A. Fox, D. E. Fox, A. Frkuska, C. Graves, J. D. Gunn, J. Henderson, T. R. Hester, J. E. Ivey, and S. E. Kleine. *Center for Archaeological Research, The University of Texas at San Antonio, Archaeological Survey Report,* No. 40.

Jackson, T. M. F., and D. W. Skelton. 1975. *Fayette Power Project: An Interim Report on the Assessment of Its Impact on the Cultural Resources.* Texas Archeological Survey, The University of Texas at Austin.

Jordan, T. G. 1966. *German Seed in Texas Soil: Immigrant Farmers in Nineteenth-Century Texas.* The University of Texas Press, Austin.

King, I. M. 1967. *John O. Meusebach: German Colonizer in Texas.* University of Texas Press, Austin.

Meinig, D. W. 1969. *Imperial Texas.* **V**

Montgomery Ward and Company. 1969. *Catalogue No. 57, Spring and Summer, 1895.* Dover Publications, Inc., New York.

Tunnell, C. D., and H. P. Jensen, Jr. 1969. Archeological Excavations in Lyndon B. Johnson State Park, Summer, 1968. *State Building Commission, Archeological Program, Report,* No. 17.

IX Battlegrounds, Forts, and Other Military Sites

Albaugh, W., III. 1958. *Tyler, Texas, C.S.A.* Stackpole Publishing Company, Harrisburg, Pennsylvania.

Baxter, E. P., and K. L. Killen. 1976. A Study of the Palo Alto Battleground, Cameron County, Texas. *Anthropology Laboratory, Texas A&M University, Report,* No. 33.

Beard, R. n.d. Fort Griffin excavation notes on file, Texas Parks and Wildlife Department, Austin.

Biggers, D. H. 1974. *Shackelford County Sketches.* Edited and annotated by Joan Farmer. The Clear Fork Press, Albany and Fort Griffin.

Black, A. 1974. Fort Lancaster State Historic Site, Crockett County, Texas, Archeological Excavations. *Historic Sites and Restoration Branch, Texas Parks and Wildlife Department, Archeological Report,* No. 18.

Boggs, W. n.d. Brazos Santiago Depot Archeological District (41CF4), Cameron County, Texas, 1980 Investigations. Notes on file, Office of the State Archeologist, Texas Historical Commission, Austin.

Bond, C. L. 1979. Palo Alto Battlefield: A Magnetometer and Metal Detector Survey. *Cultural Resources Laboratory, Texas A&M University, Report,* No. 4.

Brooks, N. C. 1849. *A Complete History of the Mexican War.* 1965 reprint. Rio Grande Press, Inc., Chicago.

Clark, J. W., Jr. 1972. Archeological Investigations at Fort Lancaster State Historic Site, Crockett County, Texas. *Texas Archeological Salvage Project, The University of Texas at Austin, Research Report,* No. 12.

Collins, M. B., T. R. Hester, and T. S. Ellezy. n.d. Excavations at Resaca de la Palma, a Mexican War Cemetery Site (41CF3), Cameron County, Texas. Notes on file, Texas Archeological Research Laboratory, The University of Texas at Austin.

Conway, W. C. (editor). 1963–1964. Colonel Edmund Schriver's Inspector General's Report on Military Posts in Texas, November 1872–January 1873. *Southwestern Historical Quarterly*, Vol. 67, pp. 559–583.

Crane, C. J. 1923. *The Experiences of a Colonel of Infantry*. The Knickerbocker Press, New York.

Crimmins, W. C. (editor). 1939. Colonel J. K. F. Mansfield's Report of the Inspection of the Department of Texas in 1856. *Southwestern Historical Quarterly*, Vol. 42, pp. 215–257.

———. 1950. W. G. Freeman's Report on the Eighth Military Department. *Southwestern Historical Quarterly*, Vol. 53, pp. 202–208.

Dickson, D. B. 1976. Archeological Research at Fort Richardson State Park, Summer, 1975. *Anthropology Laboratory, Texas A&M University, Report*, No. 28.

Fehrenbach, T. R. 1968. *Lone Star*. II

Fox, A. A. 1973. Archeological Investigations at Fort Griffin State Historic Park, Texas, February, 1973. *Texas Archeological Survey, The University of Texas at Austin, Research Report*, No. 21.

———. 1976. Archaeological Investigations at Fort Griffin State Historic Park, Shackelford County, Texas. *Center for Archaeological Research, The University of Texas at San Antonio, Archaeological Survey Report*, No. 23.

Fox, D. E. 1979. Archaeological Testing at Fort McIntosh, Laredo Junior College Campus, Laredo, Texas. *Center for Archaeological Research, The University of Texas at San Antonio, Archaeological Survey Report*, No. 68.

Francell, L. 1969. *Ft. Lancaster State Historic Park, Crockett County, Texas*. Texas Parks and Wildlife Department, Historic Sites and Restoration Branch, Austin.

Frost, J. 1850. *The Mexican War and Its Warriors*. H. Mansfield, New Haven.

Graf, L. 1942. Economic History of the Lower Rio Grande Valley. Ph.D. dissertation, Harvard University.

Graham, R. E. 1968. *Texas Historic Forts, Part IV, Griffin*. One of a series of reports submitted by the School of Architecture, The University of Texas at Austin, to the Texas Parks and Wildlife Department, Austin (See Taniguchi *et al.* 1968).

Guffee, E. J. 1976. Camp Peña Colorado, Texas, 1879–1893. Master's thesis, Department of History, West Texas State University, Canyon.

Hall, G. D., and K. A. Grombacher. 1974. An Assessment of the Archeological and Historical Resources to be Affected by the Brazos Island Harbor Waterway Project, Texas. *Texas Archeological Survey, The University of Texas at Austin, Research Report*, No. 30.

Hays, T. R., and E. B. Jelks. 1966. Archeological Exploration at Fort Lancaster, 1966, A Preliminary Report. *State Building Commission, Archeological Program, Report*, No. 4.

Hester, T. R. 1978. The Archaeology of the Lower Rio Grande Valley of Texas. In *Proceedings: An Exploration of a Common Legacy: A Conference on Border Architecture*. Texas Historical Commission, Austin, pp. 66–73.

Hole, F. 1974. The Acadia, A Civil War Blockade Runner. *Department of Anthropology, Rice University, Technical Report*, No. 1.

Holtzapple, T., and W. Roberson. 1976. Sabine Pass Battleground State Historical Park, Jefferson Co., Texas: Archeological Investigations. *Historic Sites and Restoration Branch, Texas Parks and Wildlife Department, Archeological Report*, No. 8.

Ivey, J. E., T. Medlin, and J. D. Eaton. 1977. An Initial Archaeological Assessment of Areas Proposed for Modification at Fort McIntosh, Webb County, Texas. *Center for Archaeological Research, The University of Texas at San Antonio, Archaeological Survey Report*, No. 32.

Leckie, W. H. 1967. *The Buffalo Soldiers, A Narrative of the Negro Cavalry in the West*. University of Oklahoma Press, Norman.

Lorrain, D. n.d. Daily Log. Field Notes of Fall, 1971, Excavations, Fort Lancaster, Texas, on file, Texas Parks and Wildlife Department, Historic Sites and Restoration Branch, Austin.

Luke, C. J. 1978. The Marshall Powder Mill. *Highway Design Division, State Department of Highways and Public Transportation, Publications in Archaeology*, Report, No. 11.

Metz, L. C. 1966. *John Selman, Texas Gunfighter*. Hastings House, New York.

National Archives. 1853. Survey of the Cantonments and Adjacent Grounds and Plans of Fort McIntosh Near Laredo on the Rio Grande, Texas. By Richard Delafield, Major of Engineers. Made in October and November, 1853. Record Group No. 77, Drawer No. 148-32. Washington, D.C.

Nelson, G. S. 1981. *Preliminary Archaeological Survey and Testing of Fort Inge, Texas*. Uvalde County Historical Commission, Uvalde.

Nevin, D. 1978. *The Mexican War*. Time-Life Books, Alexandria, Virginia.

Olds, D. L. 1969. *Archeological Investigations at Fort Griffin Military Post, Shackelford County, Texas*. Texas Archeological Research Laboratory, The University of Texas at Austin.

Parks, J. H. 1954. *General E. Kirby Smith C.S.A.* Louisiana State University Press, Baton Rouge.

Peck, J. J. 1970. *The Signs of the Eagle: A View of Mexico, 1830–1855*. Copely Press, San Diego, California.

Pierce, F. C. 1917. *A Brief History of the Lower Rio Grande Valley*. George Banta Publishing Company, Menasha, Wisconsin.

Ramsey, A. C. 1970. *The Other Side*. B. Franklin, New York.

Rister, C. C. 1956. *Fort Griffin on the Texas Frontier*. University of Oklahoma Press, Norman.

Roney, J., III. 1962. Marshall, Texas, 1860–1865. Master's thesis, Baylor University, Waco.

Shafer, H. J. 1974. An Archeological Reconnaissance of the Brownsville Relocation Study Area. *Anthropology Laboratory, Texas A&M University, Report*, No. 1.

Smith, G. W., and C. Judah. 1968. *Chronicles of the Gungas*. University of New Mexico Press, Albuquerque.

Taniguchi, A. Y., R. E. Graham, G. C. Hamblett, D. Green, L. Hawthorne, M. Penick, and W. E. von Rosenburg. 1968. *Texas Historic Forts*. A series of reports submitted by the School of Architecture. The University of Texas at Austin, to the Texas Parks and Wildlife Department.

Texas Parks and Wildlife Department. 1977. *Phase IV Development Plan and Program for Fort McKavett State Historic Site, Menard County, Texas*. Texas Parks and Wildlife Department, Historic Sites and Restoration Branch, Austin.

Thompson, J. H. 1965. A Nineteenth Century History of Cameron County, Texas. Master's thesis, The University of Texas at Austin.

———. 1974. *Sabers on the Rio Grande*. Presidial Press, Austin.

U. S. Army Corps of Engineers. 1876. Outline Descriptions of the Posts in the Military Division of the Missouri. Headquarters, Military Division of the Missouri, Chicago.

Weir, F. A. 1973. The Marshall Powder Mill, A Preliminary Report. *Highway Design Division, Texas Highway Department, Publications in Archaeology, Report*, No. 3.

Wesolowsky, A. B. 1982. A Note on the Human Skeletal Remains from Resaca de la Palma, 41CF3. Letter to Daniel E. Fox, September 14.

Westbury, W. A. 1976. Archeological Investigations at Fort Richardson State Park, 1976. *Anthropology Laboratory, Texas A&M University, Report*, No. 31.

X Early Industries and Factories

Anderson, T. 1980. Ceramic Analysis of a Late 19th Century Trash Midden: Nottingham, Texas. Houston Archaeological Society, *Newsletter*, No. 66, pp. 10–16.

Bandy, P. A. 1981. Choke Canyon Reservoir. **VII**

Betancourt, J., and W. M. Lynn. 1977. An Archeological Survey of a Proposed Lignite Mine Area, Shell Rockdale South

Lease, Milam County, Texas. *Office of the State Archeologist, Texas Historical Commission, Archeological Survey Report,* No. 21.

Brackner, J., Jr. 1982. The Transition from Slave Potter to Free Potter: The Wilson Potteries of Guadalupe County, Texas. In *Texana II: Cultural Heritage of the Plantation South* (Proceedings of a public humanities conference for the exploration of antebellum Texas and slavery), edited by C. Volz, pp. 39–43. Texas Historical Commission, Austin.

Briggs, A. K. 1974. The Archeology of 1882 Labor Camps on the Southern Pacific Railroad, Val Verde County, Texas. Master's thesis, The University of Texas at Austin.

Buckley, S. B. 1874. *Geological and Agricultural Survey of Texas.* A. C. Gray, State Printer, Houston.

Cartier, R. R., and F. Hole. 1972. Part I: History of the McCormick League and Areas Adjoining the San Jacinto Battleground (Cartier and Hole); Part II: Archeological Investigation of the North End of the San Jacinto Battleground (Hole). Report prepared in compliance with Permit No. 11 granted to Coastal Industrial Water Authority by the Antiquities Committee of the State of Texas.

Clark, J. W., Jr. 1976. The Sugar Industry. **IV**

———. 1978. Mission San José y San Miguel de Aguayo. **IV**

Curlee, A. 1932. Texas Slave Plantations. **VI**

Deerr, N. 1950. *The History of Sugar.* Volume 2. Chapman and Hall Ltd., London.

Dugas, V. L. 1955. Texas Industry, 1860–1880. *Southwestern Historical Quarterly,* Vol. 59, pp. 151–183.

Durrenberger, E. P. 1965. Anderson's Mill (41TV130): A Historic Site in Travis County, Texas. *Bulletin of the Texas Archeological Society,* Vol. 36, pp. 1–69.

Easton, H. P. 1947. The History of the Texas Lumbering Industry. Ph.D. dissertation, The University of Texas at Austin.

Everett, D. 1981. Choke Canyon Reservoir. **VII**

Fehrenbach, T. R. 1968. *Lone Star.* **II**

Fisher, W. L. 1963. Lignites of the Texas Gulf Coastal Plain. *Bureau of Economic Geol-*

ogy, *The University of Texas at Austin, Report on Investigations,* No. 50.

Flynn, L. M., A. A. Fox, and I. W. Cox. n.d. Archaeological Investigations at Guenther's Upper Mill, San Antonio, Texas. Center for Archaeological Research, The University of Texas at San Antonio, report in preparation.

Fox, A. A. 1970. Preliminary Survey of Pits at Mission Espada. Letter report to the State Archeologist, Texas Historical Commission, Austin.

———. n.d.a. Archaeological Investigations at Historic Sites in the Choke Canyon Reservoir Area, McMullen and Live Oak Counties, Texas. Center for Archaeological Research, The University of Texas at San Antonio, Choke Canyon Series, volume in preparation.

———. n.d.b. Archaeological Investigations at the Denton Kilns (41BX227), San Pedro Hills Subdivision, Bexar County, Texas. Field notes on file, Center for Archaeological Research, The University of Texas at San Antonio.

Fox, A. A., D. W. Day, and L. Highley. 1980. Wallisville Lake. **III**

Fox, A. A., and J. E. Ivey. 1979. Historical Survey of the Lands Within the Alamo Plaza–River Linkage Development Project. *Center for Archaeological Research, The University of Texas at San Antonio, Archaeological Survey Report,* No. 79.

Fox, D. E. 1979. Preliminary Report for Waco Suspension Bridge/Indian Spring Park. Submitted by the Center for Archaeological Research, The University of Texas at San Antonio, to the City of Waco and the Texas Historical Commission.

Freeman, M. D., and W. B. Fawcett, Jr. 1980. Stephen F. Austin Colony. **I**

Fritz, G. 1975. Matagorda Bay Area, Texas: A Survey of Archeological and Historical Resources. *Texas Archeological Survey, The University of Texas at Austin, Research Report,* No. 45.

Greer, G. H. 1977a. Groundhog Kilns—Rectangular American Kilns of the Nineteenth and Early Twentieth Centuries. *Northeast Historical Archaeology,* Vol. 6 (January–February), pp. 42–54.

———. 1977b. The Abraham Babcock Pottery Manufactory. Appendix IV in: Texana: Excavations at a Nineteenth Century Inland Coastal Town, Jackson County, Texas. by M. F. Jackson. *Texas Archeological Survey, The University of Texas at Austin, Research Report*, No. 56, *Palmetto Bend Series*, Vol. 1.

Guderjan, T. H. 1981. *Archaeological Investigations in the Forest Grove/Big Rock Areas, North-Central Texas*. With contributions by G. W. Rutenberg, M. O. Baldia, M. Irvine, P. A. Murry, L. M. Raab, and H. A. Smith. Archaeology Research Program, Southern Methodist University, Dallas.

Historic Engineering Site Survey. 1975, Texas Tech University, Lubbock.

Ivey, J. E. n.d. Historical and Archaeological Investigations at the Menger Soap Works (41BX484), San Antonio, Texas. Center for Archaeological Research, The University of Texas at San Antonio, Archaeological Survey Report, No. 79, in preparation.

Ivey, J. E., and A. A. Fox. n.d. Paseo del Rio. **V**

Jordan, T. 1966. *German Seed in Texas Soil*. **VIII**

Kendrick, G. 1963. The Antique Bottle Collector. **V**

Killen, K. L., and D. Scurlock. n.d. A Report on Preliminary Test Excavations at Mission Espada Kilns, San Antonio, Texas. Preliminary draft on file, Office of the State Archeologist, Texas Historical Commission, Austin.

Lynn, W. M., D. E. Fox, and N. O'Malley. 1977. Choke Canyon Reservoir. **VII**

Mallouf, R. J., D. E. Fox, and A. K. Briggs. 1973. Palmetto Bend Reservoir. **V**

Malone, J. M., and D. E. Fox. n.d. Lime Kilns and Brick Kilns in various parts of Texas. ·Survey notes on file, Office of the State Archeologist. Texas Historical Commission, Austin.

Malone, J. M., G. H. Greer, and H. Simons. 1979. Kirbee Kiln: A Mid-19th Century Texas Stoneware Pottery. *Office of the State Archeologist, Texas Historical Commission, Report*, No. 31.

McDowell, C. n.d. San Antonio's Mills on the River. Unpublished manuscript, Institute of Texan Cultures, San Antonio.

McEachern, M., and R. W. Ralph. 1981. McKinney Homestead. **VII**

McKearin, G. S., and H. McKearin. 1950. *Two Hundred Years of American Blown Glass*. Crown Publishers, New York.

———. 1971. *American Glass*. Crown Publishers, New York.

Meinig, D. W. 1969. *Imperial Texas*. **V**

Olmsted, F. L. 1978. *A Journey through Texas*. **VI**

Patterson, P. E. 1980. Relocation and Restoration of a Baking Oven (Site 41VV588) in Val Verde County, Texas. *Texas Department of Highways and Public Transportation, Publications in Archaeology*, No. 18.

Richner, J. J., and J. T. Bagot (assemblers). 1978. *Trinity River Basin*. **VI**

Richner, J. J., and T. R. Lee. 1976. Tennessee Colony Lake. **VII**

———. 1977. Tennessee Colony Lake. **VII**

Scurlock, D., A. Benavides, Jr., D. Isham, and J. W. Clark, Jr. 1976. Mission Parkway. **IV**

Sitterton, J. C. 1953. *Sugar Country: The Cane Sugar Industry in the South, 1753–1950*. The University of Kentucky Press, Lexington.

Skinner, S. A. 1971. Historical Archeology of the Neches Saline, Smith County, Texas. *Texas Historical Survey Committee, Archeological Report*, No. 21.

———. 1979. The Archaeology of East Texas Lumbering. *Journal of the East Texas Historical Association*, Vol. 17, No. 1, pp. 36–44.

Skinner, S. A. (assembler). 1982. Archaeology and History of Lake Ray Roberts, Vol. 2, Construction Area Testing. With contributions by L. Baird, M. B. Cliff, K. Fimple, J. Garber, K. Hahn, A. Pitchford, J. Renner, V. Scarborough, D. G. Shaddox, K. Singleton, S. A. Skinner, B. Yates, and S. Hays. *Environmental Consultants, Inc., Cultural Resources Report*, No. 82-9, Dallas.

Spratt, J. S. 1955. *The Road to Spindle Top: Economic Change in Texas, 1875–1901*. Southern Methodist University Press, Dallas.

Stenzel, H. B. 1946. Review of Coal Production in Texas. Texas Mineral Resources. *University of Texas Publication*, No. 4301, pp. 197–206.

Texas Parks and Wildlife Department. 1976. *Landmark Inn.* **VI**

———. 1980. *Preservation Plan and Program for Monument Hill and Kreische Brewery State Historic Sites, Fayette County, Texas.* Historic Sites and Restoration Branch, Texas Parks and Wildlife Department, Austin.

Toulouse, J. H. 1971. *Bottle Makers and Their Marks.* Thomas Nelson and Sons, New York.

Webb, W. P. 1964. *The Great Frontier.* University of Texas Press, Austin.

Webb, W. P. (editor). 1952. *The Handbook of Texas.* **V**

Wetzel, S. n.d. Late 19th Century Bottle-Making Techniques: And an Analysis of Glassware from a Midden at Nottingham, Galveston Island. Unpublished manuscript, Houston Archeological Society.

Whitsett, W. H., and D. E. Fox. n.d. 41HR312. Site Survey Forms and Reconnaissance Report for a Late 19th Century and Early 20th Century Brickyard on Cedar Bayou, 1980. Notes on file, Texas Archeological Research Laboratory, The University of Texas at Austin, and at the Construction Grants and Water Quality Management Division, Texas Department of Water Resources.

Wigginton, E. (editor). 1975. *Foxfire 3.* Anchor Books, Garden City.

Wilkinson, J. B. 1975. *Laredo and the Rio Grande Frontier.* Jenkins Publishing Company, Austin.

Ziegler, Jesse A. 1938. *Wave of the Gulf.* Naylor, San Antonio.

XI Urban Texas

Anderson, T. 1982. The Walls and Walkways of Ashton Villa: Permutations in House Form and Site Plan. Paper presented at the January Conference, Society of Historical Archaeology, Philadelphia.

———. n.d. The Urban Residence: Archeology Explores Victorian Domestic Life. Unpublished conference paper, Department of Anthropology, Rice University, Houston.

Barkley, M. S. 1963. *History of Travis County and Austin, 1839–1899.* The Steck Company, Austin.

Briggs, A. K. 1981. Archeological Investigations at the Grant Building and Plaza: Monitoring and Emergency Recovery In and Near the Sixth Street Historic District, Austin, Travis County, Texas. *Lone Star Archeological Services, Report*, No. 1, Georgetown, Texas.

Brown, F. n.d. Annals of Travis County and the City of Austin. Unpublished manuscript (ca. 1900), Travis County Collection, Austin Public Library.

Campbell, C. A. R. 1925. *Bats, Mosquitoes and Dollars.* The Stratford Company, Boston.

Clark, J. W., Jr. 1974a. Preliminary Investigations at Wulff House, San Antonio, Texas. *Office of the State Archeologist, Texas Historical Commission, Special Report*, No. 14.

———. 1974b. Archeological Excavations at Ursuline Academy, San Antonio, Texas: June, 1974. *Office of the State Archeologist, Texas Historical Commission, Report.*

———. n.d. Archaeological Test Excavations at the North City of San Antonio Dump of the Early 20th Century. Highway Design Division, Texas State Department of Highways and Public Transportation, Publications in Archaeology, report in preparation.

Clark, J. W., Jr., and A. M. Juarez. n.d. Urban Archaeology: A Culture History of a Mexican-American Barrio in Laredo, Webb County, Texas. Highway Design Division, Texas State Department of Highways and Public Transportation, Publications in Archaeology, report in preparation.

Cox, W. 1982. Laredo, Texas: A Gateway Community on the Texas Borderlands. Archaeological and Historical Investigations for the Laredo City Toll Plaza. 41WB36, 41WB37 and 41WB38. *Center for Archaeological Research, The University of Texas at San Antonio, Archaeological Survey Report*, No. 116.

Fox, A. A. 1977. Spanish Governor's Palace Park. **IV**

———. n.d. Preliminary Archaeological Assessment of South Parking Lot Area

(Phase I) Site of Courthouse Annex, San Antonio, Texas. Unpublished manuscript, Center for Archaeological Research, The University of Texas at San Antonio.

Fox, A. A., F. Bass, Jr., and T. R. Hester. 1976. Alamo Plaza. **II**

Fox, A. A., and J. E. Ivey. 1979. Alamo Plaza–River Linkage. **X**

Fox, D. E., D. Scurlock, and J. W. Clark, Jr. 1977. San Fernando Cathedral. **IV**

Fox, D. E., F. Valdez, Jr., and L. O. Bobbitt. 1978. Dolores Aldrete House. **V**.

Gilmore, H. W. 1953. *Transportation and the Growth of Cities.* The Free Press, New York.

Ivey, J. E. 1978a. Archaeological Investigations at the Gresser House (41BX369), San Antonio, Texas. *Center for Archaeological Research, The University of Texas at San Antonio, Archaeological Survey Report,* No. 60.

———. 1978b. Archaeological Investigations at the Mayer House (41BX326), San Antonio, Texas. *Center for Archaeological Research, The University of Texas at San Antonio, Archaeological Survey Report,* No. 59.

Ivey, J. E., and A. A. Fox. n.d. Paseo del Rio. **V**

Jones, C. J. n.d. Archaeological Investigation of the Southeast Building Complex, Old Ursuline Academy Campus, San Antonio, Texas. Center for Archaeological Research, The University of Texas at San Antonio, Archaeological Survey Report, No. 118, in preparation.

Katz, P. R. 1977. 1975 Archaeological Investigations at Old Ursuline Academy, San Antonio, Texas. *Center for Archaeological Research, The University of Texas at San Antonio, Archaeological Survey Report,* No. 34.

———. 1978. Arciniega Street Area. **V**

McGraw, A. J., and F. Valdez, Jr. n.d. Rio Rita: An Historical Cistern in Downtown San Antonio. Center for Archaeological Research, The University of Texas at San Antonio, Archaeological Survey Report, No. 57, in preparation.

McKelvey, B. 1963. *The Urbanization of America, 1860–1915.* Rutgers University Press, New Brunswick.

Moore, G. L., F. A. Weir, J. E. Keller, R. W. Jarvis, C. H. Yates, K. J. Jelks, and P. A. Bandy. 1972. Temporary Capitol of Texas, 1883–1888: History and Archaeology. *Texas Highway Department, Publications in Archaeology,* No. 1.

Olds, D. L. 1967. The French Legation Kitchen. **V**

Roberson, W. R. 1974. The Carrington–Covert House: Archeological Investigation of a 19th-Century Residence in Austin, Texas. *Office of the State Archeologist, Texas Historical Commission, Report,* No. 25.

Webb, W. P. (editor). 1952. *The Handbook of Texas.* **V**

Williamson, J. A. 1965. Ante-Bellum Urbanization in the American Northeast. *Journal of Economic History,* Vol. 25, pp. 592–614.

Willoughby, L. 1981. *Austin: A Historical Portrait.* Donning Company, Norfolk, Virginia.

XII Preserving the Evidence of Texas History

Campbell, T. N. 1972. Systematized Ethnohistory. **II**

———. 1975. The Payaya Indians. **II**

———. 1977. Coahuiltecan Populations. **II**

Fox, D. E. 1979. Lithic Artifacts. **II**

———. 1980. Professionalization for Archeology? Now Wait Just a Minute! *Practicing Anthropology,* Vol. 2, No. 4, pp. 26–27.

Guderjan, T. H. 1981. *Forest Grove/Big Rock Areas.* **X**

Hester, T. R. 1980. *Digging Into South Texas Prehistory.* **Intro**

Mallouf, R. J., H. Simons, R. L. Wilson, S. L. Andrews, J. B. Arnold III, and D. Moore. 1981. *Texas Heritage Conservation Plan, Computerization Program Manual.* Texas Historical Commission, Austin.

Rutenberg, G. W. 1981. Historic Demography in the Forest Grove/Big Rock Area. Chapter 7 in *Archaeological Investigations in the Forest Grove/Big Rock Areas, North-Central Texas,* by T. H. Guderjan. Archaeology Research Program, Southern Methodist University, Dallas.

Texas Historical Commission. 1973. *Historic Preservation in Texas: The Comprehensive Statewide Historic Preservation for Texas,* Vol. I. Published jointly by the Texas Historical Commission and the Office of Archeology and Historic Preservation, U.S. Department of the Interior.

Index

Page numbers in **boldface type** indicate illustration pages.

Notes

Notes

Notes

Notes